Richard West

has been a journalist and freelance writer for forty years, working first on the *Manchester Guardian*. He has travelled widely, and has written three books of reportage on Africa (including *The White Tribes of Africa*), two historical works, two books on Latin America, and three books on Vietnam. His other works include *An English Journey*, *River of Tears* (a study of RTZ and the politics of mining), and *Tito and the Rise and Fall of Yugoslavia*. He is married to the Irish writer Mary Kenny, and has written regularly for *Private Eye* and the *Spectator*.

Further reviews for *The Life and Strange Surprising Adventures of Daniel Defoe*:

'The story West has to tell is as good as a novel. It is rather like one of Defoe's own novels, full of immediacy, action and good sense ... West writes with admirable clarity, always keeping the story at full gallop ... it is sheer delight to read [a biography] whose author is sufficiently old-fashioned and generous to present a hero to be admired, rather than cut down to size ... Two of our masterworks of history – Macaulay's *History of England* and Trevelyan's *England under Queen Anne* – deal with the period. West can look Macaulay and Trevelyan in the face ... [an] admirable and enjoyable "Life and Times".'

ALLAN MASSIE, *Daily Telegraph*

'It is as a brilliant reporter that Richard West – who incidentally reminds us that Robinson Crusoe was a slave-trader – most admires his subject. West's own seesaw career as a distinguished, much travelled and maverick journalist fits him eminently for the task. This graphic biography is as much about Defoe's times as about the man himself ... With scant material to go on except history itself, in which he is well steeped, Richard West has produced a lively and colourful biography.'

KEITH WATERHOUSE, *Literary Review*

Further reviews overleaf

'Defoe was an imaginative genius, and the problem for a biographer is fitting the two sides together. Richard West's chatty, humane approach, backed by formidable familiarity with Defoe's massive output, goes a long way towards this, reconstructing a believable and not wholly dislikeable personality... West skilfully clarifies the complex and dangerous political world in which he struggled to survive.'
JOHN CAREY, *Sunday Times*

'Here is a gift for a biographer: a great novelist whose life was a seething broth of drama and contradiction ... A few pages into Richard West's superb *The Life and Strange Surprising Adventures of Daniel Defoe*, one wonders why Defoe is not a more significant figure in our cultural history ... West evidently likes and admires his awkward subject, and his microscopic study of Defoe's huge output ... yields more than missing historical facts ... West's Defoe is far more than the creator of *Robinson Crusoe*; though that, in itself, would be enough to win him a plinth in the gallery of immortals ... There is a strong sense, throughout this minutely researched, hugely entertaining book, of a writer being restored to his rightful place in the literary hierarchy.'
KATE SAUNDERS, *Observer*

'*The Life and Strange Surprising Adventures of Daniel Defoe* is well titled. This is a lively and entertaining study which, given the scarcity of material on Defoe's own life, provides the history of a period as well as the biography of one man.'
PETER ACKROYD, *The Times*

'Richard West, a brave and independent journalist himself, has faced the problem of explaining the politics of the day without swamping Defoe himself ... Most [readers] will find Defoe's character interesting and often impressive, and his life full of sensational ups and downs.'
JOHN JOLLIFFE, *Country Life*

'Defoe is a natural subject for Richard West, himself a good journalist who has written several books about travel and foreign tribes . . . As writers, Defoe and West are twin spirits from different ages. The affinity works.'

MALCOLM RUTHERFORD, Financial Times

'It takes a good reporter to appreciate another, and Richard West, a distinguished exponent of the trade, shows that Defoe pioneered the leading article, the gossip column and the advice or agony column . . . This much-needed biography, written with a pace and clarity of which Defoe would have approved, restores him to us as a tireless battler for the causes of free speech, fair play and tolerance.'

PETER LEWIS, Daily Mail

'What is conveyed most forcefully throughout this book . . . is the highly individual and resilient character of Daniel Defoe.'

PETER READING, Times Literary Supplement

'Defoe comes across in this detailed and sympathetic biography as a man well ahead of his time . . . [a] fascinating and exemplary biography.'

ROBERT CARVER, Scotsman

The Life &
Strange Surprising Adventures
of

DANIEL DEFOE

RICHARD WEST

Flamingo
An Imprint of HarperCollins*Publishers*

Flamingo
An Imprint of HarperCollins*Publishers*
77–85 Fulham Palace Road,
Hammersmith, London W6 8JB

Published by Flamingo 1998
9 8 7 6 5 4 3 2 1

First published in Great Britain by
HarperCollins*Publishers* 1997

Copyright © Richard West 1997

The Author asserts the moral right to
be identified as the author of this work

ISBN 0 00 638817 5

Printed and bound in Great Britain by
Clays Ltd, St Ives plc

CONTENTS

LIST OF ILLUSTRATIONS

At heart Defoe never ceased to be a Puritan; at heart he was one with that other grand Puritan creator of the novel to whom the whole world appeared as a dream. It is a striking thing that when Robert Louis Stevenson wished to describe the supreme moments in imaginative literature, he instanced only two examples from modern writers, and those two writers were Defoe and Bunyan. Crusoe recoiling from the footprint; Achilles shouting over against the Trojans; Ulysses bending the great bow; Christian running with his fingers in his ears; each has been printed on the mind's eye for ever.

JOHN R. MOORE, *Defoe in the Pillory, and other Essays*

FOREWORD

It is tempting to pretend that my interest in Daniel Defoe derives from a childhood delight in *Robinson Crusoe*, but in fact when I first read that book I was almost as old as Defoe was when he wrote it. I can remember reading *Moll Flanders* as a prurient schoolboy, for its erotic scenes were startling in that modest age before the *Lady Chatterley's Lover* trial. My fascination with Defoe really began when I read what I now regard as his masterpiece, *A Tour of the Whole Island of Great Britain*.

For as long as I can remember I have enjoyed exploring the English countryside, and then the towns and cities as well, a pleasure I later indulged as a *Manchester Guardian* reporter in the late 1950s. During the last of the three years I spent with that paper I was its Yorkshire correspondent, travelling constantly through the former three Ridings, County Durham and Northumberland. In the early 1960s I wrote for the now defunct weekly *Time and Tide* a long series of articles on the towns of Britain, and again, in the late 1970s, a similar series for the *Spectator*. In 1980, Chatto & Windus commissioned a book called *An English Journey*, which described an actual tour of the country, beginning and ending at Manchester.

From an early age I had read and enjoyed William Cobbett's *Rural Rides*, written during the 1820s, and later J. B. Priestley's *English Journey*, published in 1934, but I gradually came to regard Defoe as the master of this genre. Soon after the *Tour* appeared as a Penguin paperback in 1965, sympathetically edited and introduced by Pat Rogers, I took a copy in my airline bag on a visit to Ethiopia. During the first two nights in Addis Ababa, when I could not sleep because of the very high altitude, I read the *Tour* with ever-increasing delight. Although I did not then realize just how much the *Tour* was a work of imagination, I laughed at Defoe's account of Hampstead Heath: 'But it must be confessed, tis so near heaven that I dare not say it can be a proper situation, for any but a race of mountaineers, whose lungs have been used to a rarified air, nearer the second region, than any ground for 30 miles round it.' Reading that at an altitude of 8,000 feet, I came to see that Defoe sometimes made fun of his readers.

That first Penguin *Tour* went with me on so many journeys that it fell to pieces, as did a second copy before I turned to the fuller two-volume Everyman version, edited by the solemn left-wing economic historian G. D. H. Cole, who rather missed the point of the book. Although I never tired of the *Tour*, I increasingly came to regret the age it celebrates. Defoe had lived through and helped to achieve the transformation of England into Great Britain, a constitutional monarchy answerable to Parliament, one of the two great military powers of Europe, and heart of an ever-expanding worldwide empire. Although Britain was then largely an agricultural country, Defoe predicted the rise of industrial cities such as Manchester, Liverpool, Birmingham, Leeds, Bradford, Newcastle and Glasgow. He was the prophet of Britain as workshop of the world, as well as the heart of an empire larger than Rome's.

For someone steeped as I was in Defoe's awareness of Britain's forthcoming nineteenth-century greatness, it was sad to observe the country's decline during the twentieth century, the end of its overseas empire, the disappearance of industry and, above all, the loss of sovereignty to a European Community as abhorrent to me as Louis XIV's France was to Defoe. The conflict in Ulster during the 1970s and the renewed demands for a separate Scottish Parliament seemed to threaten the unity of the kingdom, so painfully forged three centuries earlier. In search of enlightenment, I went back to the two great books spanning Defoe's career in politics, Lord Macaulay's *History of England*, which appeared in the 1850s, and G. M. Trevelyan's *England under Queen Anne*, written eighty years later. Re-reading Trevelyan, I was amazed to be reminded just how important was the role of Defoe in English politics, particularly in obtaining the Union with Scotland. My concern about the historic relationship between the English, Scots and Irish grew still more anxious as I watched with dismay the break-up in former Yugoslavia of the federation of Serbs, Croats and Slovenes, three peoples also dear to my heart.

By the 1990s my journalistic career had fallen into one of its periodic troughs, and I no longer had the means to journey round Britain, let alone Yugoslavia, so I made up my mind to follow Defoe's example by writing books of travel from my memories. Christopher Sinclair-Stevenson kindly commissioned *Tito and the Rise and Fall of Yugoslavia*, followed by *War and Peace in Vietnam*, another part of the world I had known and loved. Then I started to write a book on Britain, following in the steps of Defoe in the *Tour*, but Christopher, now my literary agent rather than publisher, urged me to try a proper biography. At first I was discouraged by the lack of information about Defoe's private life, especially the absence of all but two letters to his family. He not only worked in the Secret Service but seemed to enjoy mystery, deception and even what we would now call 'disinformation'. Moreover, like Shakespeare, Defoe does not seem to have made any impression on his acquaintances as a remarkable or even interesting man, for he scarcely appears in any contemporary memoirs. But then I read Paula R. Backscheider's *Daniel Defoe. His Life* (Johns Hopkins, 1989), a well-researched and illuminating work, which pointed me in the direction of the rich material to be found in Defoe's minor books, pamphlets and journalism, especially the twenty-two volumes of the facsimile *Review*, the thrice-weekly journal which he wrote single-handedly from the spring of 1704 until the autumn of 1713.

Very soon I became as fascinated by Defoe the journalist and Secret Service agent as I had been by Defoe the novelist and author of the *Tour*. Although the *Review* was never accorded the lasting fame of Steele's and Addison's *Tatler* and *Spectator* or the pamphlets of Jonathan Swift, another contemporary rival, Defoe was the principal pathfinder and pace-setter in what came to be seen as the golden age of journalism. He was the first master, if not the inventor, of almost every feature of modern newspapers, including the leading article, investigative reporting, the foreign news analysis, the agony aunt, the gossip column, the candid obituary, and even the kind of soul-searching piece which Fleet Street calls the 'Why, Oh Why'.

As a journalist, as well as a novelist, Defoe excelled in the art of telling a story. He had all the basic instincts of a reporter: he was innately curious; he got straight to the point; and he never missed any quirky detail. One constantly finds in his journalism and non-fiction books the equivalent of his master stroke as a novelist – the moment when Robinson Crusoe finds on his desert island a single footprint in the sand. Defoe always knew how to time a story, first arousing his readers' curiosity, holding their interest with droll asides, then startling them with an unexpected dénouement.

Defoe's brilliance as a reporter is clearest to me when I read him on subjects that I too have tackled, although in a different age and sometimes another country. His series of articles written in the autumn of 1709, explaining why bread was expensive in London in spite of a bumper harvest, reminded me of my failure to explain, or even to understand, why the soaring cost of rice in Saigon in 1973 threatened to lose the war for South Vietnam. Reading Defoe's book on the Great Storm of 25–26 November 1703, I recognized the inadequacy of the account of a similar natural disaster which came at the end of my *Hurricane in Nicaragua*, published in 1989.

Throughout a momentous and turbulent epoch Defoe stuck doggedly to the beliefs and aims of William of Orange, later King William III, his friend and mentor. But although he was true to the principles of the 'Glorious Revolution' of 1688, Defoe was quick to adapt to circumstances, supporting either the Whigs or Tories as the occasion demanded. His independence of mind enraged both factions in politics and religion, landing him in jail and even the pillory. He grew still more unpopular when he was so often proved right. Like many a prophet crying in the wilderness, Defoe often became self-righteous and shrill. He relished being the odd man out. When Cassandra issued her warning against the wooden horse, she was first denounced by the Trojans, then raped and murdered by the Greeks – the Whigs and Tories of the time. In his independence, as in some other respects, Defoe often puts me in mind of George Orwell, who exasperated the Left still more than the Right. It was Orwell who quoted in one of his essays the lines of a nineteenth-century children's hymn, which could have been written about Defoe:

> Dare to be a Daniel,
> Dare to stand alone . . .

In Defoe's *Review* we also see the beginnings of popular tabloid journalism and even the scandal sheet, familiar to me from spells of work at the *Daily Mirror* and *Private Eye*. He was a pioneer of the bogus Letter to the Editor, foreign stories written in London, and libel by innuendo or circumlocution. He was also an outrageous author of verse lampoons and attacked by name his Old Bailey judges, accusing one of prostituting his own wife, another of being excited by whipping half-naked women, and a third of accepting bribes from highwaymen.

Perhaps most of all I identified with Defoe in his lifelong financial worries. Unlike most toilers in Grub Street – Richard Savage in Johnson's *Lives of the Poets*, for example – Defoe started life as a wealthy man, but squandered his own and his wife's fortune in reckless business ventures. He turned to writing to pay off the creditors from his bankruptcy. The modern hack, on the other hand, struggles to meet the demands of the Inland Revenue and other tax collectors.

The prospect of the bankruptcy court, the summons, the garnishee order, and even the warning note slipped under the door to say that it could be 'prison next week', now loom large in the life of every not-very-successful self-employed writer. The terror of bankruptcy and prison, which gripped Defoe until his last wretched days in hiding from his creditors, is also the inspiration and theme of most of his novels, including *Robinson Crusoe*. Anyone who has suffered over the years from chronic financial worry will recognize in *Roxana* a recurring anxiety dream. Understanding the dread and guilt which Defoe endured because of his bankruptcy, one admires still more the fortitude or, as he called it, the 'passive courage' with which he faced months spent in hiding, Newgate Prison, the pillory, the torment of a painful illness and a hideous operation, as well as the constant struggle to feed his wife and six children.

When writing the biography of a bygone figure, especially one of such strong political views as Defoe, one is tempted to offer suggestions on what he or she would think of the modern world. This generally means the biographer's own opinions. Although of course I believe that much of Defoe's writing carries a message for us in Britain today, I have tried to avoid spelling this out to readers, who naturally want to draw their own conclusions. Although I have on occasion referred to later writers, notably Dr Johnson, Dickens and Orwell, I have tried to see Defoe in the context of his time, though here again I have to admit to sympathies and antipathies, which will perhaps become apparent. Although an Anglican, not a Dissenter, I agree with Defoe on most of the issues of his age, such as Scotland, the Hanoverian Succession and the Duke of Marlborough's war with France. I disagree with him on slavery, the conservation of forests and his hostility to the Roman Catholic Irish (not least because my dear wife Mary is one herself).

When I started to write this book I received much encouragement from two old friends, both devotees of Defoe's *Tour* and both natives of Yorkshire, a part of the country on which Defoe wrote brilliantly. They are Michael Wharton, for many years 'Peter Simple' in the *Daily Telegraph*, and Keith Waterhouse, novelist, playwright and journalist. Both of them relish Defoe's tall stories, of which one in Halifax ends up, 'that tis reasonable to think that the whole tale is a little Yorkshire, which, I suppose, you will understand well enough'. While writing the chapter on Scotland, I sought the advice of a learned historian friend, John Stuart Milne, whose Roman Catholic and Jacobite views were a useful antidote to Defoe's Calvinist bigotry, especially his contempt for the medieval Church. Indeed, there were times when I sympathized with Stuart's remark: 'We've always regarded Defoe as a rotter.'

I should also like to thank that ace picture researcher Sara Waterson and many friends who have helped me with advice and knowledge. These include three residents of Defoe's Stoke Newington, Robbie Richards, Nigel Lewis and Stephen Walsh; Stephen Pickles who suggested the title; Conan Nicholas, who shares Defoe's interest in horses; Carlos Kenny of Dublin and my late, much missed brother Tony, who was a life-long fan of Defoe.

This is not intended to be a definitive, academic or even scholarly analysis of Defoe's writing. I have generally followed the Penguin or Oxford Classic texts, as being the most readily available, for the seven novels in print, and for the *Tour*, except for a few passages found in the Everyman edition. Defoe was a pioneer of simplified spelling, for example 'thro' for 'through', 'work'd' for 'worked' and ''tis' for 'it is'. Unfortunately these modernizations never caught on, and so I have often changed them back to the old but familiar archaisms. Where the form of the word is readily understandable I have retained Defoe's version – for instance, 'murther' for 'murder', and 'I will that' for 'I wish that'. Defoe often wrote 'country' for 'county', in which case I have made the alteration.

Youth in the Reign of Charles II:
1660–85

DANIEL DEFOE began his life as he was to spend it, and as he eventually ended it, in the utmost secrecy. The births of his older sisters, Mary on 13 November 1657 and Elizabeth on 19 June 1659, are inscribed in the parish register of St Giles in Cripplegate, near where his father James Foe practised his trade of tallow chandler; but Daniel's name is absent. However, there are hints in his writing that he was born in the autumn of 1660, and in that case his mother Alice Foe would have been pregnant with him during the turbulent end of Cromwell's Commonwealth, when General Monk brought an army to London to keep the peace and prepare for the Restoration of Charles II. The connection of troops with pregnancy might help to explain the opening page of Defoe's novel *The Memoirs of a Cavalier*, in which the narrator suggests that some 'extraordinary influence' had affected his birth:

> If there be anything in dreams also, my mother, who was mighty observant that way, took minutes, which I have since seen in the first leaf of her Prayer Book, of several strange dreams she had while she was with child, of her second son, which was myself. Once she noted that she dreamed she was carried away by a regiment of horse, and delivered in the fields of a son, that as soon as it was born had two wings came out of its back, and in half an hours time flew away from her: And the very evening before I was born, she dreamed she was brought to bed of a son, and that all the while she was in labour a man stood under her window beating on a kettledrum, which very much decomposed her.

Defoe had a lifelong reluctance to make public the least information about himself, and sometimes disguised his name, address and even handwriting. He never published a first-person account of his own most important experiences, such as the Battle of Sedgemoor and his spells in Newgate Prison, yet both appear in the novels. By the same token, he loved to insert imaginary happenings into what were supposed to be factual works, such *A Tour of the Whole Island of Great Britain*. He enjoyed deception, and had passed off *The Memoirs of a Cavalier* as the genuine autobiography of a Royalist officer. It would have delighted him still more to include in somebody else's bogus memoirs his own mother's account of her dreams in pregnancy during the closing year of the Civil War epoch.

Most biographers of Defoe have repeated the old suggestion that his family were the descendants of Protestant refugees from the Netherlands in the sixteenth century, who had anglicized their name to Foe, as Robinson Crusoe's father had changed his from Kreutznaer. Some have accepted Defoe's hints at kinship with one of his heroes, Sir Walter Raleigh. However, his most recent and thorough biographer, Paula R. Backscheider, failed to trace his ancestry further back than his grandfather Daniel Foe and his grandmother Rose, of Etton, Northamptonshire. Their youngest child, James Foe, the father of Daniel, was born at Etton in 1630, and followed his brother Henry into the City of London, becoming a tallow chandler in Cripplegate, a member of the Butchers' liveried company, a freeman, a wealthy merchant, and husband of Alice.

However, the year of the Restoration, 1660, which gave them their first son Daniel, was in other respects a calamity for the Foes, who were Puritans in religious faith, and Cromwellites during the Commonwealth. They were therefore objects of enmity to the now triumphant Royalists. Young Daniel, as a Dissenter or Nonconformist, was faced from his earliest years with discrimination, ostracism, harassment and threats from followers of the established Church of England. Since Defoe was to spend his life defending the rights and liberties of Dissenters, we should in fairness examine why his people were so disliked, and why most Englishmen welcomed the Restoration.

The punitive laws against the Dissenters that followed the Restoration were seen at the time as tit for tat for the persecution of Anglicans during the Commonwealth. The Puritans had banned the Book of Common Prayer, the basis of Anglican liturgy. They turned Sunday into a Pharisaical Sabbath and Christmas into a day of fasting. They abolished the staging of plays, including the works of Shakespeare, imposing fines on audiences, and having the actors whipped at the cart's tail. As Lord Macaulay says at the start of his *History of England*: 'The Puritans hated bearbaiting, not because it gave pain to the bear but because it gave pleasure to the spectators.'

Cromwell's Parliament of 1653 had introduced a rule that holders of public office must convince the House of their 'real godliness', meaning their Puritanism, so that candidates for advancement took care to affect the drab clothing, sour expression and nasal speech that were then in fashion. After the Restoration the Anglicans took their revenge by throwing the Puritans out of their government jobs, and then out of the Church itself. These measures came to be known as the Clarendon Code, after the Chancellor, Edward Hyde, first Earl of Clarendon, whose *History of the Rebellion and the Civil Wars* provided Defoe with much of his information for *The Memoirs of a Cavalier*.

The first part of the Clarendon Code, the Corporation Act, required all magistrates, officers and employees of the boroughs of England to promise their 'non-resistance' to the King, and to disclaim the Solemn Oath and Covenant, taken by men over the age of eighteen in 1645. The second stage of the Clarendon Code, the Act of Uniformity of 1662, required clergymen, 'heads, fellows, chaplains and tutors' of any halls, houses of learning and hospitals and 'every person instructing or teaching any youth in any house or private family' to subscribe to the Thirty-Nine Articles of the Church of England's doctrine, to be ordained by a bishop, and to use the new Book of Common Prayer in all services and assent 'to all and everything contained and practised in it'. It specifically banned extemporary prayers 'from the heart', which were always a feature of Puritan services. The Act of Uniformity in effect barred the Puritans from practising their religion and educating their children.

When the Act of Uniformity became law on 24 August 1662, at least 1,800 clergymen had to leave their churches. Those who preached in their own homes or meeting houses were subject to heavy fines, as were those who attended the services. A single magistrate might convict without a jury and, after a third offence, pass sentence of transportation overseas, although, by a refinement of cruelty, the Dissenters could not be sent to the New England colonies, where there were many fellow Puritans. As a result of the Act of Uniformity 15,000 families were ruined, 5,000 Dissenters died in prison, and perhaps 60,000 suffered for their religion.

Samuel Annesley, the rector of St Giles in Cripplegate, was one of the first to leave his church, and the Foes were among those who followed him. According to many accounts, including the published elegy by Defoe in 1697, Annesley was a man of outstanding courage and piety.* Within six months of leaving St Giles he was preaching illegally at his home in Stepney, and later at public meetings where thousands gathered to offer protection. After the Act of Indulgence of 1672 removed some restrictions on Dissenters, Annesley built the Little St Helens meeting house, with 'three good galleries' for the congregation, of which Defoe was a regular member.

Because of the Clarendon Code Defoe grew up in an atmosphere of suspicion, harassment and fear, against which he armed himself with piety, self-discipline and, above all, fortitude, or what he called 'passive courage'. By the time he was learning to read and write the future journalist had witnessed two of the biggest 'stories' in English history: the Plague of 1665 and the Great Fire of London in 1666. Many years later, when it became known that Defoe had written *A Journal of the Plague Year*, purporting to be the memoirs of a grown-up man, he was branded as an impostor or liar for using this harmless device to tell the story. The *Journal* is a work of imaginative re-creation, based on the printed records of what occurred at the time. But critics may be wrong to assume that a child as young as five years old would have been unaware of the terror pervading the City and gripping the minds of his parents and sisters. Even if Daniel was taken into the countryside, he must have witnessed the start of the Plague and, as he explains in the *Journal*, the sickness spread with the refugees to the furthest parts of Essex, killing more people, proportionately, in Colchester than in London. And even if he had no clear memory of the Plague Year, Defoe would have grown up listening to the stories of the disaster, still a subject of morbid fascination in 1722, which was why he wrote his book.

In the *Journal* Defoe deplores the cowardice of the King, the court and many Anglican clergymen who fled from London to places as distant as Oxford. He praises the Lord Mayor and aldermen of the City, who stayed at their posts to fight the spread of disease. No doubt thinking of Annesley, who remained in London throughout the Plague

* Defoe's elegy contains the well-known lines:

> The best of men cannot suspend their fate:
> The good die early, and the bad die late.

Year, Defoe says that Dissenting clergymen filled the pulpits of many Anglican churches, from which they were now debarred by law.* So we can take it as fairly certain that James Foe and his brother Henry stayed in London during the Plague Year, and may have provided Daniel with much of his gruesome information. The narrator of the *Journal* has the initials 'H. F.', and comes from Northamptonshire.

Even if he did not remember the Plague Year (and I find this improbable), Defoe could certainly not have forgotten the Great Fire of 1666, for his family house was one of only three left standing in his devastated neighbourhood. He never wrote a book on the Great Fire, but sometimes refers to it in his *Tour*. On the road between Guildford and Leatherhead, in Surrey, he remarks on a line of gentlemen's mansions, one of which belongs to the descendants of 'Sir Thomas Bludworth, once Lord Mayor of London, a person famous for the implacable passion he put the people of London in, by a rash expression at the time of the Great Fire: (viz) "That it was nothing, and they might piss it out."'

The Great Fire of 1666 was the catalyst for the transformation of London from a medieval city of wooden houses and Gothic churches into a modern city of brick and stone, expanding rapidly into the countryside, and graced by the classical buildings of Wren and his school. Defoe gloried in London, regarding it as the heart and engine of Britain's commerce and navy, as well as the capital of the Protestant world. Growing up in the City after the Great Fire, Defoe watched the work of rebuilding, to which he later contributed from his brickyard at Tilbury. In the part of the *Tour* devoted to London he admires the work of reconstruction:

> It is true that before the Fire of London, the streets were narrow, and public edifices, as well as private, were more crowded, and built closer to one another; for soon after the Fire, the king by proclamation, forbid all persons whatsoever, to go about to rebuild for a certain time. viz, till the Parliament (which was soon to sit) might regulate and direct the manner of building, and establish rules for the adjusting every man's property, and yet might take order for a due enlarging of the

---

* This was not the case in St Giles-in-the-Fields, the parish where the Plague first struck and later took the highest toll. The present rector, Gordon Taylor, has found from the records that his predecessor in 1665–6 remained at his post throughout.

streets, and appointing the manner of building, as well for the beauty as the conveniency of the city, and for safety, in case of any future accident; for though I shall not inquire whether the city was burnt by accident, or by treachery, yet nothing was more certain, than that as the city stood before, it was strangely exposed to the disaster which happened, and the buildings looked as if they had been formed to make one general disaster, whenever any wicked party of incendiaries should think fit.

Here Defoe alludes to his obsessional bugbear, a Popish plot, of which we will hear much more in the reign of Charles II, and as late as the reign of George I, but he later explains in more credible fashion why the Great Fire spread so fast:

The streets were not only narrow, and the houses all built of timber, lath and plaster, or, as they were very properly called paper work, and one of the finest range of buildings in the Temple, are to this day, called the Paper Buildings ... But the manner of building in those days, one story projecting out beyond another, was such, that in some narrow streets, the houses almost touched one another at the top, and it has been known, that men, in the case of fire, have escaped on the tops of the houses, by leaping from one side of a street to another; this made it often, and almost always happen, that if a house was on fire, the opposite house was in more danger to be fired by it, according as the wind stood, than the houses on either side.

Although in the new City of London there was more open ground, Defoe maintained that nevertheless more people lived in the same space. This was because most of the big, old houses were also surrounded by yards and gardens – for example, Swithen's Alleys near the Royal Exchange, which before the Fire contained a single merchant's house belonging to Mr Swithen but which now (at the time of the *Tour*) contained more than twenty houses, all of them occupied by Swithen's descendants. Copt-Hall-Court in Throgmorton Street had once been the single house of a Dutch merchant, while three more courts in the same street had been individual homes. Defoe says that 'so many great houses were converted into streets, and courts, alleys and buildings, that there are by estimate, almost 4,000 houses standing on the ground that the fire left desolate, more than stood on the same ground before'.

Even in parts of the old City left untouched by the Great Fire the inhabitants followed the same example of pulling down big, old buildings and turning the grounds into streets or squares of houses. There was a wholesale destruction of noble palaces facing the Strand, whose gardens led down to the Thames, each with its own steps and landing place. Among those demolished during Defoe's lifetime were Essex, Norfolk, Salisbury, Worcester, York and Hungerford houses, which had once stretched in a line from the Temple to modern Trafalgar Square. Defoe approved of this demolition: the new 'noble streets and beautiful houses' were 'in themselves equal to a large city'.

Defoe also witnessed the spread of London into the 'out parts', or what had been uninhabited land before the Great Fire:

> As first, within the memory of the writer hereof, all those numerous ranges of building, called Spittle Fields, reaching from Spittle-yard in Northern Fallgate, and from Artillery Lane in Bishopsgate-street, with all the new streets, beginning at Hoxton, and the back of Shoreditch Church, north, and reaching to Brick-lane, and to the end of Hare Street on the way to Bethnal Green. The lanes were deep, dirty and unfrequented; that part now called Spittlefields market was a field of grass with cows feeding on it, since 1670. The Old Artillery Ground (where the Parliament listed their first soldiers against the king) took up all these long streets . . .
>
> Brick-Lane, which is now a long well-paved street, was a deep dirty road, frequented by carts fetching bricks that way into White-Chapel from Brick-kilns in those fields, and had its name on that account; in a word, it is computed that about two hundred thousand inhabitants dwell now in that part of London, where, within about fifty years past, there was not a house standing.

There had been a similar increase in Goodman's Fields: 'the name gives evidence for it', meaning that this had been open land. The many streets between White Chapel and Rosemary Lane had all been built since 1678, but Defoe remembered the district from his childhood: 'Well Close, now called Marine Square, was so remote from houses, that it used to be a very dangerous place to go after it was dark, and many people have been robbed and abused in passing it; a well standing in the middle, just where the Danish church is now built, there the mischief was generally done.' Goodman's Fields was the scene of some of the mischief done by the juvenile thieves in Defoe's novel *Colonel Jack*.

Defoe's mother died when he was still very young, and in 1670 his father sent him to Dr James Fisher's school for Dissenters at Dorking in Surrey. His account of Dorking in the *Tour* suggests that he found the town and the countryside full of diversion and interest. It was famous, he says, for the Roman Road that could still be seen at the side of the graveyard;* for a local heath, 'which some local physicians have singled out for the best air in England'; and also for Mr Howard's vineyards, producing 'most excellent good wines, and a very great quantity of them'. Among the sights of Dorking was 'an ancient gentleman and his son, of a very good family; (viz) Augustin Bellson Esq: the father was measured seven foot and a half inch high, allowing all that he might have sunk, for his age, being seventy one years old; and the son measured two inches taller than his father.'

The schoolboy Defoe studied the operation of Dorking's famous market for poultry, 'and particularly for the fattest geese and the largest capons, the name of a Dorking Capon being known among the poulterers in Leaden-Hall Market'. The poultry were brought from as far as Sussex to be fattened up by the country people of Dorking; 'and some of these capons are so large, as that they are little inferior to turkeys: and I have seen them sold for 4s to 4s6d each, and weighing from 4lbs to 5 or 6lbs a piece.'

Defoe says darkly that some of the local Catholic gentry, including the Howards and Bellsons, were implicated in Popish plots, and no doubt he and his Nonconformist schoolboy friends believed the stories of Jesuit villainy. He and his friends also observed with disapproval the goings-on at a vault or cave at the top of nearby Box Hill. In the *Tour* he reports that each Sunday during the summer season, 'there used to be a rendezvous of gentlemen and ladies from Epsom to take the air, and walk in the box-woods; and in a word, divert or debauch, or perhaps both'. A vintner who kept the King's Arms inn at Dorking obtained permission from Sir Adam Brown, the owner of Box Hill, to furnish this vault or cellar with tables and chairs, and to sell food and wine at regular parties on Sunday evenings.

---

* Defoe gives a magisterial account of Roman road-building in the *Tour* (see Chapter Fourteen, p. 350).

After three years of this merry-making some of the local 'best governed people', meaning Dissenters, complained to Sir Adam Brown of 'the revelry and the indecent mirth ... and on the Sabbath Day too'. When Sir Adam took no notice of the complaint, 'a certain set of young men of the town of Dorking ... made an unwelcome visit to the place once on a Saturday night, just before the usual time of their wicked mirth, and behold when the coaches and ladies from Epsom appeared the next afternoon, they found the cellar or vault, and all that was in it, blown up with gun-powder . . .' This is a reference to an incident which took place in 1676, when some local youngsters (perhaps including Defoe) took this drastic action in favour of Sunday observance. Their exploit was kept so secret 'that upon the utmost enquiry it could never be heard, or found out who were the persons that did it'.

While Defoe was a schoolboy in Dorking he had occasion to see the Duke of York, the future James II, who came to hunt stags at the nearby Holm Wood: 'They have hunted the largest stags here that have been seen in England; the Duke took great care to have them preserved for his own sport.' Ten years later the duke would be hunting Defoe.

There is no record of when Defoe was in Dorking, when he began to study at Charles Morton's Academy in Newington Green, or whether he went to each of them at a different time of the year. Both his father James Foe and his minister Dr Annesley regarded Morton's Academy as the best of the places of higher learning for children of Dissenters. Like Annesley, Morton was one of the clergymen barred from his church by the Act of Uniformity. He had left his parish in Cornwall for London and, after the Act of Indulgence in 1672, had opened his private academy at Newington Green, about six miles north-west of St Paul's. This was becoming a favoured retreat from the smoke and dirt of the City, yet it was close enough for a businessman to commute to work on horseback. There is still in Newington Green today a terrace of houses dating back to the 1650s, as well as a wrought-iron gate with the monogram 'W', marking the site of the house of the Nonconformist hymn-writer Isaac Watts, the author of 'O God, Our Help in Ages Past', who also attended Dr Morton's Academy some twenty years after Defoe. This northern suburb of London was already becoming a haven for the Dissenters, and Defoe spent the last third of his life in what is today Stoke Newington Church Street.

Charles Morton, like Annesley, was renowned among the Dissenters for his piety, courage, good nature and eloquence. As well as being a Nonconformist in religion, Morton brought an enquiring mind to philosophy, politics, history, economics and natural science. As a fellow at Wadham College, Oxford, he had been one of the members of the 'invisible college', also known as the 'Oxonian Sparklers', which became the Royal Society in 1645. Among Morton's fellow 'Sparklers' were Robert Boyle, the physicist and chemist, William Petty, a pioneer economist and inventor, and Christopher Wren, who had been a physicist and astronomer before becoming the planner and principal architect of London after the Great Fire.

By teaching at his academy, Morton was breaking the 'Stamford Oath', which forbade all graduates of Oxford and Cambridge to teach in another university 'without the approval of their alma mater'. Originally introduced in 1334 to block the establishment of a rival university in the Lincolnshire town, the Stamford Oath was employed until 1828 to keep Dissenters and Roman Catholics out of Oxford and Cambridge. Because of the Stamford Oath and the Act of Uniformity Dr Morton was frequently harassed and even arrested during his years at Newington Green. Thus Defoe grew up seeing the three men he most respected – his father, Dr Annesley and Dr Morton – made outcasts by the State and the Church of England.

The curriculum at Newington Green included the Oxford and Cambridge courses in rhetoric, logic and Latin grammar, followed by arithmetic, geometry, astronomy and music, and finally Aristotle's three branches of philosophy – moral, metaphysical and natural – or what we call science. However, Morton encouraged his scholars to study a broader range of subjects. They read Locke's *Essay Concerning Human Understanding*, which was banned at Oxford, a study of metaphysics by a Jesuit, and a tract against letting a Roman Catholic sit on the throne of England. Students preparing to take holy orders read theological works by Anglicans as well as by Independent and Presbyterian divines.

Morton broke with tradition by teaching in English rather than Latin, and by introducing courses in history, geography, modern languages and physics. His laboratory at one time included air-pumps, thermometers and various kinds of mathematical instruments. Morton himself wrote a textbook for his students, *Compendium Physicae*, explaining the discoveries of Harvey, Newton, Hooke and Boyle, a work that was later used at Harvard, where Morton taught at the end of his life.

Defoe in his later writing seldom shows any interest in scientific theory or in the Royal Society, and only occasionally mentions Sir Isaac Newton. He revered Sir Christopher Wren as the architect of St Paul's, the 'most beautiful church in the Protestant world', and tells a charming story of how the old man dealt with flatterers. After defending St Paul's against those who compared it unfavourably with St Peter's in Rome, Defoe writes in the *Tour*:

> It is true, St Peter's, beside its beauty in ornament or imagery, is beyond St Paul's in its dimensions in every way larger ... And it was a merry hyperbole of Sir Christopher Wren's, who, when some gentleman in discourse compared the two churches and, in compliment to him ... suggested that St Paul's was the bigger: I tell you, says Sir Christopher, you might set it in St Peter's, and look for it a good while, before you would find it.

On one controversial topic Defoe was to prove more sensible than his teacher. In seeking to explain what happens to swallows and other migratory birds in winter, Dr Morton declared that they flew to the moon, a theory as wild as Dr Johnson's belief that they dived into rivers and slept on the bottom. In the *Tour* Defoe describes how one October he saw a huge number of swallows gathered upon the roof of the church at Southwold, on the Suffolk coast, and asked a 'grave gentleman' what this meant:

> I perceive Sir, says he, you are a stranger ... and must then understand, first, this is the season of the year when the swallows, their food here failing, begin to leave us, and return to the country wherever it be, from whence I suppose they came; and this being the nearest the coast of Holland, they come here to embark; this he said, smiling a little, and now sir, says he, the weather being too calm, or the wind contrary, they are waiting for a gale, for they are all wind-bound.

After quoting this 'grave gentleman', Defoe refuses to speculate on how the swallows know where to go, or how they navigate:

> That we must leave to the naturalists to determine, who insist upon it that brutes cannot think. Certain it is that the swallows neither come hither for warm weather, neither retire for cold, the thing is of quite another nature; they, like the shoals of

fish in the sea, pursue their prey; they are a voracious creature, they feed flying; their food is found in the air, viz. the insects; of which in our summer evenings, in damp and moist places, the air is full; they come hither in the summer, because our air is fuller of fogs and damps than in other countries.

By ignoring the abstract theories of naturalists, by listening to the wisdom of a Suffolk local, and by observing the absence of insects after the summer, Defoe was able to understand why the swallows left England in winter to 'return to the country wherever it be, from whence I suppose they came'.

Such passages demonstrate how Defoe had learnt from Morton the habit of thinking things out for himself, and then making his thoughts clear to others. 'Direct your speech,' Morton once wrote, 'not as if you intended to beat the air above men's heads, but as designing to teach and touch their hearts.' Like the great Puritan writer John Bunyan, Morton recognized the value of stories: 'Romances, and parables, or fables that have no truth in the matter, but honesty in the design, as also enlargement of stories by variety of phrases and manner of expression, or handsome oratory; the better to inculcate the virtue, or express the vice they design to represent, and are of singular use in all discourses.'

Just as Morton enlivened his sermons and lectures with fables and parables, so Defoe would use his genius as a story-teller in making a point in an article or a pamphlet. In the preface of his *Serious Reflections during the life of Robinson Crusoe* he tries to suggest that his recent and highly successful novel had a moral purpose, but he insists that 'the fable is always made for the moral, not the moral for the fable'. The same could certainly not be said of *Moll Flanders*, the bawdy tale of a courtesan, yet in the preface Defoe once more expresses the solemn hope that 'the moral will keep the reader serious, even when the story might incline him to be otherwise'. This was tongue-in-cheek humbug. Defoe knew perfectly well that *Moll Flanders* was not the kind of story that Morton had in mind when he talked of using romance 'the better to inculcate the virtue, or express the vice they design to represent'.

But the training he acquired at Newington Green was sometimes abused in casuistry, a branch of ethics designed to apply rules of religion or morality to individual 'cases of conscience'. In Defoe's lifetime most cases of conscience among the Dissenters concerned taking oaths of loyalty to the crown, and whether or not to take

Communion in the Anglican rite in order to hold public office. Casuistry, as the art of reconciling abstract principle with individual needs, easily leads to intellectual sleight of hand, which is why the word usually has a pejorative meaning.

Defoe came to pride himself on his skill at presenting opinions he did not hold. He would often write articles on the same subject for different newspapers, adopting opposing arguments. Some of his pamphlets were issued in different versions to win the support of Whigs and Tories, Anglicans and Dissenters, Jacobites and Presbyterians. In his novels he loved to project himself into the minds of people with other opinions, such as the Royalist Cavalier and the feminist Roxana. But skill at casuistry would help to land Defoe in the pillory and Newgate Prison.

Although proud of his education at Dorking and Newington, Defoe understood that it did not carry the same prestige as that acquired at, for instance, Eton and Oxford. Like many Dissenters, he felt an outsider in social position as well as religion, and was never at ease with aristocrats or the old landed gentry. Distinction of class, as well as politics, helps to explain why Defoe never mixed with famous contemporary writers such as Dryden, Addison, Steele, Swift and Pope. It may also explain his insistence on calling himself a gentleman, his dandified wig, and the diamond ring on his finger.

Before leaving Morton's Academy in 1679 or 1680 Defoe considered becoming a Nonconformist minister, then chose to follow his father into the City of London. The City then, as now, retained some of the trappings of the medieval guilds, such as its liveried companies, Lord Mayor, sheriffs, aldermen and freemen, and its Members of Parliament, who are elected by liverymen. The privileges of the City included the right of sheriffs to address the Bar of the House of Commons, and the right of the Court of Aldermen to have access to the throne. As the son of a liveryman, Defoe was a freeman by right, and no doubt entered the City as much to pursue a career in politics as in commerce.

During the struggle for power in England during the seventeenth century the City of London supported Parliament, and during the Civil War it raised trained bands, or irregular soldiers, as well as the money for the Roundhead army. Soon after the Restoration the City once more came into confrontation with the crown over politics and religion as well as over money. Yet in spite of these distractions the City was constantly growing and changing during Defoe's lifetime. The creation of the Bank of England, the Stock Exchange and financial institutions such as the East India Company and South Sea Company provided capital for the rebuilding of London after the Great Fire, the growth of trade and colonies in Asia and the Americas, the Union with Scotland, the rise of industry, and the raising of armies and navies for the wars against France. Defoe always regarded the City as both the commercial heart and the Protestant soul of the British empire, which grew in might and majesty during his lifetime.

Defoe entered the City in 1681 in the wholesale hosiery business, dealing in many kinds of knitted woollen stockings, from the warm, coarse legwear of the soldiers and agricultural workers to the fine women's hose whose patterns and colours constantly changed with the fashion. The manufacture of hosiery was a cottage industry, spread over the great wool regions of Norfolk, Devonshire and the West Riding, requiring Defoe to travel widely to order stocks for his London warehouse and sell to the local retailers. These were the first of the many journeys that gave Defoe the material for his most personal and delightful book, *A Tour of the Whole Island of Great Britain*.

Defoe established his home and warehouse in Freeman's Yard in the Cornhill, a district favoured by merchants in woollen goods, millinery and linen. Many were fellow Dissenters, who like Defoe attended the Presbyterian meeting place in Freeman's Yard and strolled in the gardens attached to the Drapers Hall. The aspiring merchant now wanted a wife, and in 1682 he began to pay court to Mary Tuffley, the seventeen-year-old daughter of a wealthy cooper, or manufacturer of the casks and barrels required for the shipping of every kind of goods – from beer and wine to sugar, tobacco, meat and gunpowder. Defoe admired the skill of the coopers, and tells in the *Tour* how a barrel of butter from Woodbridge in Suffolk travelled to the West Indies and back again, yet proved to be in perfect condition.

It was customary for a young City gentleman to woo his intended wife by presenting her with a handwritten anthology of improving texts and stories to demonstrate the principles he would bring to their marriage. In the dedication to Mary in his unpublished *Historical Collections* Defoe ventures to hope that she, the 'incomparable', 'excellent' and 'divine', will accept this offering from 'the meanest & truest of all your Adorers & Servants'. In spite of the flowery address to 'Clarinda' from 'Bellmour', the *Historical Collections* reveal Defoe's eclectic reading and skill as a story-teller. He relates how Marcus Servilius, when he saw that the Romans were 'not much moved by his words', tore off his shirt to show them his scars as proof of courage; how a sparrow fleeing from a hawk nestled in Xenocrates' bosom. While praising virtuous women, the young Defoe expresses his disapproval of harlots, especially those who use cosmetics, quoting the words of St Jerome: 'How can she weep for her sins, when fearing her tears should make furrows in her face?' Forty years later, in *Moll Flanders* and *Roxana*, Defoe was still condemning women who 'paint'.

Mary must have approved of the *Historical Collections*, for she married Defoe on 1 January 1684, bringing with her a dowry of £3,700 – worth nearly a hundred times as much in today's money. Defoe was to squander this money, and never forgave himself. Indeed, his shame and remorse over that £3,700 darkened his life and accounts for much of the brooding anxiety of the novels. Otherwise little is known of Mary. Defoe wrote to her two or three times a week from Scotland and on his journeys, but not one letter survives. From references to Mary in letters to Robert Harley, the politician, and late in life to his daughter and son-in-law, it is clear that Defoe adored his wife and was deeply grateful to her for her loyalty and her care of the children.

From Victorian times to the start of our own Permissive Society it was widely assumed that the author of such salacious novels as *Moll Flanders* must have kept company with her kind of women. In an article on Defoe published in 1949 (*Leader Magazine*, 27 August 1949) the literary critic Stephen Potter assured his readers: 'Defoe may be said to have been a strictly contemporary man, all his life. His quick-changing professions ranged from traveller to rebel, from factory owner to journalist, from family man to bastard-begetter, according to the tastes and economics of the time.' Neither Potter nor any other critic has shown as evidence that Defoe was a 'bastard-begetter', although he was once accused of this by a libellous pamphleteer. Indeed, he was not quick to beget the children by Mary, his lawful wife. Defoe's parents had waited nine years before having their first child. Defoe's eldest, Maria, was born in 1687, three years after the marriage, and the other children followed after 1690. Mary was pregnant with her last child in 1703, when Defoe was immured in Newgate Prison.

Towards the end of King Charles's reign political passions flared again as to who should succeed him, a question still unresolved at the time of his death in 1685. Meanwhile English anger against the Puritans had gradually given way to hatred and fear of those on the other doctrinal extreme, the Roman Catholics. It was known that Charles himself leaned to the Roman faith, that his younger brother and heir,

James, Duke of York, was a practising Catholic, and that both were under the sway and patronage of Louis XIV of France, the self-proclaimed enemy of the Protestant religion.

The parliamentary critics of Charles, or Whigs, as they slowly came to be called, were heartened in 1678 by widespread and frantic fears of a Popish plot against England. The leader of this scare campaign and the witch-hunt that followed was a disgraced Anglican clergyman, Titus Oates, who had spent some time on the Continent with the Jesuits. He claimed to have heard from them that the Papists had started the Great Fire of London and were now planning to burn all the ships on the Thames; that the French were about to land from Ireland; that the King would be stabbed or poisoned to death and the Protestants killed in a St Bartholomew's massacre similar to the one in France in the previous century. Oates named many Catholics who were, he claimed, involved in the plot. A Justice of the Peace, who had questioned one of the men accused by Oates, was murdered, whereupon, in the words of Macaulay: 'All the gaols were filled with Papists. London had the aspect of a city in a state of siege. The trainbands were under arms all night. Preparations were made for barricading the great thoroughfares. Patrols marched up and down the streets. Canon were placed round Whitehall. No citizen thought himself safe unless he carried under his coat a small flail loaded with lead to brain the Popish assassins.'

Many years later Defoe revealed that he too had carried a flail at the time of the Popish Plot. Early in 1712, when London was troubled by 'Mohawks', the upper-class bullies who thought it amusing to beat and humiliate peaceful citizens, Defoe wrote in his periodical *Review* for 15 March:

> I remember at the time of the Papal Plot, when murthering men in the dark was pretty much in fashion, and every honest man walked the street in danger of his life, a very pretty invention was found out which soon put an end to the doctrine of assassination, and the practice too, and cleared our streets of the murthering villains of that day, and this was the Protestant flail . . . for my part, I have frequently walked with one about me, in the old Papal days, and though I never set up for a hero, yet when armed with the scourge of a Papist, I remember I feared nothing . . . I can assure you, some honest sufferers are furnishing themselves with these Protestant flails for the

purpose and I doubt not the first Mohawk that tastes of this physic is instantly cured.

As rival demagogues joined in denouncing the Papists, Oates swore that he had heard the Queen say she would give her consent to the assassination of her husband. Several foreign priests and English Catholic laymen were sentenced to death on the word of people like Oates, and then hung, drawn and quartered. Many Dissenters, including Defoe, believed in the Popish Plot to their dying days, but the Whig politicians cynically used it in order to block the succession of James, Duke of York, by an Exclusion Bill. The man they hoped to see as the next King of England was Charles II's eldest illegitimate son, the Duke of Monmouth, who, they claimed, was the rightful heir. This was the man in whose cause Defoe was to venture his life at the Battle of Sedgemoor.

Monmouth was born in Rotterdam in 1649 to a Welsh girl, Lucy Walters, who afterwards claimed that Charles was the father, although, as Macaulay remarks, 'the lady had several admirers and was not supposed to be cruel to any'. At any rate, Charles believed her, and after his restoration showed great affection to little James Crofts, as the boy was called, later appointing him Duke of Monmouth in England, Duke of Buccleuch in Scotland, and general commanding the British troops in a war against Holland, in which he proved gallant and an acceptable officer.

A charming, handsome but vapid young man, Monmouth was seized upon by the Whigs as a Protestant alternative to the Duke of York, and soon Monmouth himself began to believe the story that his mother had secretly married Charles, and had left the proof in a Black Box, buried somewhere in Holland or England. When Monmouth travelled through Wales in 1678, and the West of England two years later, his journeys took on the character of triumphal processions, in which, in the words of Macaulay, 'he stood godfather to children of the peasantry, mingled in every rustic sport, and won foot-races in his boots against fleet runners in shoes . . .' When he arrived in London at midnight, 'the watchman was ordered by the magistrates to proclaim the joyful news through the streets of the city, the people left their beds, and bonfires were lit'.

Popular feeling in favour of Monmouth grew so strong that, when Charles summoned Parliament in 1681, he ordered it to assemble at Oxford, his father's capital during the Civil War, rather than London, the stronghold of Whigs and Puritanism. Perhaps he feared that the trainbands would intervene on the side of the Whigs, as they did on the side of the Parliament leaders in 1641. Charles triumphed at Oxford because, unlike his father, he did not depend on Parliament for the maintenance of his revenue. Some frustrated opponents, having failed to get the Exclusion Bill ratified, joined in the Rye House Plot to murder the Duke of York before he could come to the throne. The plot was detected in 1683 and the ringleaders executed, while Monmouth himself fled to Holland. During the last two years of his reign Charles II exerted his regained powers to curb the privileges of the City of London and to fill most of its offices with his own supporters – or Tories, as they had come to be called.* Defoe's first year of marriage was a desperate time for the City.

At the start of the clamour for an Exclusion Bill Charles thought it prudent to send his brother the Duke of York on a mission to Scotland, for his presence in London only inflamed resentment. However, through his behaviour in Edinburgh, first in 1679 on the Privy Council, and then from 1681 as the Royal Commissioner, James succeeded in making himself as abhorrent to the Scots as to the English. His atrocious cruelty to the Presbyterians still rankled a quarter century later, when Defoe was in Scotland, helping to bring about the Act of Union.

It was the Scots Presbyterians who, in 1639, had first taken up arms against Charles I in the series of conflicts in Britain and Ireland that came to be known as the Civil War. They called themselves Covenanters, after the pledge they had sworn to maintain the purity of their faith against attempts by the Church of England to reintroduce the hierarchy and the Book of Common Prayer. This clash between Charles and the Scots is well described in Defoe's historical novel, *The Memoirs of a Cavalier*. When the Civil War broke out in England, the Scots Presbyterians tried to play off both sides to their own advantage, but ended up beaten and harshly governed by Cromwell. At the news of the Restoration in 1660, red wine flowed from the fountains of Edinburgh. However, Charles II quickly reneged on his promises of religious toleration, provoking revolt in Dumfries, one of the Covenanting strongholds. The prisoners who had been promised quarter were sentenced to hanging, or slavery in Barbados.

---

* The Tories were nicknamed after Irish Catholic bandits; the Whigs after Scottish Presbyterian cattle rustlers and horse thieves. The nicknames stuck to the two rival parties in politics and religion.

As the Covenanters gathered to pray at secret conventicles on the open moorland, their more extreme number came to be called the Cameronians, the ancestors of the still famous regiment. In 1679 a party of Cameronians on a mission of murder came by chance on their most implacable enemy, James Sharp, the Archbishop of St Andrews, and promptly dispatched him. The authorities in Edinburgh ordered the rounding up of scores of suspects who might have information, and subjected them to the 'boot', an iron vice that crushed the foot, as well as the thumbscrews. Lord Macaulay relates how the Duke of York, the future James II of England, supervised these interrogations:

> The administration of James was marked by odious laws, by barbarous punishments, and by judgments to the iniquity of which even that age furnished no parallel. The Scottish Privy Council had the power to put people to the question. But the sight was so dreadful that as soon as the boot appeared, even the most servile and hard-hearted courtiers hastened out of the chamber. The board was sometimes quite deserted: and it was at length found necessary to make an order that the members should keep their seats on such occasions. The Duke of York, it was remarked, seemed to take pleasure in the spectacle which some of the worst men living were unable to contemplate without pity and horror.

The cruelty of James to the Scottish Presbyterians was a warning to English Nonconformists of what to expect when he came to the throne. Still more alarming were the reports of the persecution of Protestants by James's ally and patron, Louis XIV of France. The religious wars that ravaged France in the sixteenth century had been brought to an end by the Edict of Nantes, granting freedom of worship to the Huguenots or Protestants. In 1681, at the resumption of the persecution that would lead to the Revocation of the Edict of Nantes four years later, the Huguenots numbered about two million, or a tenth of the population of France. However, they had a disproportionate strength in the medical and legal professions, the civil service, the officer corps of the army and navy and, above all, in industries such as textiles, paper, printing and shipbuilding.

The persecution began with the banning of Protestant services, the closure of churches and schools, and the barring of Huguenots from most occupations. Among the punitive measures to enforce conversion were the *dragonnades*, or billeting in Protestant homes of dragoons, who were licensed to rob, rape, smash up the furniture and foul the floor with their excrement. Protestant pastors were banished from France, and those who remained to care for their flock were liable to be broken on the wheel. Lay Protestants were forbidden to leave, yet nevertheless between 100,000 and 250,000 Huguenots became refugees in Holland, the Protestant states of Germany, or in England.

Louis XIV saw the conversion of Huguenots as the prelude to his intended reconquest of Protestant Europe under the leadership of Catholic France and himself, 'the most Christian of kings'. In the closing years of the reign of Charles II of England, his patron, ally and paymaster Louis stood at the zenith of his greatness. As Macaulay writes of this ominous time for England:

> Nor was Lewis negligent. Everything at that moment favoured his designs. He had nothing to apprehend from the German Empire, which was then contending against the Turks on the Danube. Holland could not, unsupported, venture against him. He was therefore at liberty to indulge his ambition and insolence, without restraint. He seized Strasbourg, Courtray, Luxembourg. He exacted from the Republic of Genoa the most humiliating submission. The power of France at the time reached a higher point than it ever before or ever since attained, during the ten centuries which separated the reign of Charlemagne from the reign of Napoleon. It was not easy to say where her acquisition would stop, if only England could be kept in a state of vassalage.

Such was the peril facing the Protestant English in February 1685, when Charles II died and the Roman Catholic James II ascended the throne.

A Rebel Against James II

DURING THE REIGN OF JAMES II, from February 1685 until December 1688, Defoe took an active and perilous part in the great events that changed for ever the course of English history. In June 1685 he rode west from London to join the Duke of Monmouth's rebellion, almost certainly fought in the Battle of Sedgemoor, and somehow escaped the terrible retribution meted out at the 'Bloody Assizes' by Judge Jeffreys. In 1688 he wrote a brave first pamphlet denouncing James. When William of Orange landed at Brixham on 5 November 1688, Defoe rode out to greet the man who became his patron and mentor. Yet in all the millions of words he wrote, Defoe never once described or even directly acknowledged his presence at Sedgemoor, nor his services to William of Orange. This reticence seems especially odd when we think how modern journalists love to boast of 'dodging the bullets' in battle, or being on speaking terms with a prince. Yet it is in his fiction that Defoe sometimes describes the very events that he had himself experienced in the reign of James II. In his supposedly factual *Tour* Defoe mentions the Battle of Sedgemoor as he is passing through Bridgwater, but never even suggests that he had fought there, and in writing about King William III gives only a hint that he knew him personally. Yet in the fictional *Memoirs of a Cavalier* he writes a vivid account of the hero's experiences at the Battle of Edgehill, his escape in disguise from the Battle of Marston Moor, and his conversations with Charles I and Lord Fairfax, the Parliamentary general.

Defoe's silence about his activities during this time was testament to his secretive and mysterious nature; yet he also had justified fears of political retaliation. For two years after the Battle of Sedgemoor he lived in dread of arrest and the terrible punishment meted out to those found guilty of treason. He describes this dread in one of his novels,

Colonel Jack. In 1703, just after Queen Anne had come to the throne, Defoe was put in the pillory and incarcerated in Newgate Prison by Tory politicians who wanted to know of his dealings with the late King William III. The Jacobite rising of 1715 threatened to bring to the throne a Roman Catholic son of James II, and even as late as 1722 Defoe was alarmed by a Popish plot against Britain. As we can see from his novels, Defoe in his sixties still imagined that he was being hunted by grim and implacable enemies, such as Judge Jeffreys. So although the events that took place during the reign of James II appear only marginally in Defoe's own writing, they were just as important to his life as they were to England's destiny.

In the first few weeks of his reign James II took care not to alarm the majority of his subjects who were Anglican in religion and regarded him as their lawful king. His first Cabinet was formed of ministers from the previous reign, and even included two who had voted for the Exclusion Bill. James recalled Parliament for the first session since Oxford in 1681 and, thanks to the recent purge of the City of London and other boroughs, he obtained a large Tory majority in the House of Commons. Some Anglicans were shocked when James for the first time publicly attended Mass in his Roman Catholic chapel, but others praised his abandonment of pretence. Moreover, on St George's Day, 23 April 1685, James consented to be crowned by the Archbishop of Canterbury, using the Anglican rites, in Westminster Abbey.

It was not until May that James's true intentions and nature were revealed by the deeds of his terrible henchman George Jeffreys, the Chief Justice. During that month Jeffreys presided over the trial of Titus Oates; he was appointed a baron and member of the Cabinet; and he conducted the trial of Richard Baxter, an elderly and respected Nonconformist scholar. The career of Judge Jeffreys, and Macaulay's account of him, gave to generations of Englishmen an abhorrence of James II's reign, which still persists in parts of the West Country. If the very name Jeffreys is uttered with dread three centuries later, we have to understand how he appeared to Defoe, one of his possible victims.

George Jeffreys was born in Denbighshire, Wales, in 1648, educated at Shrewsbury and Westminster, called to the Bar in 1668 and three years later appointed the Common Serjeant of the City. He belonged at this time to the Puritan faction. Early practice at the Old Bailey, dealing with thieves and prostitutes, brought out his talents for bullying and abuse, which he later developed as a judge. According to Macaulay:

Impudence and ferocity sate on his brow. The glare of his eyes had a fascination for the unhappy victim on whom they fixed. Yet his brow and his eyes were less terrible than the savage lines of his mouth . . . There was a fiendish exultation in the way in which he pronounced sentence on offenders. Their weeping and imploring seemed to titillate him voluptuously, and he loved to scare them into fits by dilating with luxuriant amplifications on all the details of what they were to suffer. Thus when he had the opportunity of ordering an unlucky adventuress to be whipped at the cart's tail. 'Hangman', he would exclaim, 'I charge you pay particular attention to this lady! Scourge her soundly, man! Scourge her till the blood runs down! It is Christmas, a cold time for madam to strip! See that you warm her shoulders thoroughly!'

Jeffreys had first made a career in the Whig and Dissenting City of London, and had joined with glee in Oates's persecution of Catholics; indeed, Macaulay says, 'he had always appeared to be in a higher state of exaltation when he explained to Popish priests that they were to be cut down alive and were to see their own bowels burned, than when he passed ordinary sentences of death'. After the downfall of Oates and the Whigs Jeffreys sold his talents to James, the Duke of York, and helped to remove the Charter and privileges of the City of London, as well as condemn men falsely accused of playing a part in the Rye House Plot. Although Charles II had once declared that Jeffreys had 'no learning, no sense, no manners and more impudence than ten carted street-walkers', and had long resisted James's urgings to make him Chief Justice, Jeffreys was given the post in September 1683.

Soon after James's accession in February 1685 Jeffreys suggested to him a means by which customs revenue could be collected illegally, without the approval of Parliament. For this and other services he was made Lord Jeffreys of Wem, the first Chief Justice to be ennobled since the thirteenth century. He was now a Cabinet minister, the virtual ruler of London, and holder of all legal patronage in the land. He was the instrument of royal revenge on Titus Oates, who during his heyday had levelled atrocious accusations against James, then Duke of York, and his wife. After the fall of the Whigs in 1683 James had sued Oates for libel, winning damages of £100,000; unable to pay, Oates was thrown into prison. In May 1685 Oates was taken from prison to stand trial for the lies and perjury that had caused the death of at least thirty-four innocent people. Although Jeffreys had himself sentenced some of the Roman Catholics condemned on this testimony, he did not hesitate to hand out to Oates one of the most fearful sentences in history. He was to be whipped at the cart's tail from Aldgate to Newgate and, after a two-day pause, from Newgate to Tyburn, near the present Marble Arch. On the second day of this ordeal a witness counted 1,700 lashes. Amazingly, Oates survived to endure the second part of his punishment by standing in the pillory at various places in London. On one occasion he was almost killed by the brickbats thrown at him.

The suffering of Oates must have shocked Defoe, who always believed at least part of the story about a Popish plot. Moreover, eighteen years later Defoe would appear at the Old Bailey on charges carrying savage punishment, and stand in the very same pillory at the Temple where Oates had stood before him. Indeed, Oates may have seen him there, for after the fall of James he was freed from prison, given a state pension, and lived until 1705.

After dealing with Oates, Judge Jeffreys turned his attention to Richard Baxter, a seventy-year-old theologian who, although a Non-conformist, took a middle course between the extremes in politics and religion. When someone called him a Trimmer, after a sailor who alters his sails with the change of wind, Baxter replied that he could not join in condemning Trimmers when he remembered who it was who had blessed the peacemakers. In a recent commentary on the New Testament Baxter had dared to protest against the treatment of the Dissenters who, because they were not using the Book of Common Prayer, had been driven from their homes, stripped of their property and locked up in dungeons. An informant suggested that Baxter's writings constituted a crime against the Church and the State.

To request more time to prepare his defence, Baxter went to West-minster Mall on the very day that Titus Oates stood in the pillory in Palace Yard, provoking Judge Jeffreys to turn down his plea with a brutal outburst: 'Not a minute, to save his life! I can deal with saints as well as with sinners. There stands Oates on one side of the pillory, and if Baxter stood on the other, the two greatest rogues in the king-dom would stand together.' When the trial began and Baxter's lawyer addressed the court, Jeffreys interrupted: 'This is an old rogue, a schis-matical knave, a hypocritical villain. He hates the liturgy. He would have nothing but long-winded cant without books.' At which point Judge Jeffreys turned up his eyes, clasped his hands together, and started to sing through the nose in what he imagined was Baxter's style of praying: 'Lord we are thy people, thy peculiar people, thy dear people.' After this savage mockery, no doubt made more sinister by his Welsh intonation, Jeffreys heard with contempt the counsel's reminder that Charles II had offered Baxter the bishopric of Hereford: 'And what ailed him, old blockhead, that he did not take it?'

Judge Jeffreys then proceeded to call Baxter a dog, and said it would be no more than justice to whip such a villain through the whole city. 'Richard, thou art an old knave!' he roared at him. 'Thou hast written books enough to load a cart, and every book as full of sedition as an egg.' As the friends who had come to support him – and even his lawyers – were shaking and in tears before this onslaught, Baxter was bold enough to enquire: 'Does your lordship think that any jury will convict a man on such a trial?' Jeffreys knew that it would, for the new Tory sheriffs of London were able to pack a jury with like-minded bigots, and even honest juries quailed at the threats and commands of Jeffreys. Baxter was sent to prison for eighteen months.

The trial of Baxter, which Defoe later described as a 'beargarden', no doubt hardened his resolve to be a rebel. Facing a ban from public office in a City of London deprived of its Charter and freedoms, he now feared a persecution of Nonconformists similar to that which had taken place in France. The hopes of Defoe and the desperate Protestants now rested on Holland, where William of Orange led the resistance of Europe against the ambitions of Louis XIV. But although William distrusted James, he was married to his elder daughter Mary, and through her hoped to succeed to the throne of England by peaceful means. Moreover, in 1685 Holland stood almost alone against the military threat of France, and dared not become involved in a war against England as well. William had given asylum to Monmouth in 1683, but he had strongly disapproved of the Rye House Plot and naturally did not support Monmouth's claim to the throne of England. When Monmouth and his eighty-two followers left Holland in June to raise a rebellion in England, they did so without William's authority.

Monmouth landed at Lyme, the present Lyme Regis, on 11 June 1685. Some twenty years later, when Defoe was passing through Dorset on his Secret Service work, he reflected on Lyme's two moments of Protestant glory: 'It was in the sight of these hills that Queen Elizabeth's fleet under the command of Lord Howard of Effingham, then admiral, began first to engage in a close and resolved fight with the invincible Spanish Armada in 1588.' And this, he adds sombrely, was the landing place of 'the Duke of Monmouth and his unfortunate troop, of which I need say nothing, the history of it being so recent in the memory of so many living'.

Monmouth had chosen to raise his revolt in the West because of its Parliamentary sympathies during the Civil War and the warm reception it had given him during his tour in 1680. True to his expectations, the people of Lyme gave him a hero's welcome, with ringing of church bells and loud hurrahs, for which they would pay dearly a few months later. Monmouth read out his manifesto, drafted by one of his more extreme supporters, in which he accused King James of having burned down London – presumably meaning the Great Fire of 1666 – and of having poisoned his brother in order to succeed him. However, the proclamation did not assert Monmouth's claim to the throne but left the choice to a freely elected Parliament of the future. This manifesto still further alienated the gentry and Anglican clergy, who regarded James as their lawful king and had shown no inclination to join the rebellion.

After a skirmish at Bridport with some of the local militia, Monmouth rode into Taunton, to the acclaim of the children and grandchildren of those who had manned its ramparts for Parliament during the Civil War. Taunton was now a stronghold of the Dissenters; according to Macaulay, 'no man appeared without wearing in his hat a green bough, the badge of the popular cause'. From Taunton, Monmouth began a circuitous trip round the West Country, gathering soldiers for his army but showing uncertainty in his plan of action. He went first to Bridgwater, one of the few towns in England where there were still Whig magistrates and aldermen after the recent purges, and these lent authority to the recruitment of volunteers. Monmouth's army increased to 6,000 foot soldiers, but most of them were armed with home-made pikes, and a large proportion of his 1,000 horsemen were mounted on colts untrained for cavalry service and apt to shy at the sound of cannon or even drums. Meanwhile James's troops were moving on Somerset from Devonshire, Wiltshire and Oxfordshire.

Monmouth at first thought of trying to capture Bristol, then camped on the outskirts of Bath before moving to Frome. He could not advance on London itself without crossing Salisbury Plain and exposing his peasant army to the onslaught of James's cavalry. When he heard that the country people of Axminster had rallied to the defence of Protestantism, he decided to return once more to the nearby town of Bridgwater. On passing through Wells, the rebels displayed the ugly side of the old Cromwellian Puritanism. They not only tore the lead off the cathedral roof to melt down for bullets, an act which could be excused by the needs of war, but wantonly defaced some of the sacred ornaments. One of their captains, Grey, had to draw his sword to prevent his soldiers from desecrating the altar.

The news of Monmouth's rebellion was nowhere more welcome than in the City of London, the Protestant heart of England. Many years later Defoe remarked sourly: 'I remember, how boldly abundance of men talked for the Duke of Monmouth when he first landed; but if half of them had as boldly joined him sword in hand, he had never been routed' (*Review*, 13 March 1713). Since Defoe was one of the few hundred men from London who *joined* the rebellion, he had the right to criticize those who did not. Yet from all accounts it was hard for Monmouth's supporters to leave the City. In May, when rumours of an impending rebellion started to spread, the officers of the King were given extensive powers to arrest and search the homes of Whigs and Nonconformists. When the news of the landing reached London, the authorities sealed the exits from the City and set a patrol of boats on the Thames. Defoe never explained how or when he became one of the men who joined Monmouth 'sword in hand', and the only proof that he did so lies in the royal pardon given to him in 1687. This means that is it likely that he was present at Sedgemoor, and therefore fought in the last pitched battle on English soil.

When Monmouth returned to Bridgwater on 2 July 1685, the King's forces in the vicinity consisted of 2,500 regular troops and 1,500 men of the Wiltshire militia, most of them encamped on the plain of Sedgemoor, three miles from the town. They were accompanied by Dr Peter Mew, Bishop of Winchester, who had fought against Parliament in the Civil War, and doubtless thought that his presence in the King's camp would reassure those who were torn between horror of Popery and horror of rebellion. Although Monmouth realized that his greater numbers meant little against the King's regular troops, he took comfort from reports that the enemy army was drunk on the local Zoyland cider. He had little respect for Lord Feversham, the royal commander, and was not to know that Feversham's second-in-command, the young John Churchill, would later blossom into a military genius, the first Duke of Marlborough.

Macaulay reports that the town of Bridgwater was full of women 'who had repaired there to see their husbands, sons and lovers, and brothers once more . . . and many parted never to meet again'. A young woman Royalist, who had heard of Monmouth's plan to attack at night and thought it her duty to warn Lord Feversham, made her way to Sedgemoor:

> But that camp was not a place where female innocence could long be safe. Even the officers, despising alike the irregular force to which they were opposed and the negligent general who commanded them, had indulged largely in wine, and were ready for any excess of licentiousness and cruelty. One of them seized the unhappy maiden, refused to listen to her errand, and brutally outraged her. She fled in agonies of rage and shame, leaving the wicked army to its doom.

But the royal drunks and rapists did not get their desserts. Monmouth knew that his cause was lost, and the desperation showed in his face as he led his men out of Bridgwater at eleven o'clock at night on 5 July, in the hope of making a night assault on the King's men at Sedgemoor. Macaulay describes the prelude to battle: 'Orders were given that strict silence should be preserved, that no drums should be beaten and no shot fired. The word by which the insurgents were to recognise each other in the darkness was Soho. It had doubtless been selected in allusion to Soho Fields in London, where their leader's palace stood.'

Such was Macaulay's vivid description of the prelude to the Battle of Sedgemoor, written 160 years after it happened. Defoe, who had actually fought there, summed it up in a meagre paragraph in the *Tour*:

> He [Monmouth] went up to the top of the steeple with some of his officers, and viewing the situation of the king's army, by the help of perspectives, resolved to make an attempt upon them the same night, by way of prevention, and accordingly marched out of the town in the dead of the night to attack them, and had he not, either by the treachery of his guides, been brought to an unpassable ditch, where he could not get over, in the interval of which, the king's troops took the alarm, by the firing of a pistol among the duke's men, whether, also, by accident or by treachery, was not known; I say, had not those accidents, and by his own fate, conspired to his defeat, he had certainly cut the Lord Feversham's army all to pieces, but by these circumstances, he was brought to a battle on unequal terms, and defeated: The rest I need not mention.

The rebels were routed and fled the field even before the early midsummer dawn, desperate to escape the wrath of the victors. Macaulay describes the grim pursuit: 'The neighbouring villages long remembered with what a clatter of horsehoofs and what a storm of curses the whirlwind of cavalry went by. Before evening five hundred prisoners had been crowded into the parish church of Western Zoyland ... The next day a long line of gibbets appeared on the road leading from Bridgwater ... On each gibbet a prisoner was suspended. Four of the sufferers were left to rot in irons.' The Duke of Monmouth himself was one of the first to leave the field, and before six o'clock in the morning he had galloped twenty miles to the north. Some of his staff advised him to cross to Wales but, indecisive as ever, he headed south-east to hide in the New Forest. A few days later the King's men found him dressed as a yokel and took him to London.

Monmouth's supporters prayed he would meet his end with courage and dignity, but according to Macaulay, 'The fortitude of Monmouth was not of that highest sort of fortitude which is derived from reflection and from self-respect; nor had nature given him one of those stout hearts from which neither adversity nor pain can extort any sign of weakness.' Monmouth wrote to King James, his uncle, expressing remorse for his treason, and begging to be allowed to plead for his forgiveness in person. 'The arms of the prisoner were bound behind him with a silken cord,' Macaulay continues, 'and thus secured he was ushered into the presence of the implacable kinsman whom he had wronged. Then Monmouth threw himself to the ground and crawled to the king's feet. He wept. He tried to embrace his uncle's knees with his pinioned arms.' When Monmouth even suggested becoming a Roman Catholic, 'the King eagerly offered him spiritual assistance, but said nothing of parole or respite'. And so, in this craven manner, Monmouth went to the block, one of the many noble victims of Jack Ketch, whose name was later given to all executioners.

While Monmouth awaited death in London, his humble followers in the West were also paying the penalty of rebellion. As Lord Feversham hurried to court to receive King James's reward for victory, he left Colonel Percy Kirke in charge of the army in Somerset. Kirke's previous command had been the First Tangier Regiment, raised to make war on the infidel Muslims, its flag bearing the emblem of the paschal lamb. It was thus that his rude and ferocious men came to be known as 'Kirke's Lambs'.

Kirke's Lambs proceeded from Bridgwater to Taunton, the county town, accompanied by two carts piled high with wounded, and then a long line of walking prisoners, chained two by two. Macaulay describes what happened at Taunton: 'The signpost of the White Hart Inn served as a gallows. It is said that the work of death went on in sight of the windows where the officers of the Tangier Regiment were carousing, and that at every health, a wretch was turned off. When the legs of the dying man quivered in the last agony, the colonel ordered the drums to strike up. He would give the rebels, he said, music to their dancing.' Meanwhile the jails of Somerset and Dorset were filling up with the wretches awaiting trial at the forthcoming Western Circuit, soon to be infamous as the 'Bloody Assizes'.

Judge Jeffreys began his circuit at Winchester in Hampshire, a county almost untouched by Monmouth's rebellion. However, an elderly Hampshire gentlewoman, Alice Lisle, the widow of one of Cromwell's lords, was accused of having sheltered a fugitive from Monmouth's army, knowing him to be a traitor. Jeffreys bullied the jury into giving a guilty verdict, whereupon he ordered Alice Lisle to be burned to death that same afternoon. The Winchester clergy, the statesman Lord Clarendon, and many ladies of rank in Hampshire protested against this cruel sentence, but Jeffreys relented only so far as to change the method of execution from burning to beheading.

At Dorchester Jeffreys let it be known that the 300 rebels awaiting trial in Dorset had no hope of a pardon or respite unless they pleaded guilty. Seventy-four of them were sentenced to death. In Somerset, the heart of the Monmouth Rebellion, Jeffreys ordered 233 prisoners to be hung, drawn and quartered. Macaulay explains how their fate was made an example to the county:

At every spot where two roads met, on every market place, on the green of every large village which had furnished Monmouth with soldiers, ironed corpses clattering in the wind, or heads and quarters stuck on poles, poisoned the air, and made the mind sick with horror. In many parishes the peasants could not assemble in the house of God without seeing the ghastly face of a neighbour grinning at them over the porch.

The savagery of Jeffreys was not confined to hanging, drawing and quartering. At Dorchester he sentenced John Tutchin, a radical journalist, to be whipped once a fortnight through each market town in the county. He also condemned 841 of the Monmouth rebels to transportation servitude, not in New England or Virginia, where they might find a congenial climate and company, but in one of the West Indian islands, toiling alongside African slaves. Macaulay says that at least a fifth of these convicts died and were thrown to the sharks before they reached the Caribbean, and many more died of disease before completing their ten-year sentence. Along with many others at court James's French queen was given the right to sell these slaves to their future West Indian owners, and she is said to have made 1,000 guineas on the transaction. Most of these West Country rebels went to Barbados, where their descendants still form a tenth of the island's population. Indeed, these white Bajans still speak with an antiquated 'Zummerzetshire' accent. Some of the convicts were later freed and came back to England, and may have contributed to Defoe's account of a West Indian island in *Robinson Crusoe*. Although Crusoe's island is said to be near the mouth of the Orinoco, like Trinidad and Tobago, in climate and vegetation it more closely resembles the healthier, cooler Barbados. Like Crusoe's island, Barbados differs greatly on its windward and leeward coasts.

As already mentioned, the only evidence that Defoe took part in the Monmouth Rebellion is the royal pardon given to him on 31 May 1687, now published in the *Calendar of State Papers Domestic Series*. Just as we do not know how he came to be at the Battle of Sedgemoor, we can only surmise how he escaped from the wrath of Kirke's Lambs and Judge Jeffreys. He had the primary requisite for escape – a horse. He also possessed a valid reason for travelling in the West Country, since Devon and Somerset were among the places he visited in order to buy hosiery. Some of Monmouth's supporters escaped the country and lived for a time in Holland and Germany, and it is possible that Defoe was among them. This would account for the references in the *Tour* to his widespread travels in Europe; but there is no shred of evidence that Defoe ever went further abroad than Scotland. His very reticence on the Monmouth affair is perhaps the surest proof of its importance to him. The defeat at Sedgemoor, the frantic escape and then two years spent in dread of arrest and appearing before Judge Jeffreys would have tested the courage of any man, and undoubtedly left their mark on Defoe. His experience gave him the lifelong sense of being a lone fugitive in search of a hiding-place. This feeling of being pursued is experienced at one time or another by all Defoe's fictional heroes and heroines, even by Robinson Crusoe when he finds he is not alone on his island. In two of his novels, *The Memoirs of a Cavalier* and *Colonel Jack*, Defoe describes an escape from pursuers after defeat in battle. The Cavalier disguises himself as a yokel to escape Cromwell's troopers after the Battle of Marston Moor, and Colonel Jack has taken up arms for the Old Pretender in 1715. In the characters of a Cavalier and a Jacobite, Defoe describes his feelings as a fugitive on the other side.

King James's triumph at Sedgemoor did not destroy the will of his opponents, even in Dorset and Somerset, which had endured the Bloody Assizes. Defoe writes in his *Tour* of the people of Taunton: 'They suffered deeply in the Duke of Monmouth's rebellion, but paid King James home for the cruelty exercised by Jeffreys among them; for when the Prince of Orange arrived the whole town ran in to him, with so universal a joy, that, twas thought, if he had wanted it, he might have raised a little army there, and in the adjacent part of the country.'

Taunton was a Dissenting town, but James's cruelty after the Battle of Sedgemoor had dismayed and shocked many loyal High Churchmen, notably Thomas Ken, the Bishop of Bath and Wells, whose cathedral had been vandalized by Monmouth's soldiers, Bishop Ken is still remembered as the author of some of our simplest and dearest hymns, such as:

> Awake my soul, and with the sun
> The daily stage of duty run . . .

As one of the royal chaplains at Winchester, Ken had forbidden the use of his house to Nell Gwyn, King Charles II's mistress, saying that a woman of ill repute should not be seen in the house of a clergyman. The affable Charles bore him no ill will and afterwards offered the see of Bath and Wells to 'the little black fellow that refused his lodgings to poor Nelly'. Macaulay describes how in the aftermath of Sedgemoor, when the jails of Somerset and Dorset were filling up with the wretches awaiting trial by Jeffreys, Bishop Ken showed kindness to the prisoners.

Three years after the Monmouth Rebellion Ken and six other bishops were put in the Tower of London by James II for refusing to support a Declaration of Indulgence, which greatly increased the power of the Roman Catholic Church. In order to weaken the Church of England James suspended the penal laws against not only the Catholics but also the Protestant Nonconformists, and actually wooed their support. This extraordinary volte face caused a crisis of conscience among the Dissenters, inspiring Defoe's first known pamphlet.

An earlier Declaration of Indulgence during the reign of Charles II permitted the Roman Catholics to worship in private dwellings, though even this aroused fears of a 'papal plot'. King James II's Declaration permitted them to build and decorate temples, and even walk in procession along Fleet Street with crosses, images and censers. Then the King and the Church both began to bid against each other for the favour of the Protestant Dissenters, hitherto a despised class.

King James released from prison and tried to win the support of Richard Baxter, whom Jeffreys had called at his trial 'an old rogue, a schismatical knave, a hypocritical villain'. Not surprisingly, Baxter turned down this offer of friendship. James, through his agent Lord Aylesbury, even offered a government post to John Bunyan, author of *The Pilgrim's Progress*, who had spent twelve years in Bedford jail for his Puritan opinions. Bunyan resisted these blandishments, but managed to secure some seats on Bedford Corporation for followers of his independent church. King James had more success with the Quaker William Penn, whose father had been a friend and fellow naval officer; because of his favourable treatment during the reign Penn was later imprisoned by the Whigs and vilified by Macaulay.

The large Dissenting community in the City of London was fearful of Popery, but tempted to get its own back on the Church of England. Soon after the Declaration of Indulgence in August 1687 a number of Nonconformist bodies sent a 'Letter of Thanks' to James, but the following year, when Bishop Ken and his colleagues were in the Tower, the majority of Dissenters rallied to their support. It was during this time of acute political and religious turmoil that Defoe published his first pamphlet, *A Letter to a Dissenter, from his Friend at the Hague, Concerning the Penal Laws and the Test; showing that the Popular Plea for Liberty of Conscience is not concerned in that Quarter*. The title page carries the imprint 'Tot de Hague, gedrucht door Hans Verzaeght', or 'Printed at The Hague by Hans Verzaeght', but this could be a device for concealing the name of an English publisher. Since Defoe had been pardoned in 1687, and was busy in trade in London in 1688, it seems unlikely that he went to Holland to write this imaginary letter. His first pamphlet begins in the lucid, forceful and carefully reasoned manner that he sustained all his life:

I suppose you are very busie about the choice of Parliament-Men and all are hard at work to elect such members as may comply with the great design to repeal the Penal Laws and the Test. The pretence I confess is very plausible, for all men

are fond of liberty of conscience, who dissent from the established religion; but you and I have lived long enough in the
world to observe that the most pernicious designs have been
carried on under the most plausible pretences; and that is
reason enough to enquire whether there be no danger of it
now.

Defoe sees King James's offer as an attempt to 'wheedle unthinking
people and to catch them with a very inviting bait'. The only purpose
of the repeal of the Test Act 'must be to give a legal qualification to
Papists to possess all places of honour, profit and trust in the nation;
that is to put your lives and liberties in their hands.' Defoe advises his
fellow Protestants not to believe in Papist offers of toleration: 'For it
would be very surprising to find a Roman Catholic prince, whose
conscience is directed by a Jesuit, to be really zealous for liberty of
conscience, when all the world knows what opinion the Church of
Rome has about liberty of conscience: witness the mild and gentle
usage of the French Protestants by a king whose conscience is directed
by a tender-hearted Jesuit.'

Defoe was proud of this early pamphlet, and sometimes referred to
it in his newspaper, the *Review*, during later religious debates. For
instance, on 24 September 1711 he boasts of having protested openly
against the address of thanks to James II, although this annoyed some
Dissenters: 'I had their anger again when in print, I opposed at the
utmost hazard, the taking of the Penal Law and Test, and had the
discouragement to be told by some grave, but weak good men, that I
was a young man, and did not understand the Dissenters' interest, but
was doing them harm instead of good; to which, when time undeceived
them, I only returned the words of Elijah to Job, for which God never
reproved him – Old men are not always wise, neither do the aged
understand wisdom.' In the *Review* of 1 May 1712 he recalls how in
1688 the Church of England had grovelled to the Dissenters in hope
of drumming up support: 'Read their whining, fawning, truly canting
sermons.' Not that he would have had the Dissenters join with King
James: 'No, no, I thank God I was of age then to bear my testimony
against them, and to affect some of those that were of that opinion.'

By the autumn of 1688 the opposition to James included most of
the nation, and several prominent Tories signed the appeal to William
of Orange to come to England. The crisis came to a head when James,
in an attempt to hold on to his throne and defend his religion, brought

Irish troops over to England. In his *Tour* Defoe describes some of the skirmishes between James's Irish troops and William's advancing army. He also traces the origins of the panic fear of the Irish that swept through England during that year of the Glorious Revolution, and persisted into the eighteenth century, and even beyond.

Modern history books have taught the English to think of themselves as wicked oppressors of Ireland from the sixteenth century onwards. The Protestant side of the story, though it is well remembered in Ulster, is almost unknown to the modern British. The Catholic Irish revolt began in October 1641, just before the start of the Civil War in England, since the rebels believed, with reason, that victory for the Puritans would mean an assault on their religion, and further seizure of land. A massacre of the Protestants took place in the winter of 1641–2, especially in Antrim and Derry, and the horrified British public read stories of settlers burned alive, disembowelled and hanged, of women raped, and children spitted on knives or drowned in bogs. Although the number of killed was nowhere near the 100,000 claimed by Protestant pamphleteers, a massacre certainly took place.

Parliament had believed from the start that Charles I was on the side of the Irish rebels. In 1643 he agreed to an armistice with the Irish leaders in order to free the government troops for service in Britain and, as his position grew worse, he tried to recruit a Catholic Irish army. In July 1644 1,000 Irish warriors landed at Ardnamurchan in Scotland, bringing with them their wives, children, cattle and priests, a band of crusaders who never sat down to eat without first hearing a Latin grace and never went into battle without first taking the sacrament. In his *Memoirs of a Cavalier* Defoe suggests that this Irish invasion horrified many of Charles's supporters:

> But the King was persuaded to make one step further; and that, I confess, was unpleasing to us all; and some of his best and most faithful servants took the freedom to speak plainly to him of it; and that was bringing some regiments of the Irish themselves over. This cast, as we thought an odium upon our whole nation, being some of those very wretches who had dipped their hands in the innocent blood of the Protestants, and with unheard of butcheries, had massacred so many thousands of English in cold blood.
>
> Abundance of gentlemen forsook the King upon this score; and seeing they could not brook the fighting in conjunction

with this wicked generation, came into the Declaration of the Parliament, and making composition for their estates, lived retired lives all the rest of the war, or went abroad.

From the start of the reign of James II Catholic Ireland was once more a cause of alarm and contention in Protestant Britain. The new King appointed Richard Talbot, the Earl of Tyrconnel, as head of the Irish army, with free rein to advance the careers of his fellow Roman Catholics. As Lord Deputy from 1687, Tyrconnel still further subverted the Protestant hold on power. In the autumn of 1688 rumours swept Ireland that the Catholics were planning another massacre, worse than that of 1641, and hundreds of Protestants fled the island, including Defoe's future antagonist, Jonathan Swift. At this point, when leading statesmen in England had already invited William of Orange's intervention, James decided to call in Irish troops. This had been urged on him by the Queen and the French Ambassador, but James must have understood the folly of what he was doing, for he dithered, and ended up by defeating his purpose. Lord Macaulay describes his indecision at the start of one of his great bravura passages:

He brought over Irishmen, not enough indeed to hold down the single city of London, or the single county of York, but more than enough to excite the alarm and rage of the whole kingdom from Northumberland to Cornwall. Battalion after battalion raised and trained by Tyrconnel, landed on the west coast and moved towards the capital; and Irish recruits were imported in considerable numbers to fill up the vacancies in the English regiments. Of the many errors which James committed, none was more fatal than this.

Not even the arrival of a brigade of Lewis's musketeers would have excited such resentment and shame as our ancestors felt when they saw armed columns of Papists, just arrived from Dublin, moving in military pomp along the high roads . . . No man of English blood then regarded the aboriginal Irish as his countrymen. They did not belong to our branch of the great human family . . . When they talked English their pronunciation was ludicrous; and their phraseology was grotesque . . . They were therefore foreigners; and of all foreigners the most hated and despised; . . . the Englishman felt proud when he compared his own fields with the desolate bogs whence the Rapparees [brigands] issued forth to rob and murder, and his own dwelling with the hovels where the peasants and the hogs of the Shannon wallowed in filth together ... The English felt as the white inhabitants of Charleston and New Orleans would feel if those towns were occupied by negro garrisons.

When William of Orange landed at Brixham on 5 November 1688, some of these Irish troops were deployed to stop his advance on London – initially at Newbury, according to Defoe's *Tour*:

> Here it was that the vanguard, or first line of the Prince of Orange's army was posted, when the Irish dragoons, who were posted in Reading, finding that they should be attacked in a few days, had put the town's people into such a fright, by threatening to burn and plunder the town, and cut all the people's throats, that they sent express messengers to the Dutch general officer Grave van Nassau for help, who sent them a detachment of but two hundred and eighty dragoons, though the troops in the town were near seven hundred men.

On reaching Reading, Defoe continues his *Tour* with the story of how the Irish had planned to 'murther and plunder' the townspeople:

> It was on a Sunday morning, that the Irish dragoons had resolved on the designed mischief, if they really intended it: In order to do it, they posted at the principal church in the piazza there, and might, indeed, easily have locked all the people in it, and have cut all their throats; also they placed a company of foot in the church yard of another church, over against the Bear Inn ... so that if they really did not intend to massacre the people, as their officers said they did not, yet that way of posting the men, joined to the loud oaths and protestations, that they would do it, made it look as much like such a design, as anything unexecuted, or unattempted, could do.

Defoe seems to suggest that the Irish were on the point of beginning the massacre when they were taken by surprise:

> The Irish had placed a sentinel on the top of the steeple of the great church, with orders, if he saw any troops advance, to fire his piece, and ring the bell; the fellow, being surprised with the sight, for he discovered the Dutch but a little before

they reached the town, fired his musket, but forgot to ring the bell, and came down. However, his firing gave the alarm sufficiently, and the troops in the town, who were all under arms before, whether for the designed execution, or not, I will not determine ... had little more to do, but to post their troops, which they did with skill enough, being commanded by Sir John Lanier, an experienced officer, and colonel of a regiment of horse in King James's army; and had the men done their duty, they might easily have repulsed the few troops that attacked them; but the Dutch entering the town in two places, one by the ordinary road from Newbury, and the other by the Broad Street near where the horse-fair is kept, forced both the posts, and entered the market-place, where the main body of the Irish troops were drawn up.

More than eighteen months before the Battle of the Boyne and other encounters in Ireland the Protestant Dutch first bested the Catholic Irish at Reading:

The first party of the Dutch found a company of foot drawn up in the church-yard over against the Bear Inn, and a troop of dragoons in the Bear Inn yard; the dragoons hearing the Dutch were at hand, their officer bravely drew them out of the inn yard, and faced the Dutch in the open road, the church yard wall being lined with musketeers to flank the street; the Dutch, who came on full gallop, fell in upon the dragoons, sword in hand, and with such irresistible fury, that the Irish were immediately put into confusion, and after three or four minutes bearing the charge, they were driven clear out of the street. At the very same instant, another party of the Dutch dragoons, dismounting, entered the church-yard, and the whole body posted there, fled also, with little or no resistance. After this, the dragoons mounting again, forced their squadrons, and entered the market place.

Defoe goes on to claim, as an 'eye-witness', that here at Reading 'began the universal alarm that spread over the whole kingdom (almost at the same time) of the Irish being come to cut every bodies throats'. As the threats of the Irishmen had obliged the magistrates of the town to apply to William of Orange's army for help, 'so you cannot doubt, but that many of the inhabitants fled for their lives by all the ways that they could; and this was chiefly in the night; for in the day, the soldiers, who had their eyes everywhere, stopped them, and would not permit them to stir, which still increased their terror.' The refugees not only spread but embellished stories of horror:

> Those that got away, you may be sure, were in the utmost fright and amazement, and they had nothing less in their mouths, but that the Irish would (and by that time had) burnt the town, and cut the throats of all the people, men, women and children. I was then at Windsor, and in the very interval of all this fright, King James being gone, and the army retreated from Salisbury, the Lord Feversham calls the troops together, and causing them to lay down their arms, disbands them, and gives them leave, every man, to go whither they would.

This was the same Lord Feversham who had beaten Monmouth's army at Sedgemoor.

The Irish dragoons who had been beaten at Reading first rallied at Twyford, then marched towards Colebrook and Staines, meanwhile spreading alarm ahead to Kingston, Hounslow, Brentford, Egham, Uxbridge and London itself. On their way to Colebrook the Irish as usual blustered about how they would burn and plunder the town, although it was occupied by Scottish troops in the service of James. The Scottish colonel, whose name Defoe regrets that he cannot remember, refused to admit the Irish, and swore to defend the town to the last man. The enraged and frustrated Irish then headed for Staines, once more swearing to kill every man, woman and child they found there. Once the Colebrook people had recovered from their own terror, they sent warning ahead to Staines of the danger:

> It is impossible to express the consternation of the people [of Staines]. Away they run out of the town, dark and rainy, and midnight as it was, some to Kingston, some over the heath to Hounslow, and Brentford, some to Egham, and some to Windsor, with the dreadful news; and by that time they reached those places, their fears had turned their story from saying, they would burn and kill, to they had burned and killed, and were coming after you to do the like.

The same alarm was carried by others from Colebrook to Uxbridge ... and thus some one way, and some another, it spread like the undulations of the water in a pond, when a flat stone is cast upon the surface: From Brentford and Kingston, and from Uxbridge, it came severally and by different roads, to London, and so, as I may say, all over England; nor is it wonderful, that it seemed to be all over the nation in one day.

Defoe appears to have traced the course of these rumours:

I rode the next morning to Maidenhead: at Slough they told me Maidenhead was burned, and Uxbridge, and Reading, and I know not how many more, were destroyed; and when I came to Reading, they told me, Maidenhead and Okingham were burnt, and the like. From thence I went to Henley, where the Prince of Orange, with the second line of his army, entered that very afternoon, and there they had the same account, with the news of King James's flight; and thus it spread every way insensibly.

This is followed by a vivid account of the spread of rumour, as refugees embellish stories of horror in order to justify their flight. But it is doubtful whether the fear of the Catholic Irish originated at Reading. Stories of an impending massacre of the Protestants had spread through Ireland during the autumn of 1688 and were carried to England by fugitives, gathering more credibility as the first of Tyrconnel's battalions set foot in this country. Fear of an Irish Papist terror was propagated not through the printed word, but through the ditty and tune of 'Lillibullero', which, like 'La Marseillaise', was one of those songs that altered history. In this cod Irish ballad a Papist congratulates one of his fellow 'teagues' on the news of the appointment as Lord Deputy of Richard Talbot, the Earl of Tyrconnel:

Say brother Teague, hast heard the decree,
That we shall have a new deputee?

He goes on in his barbarous brogue to predict the coming triumph of Popery and the exclusion of Protestant officers; the Great Charter (Magna Charta) and the 'prater' who administers it will be hung on the same rope, and Talbot will cut the throats of the Englishmen. Soon 'Lillibullero' was sung or whistled all over England, particularly in the army, which greatly resented the new Irish troops who had been foisted on them. Lawrence Sterne, in his novel *Tristram Shandy*, written more than seventy years after the Glorious Revolution, remarks that the old soldier Uncle Toby would always respond to a difficult question by 'whistling half a dozen bars of Lillabullero'.

By mid December James and Judge Jeffreys realized that the game was up, and tried to escape to France by boat. Jeffreys disguised himself as a sailor and boarded a ship off Wapping, but was then overcome by the need for a drink and was recognized at the Red Cow Tavern. He died in prison the following year before he could stand trial for his crimes. James got as far as the mouth of the river Swale on the Kent coast, where he was apprehended by fishermen and taken to Faversham. In his *Tour* Defoe reproaches the town

> that the fishermen and rabble can never be excused, who treated the king, even after they were told who he was, with the utmost indecency, using his majesty; (for he was then their sovereign, even in the acknowledged sense of his enemies) I say, using him with such indignity in his person, such insolence in their behaviour, and giving him such opprobrious and abusive language, and searching him in the rudest and most indecent manner, and indeed rifling him; that the king himself said, he was never more apprehensive of his life than at that time . . .

The expression of concern over the treatment of James was no doubt inserted to please Tory readers; perhaps it was one of Defoe's private jokes. James was taken to London, politely treated by William, his son-in-law, then made a successful escape to France. He went on to raise a Catholic revolt in Ireland, whose bloody failure helped to create the suspicion and hatred that still bedevil our islands today.

Bankrupt and Pamphleteer

THE LANDING OF William of Orange on 5 November 1688 and the Glorious Revolution that followed, were hailed by Defoe and celebrated by generations of Englishmen as the guarantee of parliamentary government, constitutional monarchy, religious toleration and economic prosperity. William's triumph at the Battle of the Boyne on 1 July 1690 and his subjugation of Catholic Ireland have made 'King Billy' the hero of Protestant Ulstermen to the present day: his figure on horseback adorns numberless banners and gable-ends. Yet William cared little about the future of England or Ireland, and intervened in these countries only in furtherance of his war against France.

A descendant of William the Silent of the house of Nassau, the liberator of Holland in the sixteenth century, William of Orange was called to his country's rescue in 1672, when Louis XIV's armies had occupied four of the seven United Provinces. Appointed Stadtholder at twenty-two, Prince William was able to save the province of Holland only by breaking the dykes and flooding the land approaches to Amsterdam and The Hague. In that terrible year of 1672 the Dutch were fighting the English at sea, as well as the French on land, for Charles II had sent his fleet to the assistance of his patron Louis XIV. The experience taught William the overriding importance of friendship with Protestant England. He was, through his mother, the grandson of Charles I, and in 1677 he strengthened the English connection by wedding his cousin Mary, the daughter of the Duke of York, the future James II. Through Mary, William hoped one day to obtain by rightful succession the throne he would later seize by force.

During his early years as Stadtholder William drove the French from the seven United Provinces, and by 1678 had won a favourable peace at the Treaty of Nijmegen. Meanwhile he had built up a large and well-disciplined army recruited from every Protestant country in

Europe, and forged an alliance with Roman Catholic Austria, Spain and the Pope himself. These allies supported William when he invaded England and turned out the Catholic King James. They supported him when he invaded Ireland and put down a Catholic rebellion. The bells of the Vatican rang with joy at the news of King William's victory at the Boyne in 1690.

William's domestic policy was to keep the English able and willing to fight the French through the exercise of their natural political talents. The Bill of Rights and later an Act of Settlement established the principle of a constitutional, Protestant monarchy whose ministers were responsible to Parliament. The creation of the National Debt, the Bank of England and a growing supply of capital in the City enabled William to raise the money to fight his war without resort to coercion. A relaxation of the constraints on the Press and religious Nonconformists contributed to a spirit of tolerance and harmony. Although a Calvinist by religion, William distrusted the Whigs as descendants of the men who had cut off the head of his grandfather, Charles I, and suspected them of republicanism. He preferred the Tories, except that their enmity to Dissenters split the country in time of war and could lead to trouble with Holland.

After the first rapturous welcome the English did not take kindly to William. The Whigs, who had hoped he would be their king, as Charles II had been the king of the Tories, were swiftly disappointed. The Tories accepted William as long as Mary shared the throne, for she was a Stuart and therefore a lawful sovereign, but after her death in 1694 they grew increasingly hostile. William's poor knowledge of English, his bleak manner and humourless personality did not endear him to his new subjects. At Brixham, where he was carried ashore on the back of a local fisherman it was said that he began his speech to the crowd, 'I haff come for your goots . . .', meaning the good of the country, at which one of his hearers interjected, 'Aye, and our chattels too . . .' Although the story is no doubt apocryphal, it sums up the later English opinion of William, even in Nonconformist Brixham. As a soldier, statesman and leader of men, William enjoyed every attribute – except charm. In this he was the opposite of the Duke of Monmouth, who had landed in England three years earlier. Monmouth had an abundance of charm, but little or none of William's courage, endurance, wisdom and foresight. Even Lord Macaulay, who made William the hero of his *History of England*, has this to say of his manner at Court:

He seldom came forth from his closet; and when he appeared in the public rooms, he stood among the crowd of courtiers and ladies, stern and abstracted, making no jest and smiling at none. His freezing look, his silence, the dry and concise answers he uttered when he could keep silence no longer, disgusted noblemen and gentlemen who had been accustomed to be slapped on the back by their royal masters, called Jack or Harry, congratulated about race cups or rallied about actresses.

The most heartfelt welcome came from people such as Defoe in the City of London, the stronghold of Protestantism and parliamentary government. The City had lost its Charter for its resistance to Charles II, and lived in danger during the three-year rule of James II. In his *Tour* Defoe speaks of the former 'emulation' or rivalry between the Court and the City, 'for the Court envied the City's greatness, and the citizens were ever jealous of the court's designs.' By 'the Court' he meant also those Whig and Tory politicians who squabbled for power and preferment after the Glorious Revolution and joined in accusing William of ingratitude.

When William entered the City to hear a proclamation of loyalty read at the Guildhall, four regiments of militia lined the way up Ludgate Hill, round St Paul's Cathedral and along Cheapside. Defoe could well have served in one of those regiments, for we know that he took part in a military pageant in honour of William and Mary on 29 October 1689, the first Lord Mayor's Show after the Glorious Revolution. A rival journalist, John Oldmixon, described the event:

The City of London, in gratitude for the Care his Majesty took of their Liberties ... prepared [a Balcony] for them at the Angel in Cheapside to see the Show, which, for the great number of Livery men, the full appearance of the Militia and Artillery Company, the rich adornments of the pageants, and the splendid and good order of the whole proceeding, out-did all that had been seen before upon [Lord Mayor's Day]; and what deserved to be particularly mentioned ... was a Royal Regiment of Volunteer Horse, made up of the chief Citizens, who being gallantly mounted and richly accoutred, were led by the Earl of Peterborough ... Among these Troopers, who were for the most part Dissenters, was Daniel Foe, at that time a Hosier in Freeman's Yard, Cornhill.

This Royal Regiment attended the King and Queen from Whitehall to the Guildhall, where they joined in the Lord Mayor's feast. Defoe belonged to a regiment chosen to be 'the guards for their Majesties persons', although it was open to those 'who cannot take the Test as related to the Sacrament' – that is to say, Dissenters. The regiment was commanded by Charles Mordaunt, the Earl of Peterborough, one of the Council of Nine who advised Queen Mary whenever William was abroad. The captains of the regiment included the grandest names in the City. Its prominence at the Lord Mayor's Day of 1689 was seen by contemporaries as a sign of royal respect to the City and the Dissenters.

> The nobler citizens themselves present,
> To guard his person and his government
> No Hireling Soldiers for their Countries good,
> But freely spend their treasure as their blood.

Inevitably, the Royal or City Regiment also attracted jeers, like this from a balladeer, Joseph Haynes:

> Some smoking, some whistling, all meaning no harm
> Like Yorkshire attorneys, coming up to a term.
> On bobtails, on longtails, on trotters and pacers!
> On pads, hawkers, hunters, or higglers and racers.

In the following year, 1690, when William considered taking the Royal Regiment to fight in Ireland, Haynes pretended to believe that these ceremonial troopers were frightened sick at the prospect of battle. Defoe's service as a trooper was held against him thirty years later in one of the satires on *Robinson Crusoe* in 1719. The author, Charles Gildon, imagines Defoe confessing: 'I was most damnably frightened with the dream; nay, more than ever I was in my life, even more than when we had news that King William designed to take into Flanders the Royal Regiment.'

Defoe's rival journalists were probably unaware of the fact that he had served in the brief Monmouth Rebellion. However, we can be certain that Defoe's participation in the Battle of Sedgemoor was known to his captain of horse, to Lord Peterborough, the Lieutenant-Colonel of the regiment and probably to King William himself, whose main concern was the army. As we shall see, there is evidence that towards the end of his reign, William employed Defoe as a pamphleteer, adviser and informant, though characteristically Defoe gives misleading accounts of this. However, at several points in the *Tour*, Defoe suggests that he also knew William and Mary early on in their reign, when they were making their homes and planting their gardens at Hampton Court, Windsor Castle and Kensington Palace. Moreover, he writes with what is apparently inside knowledge of William's fondness for painting and Mary's innovations in furniture, dress and interior decoration. Clearly Defoe looked upon his hero and heroine as arbiters of the country's taste and fashion, as well as the saviours of its freedom. So we can fairly assume that Defoe, as one of the bright young troopers of Lord Peterboroughs' Royal Regiment, attended the King and Queen as a kind of escort or equerry. Most kings and queens, before and since, have chosen military courtiers from titled young men in one of the grander regiments; William and Mary were just as content with a merchant and Dissenter, especially one who had fought at Sedgemoor. Defoe must have reminded William of one of those Dutch burgher soldiers that Rembrandt portrayed in *The Night Watch*. His intelligent conversation on history, military science, religion and even gardening, would have made him agreeable to his serious-minded King.

In the second circuit of his *Tour*, which takes him through south-east England, Defoe remarks that the beautiful buildings and gardens on either side of the Thames between Richmond and London are unsurpassed by any place in the world, 'no not the country for twenty miles round Paris, though that indeed is a kind of prodigy'. He mentions gardening as one of the four innovations brought to this country by William and Mary. The Queen, he says, introduced the rage for East Indian calico, which later became so popular that it threatened English textiles. Defoe had himself played a part in getting through Parliament the Calico Act of 1721, which banned these imports. Mary also 'brought in the custom or humour, as I may call it, of furnishing houses with China-ware, which increased to a strange degree afterwards, piling their china upon the tops of cabinets, scrutores [escritoires] and every chimney-piece, to the tops of the ceilings, and even setting up shelves for their china-ware ... till it became a grievance in the expense of it, and even injurious to the families and estates.' One can imagine that many husbands shared Defoe's anger at the piling up of this china-ware in their homes.

Defoe credits to William the English love of painting, a dubious claim when one thinks of the patronage shown by Charles I to Lely and Van Dyck. At this stage of his journey Defoe mentions how William introduced evergreens, which before his accession had been planted only in Sir Stephen Fox's garden at Isleworth and in Sir William Temple's at East Sheen. When William saw the latter, he 'was so pleased that according to his Majesty's usual expression when he liked a place very well, he stood and looked around him from the head of one of the canals, Well says his majesty, I could dwell here five days.' Defoe's obviously first-hand account captures William in one of his rare displays of pleasure. After William had planted the garden at Hampton Court, 'the gentlemen followed everywhere with such a gust [gusto or relish] that the alteration is indeed wonderful thro the whole kingdom; but no where more than in the two counties of Middlesex and Surrey, as they border on the River Thames; the beauty and expanse of which are only to be wondered at, not described.'

William and Mary spent as much time as they could in the Thames Valley or Kensington, away from the acrid smoke of London. William suffered from chronic asthma and found Whitehall Palace intolerable; Mary also complained of feeling confined by its walls. The royal couple were particularly fond of the palace at Hampton Court, which Cardinal Wolsey had built for himself before he fell out of favour with Henry VIII. William and Mary kept most of the Tudor buildings but asked Sir Christopher Wren to add a classical façade to the east wing. It was here that they established their most famous garden.

When Defoe reaches Hampton Court in the *Tour*, he remarks that the clergy were excellent judges of where to build, for Wolsey had chosen the finest stretch of the Thames between Staines and Windsor bridges, with gardens extending down to the water yet never flooding, the river high enough to be navigable yet low enough to be 'a little pleasantly rapid, so that the stream looks always cheerful, not slow and sleeping, like a pond'. This meant that the waters were always clear and keen, the bottom in view, the fish playing, and in sight; 'and in a word, it has everything that can make an inland, or as I may call it, a country river, pleasant and agreeable.'

The original Hampton Court was, Defoe acknowledges, a building fit for a king and, although not a masterpiece by modern standards, left room for expansion and improvement. Queen Mary liked it so much that even while Wren was at work on the new state apartments she made a temporary home in the Water Gallery by the river, and filled it with all her favourite things, such as her Delft ware, her china, and the portraits she had commissioned of her ladies-in-waiting. Mary had made her new home, Defoe adds, on a sentimental note, 'as if she had been conscious that she had but a few years to enjoy it'. She died in 1694 and was buried in Westminster Abbey, to funeral music by the organist Henry Purcell, who died a few months later.

At Hampton Court Defoe once more claims that King William 'brought into England the love of fine paintings', and cites as examples the two cartoons he saw there – St Paul 'preaching on Mars-hill to the self-wise Athenians', and St Peter passing sentence of death on Ananias: 'These two strike the mind with the utmost surprise; the passions are so drawn to the life, astonishment, terror and death in the face of Ananias; zeal and a sacred fire in the eyes of the blessed apostle; fright and surprise upon the countenance of the beholders in the piece of Ananias.' Defoe neglects to say that the two cartoons were by Raphael, and had been brought to this country not by his hero William III but by one of the monarchs he did not approve of, Charles I. They are now in the Victoria and Albert Museum.

According to Defoe, William and Mary agreed on the grand design for the Privy Garden at Hampton Court, except that the 'scrolls and bordure of the garden were at first edged with box; but on the queen's disliking the smell, the edgings were taken up, but have since been planted again'. Like most baroque gardens, Hampton Court's was designed to be seen at a single glance. William wanted the whole breadth of Wren's south façade to greet his visitors as they arrived by river, and equally he wanted a clear view of the Thames from his first-floor apartment. The recent restoration of Hampton Court garden has followed the planting lists and the pressed flower collections left by William and Mary. As in their time, the bulbs of the 2,000 tulips, 2,000 white narcissi, 2,000 crocuses and 300 irises were all brought over from Holland. The restorers of the Privy Garden have noticed how its colours echo those of Wren's south façade. Just as the garden was composed of three predominant tones – green grass, orange sand and gravel – so the building blends red brick, white Portland and yellow sandstone. Defoe, who later ran a successful brickyard and constantly advocated the use of Portland stone, certainly understood the relationship of buildings to gardens like the one that he kept at his home in Stoke Newington.

Defoe may have attended Queen Mary at Windsor, 'the most beautiful and most pleasantly situated castle, and royal palace in the whole isle of Britain', for he tells us how she refurnished the royal apartments:

> In one of these lodgings, the late Queen Mary set up a rich atlas [satin silk from the East] and chintz bed, which in those

times was invaluable, the chintz being of Masalapatan, on the coast of Coromandel, the finest thing that was ever seen before that time in England . . . also here was, some time before this, the picture of the late Duchess of Portsmouth [Charles II's French, Catholic mistress] at full length, a noble piece, and of which King Charles would say, twas the finest painting of the finest woman in Christendom; but our English ladies of Queen Mary's court, were of another opinion, and the Gallery of Beauties, as it was called, which her majesty placed in the water gallery at Hampton Court, shows several as good faces and as good painting.

The site of Windsor Castle, he continues, may have been chosen by William the Conqueror, 'who delighted in hunting' and saw it as good sporting country, but he adds that it was largely built by Edward III, who 'committed the overseeing and direction of the works to William of Wickham, or, if you please, William of Wickham was the Sir Christopher Wren of that court; for William was then a layman, not having had a liberal education, but had a good genius, a mighty love of building, and had applied his head much that way'. At Windsor – indeed, everywhere he went – Defoe always looked to history, especially its heroes and villains. He regarded William the Conqueror as a tyrant who threw the peasants off their land in order to enjoy his hunting. Defoe used his time at Windsor to study the life of his favourite Protestant woman: 'On the outside was added the terrace walk, built by Queen Elizabeth, and where she usually walked for an hour every day before her dinner, if not hindered by windy weather, which she had a particular aversion to; for as to rainy weather, it would not always hinder her; but she rather loved to walk in a mild, calm rain, with an umbrella over her head.'

In describing the Royal Chapel at Windsor, 'the neatest and finest of its kind in England', Defoe poses as an Anglican in order to put forward a Dissenting view:

I remember that going with some friends to show them this magnificent palace, it chanced to be at the time when the Dissenters were a little uneasy at being obliged to kneel at the Sacrament; one of my friends who, as I said, I carried to see Windsor Castle, was a Dissenter, and when he came into the chapel, he fixed his eyes upon the altar-piece with such a fixed, steady posture, and held it so long, that I could not but take notice of it, and asked him, whether it was not a fine piece. Yes, says he, it is; but, whispering to me, he added, how can your people prosecute us for refusing to kneel at the Sacrament? Don't you see there, that though our Saviour himself officiates, they are all sitting about the table.

I confess it surprised me, and, at first, I knew not what answer to make to him, but I told him, That was not a place for him and I to dispute it, we would talk of it afterwards, and so we did, but brought it to no conclusion, so tis useless to mention it any more.

That is a fine example of how Defoe could bemuse his readers, even in the supposedly factual *Tour*. He pretends to be an Anglican, unable to answer the arguments of a Dissenter, and this at a time when Nonconformists were under pressure to kneel at the Sacrament. Yet it is most improbable that Defoe entered the Royal Chapel at Windsor except during the reign of William and Mary, when the Dissenters enjoyed unaccustomed liberty. It is probable that in 1703, when Defoe was serving an indeterminate sentence in Newgate Prison, he was brought to Windsor to plead for a pardon from Queen Anne, but if so, the visit did not include a tour of the sights of the castle.

Defoe writes with affection and pride of Kensington Palace and its still delightful gardens, now one of the Royal Parks: the palace 'may be called entirely new, though it was originally an old house of the Earl of Nottingham's of whom the late King William bought it and then enlarged it as we see; some of the old building still remaining in the centre of the house'. Kensington Palace was then famed for the garden that fronted it on three sides and reached 'quite from the great road to Kensington town, to the Acton Road north', now Bayswater Road. Here, and only here, Defoe coyly reveals that he knew Queen Mary:

The first laying out of these gardens was the design of the late Queen Mary, who finding the air agreed with, and was necessary to the health of the king, resolved to make it agreeable to herself too, and gave the first orders for the enlarging of the gardens; the author of this account, having had the honour to attend her majesty, when she first viewed the ground, and directed the doing it, speaks this with the more satisfaction.

The fire at Kensington Palace in November 1691, which burned down much of the south wing, is described by Defoe with apparent authority: 'The Queen was a little surprised at first, apprehending some treason, but King William, a stranger to fear, smiled at the suggestion, cheered her majesty up, and being soon dressed, they both walked out into the garden, and stood there some hours until they perceived the fire by the help that came in, and by the diligence of the foot guards, was gotten underfoot.' The diarist John Evelyn, who was not writing for publication in his lifetime, claims that during the fire the King and Queen 'stood laughing heartily as the ladies of the court rushed about *en chemise* with needless alarm'. On taking his leave of Kensington in the *Tour*, Defoe says the palace 'has lost much of its pleasantness on one account, namely, that all the princes that ever might be said to have singled it out for their delight, had the fate to die in it; namely King William, Prince George of Denmark [Queen Anne's consort], and lastly Queen Anne herself.'

Defoe's visits to Kensington Palace, Windsor Castle and Hampton Court did not keep him from leading a busy life in the City. He was a liveryman of the Butchers Company, a member of the Cornhill Grand Jury, and a patron of Chew's and Smith's coffee houses, where most of the company were Dissenters. It was at about this time that he started to write his name as 'Defoe', though he always used the initials 'D. F.' rather than 'D. D.' He was trying his hand at pamphlet writing, though this was only a sideline to his merchant ventures, which now occupied more of his time than hosiery.

Under the guidance of his father-in-law, Defoe started to trade in beer, wine, spirits, tobacco and textile goods, buying from Portugal and America and reselling to towns in the British Isles. In the days of the sailing ship, widespread piracy and only a fledgling system of marine insurance, the mounting of such hazardous ventures required experience, caution and large financial resources, in all of which Defoe was wanting. He suffered considerable losses on ill-timed ventures to buy tobacco in Maryland and to sell a cargo of beer and wine in Belfast. When war resumed in 1689 a French privateer captured a ship in which Defoe had a major share. All these misfortunes were followed by litigation against him. Yet rather than cutting his losses and sticking to the safe trade of hosiery, Defoe borrowed heavily from his friends and relations to back ever more hazardous foreign ventures.

By 1691 he was borrowing to meet the payment dates on earlier loans and to recoup his fortunes with a spectacular deal. He later described the state of mind of a man on his way to financial ruin: 'If

I were to run through the infinite mazes of a bankrupt, before he comes to the crisis; what shifts, what turnings, what windings in trade, to support his dying credit; what buying of one to raise money to pay another; what discounting of bills, pledgings and pawnings; what selling at loss to present supply; what strange and unaccountable methods to buoy up sinking credit.' Yet in spite of his guilt and worry, and his sense of approaching disaster, in 1692 Defoe was ready to squander more money on civet cats and a diving bell. He bought the seventy cats for about £850, in the hope of making scent from the musk of their anal glands, as the Dutch had been doing for years with great success. His creditors took back the beasts before their glands had gone into production. The experience gave Defoe a loathing of civet cats, which we can discern when the hero of his novel *Captain Singleton* tries to eat one of these creatures and finds the flesh 'the worst of carrion'. At about the time he bought the cats Defoe invested £200 in a scheme to raise sunken treasure by means of a diving bell. He also became general secretary to a company formed to finance a diving expedition. Although similar syndicates had enriched themselves on the Spanish Main, and Defoe's own brother-in-law had been diving off Cornwall, there were insufficient investors to fund an expedition. Meanwhile the bell's inventor sued Defoe for the cost of repairs and maintenance. The project is mentioned ruefully in the *Tour*, when Defoe stops at Land's End and looks across at the Scilly Isles.

In the year of the civet cats and the diving bell Defoe's other creditors lost patience and made him bankrupt for the enormous sum of £17,000, as well as committing him to the Fleet Prison on 29 October 1692. He was transferred to the King's Bench Prison, discharged and later detained once more as the courts considered the claims of a string of creditors. Bankrupts could be kept in jail until they had paid all their debts, as well as the mounting prison fees, but creditors normally wanted to see them earning money to pay back what they owed, or at least a part payment in 'composition'. Defoe's creditors for this 1692 bankruptcy were to hound him for money until the day he died in 1731.

Within a few months of his first arrest Defoe was free from the danger of prison, but he was now a broken and changed man. He had squandered all his money, including his wife's dowry of £3,700, and saw no prospect of earning the necessary £17,000. He had lost his house and hosiery store in Freeman's Yard, and had gone with his family to stay at his mother-in-law's near London. Because of his bankruptcy he was no longer eligible for a public career. Moreover, the torment of mind he suffered before and during the bankruptcy, in addition to the subsequent burden of debt, had condemned him to a lifetime of misery, fear, loneliness and remorse, from which he could only escape through prayer, the love of his family and eventually by writing books.

Like all the major experiences of his life – the Plague, the Great Fire, the Monmouth Rebellion, the Glorious Revolution, the pillory, Newgate and his work for the Secret Service – Defoe's financial disaster figures large in his novels and the autobiographical *Tour*. One sees in his writing four separate, though interrelated horrors attending the bankruptcy: the nightmarish succession of failures in his career as an overseas trader; the shame of the Fleet and the King's Bench prisons; the relentless persecution by his creditors, and lastly, his remorse at having ruined his loyal and loving wife.

Most of the heroes and both the heroines of Defoe's principal novels are at one time or another merchants, fearful of shipwrecks, piracy, damaged cargoes and theft; worried, above all, about getting their money and valuables back to London. Even Robinson Crusoe leaves his island only to become obsessed with the problem of transporting his wealth from Brazil to Lisbon, and then over the Pyrenees, where he and Man Friday fight off a pack of ravenous wolves.

Although the Fleet and the King's Bench prisons were not as dreadful as Newgate, which he describes in *Moll Flanders*, Defoe understood the peculiar horror of jail for debt. In the section on London, the *Tour* refers to 'tolerated prisons' or 'sponging-houses', where debtors were held until their committal to prison: 'All these private houses of confinement are pretended to be little purgatories, between prison and liberty, places of advantage for the keeping of prisoners at their own request, till they can get funds to deliver them and so avoid going into public prisons, though in some of them, the extortion is such, and the accommodation so bad, that men choose to be carried away directly.' When he wrote this, Defoe had seen the inside of sponging houses as well as the Fleet, King's Bench and Newgate, and would soon be spending his final years on the run from one of these 'tolerated prisons'.

The anxiety of the chronic debtor pervades Defoe's novels, expressing itself in a sense of being hunted by real or imagined enemies; in constant changes of residence and disguise; and, above all, in fantasies of acquiring a fortune, like this in *Roxana*:

So we opened the box ... and he produced in goldsmith's bills, and stock in the English East-India Company, about sixteen thousands pounds sterling; then he gave into my hands, nine assignments upon the Bank of Lyons in France, and two upon the rent of the town-house in Paris, amounting in the whole to 5,800 Crowns ... and lastly the sum of 30,000 Rixdollars, in the Bank of Amsterdam; besides some jewels and gold in the box, to the value of about £15 or £16,000, among which was a very good necklace of pearl, of about £200 value; and that he pulled out and tied about my neck.

Defoe understood how debtors attempt to escape from their misery by indulging in joyless debauchery. When Moll Flanders goes to live in the Mint, a debtors' haven, she meets men 'who wanted half a crown in the pound to pay their creditors', but are ready to buy her dinner:

It was indeed a subject of strange reflection to me to see men who were overwhelmed in perplexed circumstances, who were reduced some degrees below being ruined, whose families were objects of their own terror and other people's charity, yet while a penny lasted, nay, even beyond it, endeavouring to drown their sorrows in their wickedness, heaping up more guilt upon themselves, labouring to forget former things, which now it was the proper time to remember, and sinning on, as a remedy for sin past.

Although, in the dealings that led to his bankruptcy, Defoe was never accused of fraud or any criminal conduct, he knew that he had behaved dishonourably, as is clear from this passage in *The Complete English Tradesman*, published in 1727:

I might instance here the miserable, anxious perplexed life, which the poor tradesman lives under before he breaks ... how harassed and tormented for money ... how many, little, mean, and even wicked things will even the most religious tradesman stoop to in his distress to deliver himself? even such things, as his very soul would abhor at another time; and for which he goes, perhaps with a wounded conscience all his life after?

Defoe's anguish at having squandered his wife's money is made explicit in one of the letters he wrote to his Secret Service employer, Robert

Harley, and it appears with tragic intensity in *Roxana*, whose heroine is started on her career of vice by the bankruptcy of her profligate husband. It would not be too far-fetched to suggest that Defoe's bankruptcy led him to become a novelist. His failure as a merchant meant that henceforth he had to earn a living from his brickworks, his Secret Service employment, but above all by writing pamphlets, articles and finally books. When he turned to fiction in 1719, Defoe naturally drew on his own experiences, of which the most powerful was bankruptcy.

Although frequently 'floored' by debt, Defoe would rapidly pick himself up to try a new wheeze for making money. Thanks to a friend called Thomas Neale, who held the government post of King William's Groom Porter, Defoe was appointed manager-trustee for some of the private lotteries under licence from the crown. A handbill advertisement for one of these lotteries promised 250 prizes after a draw 'round a table in a great room at Freeman's Yard, Cornhill', near Defoe's former house and business. Perhaps through Neale, Defoe secured the job of accountant to the Commission on glass duty, collecting the tax on bottles and glasses – though not the later window-tax, whose effect can be seen in the bricked-up windows of many eighteenth-century houses.

In spite of his bankrupt condition, Defoe was able to keep and exploit a plot of land at Tilbury in Essex on the Thames estuary. His father had some connection with Tilbury, and Defoe's biographer Paula Backscheider mentions the possibility that Defoe was the 'Daniel son of a stranger', baptized at nearby Chadwell on 27 July 1662. Tilbury was especially dear to Defoe because his heroine Queen Elizabeth had made a famous speech there before the Armada arrived in 1588: 'I know I have the body of a weak and feeble woman, but I have the heart and stomach of a king, and a king of England too; and think foul scorn that Parma or Spain, or any prince of Europe should dare to invade the borders of my realm.' In his *Tour* Defoe calls Tilbury Fort 'the key of the river of Thames, and consequently the key of the city of London', whose mighty bastions stood as firm as the rock on which they were founded. Overlooking the Thames were 106 cannon, capable of firing a 46-pound ball, 'a battery so terrible that they must be bold fellows who venture in the biggest ship the world has heard of, to pass such a battery, if the men appointed to serve the guns, do their duty like stout fellows'.

Defoe had acquired the land at Tilbury for corn and cows, but later went into partnership in the manufacture of bricks and pantiles, the S-shaped roofing tiles recently introduced from Holland. Bricks were in constant demand for the development of London, and some of Defoe's were used in Wren's magnificent Greenwich Naval Hospital. The glazed red pantiles, because of their shape, required no mortar to fit them on to a roof. They were so widely used on the Non-conformist chapels and meeting houses that sprang up during William's reign that some country people referred to Dissenters as 'pantilers'. In her study of the Tilbury business Paula Backscheider remarks that there were no complaints about the quality of the produce, from which she concludes that unlike most brickmakers Defoe did not 'mix soil called "Spanish" in the bricks, or use ashes and cinders, "breeze", instead of pure coal in the kiln'.

In a letter to Robert Harley, who released him from prison in 1703, Defoe says that King William had helped to finance the Tilbury brickyard: 'All my prospects were built on a manufacture I had erected in Essex; all the late king's bounty to me was expended there.' That is the only evidence we have that Defoe was in the paid employ of William. Moreover, judging by another letter he wrote to Harley, it seems that Defoe dealt directly with William rather than with one of his ministers.

This would tend to confirm the supposition already advanced, that Defoe had been an acquaintance of William and Mary early on in their reign, when they were moving into their homes at Hampton Court, Windsor Castle and Kensington Palace. Defoe revered William as the greatest soldier of his time, a statesman standing above the squabbles of Whig and Tory politicians, and a pious Calvinist who nevertheless upheld the freedom of worship for people of other faiths. In another letter to Harley Defoe claims that William asked for and listened to his advice on English affairs, but he probably earned most of 'the late king's bounty' by writing pamphlets favourable to his interests. In the tolerant mood of the Glorious Revolution there was a growing market for books and pamphlets on topical subjects like trade, travel, military history, English and European politics and religious disputes. Booksellers sometimes doubled as publishers and printers, and took in each other's titles to increase their trade.* Defoe, with his well-stocked mind and facile pen, was able to churn out pamphlets at two or three guineas a time, on top of the fee he took from a patron – in this case the King.

* Although these pamphlets were generally anonymous, the rival publisher probably knew who the authors were, as did the more discerning reader.

Defoe wrote several pamphlets supporting William's arguments for a standing army in England, to match the one maintained by the Dutch on the Continent. But Defoe's most famous and best-selling pamphlet, the verse satire *The True-Born Englishman*, was published in 1700 as a personal defence of William against a recently published verse attack by John Tutchin. The King had never endeared himself to the English public, and he seemed still more remote and foreign after the death of Queen Mary in 1694. The behaviour of some of the King's Dutch friends, notably William Bentinck, the first Earl of Portland, confirmed the popular English view that the Dutch were uncouth and avaricious, especially when they were given a disproportionate share of the land seized from the Catholics in Ireland. In his light-hearted and often amusing satire, Defoe reminds his xenophobic and bigoted fellow-countrymen that they themselves are a mongrel race, possessing all the vices that they attribute to foreigners.

In the prose introduction Defoe says he expects that hostile readers will call him a Dutchman, in which they are mistaken. He is an Englishman: 'But I am one that would be glad to see Englishmen behave themselves better to strangers ... and it cannot be denied that we are in many cases, and particularly to strangers, the churliest people alive. As to vices, who can dispute out intemperance, while an honest drunken fellow is a character in a man's praise.' The poem begins with a survey of Europe, showing how Satan has given each people their own peculiar vice or sin:

> Pride, the first peer and president of Hell
> To his share Spain, the largest portion fell ...
> Lust chose the torrid zone of Italy
> Where blood ferments in rape and sodomy.
> Drunkenness, the darling favourite of Hell
> Chose Germany to rule, and rules it well.
> Whether by Luther, Calvin or by Rome
> They sail for Heaven, by wine he steers them well.
> Ungoverned passion settled first in France,
> Where mankind lives in haste, and thrives by chance ...
> Rage rules the Portuguese, and fraud the Scotch,
> Revenge the Pole, and avarice the Dutch

Some of Defoe's assessments of national character may strike us as odd. He calls the Spanish proud because they disdain to go into commerce, leaving the trade with Peru and Mexico to Dutch and English merchants, acting under licence. England's right to trade directly with Latin America was a favourite hobby-horse of Defoe's, appearing frequently in his articles and at least three of the novels, including *Robinson Crusoe*. His aspersions on the sexual habits of the Italians are repeated even more forcefully in *The Memoirs of a Cavalier*, when a courtesan invites the English hero to use her 'as a lady, or as —', clearly implying sodomy. When Defoe describes the Germans as drunkards on wine, he must have been thinking of Rhinelanders, or perhaps he had chosen beer as the English vice. He concedes the vice of avarice to the Dutch, yet later denies it in his novel *Roxana*.

After this survey of Europe Defoe examines the origins of the English:

> The Romans first with Julius Caesar came,
> Including all the nations of that name,
> Gauls, Greeks and Lombards; and by computation
> Auxiliaries and slaves of every nation.
> With Hengist, Saxons; Danes with Sweno came
> In search of plunder, not in search of fame.
> Scots, Picts and Irish from the Hibernian shore,
> And conquering William brought the Normans o'er.
> All these their barbarous offspring left behind
> The dregs of armies, they of all mankind . . .
> From this amphibious, ill-born mob began
> That vain, ill-natured thing an Englishman . . .
> These are the heroes that despise the Dutch
> And rail at new-come foreigners so much,
> Forgetting they themselves are all derived
> From the most scoundrel race that ever lived . . .
> The Pict and painted Briton, treacherous Scot,
> By hunger, theft and rapine hither brought,
> Norwegian pirates, buccaneering Danes,
> Whose red-haired offspring everywhere remains,
> Who joined with Norman-French compound the breed
> From whence your True-Born Englishmen proceed.

To those Englishmen who complain of William's foreign cronies, Defoe points out that two of the Stuart kings had brought in much less worthy favourites. He says of the Scots who arrived with James I:

Thick as the locusts which in Egypt swarmed
With pride and hungry hope completely armed . . .

And he enjoys himself at the expense of Charles II:

The royal refugee our brood restores
With foreign courtiers and with foreign whores
And carefully repeopled us again
Throughout his lazy, long lascivious reign . . .

After mentioning some of the minor vices of the English, such as a passion for ale, Defoe condemns their ingratitude to the saviour of the nation:

William the Great Successor of Nassau
Their prayer heard and their oppression saw;
He saw and saved them; God and him they praised,
To this their thanks, to that their trophies raised.
But glutted with their own facilities
They soon their new deliverer despise . . .
But English gratitude is ever such
To hate the hand that does oblige too much.

He then confronts head on the main English objection to William:

We blame the king that he relies too much
On strangers, Germans, Huguenots and Dutch;
And seldom does his great affairs of state
To English counsellors communicate.
The fact might very well be answered thus,
He has so often been betrayed by us
He must have been a madman to rely
On English gentlemen's fidelity.

Whatever King William paid Defoe for writing *The True-Born Englishman*, it was money well spent, for the satire became an instant and lasting best-seller, eventually entering forty editions over as many years. Throughout his life Defoe was better known for this early work than for any subsequent book, and even today it provides most of his entries in *The Oxford Dictionary of Quotations*, including the once well-known lines:

Wherever God erects a house of prayer,
The Devil always builds a chapel there,

> And 'twill be found upon examination
> The latter has the largest congregation.

Yet modern readers may wonder how Defoe's artless and sometimes doggerel verse could compete with the works of contemporary poets as great as Dryden and Pope, or as elegant as Congreve, Prior and Addison. The reason is that *The True-Born Englishman* displays to the full Defoe's two great qualities as a writer: his common sense and his clarity of expression. When the satire was published in 1700, many Englishmen grumbled about King William's rule, but few except Jacobites really regretted the Glorious Revolution or queried the need to resist French aggression. Moreover, the English then were more aware than they are today of the mixture of races that made up the nation, and of the conflict caused by the Norman invasion. Defoe liked to play on Anglo-Saxon resentment of William the Conqueror and his forest law, which later inspired the legend of Robin Hood. The conquering race in England had also become its upper class, as Tennyson wrote in the nineteenth century:

> Kind hearts are more than coronets
> And simple faith than Norman blood . . .

Thoughtful Englishmen knew that the mixture of races had helped to give them their greatest national asset, the English language, combining the riches of Anglo-Saxon and Norman French. Although, by 1700, English was probably spoken much as it is today, the written language tended to stress the French rather than the Anglo-Saxon in syntax, rhythm and choice of words. A Latinate style reflected the classical education received by most of the literary men of the seventeenth and eighteenth centuries – for example, Milton, Dryden, Pope, Dr Johnson and Gibbon. Although he knew Latin and French, Defoe was one of the first successful authors to write in the Anglo-Saxon mode, whether in poetry or prose. He wrote as he spoke, which is why in the novels one scarcely discerns a difference between narrative and quoted speech. In *The True-Born Englishman*, as in his prose works, Defoe was addressing his readers in a language they spoke and understood. The popularity of his verses does not mean that Defoe was a great poet, or even a poet at all.

The huge popularity of *The True-Born Englishman* rallied support for William during the last gruelling year of his life, when he toiled to ensure that after his passing the country retained a Protestant monarch, hostile to France. William's almost personal war against Louis XIV had started in 1672, had paused for a truce after the Treaty of Nijmegen in 1678, and again at the Peace of Ryswick in 1697, and was now about to resume as Louis's grandson succeeded to the Spanish throne. There is no need to explain here the dynastic rivalries that led to what historians call the War of the Spanish Succession. It is enough to say that France's claim to be ruler of Spain and all her possessions was seen by Englishmen such as Defoe as a mortal danger.

The French acquisition of Spain and its possessions in Italy and the Netherlands would upset the balance of power in Europe, which England saw as the guarantee of its independence. The Dutch and the English, the two main commercial and maritime countries in Europe, would suffer a ruinous blow to their trade if Spain was to come under French domination. Because the Spanish disdained to go into commerce and industry, as Defoe had pointed out in *The True-Born Englishman*, they allowed English and Dutch merchants, thinly disguised under Spanish names, to trade between Spain and its colonies, using Cadiz as a depot. Cloth woven in England was imported on an enormous scale into Spain and its colonies in America, Italy and the Netherlands. French rule at Madrid would mean England's exclusion from these markets and from the whole of the Mediterranean. In addition to economic ruin, England faced a threat to its independence and sovereignty if the French established themselves in the Spanish Netherlands, or what is now Belgium. The Dutch would once more face Louis's army across the Schelde and the Maas.

After the death of the old Spanish King in November 1700, and Louis's decision to take the crown for France, William devoted himself to seeing through Parliament an Act of Settlement, fixing the English crown on the Protestant House of Hanover after Anne's death, and at the same time rebuilding a Grand Alliance in Europe to meet the expected attack from France. The English were reluctant for war until Louis himself aroused them to action in February 1701, when he ordered his army into the Spanish Netherlands and occupied all the fortresses, including Nieuwpoort and Ostend, facing the English coast. Like the Kaiser's invasion of Belgium in 1914, this brought the danger close to home.

Soon afterwards, Louis threatened an English economic interest dear to Defoe's heart and a major theme of *Robinson Crusoe*. France compelled Spain to hand over the Asiento (the contract for the supply of African slaves to Latin America), enforcing its new monopoly with ships of the French navy. The previous government of Spain had allowed English merchants to transport slaves, and with them other goods, like cloth, to Spanish America. The loss of the Asiento was one of England's bitterest grievances during the War of the Spanish Succession, and into the reign of George II.

To win support for his policies in a largely Tory Parliament, William relied on the Speaker of the House of Commons, Robert Harley, who later became the patron and Secret Service employer of Defoe. Although a Tory, Harley was more of a manager than an ideologue in politics, and tried to unite the country behind the coming war. In June 1701 he steered the Act of Settlement through Parliament, and by September had won the support of the House for a Treaty of Grand Alliance. Most Tory doubts were swept away when, on 13 November 1701, Louis XIV stood by the deathbed of James II of England and swore to acknowledge his son as James III. This blatant affront to the English King and Parliament united the country in indignation. It was the High Tory leader, Sir Edward Seymour, who in January 1702 moved in the House of Commons that a clause be added to the Treaty of Grand Alliance, binding the signatories not to make peace until Louis acknowledged the Protestant Succession.

Assured of the support of Parliament and the English people, William devoted his last painful months to grooming the man he had chosen as his successor to lead the struggle against the French. This was John Churchill, then Earl and soon to be Duke of Marlborough. Hitherto Marlborough's career had owed more to his skill and charm as a courtier, politician and diplomat than to prowess on the battlefield, and there were many who thought him disloyal to William. Born in 1650, the son of a West Country squire named Winston Churchill, Marlborough obtained his first job at Court as page to the Duke of York, the future James II. The handsome and attractive young man won the favour of Charles II's mistress, the Duchess of Cleveland, who secured him an ensigncy in the Guards and a gift of £5,000 in return for certain unnamed services. Thanks to his cousin Arabella, who was one of the Duke of York's mistresses, the young Churchill rose to be colonel. He served under the Duke of Monmouth in Holland, and in 1678 carried out a diplomatic mission to William of Orange, for which he was made Baron Churchill of Eyemouth.

Even early on in his career Marlborough was seen to waver between the Protestant-Dutch and Catholic-French parties in English political life. He helped to win James's victory over the Duke of Monmouth at Sedgemoor in 1685; yet soon he switched his allegiance to William and helped him to trounce the Irish at Cork. Marlborough fell from favour with William when it was discovered that he had been in touch with the exiled Jacobites in France, but his closest political ties were with Princess Anne, James II's younger daughter and heir to the throne, whose friend and confidante was Sarah, the Duchess of Marlborough. It was typical of William's magnanimity that he entrusted the future of England and Holland to Anne and the Marlboroughs, who had formerly been members of the 'anti-Dutch' political faction. Indeed, it was known that Anne, as a princess, often referred to King William as 'Mr Caliban', after the savage in Shakespeare's *The Tempest*.

In July 1701 King William took Marlborough to The Hague to acquaint him with the work of the Grand Alliance and with his Dutch opposite number, Antoine Heinsius, Grand Pensionary of Holland. The two men formed a mutual liking and understanding that was to survive all the efforts of politicians to split them. Meanwhile Marlborough studied the diplomatic and military map of Europe, and learned to deal with allies as various as the hidebound Habsburgs of Austria and the semi-barbarous Swedes. Marlborough was as great a diplomat as he was a soldier, delighting the salons of The Hague with his graceful manners and charmingly bad French. Between that summer of 1701 and the start of the War of the Spanish Succession Marlborough took care to make his policies and decisions acceptable to the English government and Parliament. As G. M. Trevelyan observed in *Blenheim*, the first of his three volumes of *England in the Reign of Queen Anne*: 'Marlborough would not have been England's greatest leader in war if he had not understood the necessary relation between her war effort and her civil constitution. In that understanding he was not surpassed by Chatham himself.'*

As excitement mounted in 1701, Defoe lent his skills as a pamphleteer to the Whigs and the merchants who clamoured for war, and blamed the Tories for England's state of unreadiness. From Kent, the county nearest to Louis's armies in Ostend and Calais, the Grand Jury and freeholders at Maidstone Quarter Sessions petitioned the House of Commons to send urgent financial relief to the Dutch so that 'his

---

* Trevelyan wrote those words in 1930. Ten years later an even greater wartime leader of England, the Duke of Marlborough's descendant Winston Churchill, displayed his loyalty to the civil constitution by justifying his policies from the floor of the House of Commons.

most sacred Majesty may be enabled powerfully to assist the allies before it is too late'. Although this 'Kentish Petition' was lawful under the Bill of Rights, the Tories were stung by its imputations and called the document 'scandalous, insolent and seditious', before locking up five of the men who presented it. Defoe responded by writing a second petition, *Legion's Memorial*, in which he threatened the House of Commons: 'Thus Gentlemen, you have your duty laid before you ... but if you continue to neglect it, you may expect to be treated according to the resentment of an injured nation, for Englishmen are no more to be slaves to Parliament than to a king.'

Whether or not Defoe presented it to the House of Commons, *Legion's Memorial* was far more bold and aggressive than the 'Kentish Petition'. Moreover, he followed it up with still bolder pamphlets such as *The History of the Kentish Petition* and *Legion's New Paper*, asserting the will of the people, and even proclaiming the right to the crown of the Duke of Monmouth's son. With *Legion's Memorial* following on the success of *The True-Born Englishman*, Defoe was becoming a famous pamphleteer, but at the cost of making a host of enemies. He attacked by name a number of MPs whom he accused of winning their seats by electoral fraud or corruption. Nor did he shrink from abusing hypocrites among the City Dissenters.

His enemies named Defoe 'the Devil' after the unclean spirit in Mark 5.30, who says, 'My name is Legion: for we are many', before he enters the Gadarene swine. Defoe had probably taken his title from Milton's use of the word, on behalf of the 'free-born people of England' in their resistance to 'destructive' governments. His enemies seized on the gospel, meaning to brand Defoe as a devil of mischief who set the people of England at each other's throats. He was caricatured in pamphlets, doggerel ballads and prints, such as 'Daniel Defoe and a Devil at Leap-frog'. It was assumed by the Tories and some of the Whigs that Defoe was writing his pamphlets on behalf of a government paymaster. The enemies made by Defoe during the final year of William's reign were to get their revenge in full in the opening year of Queen Anne's.

At the end of the final volume of his *History of England* Lord Macaulay describes the physical state of his hero William of Orange late in 1701:

> He could not last long. It had, indeed, often been prophesied
> that his death was at hand; and the prophets had hitherto been

mistaken. But there was now no possibility of mistake. His cough was more violent than ever; his legs were swollen, his eyes once bright and clear as those of a falcon, had grown dim; he who, at the banks of the Boyne, had been seven hours on the backs of different horses, could now with great difficulty creep into his stage coach. The vigorous intellect and the intrepid spirit remained; but on the body fifty years had done the work of ninety.

When he wrote those words, Macaulay himself was dying, and did not live to revise the final chapter. He tells the well-known story of how William, who had ridden unscathed through many battles, was felled when his horse tripped on a molehill in Hampton Court park. He broke nothing worse than a collar-bone, but the shock to his system was fatal. While he lay fevered and dying in Kensington Palace, William composed a final message to Parliament, recommending the Union with Scotland, in which Defoe was to play a large part. Macaulay ended his life's work with a bald account of William's death on 8 March 1702: 'When his remains were laid out, it was found that he wore next to his skin a simple piece of black silk riband. The lords in waiting ordered it to be taken off. It contained a gold ring and a lock of the hair of Mary.'

Since Macaulay never wrote William's obituary, perhaps we should leave this to G. M. Trevelyan, Macaulay's great-nephew and maybe the last historian in that Whig or liberal tradition which regarded William of Orange as the saviour of English freedom. Trevelyan writes of him in *Blenheim*:

He was remembered as the Deliverer, often with religious thankfulness; but warmth of feeling for him, on this side of St George's Channel, was found chiefly in the army, among the men who had seen his soul taking fire under the stresses of battle. Uncle Toby, when he remembered the look of William galloping past him at Landen to rally his shaken squadron for another charge, forgot the king and cried 'gallant mortal'.

4

The Pillory and Newgate Prison

THE DEATH OF WILLIAM delighted the Jacobites and the friends of France, who long afterwards toasted 'the little gentleman in velvet' – the mole responsible for his fall in Hampton Court park. But his death dismayed his friends such as Defoe, who feared that Queen Anne would return to the ways of Charles II or even James II. She was James's daughter, and sister to the Pretender, a High Church Anglican and a Tory. By the time she came to the throne she was worn out by the pain and sorrow of bearing and then losing fifteen children, as well as by fits of gout and dropsy. Her husband, King George of Denmark, was kind but dull, and a drunkard. Anne too consoled herself with the brandy bottle or 'cold tea' as well as with devotional books and the brilliant talk of her friend Sarah, the wife of Marlborough.

The enemies of the Duke of Marlborough, from his contemporary, Swift, to Thackeray in his historical novel *Henry Esmond*, have always suggested that Sarah exploited her hold on Anne to advance the career and fortune of her husband. Yet as we know from her letters, the Duchess regarded Anne with solicitude and affection; moreover, the Duke would not have remained as head of the Allied armies if he had not amply proved himself a commander of genius. However, the friendship between the Marlboroughs, or 'Mr and Mrs Freeman', as they called themselves in their private language, and 'Mrs Morley', the Queen, undoubtedly helped to shield the Duke from the malice of his enemies.

With the encouragement of the Marlboroughs, from the moment she ascended the throne Anne made it plain that she would adhere to the ideals of her predecessor. On the Sunday morning that William died she summoned her Privy Council and told them that she stood by the Protestant Succession and resistance to France. On the same day the two houses of Parliament met to express their loyalty and give wholehearted support to the principles she had just announced. On Tuesday 10 March 1702, only forty-eight hours after William's death, Marlborough departed for Holland as Anne's Ambassador Extraordinary and Captain-General of the intended English Expeditionary Force. G. M. Trevelyan tells us that 'the swift sequence of these steps towards vigorous warfare on the Continent, by no means desired by everyone ... must have been arranged between Anne and the Churchills while William was still drawing painful breath'.

When Marlborough arrived at The Hague he found the Dutch still in a state of grief at the death of William, their Stadtholder, and half expecting to be betrayed by their English allies. Marlborough reassured them, then broached the question of who should command the Allied army. He wanted the job himself, of course, and the Dutch, who provided most of the money and troops, were prepared to accept the man chosen by William. However, Queen Anne wanted her husband, Prince George, to lead the Allies, with Marlborough commanding only the English Expeditionary Force, and it was not until May that she dropped her demand.

As Marlborough prepared for the first of his many campaigns, which usually lasted only from spring to autumn, he still did not have the confidence of the Dutch generals and parliamentary deputies, who were attached to his staff as observers. The Dutch were loath to risk the lives of their well-paid mercenaries in a set-piece battle, preferring to use them in sieges and similar minor operations. But Marlborough had learned from the two greatest generals of the seventeenth century, Gustavus Adolphus and Oliver Cromwell, that victory has to be won in the open field. Here he had the support of the Dutch Grand Pensionary, Heinsius, who said that to retake the Spanish Netherlands with only two sieges a year would mean another Thirty Years War. Among those who supported Marlborough's strategy was Defoe, who had fought against him at Sedgemoor in 1685. In the fictional *Memoirs of a Cavalier*, a book that displays considerable knowledge of military science, Defoe praises Gustavus Adolphus and Cromwell, and argues that their open battles were in the end less costly in dead and wounded. He applauded Marlborough's brilliant campaign of 1702, which won back from France the Maas and Lower Rhine valleys – 'Marlbrook s'en va-t-en guerre!' as the French soldiers ruefully sang.

As well as conducting the summer campaigns in northern Europe, Marlborough remembered William III's insistence on the importance of the Mediterranean. At the start of the war in 1702 the French controlled the kingdoms of Spain and Naples, and therefore could close the Mediterranean to English naval and merchant ships. Through the conquest of Gibraltar and then Port Mahon (Minorca), Marlborough's strategy re-established English control of the inland sea. The battle off Málaga in 1704 was the last occasion on which the French Grand Fleet ventured to meet the English, and two years later it was destroyed in Toulon harbour. In the opinion of Trevelyan, 'The creation of British naval and commercial supremacy on a footing that proved permanent for more than two hundred years, might not unreasonably be regarded as the most important outcome of the reign of Anne. But it passes little notice in English popular tradition, being associated with no stirring name like the Armada, La Hogue or Trafalgar; no supreme seaman like Drake, Blake or Nelson.'

Marlborough's Mediterranean strategy, which he inherited from his mentor William, was most unpopular with the High Tories, who favoured the 'blue water school' of naval warfare, which involved making raids on the enemy on the distant oceans. Those who hated the Calvinist Dutch could never accept Marlborough's policy of a continental alliance, whether in northern Europe or in the Mediterranean. This was part of the criticism later levelled against Marlborough in Swift's devastating but unfair *Conduct of the Allies*. Defoe wholeheartedly backed Marlborough's European strategy in his pamphlets, articles, his Secret Service papers and, retrospectively, in the *Tour*.

Until near the end of the War of the Spanish Succession Defoe supported Marlborough and the government against their English political enemies. Even before he began his first campaign in 1702 Marlborough had asked Queen Anne, as a condition of his service, to appoint his kinsman Sidney, Lord Godolphin, as Treasurer and, in effect, Prime Minister. Besides being a loyal friend, Godolphin had the financial skills to provide the money for Marlborough's campaign. His ally and second-in-command, first as Speaker in the Commons and then as senior Secretary of State, was Robert Harley, who had the task of maintaining support for the war in Parliament and the country, for which he later employed Defoe. These three moderate Tories, Marlborough, Godolphin and Harley, were England's ruling triumvirate for the first five years of the War of the Spanish Succession.

Thanks to Marlborough's diplomacy, the Dutch as well as the English politicians were sinking their differences in the face of the danger from France. Grand Pensionary Heinsius was now on such excellent terms with Marlborough that he ventured a word of advice on English politics, urging him not to join in a High Tory vendetta against the Whigs and Dissenters, but to follow the Dutch in preferring 'moderate sentiments' to unite the people in time of war. Marlborough expressed his sincere agreement, for he, Godolphin and Harley all opposed the High Church wing of the Tory party. However, in 1702, when Heinsius was giving his good advice to Marlborough, the English political scene was upset by a hate campaign against the Dissenters.

The accession of Anne had encouraged some of the High Church Tories to call for a tightening of the existing laws against the participation in public life of those who did not subscribe to the Church of England's doctrines. A cantankerous Oxford clergyman, Dr Henry Sacheverell, preached a sermon declaring that government should be based on religion; that schism and heresy led to rebellion; and that rather than surrender to 'a party that is so open and avowed an enemy of our religion' – meaning the Whigs and Dissenters – he would 'hang out the bloody flag of defiance'. Above all, Dr Sacheverell castigated 'occasional conformists', or those who held public office by making a token Communion in the Church of England but afterwards worshipped in a chapel or meeting house. He called them 'insidious persons who can creep to our altars in order to destroy the Church'.

As Dr Sacheverell and other High Churchmen whipped up popular rage against the Dissenters, the Tories in Parliament introduced an Occasional Conformity Bill designed to exclude from even the humblest public office all those who worshipped outside the Church of England. The Bill, had it passed into law, would have excluded Dissenters from government agencies such as the Customs, Excise and Royal Forests. Since Dissenters would be barred from supplying government institutions, Defoe might have lost his contract for bricks in the building of Greenwich Hospital. The Bill would have hurt the Dissenters most in their stronghold, the Boroughs, effectively preventing them from becoming mayors, aldermen, magistrates, bailiffs, common councillors or even refuse collectors.

The Tories in Parliament backed the Occasional Conformity Bill because it would strengthen the party's hold on power and privilege in the Boroughs, and ultimately in the House of Commons. The Whigs rejected it for those very same reasons. The moderate Tories such as Godolphin, Harley and Marlborough supported the Bill in public but disliked it privately, because it divided the country in time of war. The Lutheran Prince Consort, George, who was made to vote for the Bill in the House of Lords by the High Tory Anne, was heard to whisper to one of the Whig opponents: 'I am wid you.' In the winter of 1702–3 the Bill passed easily through the House of Commons but was turned down by the Lords. As Trevelyan points out, the excitement over Occasional Conformity might never have been remembered but for 'its effect upon the fortunes of an obscure inhabitant of Grub Street . . . because it set Daniel Defoe in the pillory.'

Defoe's suffering in the pillory and in Newgate Prison, on top of the misery of his bankrupt condition, completed his transformation from a conventional City merchant into a lonely, hunted and secretive outsider. But far from breaking Defoe's spirit, the dreadful experience gave him the courage, patience and resolution he needed during the difficult years ahead. With two outspoken pamphlets on Occasional Conformity Defoe outraged his former Dissenting friends as much as his Tory enemies, leaving him a pariah. Yet far from becoming bitter, he slowly changed from a cocksure young pamphleteer into the wiser, kinder author of *Robinson Crusoe*, *Moll Flanders* and the *Tour*. He endured the pillory and Newgate because he had mocked and denounced both sides in the argument on Occasional Conformity; because he believed in freedom of conscience. As a reward for this he was sprung from prison and then employed by Harley and Godolphin, the two leading men in a government dedicated to healing the political and religious feuds of the seventeenth century.

Several contemporaries thought that Defoe himself had stirred up the rage that landed him in the pillory when, in 1698, he wrote a pamphlet called *An Enquiry into the Occasional Conformity of Dissenters, In Cases of Preferments*. During the tolerant reign of William III many Dissenters who held public office complied with the Test Act of 1673 by at least once taking Holy Communion in the Church of England, yet continuing to worship at a Nonconformist chapel. Defoe cited as an example Sir Humphrey Edwin, the Lord Mayor of London, who on two consecutive Sundays went to St Paul's in the morning and to Pinner Hall Conventicle in the afternoon, on all four occasions dressed in his mayoral robes, with the sword of office carried before him. Indeed after the second Sunday his sword-bearer lodged an official complaint that Edwin had locked him into a pew at Pinner Hall to prevent him from leaving.

In the *Enquiry* Defoe distinguished between religious Dissenters who would not compromise their beliefs, and 'Politick Dissenters' who occasionally conformed to gain 'publick advancement, and glittering gawdy honours of the age'. He accused the Dissenting clergy of admitting Edwin 'because of his gold ring and fine apparel', and Edwin himself of apostasy 'upon the occasion of preferment', and of making 'the sacred institutions of Christ Jesus, become pimps to secular interest'. He condemned the behaviour of Edwin and his kind as playing a 'loose game of religion', 'bantering with religion' and even 'playing Bo-peep with God Almighty', a reference to the children's game in which a player pops up in an unexpected place, as Edwin had done at St Paul's and then Pinner Hall. In November 1700 another Dissenting Lord Mayor, Sir Thomas Abney, also attended St Paul's in the morning and a meeting house in the afternoon. Defoe issued a new edition of the *Enquiry*, including a strong attack on Abney's preacher, John How, who answered it in a pamphlet, which led to a further exchange on Occasional Conformity. The quarrel among the Dissenters delighted their High Church enemies.

Defoe was taking a principled stand, and indeed he was said to have nailed his pamphlet to the door of St Paul's when Edwin was due to attend a service there, just as Luther had nailed his theses to the door of the church at Wittenberg. Defoe blamed the Test Act of 1673 for debasing Communion, 'the most sacred thing in the world into a political tool and engine of state'. He thought that the Act weakened Dissent by tempting the faithful to compromise their beliefs for the sake of worldly ambition. He must have recalled how the family preacher Annesley had suffered and gone to prison during the reign of Charles II; how his teacher Dr Morton was forced to emigrate to America; how he and his friends from school had risked their lives in the Monmouth Rebellion. Men like Edwin and Abney betrayed the sacrifices of an earlier generation, and sullied the purity of the Nonconformist faith.

Defoe's *Enquiry* hurt and angered many Dissenters just because they recognized its truth. Defoe was playing the old and unloved role of the Hebrew prophet denouncing the sins of a generation of vipers, a Brutus recalling the virtues of an earlier Rome, or a cloth-cap socialist reproaching his former comrades for sending their children to fee-paying schools. Like most men who ostentatiously stand on principle, Defoe had a self-righteous and priggish streak, which enraged the victims of his attacks. Many Dissenters also accused him of giving ammunition to their High Church enemies. Certainly it was Defoe and not the Tories who first stirred up a debate on Occasional Conformity, and pointed the finger of scorn at men like Edwin and Abney.

When Dr Sacheverell and the other 'high fliers' called Occasional Conformists apostates and hypocrites, they were able to cite Defoe as proof that many Dissenters agreed with them. But if Defoe with his first pamphlet alienated his fellow Dissenters, he landed himself in the pillory and Newgate Prison with a far more sensational blast against the High Church Tories.

After July 1702, when Dr Sacheverell raised the 'bloody flag of defiance', the High Church Tories became increasingly violent in their attacks on Dissenters, and in their demands for an Occasional Conformity Bill. In the Press and the Church of England pulpits the 'high fliers', as they were called, denounced Dissenters as regicides and enemies of religion, comparing them with vermin, snakes, cancers and pestilence. The savagery of this verbal assault was worse than anything the Dissenters had known in the reigns of Charles II and James II, and led them to fear that they might be the victims of persecution and massacre, like the Huguenots in France.

It seems that even Defoe was alarmed by the intensity of the anger, which he had helped to arouse with his pamphlet on Occasional Conformity four years earlier. In November 1702 he published a third and very much altered edition called *An Enquiry into Occasional Conformity, Showing that the Dissenters are in no Way Concerned in it*, in effect putting the blame entirely on the Act of Conformity of 1662 and the Test Act of 1673. The pamphlet begins with a rueful remark on the general dislike of Defoe's point of view: 'Tis hard for a man to say, all the world is mistaken but himself, but if it be so, who can help it?'

When reasonable arguments had no effect on public opinion, Defoe as a last resort turned to satire, writing an outrageous parody of a High Tory pamphlet, *The Shortest Way with [the] Dissenters* – meaning, to kill them all. In this brilliant, ferocious diatribe against his own religion, Defoe reproduces the arguments and the accusations of men such as Dr Sacheverell, even some of his slogans like the 'bloody flag of defiance', but he carries their bigoted rage to its logical and as yet unprinted conclusion. While High Church clergymen had compared Dissenters with snakes and toads, leaving their congregations to draw their own inference from this, Daniel spells out to his readers their painful duty: 'It is cruelty to kill a snake or a toad in cold blood, but the poison of their nature make it a charity to our neighbours to destroy these creatures.'

Defoe understood that the Tory hatred of the Dissenters' religion was mingled with envy of their wealth and, as he did in *The True-Born*

Englishman, he mocks the belief of the country squires that Dissenters were Dutchmen and Huguenots, newly arrived in this country to spoil its racial purity. One passage splendidly catches the brutal and hearty tone of a backwoods Tory, complaining about the leniency shown to Dissenters: 'Tis vain to trifle in this matter. The light, foolish handling of them by mulcts, fines etc., tis their glory and advantage. If the gallows instead of the counter [prison] and the gallies instead of the fine were the reward of going to a conventicle, to preach or hear, there would not be so many sufferers. The spirit of martyrdom is over.'

Unhappily for Defoe, his parody of the High Church Tories was much too accurate. He had yet to learn that irony is a weapon that should be handled with care, as shown by Swift in his later pamphlet, *A Modest Proposal for preventing the Children of poor People in Ireland from being a burden to their parents or country and for making them beneficial for the Publick* – in other words, by fattening them to be eaten. The very outrageousness of his title is a signal from Swift to even his stupidest readers that what they are going to enjoy is a satire that should not be taken literally. But *The Shortest Way with Dissenters* never gives any indication that it is not in earnest. Nobody in England seriously thought of eating Irish children, but many Tories agreed with hanging Dissenters, as Judge Jeffreys had done at the Bloody Assizes. If Louis XIV had turned thousands of Huguenots into galley-slaves, was it strange to suggest that Queen Anne do the same to Dissenters?

The effect of *The Shortest Way with Dissenters* was like that of a double-barrelled shotgun. With his first blast, Defoe destroyed his intended target, Dr Sacheverell and his friends; with his second blast, the gun blew up in his face. When it was first published everyone thought that a High Church Tory had written the pamphlet. Many of Dr Sacheverell's friends welcomed this brilliant new statement of his position, and in Oxford and Cambridge, so it was said, *The Shortest Way* was set next to the Bible on many a college table. More sensible Tories were shocked by the savagery of the language, while the Whigs and Dissenters were at first filled with alarm. Then anger succeeded fear; some of the High Church Tories had to endure the abuse that they had so recently handed out to Dissenters. The 'bloody flag of defiance' was soon pulled down, and the Occasional Conformity Bill was dropped by the Lords and then for a time forgotten.

From the moment of publication everyone wanted to know who had written *The Shortest Way*. According to Robert Harley, the Speaker of the House of Commons, no one at first suspected that the author was not a Tory, and that the pamphlet was a hoax. When the politicians, especially the Tories, realized they had been fooled, they united in rage against the unknown pamphleteer. Harley wrote to Godolphin, the Treasurer, saying that it was 'absolutely necessary for the service of the government' to discover and punish the author.

The man assigned to this task was the Earl of Nottingham, a stern High Church Tory, who had been horrified by *The Shortest Way*, and certainly did not regard it as a joke. He hauled in the printer and bullied from him the name of the author. On 30 December 1702 Nottingham issued a warrant for Defoe's arrest 'for high crime and misdemeanour', with orders that he be brought to him personally for interrogation. Nottingham wanted to find out if Defoe had any accomplices among the Whigs, or even among his moderate Tory rivals, such as Harley. He also knew that Defoe had been an adviser to William III and might be forced to betray some useful secrets.

Defoe went into hiding but sent his wife to plead with Nottingham, who advised her to make her husband surrender. Defoe afterwards claimed that Nottingham, or 'Don Dismal', as he referred to him,* had tried to cajole and bully the hapless Mary, but Trevelyan thinks this would not have been in character. Then Defoe, from his hiding place, sent Nottingham a bold, even arrogant letter:

> To flee from her majesty's justice seems, my lord to be a kind of raising war against her, and is very irksome to me. I beseech your lordship to assist me in laying down these arms, or at least in making such a truce as may through her majesty's condescension obtain a pardon.
>
> I was informed, my Lord, that when my distressed wife made appeal to your lordship, you were pleased to direct I should surrender and answer to such questions as should be asked me. But my lord, if after this I should still have the misfortune to remain under her majesty's displeasure, I am then her most humble petitioner that she will please to remit the rigour of prosecution, and that pleading guilty I may reserve a sentence for her particular justice, a little more tolerable to me as a gentleman, than prisons pillory and such like, which are worse to me than death.

---

* Nottingham's self-righteousness, as well as his gloomy manner, had earned him the nickname Dismal.

I beg leave to observe to your lordship that felons and thieves whose punishment is death, are frequently spared upon entering into her majesty's service. If her majesty will be pleased to order me to serve her a year, or more at my own charge, I will surrender myself a volunteer at the head of her armies in the Netherlands, to any colonel of horse, her majesty shall direct, and without doubt my lord, I shall die there much more to her service than in prison.

Lord Nottingham filed this letter, but his only reply appeared the following day in the first of two advertisements in the *London Gazette*, offering £50 to 'whosoever shall discover [Defoe] ... so he may be apprehended'. The second advertisement on 14 July 1703 carried the fullest description we have of Defoe's appearance: 'He is a middle siz'd spare man, about forty years old, of a brown complexion, and dark brown-coloured hair, but wears a wig; a hooked nose, a sharp chin, grey eyes and a large mole near his mouth.' That pen portrait is far clearer than the engravings of Defoe in the frontispieces of some of his books. He was not a man who wanted his likeness known to the public. In this second advertisement he is called Daniel de Foe, alias de Fooe, suggesting that he was now widely known by the longer version of his name.

On 24 February 1703 Defoe was indicted in his absence in the Justice Hall at the Old Bailey on charges of scheming to deny religious toleration to Dissenters – in fact the very reverse of what he intended. On the following day the House of Commons lodged a formal complaint claiming that *The Shortest Way with Dissenters* was 'full of false and scandalous Reflections upon this Parliament', and tended to 'promote sedition', whereupon they ordered it to be burned by the common hangman. Neither the legal officers of the crown nor the members of the House of Commons took into account that the pamphlet was a satire, and not an attack on Dissenters. Defoe's real crime was to make the politicians look ridiculous.

Defoe knew that he was just as unpopular with the men who would sit in judgement upon him, if and when he appeared on trial at the Old Bailey. A few months earlier they had sentenced another Dissenting pamphleteer, William Fuller, to three days in the pillory, a fine of 1,000 Marks (approximately £660) and hard labour in Bridewell until he had paid it. Fuller was whipped on his first day in Bridewell and pelted with stones and rotten eggs as he stood in the pillory.

Although he was a brave man, as he was shortly to prove, Defoe knew in his heart that he did not deserve such treatment, and felt that to surrender himself would be an admission of some ignoble motive in writing *The Shortest Way*, rather than making a plea for religious toleration. Perhaps he already knew that Harley was sympathetic, for he seems to have made an approach to him through William Paterson, a Scottish merchant and one of the founders of the Bank of England. In a letter to Paterson, written at this time, Defoe complained that even the people he wanted to help had turned against him:

> Even the Dissenters, like Casha [*sic*] to Caesar, lift up the first dagger at me; I confess it makes me reflect on the whole body of the Dissenters with something of contempt, and gives me the more regret that I suffer for such people. Shall I own to you that the greatest concern I have upon me is that the government whom I profess I did not foresee would be displeased, should resent this matter? I had it not in my thoughts that the Ministers of State would construe that as pointing at them, which I levelled only at Dr Sacheverell, Dr Stubbs and such people. Thus like old Tyrell who shot at a stag and killed the King, I engaged a Party and embroiled myself with the Government.

The metaphor was unfortunate, since from 1100 onwards many had believed that Tyrell or someone else had deliberately aimed an arrow at William II. But Defoe was learning the hard way the danger of telling the truth. He had exposed the Dissenters as time-serving hypocrites, the High Church clergymen as brutal bigots, and most of the politicians as self-important fools. He should not have been surprised that they did not like him.

Defoe remained in hiding until 21 May 1703, when he was apprehended in Spitalfields at the house of a weaver, Nathaniel Sammen. He was taken straight to Lord Nottingham, who subjected him to a two-day interrogation about his accomplices and his secret work for William III. When Defoe refused to give the expected information, he was taken to Newgate, the most dreaded of London's twenty-seven jails, and the one commonly filled with men and women awaiting execution. In *Moll Flanders* he gives an indication of the agony of mind that he must have known during his months there:

That horrid place, my very blood chills at the mention of its name ... tis impossible to describe the terror of my mind, when I was first brought in and when I looked on myself as lost and that I had nothing to think of but of going out of the world, and that with the utmost infamy; the hellish noise, the roaring, swearing and clamour, the stench and nastiness, and all the dreadful crowd of afflicting things that I saw there, joined to make the place seem an emblem of hell itself, and a kind of entrance into it ... In the next place, how did the hardened wretches that were there before me triumph over me!

Alexander Solzhenitsyn, in *The Gulag Archipelago* and his novel *The First Circle*, has described the terror and shock experienced by Russian political suspects pitched suddenly into the hell of somewhere like the Lubianka jail and put at the mercy of the *zeks*, the criminal prisoners. The experience softened them up to make the confessions required by Stalin's secret police. In the same way Defoe was committed to Newgate to make him more ready to answer the questions put to him by Lord Nottingham. After a first brief stay he was released on bail to await his trial at the Old Bailey, now set for 7 July 1703. Defoe realized that a prison sentence would ruin his business and leave his family once more destitute. Thanks to the flourishing Tilbury brickyard, he had been able to pay off some of the debts from his bankruptcy, to buy a fine house in Hackney, and even to keep a carriage. He was now the father of two boys and four daughters, the youngest of whom, Sophia, was only two years old, and he must already have known that his wife was pregnant again. If he was sent back to Newgate, his suffering would be made still worse by the knowledge that he had once more ruined his wife and children.

The trial of Defoe at the Old Bailey on 7 July 1703 attracted a huge attendance from the legal profession, politicians, the grandees of the City of London, and the general public, who paid a shilling a head to see what happened to the author of *The Shortest Way with Dissenters*. The verdict of the jury was a foregone conclusion, since on the advice of his counsel Defoe pleaded guilty to the nebulous offence of 'seditious libel', and threw himself on the Queen's mercy. Queen Anne herself was cross with Defoe at the time, but she was not vindictive; however, the Old Bailey court was entirely hostile. The case for the prosecution was made by Sir Simon Harcourt, the Solicitor-General and a High

Church Tory MP – although, as Defoe had on several occasions intimated in print, he was privately a Deist or Atheist. The records of the proceedings are lost but it is known that two of the judges present were the Lord Mayor, Sir Thomas Dashwood, who presided, and the Recorder, Sir Salathiel Lovell, who managed the trial and afterwards read out the sentence. All the six circuit judges had the right to sit on the bench at the Old Bailey, and almost certainly would have attended a case of such notoriety. Moreover, the bench was open to all the senior aldermen of the City of London, the wealthy and self-important body who held office for life. In his essay *Defoe in the Pillory*, published in 1939, J. R. Moore suggests that among the aldermen sitting as judges that day were Sir Humphrey Edwin, Sir Thomas Abney, Sir Robert Clayton and Sir Robert Jeffreys, who was no relation of the 'Bloody Assizes' judge but had probably been a friend of his, and undoubtedly shared his predilection for cruelty.

All those mentioned, and probably everyone on the bench that day, disliked what Defoe had written on Occasional Conformity. The Dissenters Edwin and Abney were the two former Lord Mayors whom Defoe had denounced for attending St Paul's in the morning and their conventicles in the afternoon. The majority of the aldermen were High Church Tories, whose self-esteem had been hurt by the mockery of *The Shortest Way*. Besides offending against their principles, Defoe had in certain cases attacked the morals and character of the people now sitting in judgement on him, for as well as writing pamphlets on politics and religion he had been trying his hand at the well-paid art of the verse lampoon, of which some of the masters during his lifetime were Dryden, Pope, Congreve and Swift. At least one of these satires, Dryden's *Absalom and Achitophel*, is still widely read today, although we forget the politicians behind the biblical names. Much of this verse satire strikes us today as scurrilous, savage and, above all, libellous. And the most outrageous satirist of his age was Defoe himself.

The success of *The True-Born Englishman* had proved to Defoe that the public enjoyed his down-to-earth, easily comprehensible rhyming couplets, as well as his trenchant opinions and broad humour. He was no respecter of persons and grandly took it upon himself to expose the scandalous private lives of those in high places, especially the Church, the legal profession and Parliament. In 1702, before writing *The Shortest Way with Dissenters*, he had published an anonymous verse satire, *The Reformation of Manners*, to which he added a sequel, *More Reformation*, in 1703, while he was hiding from Lord Nottingham. As he stood in the dock at the Old Bailey on 7 July, Defoe saw sitting in front of him on the bench some of the men he had grossly lampooned only a few months earlier. Among them was the Recorder, the eighty-four-year-old Sir Salathiel Lovell, a savage, arrogant brute in the worst tradition of Judge Jeffreys. Like Jeffreys, Sir Salathiel loved to harangue and torment the wretch on whom he had just passed sentence. Like Jeffreys too, Lovell was widely reputed to take bribes and even to share the spoils of highwaymen to whom he had given a lenient sentence. Yet even if what he says is true, Defoe's effrontery takes one's breath away. He begins his account of Lovell in *The Reformation of Manners* by comparing him to a pandour – a plundering Croat soldier in the Austrian army:

> L — the Pandor of thy Judgment Seat
> Has neither Manners, Honesty nor Wit,
> Instead of which, he's plenteously supplied
> With nonsense, noise, impertinence and Pride . . .
> Definitive in law, without appeal
> But always serves the hand who pays him well;
> He trades in justice and the souls of men
> And prostitutes them equally to gain.
> He has his public book of rates to show
> Where every rogue the price of life may know;
> And this one maxim always goes before,
> He never hangs the rich nor saves the poor . . .
> Fraternisation of villains he maintains,
> Protects their robberies and shares their gains.

One can hardly imagine a more lethal mixture of criminal libel and contempt of court. To make matters worse, Defoe mentions in *More Reformation* that Lovell had been displeased by what he had written about him, and adds that Satyr's fate is sealed if he ever appears in Lovell's court:

> Twill be in vain to make a long defence,
> In vain twill be to plead thy innocence.
> His breath concludes the sentence of the day,
> He kills at once, for tis the Shortest Way.

Although *More Reformation* did not appear until ten days after the trial, Defoe had correctly predicted that Lovell would read out a savage sentence on 'Satyr'.

Another of Defoe's satirical targets now sitting in judgement on him was Sir Robert Clayton, a seventy-four-year-old Whig politician and businessman, who had been Lord Mayor of London in 1679, when he was also involved in some sort of scandalous contract with his wife. Clayton had been financial adviser to Nell Gwyn, King Charles II's mistress, and he plays a similar role in Defoe's novel *Roxana*. There is also a reference to him in *A Journal of the Plague Year*, and he appears as Ishban in Dryden's *Absalom and Achitophel*. Defoe would have most disliked Sir Robert Clayton as the friend, patron and father-in-law of Judge Jeffreys, but in his satire *The Reformation of Manners* he charges him only with fondness for money:

> And yet he covets without rule or end,
> Will sell his wife, his master or his friend.
> To boundless avarice a constant slave,
> Unsatisfied as death, and greedy as the grave.

Sir Robert Clayton would not have warmed to Defoe in the dock. Nor would his nonagenarian fellow alderman Sir Robert Jeffreys, who still presided over the whipping of half-naked prostitutes at the Bridewell house of correction, of which he was president. A hundred years earlier Shakespeare had railed at the cruel vice of men such as Sir Robert Jeffreys:

> Thou rascal beadle, hold thy bloody hand!
> Why doest thou lash that whore? Strip thine own back!
> Thou hotly lusts to use her in that kind
> For which thou whipst her.

Defoe, in his *Reformation of Manners*, suggests that Jeffreys is now too old to enjoy the whores in the way he used to do, and is only aroused by superintending their punishment as the justice of the night, and by bawdy talk with his cronies:

> Old venerable Jeph, with trembling air,
> Ancient in sin and father of the chair.
> Forsaken by vices he had served so long
> Can now be vicious only with his tongue.
> Yet talks of ancient lewdness with delight
> And loves to be the justice of the night.
> On bawdy talk with pleasure he reflects
> And lewdly smiles at vices he corrects.

In his condemnation of brutal punishment Defoe was especially courageous, since as a notorious pamphleteer and satirist he was himself at risk. It appears that at Defoe's trial the Solicitor-General, Sir Simon Harcourt, asked for a 'whipping sentence' to be added to the penalties. However, the judges stopped short of adding more barbarity to the sentence of three days in the pillory, a fine of 200 Marks (approximately £130) and 'to remain in prison till all be performed' – a vaguer, more sinister term than the usual 'at the Queen's pleasure'. Defoe was also bound under heavy sureties for seven years' good behaviour, so that right up until 1710 he was often in danger of arrest because of complaints from such diverse people as the Russian ambassador, an admiral, a judge and a Devonshire magistrate who objected to something Defoe had written or said.

Defoe was to stand in the pillory for the first time on 19 July, but meanwhile Lord Nottingham hoped that in exchange for remitting this part of the sentence he might discover Defoe's accomplices. The famous Quaker William Penn was one of those who intervened on Defoe's behalf, or perhaps in the hope of getting a confession. Defoe thanked Penn for his solicitude to an 'unknown captive', but insisted that he had acted alone in writing *The Shortest Way*. He complains that Nottingham's attempt at 'discovering parties, is the same, which his Lordship has often put upon me before', and would mean betraying what friends had said in private conversation. The Queen herself agreed with Nottingham that Defoe had written his pamphlet on behalf of some dangerous plotters against her government, and she had him brought from Newgate to Windsor to make a confession in person. Whatever he told her was not enough. 'As to de Fooe', wrote Godolphin later, 'the Queen seems to think that the confession amounts to nothing.'

Queen Anne, Lord Nottingham and the High Church Tories were what we would now call 'conspiracy theorists', and could not believe that Defoe had acted alone. They knew that he had been the adviser and confidant of the late King William, and therefore assumed that he had worked with some of the Whigs who were ministers during his reign. It is possible that Lord Nottingham may have suspected his moderate rival Harley of having commissioned Defoe to write the pamphlet that had so effectively dished the High Church faction. Conspiracy theorists cannot accept that men like Defoe are natural loners, distrustful of parties, factions and plots. Even in his opinions, Defoe was increasingly on his own.

Whereas conspirators are by their nature trying to overthrow the established regime, Defoe by his nature tried to defend it. As a young man he had taken up arms against someone who was, in his eyes, an unlawful king, but he had since been a loyal supporter of William III and now Queen Anne. He had written *The Shortest Way* to protect the triumvirate against what he saw as a plot by the Jacobites, under the guise of High Church Tories. In the carrying out of confidential services for William III, and later for Harley and Godolphin, Defoe was not a conspirator but a seeker-out and foiler of conspiracies. And in this secret policeman's role he proved very much abler than Nottingham for, unlike Nottingham, he could distinguish between a plot against the State and a plea for religious toleration. He had written *The Shortest Way* as a protest against the Test Act. He later defended the freedom of worship for Roman Catholics in England, for Episcopalians in Scotland, and even for cannibal heathens on Robinson Crusoe's island. Like many men who challenge the received ideas of their time, Defoe suffered ostracism, abuse and even persecution. And so, when he still refused to name any accomplices, he was made to suffer the cruellest part of his sentence for 'seditious libel'. With characteristic fortitude he even composed and had printed a *Hymn to the Pillory*, which was sold or handed out to spectators of his ordeal at the Royal Exchange on 29 July 1703, at Cheapside the following day, and at Temple Bar on the final day of the month.

It is hard for modern people to understand why the pillory was such a dreaded punishment in an age when political rebels could be hung, drawn and quartered, whipped through every town in the county, or sent to Barbados as plantation slaves. Compared to such horrors, not to mention the 'boot' and the thumbscrew used on the Scottish Covenanters, the pillory sounds no worse than the stocks, the ducking-stool or the scold's bridle. It had been introduced in Anglo-Saxon times to punish antisocial behaviour such as slander, loading dice, or begging with somebody else's child, and in Defoe's time it was meted out to perjurers and rioters.

It was largely because of the shame attached to standing in the pillory that prisoners feared it more than fines and imprisonment, but the punishment also carried the risk of severe and even fatal injuries from a hostile crowd. Titus Oates came nearer to death from the brickbats hurled at him as he stood in Temple Bar than he did from being whipped from Newgate to Tyburn. The pamphleteer William Fuller also said that the pillory had been worse than the thirty-nine lashes he received in Bridewell: 'Never was a man among Turks or Barbarians known to be worse used ... I was stifled with all manner of dirt, filth and rotten eggs; and my left eye was so bruised with a stone ... that I fell down and hung by the neck ... I was all over bruised from head to heels; and on the small of my back as I stood stooping, a stone struck me which weighed more than six pounds.' Knowing what had happened to Fuller a few weeks earlier, Defoe still refused to escape his fate by telling the Queen the names of any real or imagined accomplices. His courage was amply rewarded, for on all three days that he stood with his head and hands clamped in their wooden case he was surrounded by cheering supporters, and if he was pelted it was with flowers. Even the Tory Press acknowledged his friendly reception, which they sourly attributed to bribes from a 'party', meaning the Whigs or Dissenters.

Since Defoe had no party behind him, we have to assume that the people of London admired the man who had cheeked the high and mighty, especially the judges and aldermen of the City. Many among the crowd had probably suffered at the hands of sadists such as Sir Robert Jeffreys or crooks like Lovell. They bought and clearly enjoyed the *Hymn to the Pillory*, which was hawked among the spectators of Defoe's ordeal. The *Hymn* is not a great poem; it is not even up to the standard of Defoe's usual verse, but it stands as lasting testament to his honesty and courage. When he composed it Defoe was serving an indeterminate sentence in Newgate Prison, he was financially ruined and worried about his pregnant wife, and he was shortly to brave the London mob which only a few weeks earlier had savagely stoned another pamphleteer. Yet rather than begging for mercy or sinking into despair and lethargy, he had the guts and the gall to write a lampoon on his judges, suggesting that it was they who should stand in the pillory.

Defoe begins by praising earlier occupants of the pillory, such as William Prynne, who had also had his ears cut off for impugning the virtue of the wife of Charles I. He gives pride of place in the pillory to the High Church clergyman Dr Sacheverell:

> There would the famed S—ll stand
> With trumpet of sedition in his hand . . .
> He from a Church of England pulpit first
> All his Dissenting brethren cursed.

He goes on to attack Sir Robert Jeffreys:

> Let no such Bridewell Justices protect
> As first debauch the whores whom they correct.

He bravely defies Sir Simon Harcourt, the Solicitor-General, who wanted to add a whipping to Defoe's Old Bailey sentence:

> In vain he struggled, he harangued in vain,
> To bring in whipping sentences again
> And to debauch a milder government
> With abdicated kinds of punishment . . .

Defoe triumphed over the pillory, but the experience made him even more of a loner, an outsider despised and rejected even by other literary men. Jonathan Swift called him 'one of those authors, the fellow who was pilloried, I have forgotten his name', while in a satire by Addison he is advised by a judge that if he values his ears he should 'forebear uttering such notorious falsehood'. Pope also thought it amusing in *The Dunciad* to suggest that Defoe had suffered the fate of Prynne:

> Earless on high stood unabashed Defoe,
> And Tutchin, flagrant for the scourge below.

Defoe's ordeal in the pillory ended on 31 July 1703, but he still faced an indeterminate sentence in Newgate Prison, 'an emblem of hell itself, and a kind of entrance to it'. His Tilbury brickyard was ruined; he no longer had any means of helping his wife and children; and every day that he spent in prison increased the burden of debt from his bankruptcy. Some of the verse he composed in Newgate and published after his release shows that even Defoe occasionally lost heart and thought of hanging himself. In his *Aspects of the Novel* E. M. Forster suggests that Defoe had some kind of revelation in Newgate: 'We do not know what it was, and probably he himself did not know afterwards, for he was a busy, slip-shod journalist and a keen politician. But something occurred to him in prison and out of its vague, powerful emotion, Moll Flanders and Roxana are born.'

This spell in Newgate obviously helped Defoe when he came to *Moll Flanders*; however, his bankruptcy is likely to have been a more traumatic experience than prison or the pillory, and should be seen as the key to his novels. If Newgate did not turn Defoe into England's first great novelist, it helped to make him its first great journalist, as well as a Secret Service agent. While he was still in Newgate it came to Defoe in a dream that he should set up a journal, the *Review*. It was also while he was in Newgate Prison that Harley decided to hire him as a spy, propagandist and confidential adviser.

During the autumn of 1703 Harley was rapidly gaining in influence over the High Church Nottingham, and would soon replace him as one of the two principal Secretaries of State. He suggested to Godolphin, the Treasurer, that Defoe was too gifted a man to languish in prison, because 'if his fine be satisfied without any other knowledge but that it is the Queen's bounty to him and grace, he may do service and this may engage him better than after rewards and keep him more under the power of obligation'. Godolphin replied: 'I have found it proper to read some paragraphs of your letter to the Queen. What you propose about Defoe may be done when you will and how you will.' On the advice of Godolphin, Queen Anne paid Defoe's fine, and apparently on her own initiative sent some relief to his wife and children. Defoe was released from Newgate early in November, and on the ninth of the month he wrote to Harley a deeply grateful letter from 'a mortified stranger', signing it, 'your most obedient, infinitely obliged humble servant, Daniel Defoe'. Although the tone of the letter is almost embarrassingly fulsome, there is no doubt of Defoe's deep and lasting gratitude to Harley, as to his previous friend and employer, William III. Proud and lonely as he was, Defoe responded warmly to kindness.

5

On Her Majesty's Secret Service

AFTER ALMOST A YEAR spent in hiding or in Newgate Prison, Defoe was back at home with his wife and children, enjoying the comfort of freedom and peace, when he grew aware that a new disaster was looming, though this time a natural one. An uncommonly fierce and persistent south-westerly gale developed during the night of 25–6 November 1703 into the Great Storm, which devastated the South of England and almost destroyed its naval and merchant fleets. After surviving a night of terror in his house in Hackney, Defoe set out to inspect the damage and to question his fellow Londoners on their experiences of the hurricane. He placed an advertisement in the *London Gazette*, appealing to readers to send in accounts of how the storm had affected different parts of the country and coast. Within days he began to write what we would now call an 'instant book' of about 75,000 words, *The Storm: or a Collection of the most Remarkable Casualties and Disasters which Happened in the late dreadful Tempest both by Sea and Land*. As a piece of reporting, *The Storm* is a masterpiece, which puts to shame all modern accounts of disaster, whether in books, newspapers, radio or television. In most respects the factual *Storm* is even more gripping than the fictional *Journal of the Plague Year*, and fully deserves to be published again, if only for students of journalism.

As in all his later writing, Defoe sets out to satisfy every kind of reader. For the pious Christian, he quotes from Nahum 1.3, 'The Lord hath his way in the whirlwind and in the storm', and asks if this was a punishment for our sins. For the scientifically minded, he writes on 'the natural causes of wind', with reference to Aristotle, Robert Boyle and Sir Walter Raleigh. For the merchant class, he examines the damage done to ships, and for landowners, the number of trees brought down. For the very large class of readers who love to see their names in print, Defoe credits all those who replied to his advertisement.

In *The Storm*, as in *A Journal of the Plague Year*, Defoe does not rush into the climax of his narrative. These islands, he starts off, had long been 'distinguished from all the world by impassable seas and terrible north winds, which made the Albion shore dreadful to sailors'. The Greek and Phoenician ships could not have survived our waters: 'And in more modern times, we have a famous instance in the Spanish Armada; which after it was rather frightened than damaged by Sir Francis Drake's machines, not then known by the name of fire-ships, were scattered by a terrible storm, and lost upon every shore.' Defoe then describes how the storm had been building up since about 10 November, or only a few days after he left Newgate Prison:

> It had been exceedingly hard for about fourteen days past, and that so hard that we thought it terrible weather, several stacks of chimneys were blown down, and several ships were lost, and the tiles in many places were blown off the houses; and the nearer it came to the fatal 26th of November, the tempestuousness of the winds increased . . . The collector of these sheets narrowly escaped the mischief of a part of a house which fell in the evening of that day [24 November] by the violence of the wind.
>
> On Friday morning, it continued to blow exceedingly hard, but not so as that it gave any apprehensions of danger within doors; towards night it increased, and about 10 a clock, our barometers informed us that the night would be very tempestuous; the mercury sunk lower than ever I had observed it on any occasion whatsoever, which made me suppose the tube had been handled and disturbed by the children.

We see there the touch of a great, and not just a good reporter. To understand what follows, one should bear in mind that people in those days slept at the top of the house.

> It did not blow so hard till twelve a clock at night, but that most families went to bed; though many of them not without some concern at the terrible wind. But about one, or at least by two a clock, tis supposed, few people, that were capable of any sense of danger, were so hardy as to lie in bed. And the fury of the tempest encreased to such a degree, that the editor

of this account being in London, and conversing with the people the next days, understood, most people expected the fall of their houses.

And yet in this general apprehension, nobody durst quit their tottering habitation, for whatever the danger was within doors, twas worse without; the bricks, tiles and stones from the tops of the houses, flew with such force, and so thick in the streets, that no-one thought fit to venture out, though their houses were near demolished within.

The author of this account was in a well-built brick house in the skirts of the city; and a stack of chimneys falling in upon the next houses, gave the house such a shock, that they thought it was just coming down upon their heads; but opening the door to attempt an escape, the danger was so apparent, that they all thought fit to surrender to the disposal of Almighty Providence, and expect their grave in the ruins of the house, rather than to meet more certain destruction in the garden: for unless they could have gone about two hundred yards from any building, there had been no security; for the force of the wind blew the tiles point blank, though their weight inclines them downward: and in several very broad streets we saw the windows broken by the flying of tile-sherds from the other side: and where there was room for them to fly, the author of this has seen tiles blown from a house above thirty or forty yards, and stuck from five to eight inches into the solid earth. Pieces of timber, iron and sheets of lead, have from higher buildings been blown much further.

Many people in England said they experienced earthquakes and storms of fire, on which Defoe keeps an open mind: 'And yet tho I cannot remember to have heard thunder, or that I saw any lightning, or heard of any that did in or near London, yet in the countries [counties] the air was seen full of meteors and vaporous fires: and in some cases both thundering and unusual flames of lightning, to the great terror of the inhabitants.'

Since Mary Defoe had recently given birth, the following passage has a particular poignancy: 'Several women in the city of London who were in travail, or who fell into travail by the fright of the storm, were obliged to run the risk of being delivered with such help as they had; and midwives found their own lives in such danger that few of them

thought themselves obliged to show any concern for the lives of others.'
The terror of that night then reached its climax:

> From two of the clock, the storm continued and encreased till
> four in the morning; and from five, to half an hour after six,
> it blew with the greatest violence ... In this last part of the
> time the greatest part of the damage was done: several ships
> that rode it out till now, gave up all, for no anchor could hold.
> Even the ships in the River of Thames were all blown away
> from their moorings, and from Execution Dock to Lime-house
> Hole, there were but four ships that rode it out, the rest were
> driven down into the Bite as the sailors call it, from Bell-Wharf
> to Lime-House; where they were huddled together and drove
> on shore, heads and sterns, one upon another, in such a manner
> as anyone would have thought it had been impossible ...
> Together with the violence of the wind the darkness of the
> night added to the terror of it.

It was not until eight o'clock on the morning of 26 November that
the storm had abated enough for people to venture outside to enquire
after their friends and relations and to inspect the damage. Defoe, who
had only recently owned a factory making bricks and pantiles, must
have found the sight heartbreaking.:

> The streets lay so covered with tiles and slates, from the tops
> of the houses, especially in the Out-Parts, that the quantity is
> incredible, and these houses were so universally stripped that
> all the tiles in fifty miles round would be able to repair but a
> small part of it.
>
> Something may be guessed at on this head, from the sudden
> rise of the price of tiles; which rose from 21s per thousand to
> £6 for plain tiles; and from 50s per thousand for pantiles to
> £10 and bricklayers labour to 5s a day. And though after the
> first hurry the prices fell again, it was not that the quantity
> was supplied but because ... the charge was so extravagant
> that an universal neglect of themselves, appeared both in land-
> lord and tenant; an incredible number of houses remained all
> the winter uncovered, and exposed to all the inconvenience of
> wet and cold.

Most of *The Storm* was compiled from reports from those who had
answered Defoe's advertisement in the *Gazette* or from information

given by the Admiralty and other government offices; but Defoe himself described what had happened in London. Surprisingly, only twenty-one people were killed in the City, most by falling chimney stacks, and often because they had stayed in their beds at the top of the house:

> In Threadneedle Street, one Mr Simpson, a scrivener, being in bed and fast asleep, heard nothing of the storm, but the rest of the family being more sensible of danger, some of them went up and waked him; and telling him their own apprehensions, pressed him to rise; but he too fatally sleepy, and consequently unconcerned at the danger, told them, he did not apprehend any thing; and so, notwithstanding all their persuasions, could not be prevailed with to rise; they had not been gone many minutes out of his chamber, before the chimneys broke through the roof over him, and killed him in his bed.

The lead on church roofs was rolled up like parchment 'and blown in some cases clear off from the buildings; as at Westminster Abbey'; seventy trees were down in Moorfields, and more than 100 elms in St James's Park, 'some of which were of such growth as they tell us they were planted by Cardinal Wolsey, whether that part of it be true or not, is little matter, but only to imply that they were very great trees.'

Defoe could never resist an odd or amusing story, even when it is not entirely believable:

> And twas observed that in the morning after the storm was abated, it blew so hard, the women who usually go for milk to the cow-keepers in the villages round the City, were not able to go along with their pails on their heads; and one that was more hardy than the rest, was blown away by the fury of the storm, and forced into a pond, but by struggling hard got out, and avoided being drowned; and some that ventured out with milk the evening after, had their pails and milk blown off their heads.

Writing *The Storm* probably helped Defoe to forget his private worries and grievances, especially the ceaseless attacks on him by scurrilous journalists and pamphleteers. His wretchedness is expressed in a poem in which the hurricane is a metaphor for his affliction and persecution, *An Elegy on the Author of the True-Born Englishman, with an Essay on the late Storm.* He tells us that he had gone to the country – no doubt to his mother-in-law – to get away from the ribaldry and the bear-garden abuse which was heaped on him, 'a poor abdicated author': 'I tried retirement and banished myself from the town. I thought, as the boys used to say, twas but fair they should leave me alone, while I did not meddle with them. But neither a country retreat any more than a stone doublet, can secure a man from the clamour of the pen.'

This unaccustomed tone of self-pity is also heard in the poem itself, where Defoe complains of that part of the Old Bailey sentence which bound him under heavy sureties to seven years' 'good behaviour'. He saw this as a judicial check on his freedom of speech and writing:

> Circled in Newgate's cold embrace,
> And reconciled to death by such a place,
> I from the horrid mansion fled
> And, as concerning poetry, am dead
> To seven long years of silence I betake
> Perhaps by then I may forget to speak
> And then I died, and yield satiric breath,
> For to be dumb, in poetry, is death.

He also complains of the law's attempt to break him financially, yet boasts:

> I'm satisfied it never shall be said
> But He that gave me brains will give me bread.

Defoe knew he could live by writing and government work, but must have regretted the money he could have made by selling pantiles after the Great Storm. He rails at government lawyers, and at himself for having

> ... ventured to believe
> Men whose profession is to deceive.
> If among poets there remains a fool
> That scorns to take this notice for a rule
> But ventures the fidelities
> Of those whose trade and custom tis to lie
> Let me no pity to him show
> Let him to Bedlam not to Newgate go.

In the *Essay on the late Storm*, which follows on from the *Elegy*, Defoe likens it to the factiousness of the English, which had so distressed the late King William III. And here – in his published writing a rare occurrence – Defoe thanks William for his personal kindness, which, as we know from a private reference, consisted of subsidizing his brick and pantile works:

> It brought my hero to my mind,
> William the Glorious, Great and Good and Kind,
> Short epithets to his just memory
> The first he was to all the world, the last to me.
>
> The mighty genius to my thought appeared
> Just in the same concern he used to show
> When private tempests used to blow,
> Storms which the Monarch more than death in battle feared,
> When Party fury shook his throne
> And made their mighty malice known
> I've heard the sighing monarch say
> The publick peace so near him lay,
> It took the pleasure of his crown away.
>
> When to the Queen the sceptre he resigned
> With a resolved and steady mind
> Tho he rejoiced to lay the trifle down
> He pitied her to whom he left the crown.
> Foreseeing long and vigorous wars,
> Foreseeing endless, private, party Jarrs
> Would always interrupt her rest
> And fill with anxious cares her royal breast.

In the *Elegy* we recognize the obsessions which drove Defoe to write half a million words in the year after leaving Newgate. There was first the imperative need for money to make good his boast that 'he that gave me brains will give me bread'. This is why he refers to himself as the author of *The True-Born Englishman*, by far his most popular work, when this is in fact an elegy for the author of *The Shortest Way*, the pamphlet that landed him in 'Newgate's cold embrace'. Defoe was also determined to prove that the pamphlet was right, and that he, the friend of the late King William, was equally loyal to Anne, to her moderate government, and to the cause of the English war against

France. Finally, he was obsessed by the seven-year ban, which prevented him from getting his own back on the High Church journalists, who called him an 'insolent scribbler', 'foul mouth' and 'prostitute'.

For all these reasons, Defoe decided early in 1704 to realize the dream, which had come to him in Newgate, of starting a journal of current affairs to propound the ideals of William and of the Glorious Revolution. The result was the *Review*, which he wrote single-handedly first in weekly, then bi-weekly and soon tri-weekly issues from 13 February 1704 until 11 June 1713, the longest-running, the liveliest and most influential paper in what would prove to be the golden age of journalism.

The relaxation of censorship or prosecution of writers in 1695 had encouraged the setting up of at least ten newspapers in addition to the official *London Gazette*. These early papers supplemented the 500 coffee houses of London as sources of home and foreign intelligence, shipping and business news, and gossip. By the time Queen Anne came to the throne the average newspaper consisted of one sheet of two printed sides, sometimes folded into four. Some papers gave a Tory slant to the news, like the *Postboy*, or a Whig slant, like the *Postman*, but none carried a leading article.

Defoe's *Review* appeared in the same four-page format but gave almost all its space to comment rather than news. For some years its only rivals in this field were the Whig *Observator*, largely written by John Tutchin, who like Defoe had joined the Monmouth Rebellion, and its enemy the High Tory *Rehearsal*, largely written by Charles Leslie, a Jacobite. As we shall see, both Tutchin and Leslie, from their extreme positions, detested the moderate stance of Defoe. It was not until the period 1709–13 that first Richard Steele, then Joseph Addison and Jonathan Swift, followed the model of the *Review* to produce the *Tatler*, the *Spectator* and the *Examiner*. As a journalist, Defoe never received the acclaim of the other three, for he was neither a graceful nor a polished writer, and did not address such a learned readership. Although the political articles in the *Review* were read by statesmen in Westminster, as well as by Marlborough in his tent, Defoe wrote for his own people – the tradesmen, Dissenters and middle class of London and other towns.

Within two months of the first edition Defoe's printer was selling 200 copies, first at a penny and then at halfpence a time, as well as taking advertisements for serious books, cosmetics, wigs, rupture appliances and VD cures. In the General Election year of 1705 the government subsidized the *Review* by buying and distributing many copies, bringing the circulation up to 1,500.

Besides writing an article on the war, foreign politics or the state of trade, Defoe soon introduced a feature called 'Advice from the Scandalous Club', instructing his readers on manners and morals in what was a prototype of the agony aunt as well as the gossip column. Here he denounced such vices as duelling, swearing, displays of drunkenness by the clergy (especially Dr Sacheverell) and lust masquerading as gallantry. As in some of the later novels, the puritanical message of the 'Scandalous Club' is heavily overlaid with ribaldry and salaciousness. Defoe quickly perfected the art of identifying those who were guilty of bad behaviour, while at the same time pretending to keep their names secret. In the issue of 7 November 1704 he tells a reader that he cannot possibly print his story about a City treat or drinking party: 'with a list of how many magistrates were drunk there; how many bawdy songs were sung there; who p . . . . t over the balcony on the people's heads, and who were so drunk, they were obliged to do it in their breeches.' One can be certain that many *Review* readers soon ascertained who these magistrates were, and passed on their names to coffee-house friends.

In the 'Advice from the Scandalous Club' on 14 December 1704 Defoe prints a letter purporting to come from one of a group of gentlemen:

> The question arising in company whether the woman that would permit a man to set upon her bed, after she is in it, and the whole family before that time being gone to bed, would not in all likelihood, admit him at some time into the same? I offered to lay, that by the frequent permission of the man, the virtue of the woman might be seduced and she therefore become a prostitute. The case being argued since, a wager of two guineas for a handsome treat has been laid thereupon, both parties agreeing to stand by the decision of the society. You are therefore desired not to fail of answering this in the next Review, because Monday is the day appointed for the money to be spent.

To this, the Society – that is, Defoe – delivers a judgement calling the censure 'unjust and too severe', though warning the persons involved of the risk they took. Here, as frequently in the 'Scandalous Club', Defoe appears as an early champion of women's rights in social behaviour, the choice of a husband, education and the control of property, which is also a central theme of *Roxana*. He not only discerned that women had minds of their own, but probably hoped they would buy his paper.

During the first few months of the *Review*'s publication England was preparing itself for the summer campaign in Europe, which was to end gloriously in the Battle of Blenheim; but the High Church Tories were doing their best to frustrate Marlborough's plans. Defoe's enemy Lord Nottingham had transferred 2,000 troops from the Netherlands to Portugal, without consulting Marlborough, who was furious. Nottingham's High Church crony Sir Edward Seymour, who also became an enemy of Defoe, had done his best to stop Parliament voting supplies to the army in the Netherlands, causing Marlborough to say in a letter to Sarah: 'We are bound not to wish for anybody's death but should Sir Edward Seymour die, it would be no great loss to the Queen nor to the nation.'

By February 1704 it was becoming apparent to Marlborough that France and its ally Bavaria were in a position to march on Vienna and threaten the very existence of the Austrian empire, which was also convulsed by a Protestant rising in Hungary. By April Marlborough had made up his mind to move his army from Holland, up the Rhine, then across to the Danube, to come to the help of Vienna. He and his brilliant Austrian opposite number, Prince Eugene of Savoy, were aware of the need to keep their strategy secret. If the French got wind of it, they would march to forestall them in Bavaria. If the Dutch politicians heard that Marlborough was leaving the Netherlands, they might withdraw their troops from his army, or even conclude a separate peace with France.

Above all, Marlborough had to keep his plans secret from Nottingham and the other High Tories in the government, who would be certain to raise the alarm and cut off supplies of money. Only the Queen and Godolphin knew and approved of Marlborough's plan. Before he sailed from Harwich on 8 April 1704 he wrote to Godolphin, telling him that Nottingham was unremittingly hostile and wanted to make supplies to the army conditional on a revived Occasional Conformity Bill. No wonder Nottingham hated Defoe for having scuppered this Bill in the previous year. At the end of April the Queen at last got rid of Nottingham and the other High Church ministers; yet as late as June, and only six weeks before the Battle of Blenheim, Sir

Edward Seymour was ranting against the waste of English blood in Germany, and even demanded Marlborough's impeachment.

Defoe called his first issue the *Weekly Review of the Affairs of France*, and even when it became a tri-weekly journal, and gave most of its space to Britain and other countries in Europe, the word 'France' lingered on in the title. Defoe's purpose, as we can see from the second number (18 February 1704), was to challenge English complacency, based on victories over the French at Crécy, Poitiers and Agincourt in the Hundred Years War: 'But whatever the French were in former days, however effeminate the kings or people . . . we find them to our loss, a bold, adventurous, wise, politick and martial people.' Although he detested the French regime, especially its persecution of Huguenots, Defoe admired certain of Louis's innovations, especially the ban on duelling. Much of the early 'Advice from the Scandalous Club' used the example of France to denounce recent duels in London, especially the one involving the High Tory Admiral Sir George Rooke, whose friend had challenged Defoe's lawyer William Colepepper.

When Marlborough's summer campaign began, Defoe warned his readers not to be too optimistic: 'If I am asked what is the true occasion why the French have so many turns [successes], and how they maintain a war with so much advantage, against all the united powers of Europe, I should answer tis because the Powers are united and not united . . . the Croats in Hungary refuse to fight, and deserting their general is a fresh instance of this' (13 May 1704). The Croats, or Crabats, as it was sometimes written, were South Slav infantry, who figure large in Defoe's historical novel *The Memoirs of a Cavalier* and in all the bitter controversy of the War of the Spanish Succession. The Serbo-Croat word for these soldiers, *pandur* or 'follower of a banner', had been anglicized as 'pandour', meaning a robber, the name Defoe had applied to the Old Bailey Recorder, Sir Salathiel Lovel. The rapacity and ruthlessness of these troops in the Austrian army were constantly referred to by Jonathan Swift as a means of attacking the Duke of Marlborough; they crop up again in Thackeray's novel *Henry Esmond*, set in the reigns of William III and Anne.

These Croats were *Grenzer*, or guardians of the Military Frontier, established in 1522 to protect the Habsburg empire against the Turks, who by then had occupied what is now Serbia and Bosnia-Hercegovina. The *Grenzer* or Frontiersmen served the same purpose in central Europe as did the Cossacks in the east, and during the nineteenth century came to acquire a similar reputation as agents of despotism, especially in crushing the revolutions of 1848. Although originally called 'Croats', these warriors of the Military Frontier (in Serbo-Croat, *Vojna Krajina*) were almost exclusively Eastern Orthodox Christians, and during the twentieth century came to be known as 'Serbs'.

In the issue of 6 June Defoe mentions another nation he sees as a weak link in the Grand Alliance:

> The Italians are so despicable in their character in the field that the present French Army above mentioned, now in Italy, suppose it to be 50,000 men, would think themselves a match, and make no scruple to fight 100,000 of the best Italian troops now in the field. So much has sloth, bigotry and debauchery, effeminated the gallantest and most magnanimous nation in the world, who should travel into Italy and see that people now would imagine that they should be the remains of the Ancient Romans, the glory and the conquerors of the world?

This article repeats the calumnies against the Italians that Defoe expresses in his verse satire *The True-Born Englishman* and in his novel *The Memoirs of a Cavalier*.

Many readers of the *Review* were puzzled and angered by its constant references to the power of France, with its 'impregnable fortifications', 'disciplined soldiers', 'experienced officers' and 'bottomless supplies'. Among the disgusted readers was the Treasurer, Godolphin, who asked his colleague Harley to 'find out the author of the *Review*' and take appropriate action, for his 'magnifying of France is a thing so odious'.

The next two issues of the *Review* show that Defoe has heeded the warning: on 4 July he writes an amusing apologia: 'Those who pretend to charge me with favouring the French interest and being bought and bribed with French money, would do well to go into France and present themselves to the French king, as the authors of the *Review* and plead the merits of it; I freely give them liberty to make use of my name, and am satisfied his majesty will reward them with the wheel or the halter [breaking on the wheel, or hanging].' He compares himself to the geese on the capitol of ancient Rome, who were meant to sound the alarm when an enemy was approaching but were often accused of disturbing the sleep of the citizens: 'If I, like an honest Protestant goose, have gaggled too loud of the French power, and raised the country; the French indeed may have reason to cut my throat if they could; but tis hard my own countrymen, to whom I have shown their danger and who I have endeavoured to wake out of their sleep, should take offence at the timely discovery.'

There is no doubt at all that Defoe acted in good faith in warning against the danger of France. This was the lesson he had learnt from his hero William of Orange, who had dedicated his life to resisting Louis XIV. Besides, at the time that Godolphin wrote to Harley about the *Review*, Defoe had almost certainly entered Harley's service. Within a few months Godolphin himself was asking Defoe for the names and addresses of all the Jacobites in London who were thought to be in correspondence with the Pretender in France; and later he offered to take over from Harley the cost of Defoe's employment, which had already proved so valuable to the government. After his first effusively grateful letter to Harley in November 1703, Defoe appears to have waited six months before he was offered a job. Then in May or June 1704 he wrote to Harley this extraordinary letter, revealing the pain and frustration of his tormented life:

All my prospects were built on a manufacture [the brickyard] I had erected in Essex; all the late king's bounty to me was expended there. I employed a hundred poor families at work, and it began to pay me very well. I generally made six hundred pounds profit per annum. I began to live, took a good house, bought me coach and horse a second time; I paid large debts gradually, small ones wholly, and many a creditor after composition [a percentage accepted by a bankrupt's creditors in lieu of full payment], whom I found poor and decayed I sent for and paid the remainder to, although already discharged. But I was ruined by *The Shortest Way* and Sir, had not your favour and her Majesty's bounty assisted, it must have been one of the worst sorts of ruin! That I shall never want that, but a large and promising family, virtuous and excellent mother to seven beautiful and hopeful children, a woman whose fortune I have ruined, with whom I have had £3,700, and yet who in the worst of my afflictions, when my Lord N[ottingham] insulted her then tempted her, scorned so much as to move me to comply with him, and rather encouraged me to oppose him . . .

Seven children, Sir, whose education calls on me to furnish

their heads if I cannot their purses, and which debt if not paid now can never be compounded hereafter is to me a moving article and helps very often to make me sad. But Sir, I am thank God furnished with patience. I never despaired and in the worst condition always believed I should be carried through it, but which way, has been and yet remains a mystery of providence unexpounded. I beg heartily your pardon for this tedious epistle. The miserable are always full of their own cases, and think nothing impertinent. I write this for tis too moving for me to speak it.

Here, for the first time, we see the unhappy, lonely and hunted man behind the mask of fortitude and defiance: the misery caused by his debts, and his anguish at having squandered his wife's money are shown in the way he makes himself write down the exact sum – £3,700. All the doubt, fear and wretchedness he had kept bottled up during the previous eighteen months come welling out in this passionate, almost incoherent letter.

Who was this man Harley, that he could so quickly win the devotion and trust which Defoe had previously given only to William of Orange? He was about the same age as Defoe, from a similar Nonconformist background, and had first entered Parliament as a Whig in 1689. He had later become an Anglican and a Tory, but was always a man of the centre, in religion as in politics. He was helped in his career by his cousin Abigail Hill, or Mrs Masham, who was also related to Sarah, Duchess of Marlborough, and later supplanted her as Queen Anne's favourite.

From all accounts, Harley was affable, easy tempered, dilatory and secretive, the sort of man of whom it is commonly said that he holds his cards close to his chest and never lets his right hand know what his left is doing. He was happiest with a glass of wine and a book from his famous library, now the Harleian Collection in the British Museum. Although a poor writer himself, Harley enjoyed the company of literary men, and on his retirement joined the Scribblers Club, receiving invitations in verse by Swift and Pope. Although he could not have known in 1704 that the bankrupt pamphleteer he employed would become a world-famous author, he may well have spotted Defoe's genius. Harley's greatest gift as a politician was understanding and sound judgement of people's character, as he had shown as Speaker of the House of Commons. As Secretary of State he tried to assess the character and loyalty of all the important people of every county and borough of England, and later Scotland.

Harley had chosen Defoe to help him compile this character study of British political life; but first he had studied Defoe. Unlike Nottingham and the Queen, Harley seems to have understood from the start that Defoe was an utterly independent man, who could not be bullied or bought by the government but might respond to an act of kindness. Having served as a minister during the previous reign, Harley may have known of Defoe's devotion to William III for the kindness shown to him. The fulsome letter that he received from Defoe on his release from Newgate proved Harley right, but he prudently refrained from making an immediate offer of employment, which might have weakened Defoe's sense of obligation.

It would be wrong to infer from this that Harley was cynical. The cynic has a contempt for human beings, and thinks they can all be bribed, bullied or blackmailed into service. Harley was an unusual politician because he discerned and exploited the better side of human nature. He knew that an independent man, bound to him by gratitude, was worth a hundred who had been bought or cajoled. Moreover, Harley, as much as Defoe, sincerely believed in the cause for which they worked together over the years. G. M. Trevelyan has well described the coming together of Harley and Defoe:

> Perhaps because he himself was so little of an orator in Parliament, Harley realised sooner than any of his colleagues or rivals the relation of public opinion to political power in Post-Revolution England. It was not only the Queen but her subjects whom he approached by the back-stairs. He found the observer, agent and journalist he wanted in Daniel Defoe, a man of shifty and secret ways like himself, of moderate views and kindly nature like himself, like himself of Puritan upbringing, but with a style of writing as lucid and telling as Harley's was slovenly and confused . . . And Harley now employed him to travel round England and report. Moving about under an assumed name, he communicated with the Secretary of State by stealth. Defoe was still so unpopular with all parties in Church and State that Harley dared not own him in public. Moreover both men loved mystery for its own sake. Defoe became Harley's Man Friday, and remained so for long years to come, through many changes of men and measures.

On 31 July 1704, the anniversary of Defoe's day in the pillory at Temple Bar, Godolphin wrote to Harley: 'I return you the blank warrant signed by the Queen for D—'s pardon. Her Majesty commands me to tell you she approves entirely of what you have promised him, and will make it good.' By this time Defoe was busy at work for Harley, briefing him on the affairs of Sweden and Russia, advising him to sack Sir George Rooke, the Tory admiral, and preparing for a trip to East Anglia, 'which I fully believe may be the foundation of such an intelligence, as never was in England'.

In another long letter Defoe outlines his plan for a greatly enlarged and improved Secret Service, embracing intelligence-gathering abroad, with counter-intelligence in this country, the jobs now performed by MI6 and MI5 respectively. Defoe had read a biography of the French master spy Cardinal Richelieu, and seems to have studied some English practitioners of the art. He admires Thomas Cromwell, Henry VIII's devious henchman, now chiefly known for his part in the dissolution of the monasteries and for a reign of terror whose victims included Sir Thomas More. He recommends to Harley one of his predecessors as Secretary of State, Queen Elizabeth's servant Sir Francis Walsingham, whose spies enabled him to detect the treason of Mary Queen of Scots and to learn the plans for the Spanish Armada. Defoe calls his fellow Puritan 'the greatest master of intelligence of the age', adding that Walsingham, like Thomas Cromwell, died poor.

Apart from Richelieu, most of Defoe's favourite spy-masters were Protestants. He says that Gustavus Adolphus, 'the king of Sweden in his German wars, always employed trusty persons in the towns and cities he reduced, to inform themselves of any known case where one was oppressed, or any family that had the general pity'. In the modern term, Gustavus wanted to 'win the hearts and minds' of the German people. Defoe praises the intelligence work of the poet John Milton, who during the Commonwealth held the office of Latin Secretary, expounding Oliver Cromwell's policy to the governments of Europe. According to Defoe, Milton kept 'a constant epistolary conversation with several foreign ministers of state, but so woven with political observations, that he found it as useful as any of his foreign correspondence'.

As he warms to his subject, Defoe clearly imagines himself as the man controlling a network of agents at home and abroad: 'A hundred thousand pounds per annum spent now for three years, might be the best money ever the nation laid out, and I am persuaded I could name two articles where if some money had been well applied, neither the insurrection in Hungary, nor the war in Poland, should have been so fatal to the confederacy as now they are.' He had read almost every available book on eastern and northern Europe, and often discussed it in the *Review* and in secret reports to Harley, who as Secretary of State for the Northern Department took care of policy to these countries as well as to Scotland. More than two years before he was sent up to Edinburgh Defoe observed: 'A settled intelligence in Scotland, a thing strongly neglected there, is without doubt the principal cause of the present misunderstanding between the two kingdoms.'

In his survey of the intelligence scene Defoe did not forget the war with France, and suggested appointing merchants as spies in Toulon, Brest and Dunkirk, the enemy's principal naval bases. He also chides Harley for lack of security in his own department: 'I have been in the Secretary's office of a post night, when had I been a French spy, I could have put in my pocket my Lord N—'s letters to Sir Geo Rook and to the Duke of Marlborough, laid carelessly on a table for the doorkeeper to carry to the Post Office.' If such laxity was corrected, Defoe continues, the Secretary's Office, under an active and ambitious chief with a proper system of intelligence, could become the clearing place of the nation's business instead of the Treasury, and 'be thus the only Cabinet . . . Here would be a Prime Minister without a grievance.' Defoe is suggesting that, if he was properly organized and backed by a proper intelligence service, Harley could replace Godolphin as Treasurer, and therefore head of the government.

Harley's failure to heed this almost clairvoyant warning nearly cost him his job and even his life, and helps to explain his later disgrace and imprisonment in the Tower of London. In the autumn of 1707, when he had quarrelled with Godolphin and was beset with political enemies, a clerk in the Secretary's Office was bribed by the French to purloin a letter from Anne to the Austrian Emperor. When the culprit, William Greg, was caught and sentenced to be hung, drawn and quartered, he was repeatedly offered commutation of his sentence if he would implicate Harley in his treason. Greg was kept in Newgate for three months, but in the end went to the scaffold, protesting Harley's innocence.

In the same astonishing letter in which he warns Harley against French spies Defoe gives details of the kind of information he plans to gather during his forthcoming travels in England.

1st A perfect list of all the gentry and family of rank in England, their residence, characters and interest [political faction].

2. Of all the clergy of England, their benefice, their character and morals, and the like for the Dissenters.

3. Of all the leading men in the cities and boroughs, with the parties they report [support].

He began to compile this 'perfect list' on a trip to East Anglia in the late summer of 1704, at the same time giving Harley detailed reports on the political climate there. He writes of Hertfordshire: 'That part adjoining to Bedford and Buckingham is whiggish and full of Dissenters. That part adjoining to Huntingdon, Cambridge and Essex is entirely Church and all of the High sort.' The gentlemen of the Royston Club, he says, 'settle all the affairs of the county and carry all before them', but are not quite so drunken as they were when he lampooned them in *The Reformation of Manners*.

On this journey Defoe went as far as Norfolk, but did not venture into the city of Norwich, where apparently he was frightened of meeting a creditor. While staying at Bury St Edmunds, he asked Harley to send letters addressed to him as 'Alexander Goldsmith', but in spite of this subterfuge he was in trouble again, as we see from this advertisement in the *Review* (7 November 1704):

> Whereas in several written News-Letters dispersed about the countries, and supposed to be written by one Dyer, a News-Writer, and by Mr Fox, bookseller in Westminster Hall, it has falsely, and by meer malice, scandalously been inserted, that Daniel de Foe was absconded, run away, fled from justice, had deserted his security, forfeited his behaviour, had been searched for by messengers ... the said Daniel de Foe being in St Edmunds Bury when the first of these papers appeared.

Defoe was understandably frightened of violating the order for seven years' 'good behaviour' imposed on him by the Old Bailey judges, though it must have been hard for him to explain what he was doing at Bury St Edmunds under the name 'Alexander Goldsmith'.

In August 1704 Defoe and the rest of the nation heard the news of Marlborough's victory at what came to be known as the Battle of Blenheim, as well as the capture of Marshal Tallard, the French commander. In the *Review* of 19 August Defoe had to admit that the French defeat did not square with his earlier forebodings: 'The objectors to our arguments seem to reply with some advantage, that French power seems to be less formidable, than at the beginning of these papers I presented it, and that all the terrible things which I foretold of it are dash't at one blow . . .' Nevertheless, he is clearly delighted that Marlborough has proved him wrong, and he calls the battle 'the greatest, most glorious and most complete victory that I can find in history, for about 200 years past'.

Within three weeks of hearing the news of Blenheim Defoe had written and published *A Hymn to Victory*, in which he points out that Marlborough had won by choosing to fight in the open field, in the manner agreed with Heinsius two years earlier. If Tallard had hoped to beat the English, he should have pursued a war of attrition and siege:

> He'll find it must not be a fighting war
> If he will Englishmen subdue.
> He must his way of spinning war renew
> Fatiguing marches, harass and surprises,
> Long campings, dodgings and delays
> That baulk an Englishman and make him mad.

Defoe also sees Blenheim as a triumph by Marlborough over his enemies in England, especially 'empty Nottingham', who had divided the country over the Occasional Conformity Bill. Although he modestly does not mention *The Shortest Way with Dissenters*, Defoe points out, with reason, that the scuppering of the Bill had helped to make Blenheim possible:

> The willing Lords close with the Royal word
> And damn the Bill as cruel and absurd
> Twas now that Victory returned,
> The flame of civil strife too long had burned . . .

At the end of *A Hymn to Victory* he addresses the Duke of Marlborough:

> The battles which you fight abroad procure
> New peace at home and make that peace secure
> The enemies you conquer on the Rhine
> Make our worst enemies at home decline . . .

For the first few weeks after the Battle of Blenheim most of the country united in joy, and even the Tory squires forgot to grumble about the Land Tax, the principal source of revenue for the war. Ned Ward, a popular Tory rhymester, exploited the battle for party ends by comparing the triumphs under the High Church Anne with the fruitless wars under the Dutch King William:

> But thou, Great Marlborough, hast on two campaigns
> Made happy Ann's surpass all other reigns,
> And by thy conduct, at a moderate cost,
> Retrieved that honour fourteen years had lost.

If the Tories could have turned Marlborough into their party's hero, they might have made peace to England's advantage. However, the High Church faction of Nottingham and Seymour were still incensed with Marlborough and Godolphin for having frustrated them on the Occasional Conformity Bill, and for driving them out of office at the beginning of the year. According to the Duchess of Marlborough, after the news of Blenheim the High Tories spoke as if her husband 'instead of beating the French had beaten the Church'. Soon Nottingham and Seymour were exploiting the recent successes at Málaga and Gibraltar to exalt Rooke and the navy at the expense of Marlborough and his redcoats. At the end of September Defoe wrote to Harley from Bury St Edmunds:

> The High Church Party look on Sir George Rooke as their own. The victory at sea they look upon as their victory over the Moderate Party, and his health is now drunk here by those who won't drink the Queen's, nor yours. I am obliged with patience to hear you damned, and he praised, and Her Majesty slighted, and the sea victory set up against the land victory; Sir George exalted above the Duke of Marlborough, and what can the reason of this be that they conceive some hopes from this that their High Church Party will revive under his patronage.

As Marlborough grew unpopular with the High Church Tories so, in Trevelyan's phrase, 'he became the hero of the Whigs, though he was never a Whig hero'. Godolphin too was looking for allies in that direction. When Marlborough was due to make his triumphal return to England, Godolphin commissioned a celebratory poem from Joseph Addison, a protégé of the Whig grandee Lord Halifax, called the Maecenas of his age after the rich Roman patron of Virgil. Thanks to Godolphin, Addison got a sinecure in the Excise department at £200 per annum, as well as immense publicity for his poem *The Campaign*. Addison was a much better poet than Defoe, who was nevertheless riled by his preferment; he had hoped for government sponsorship of his own *The Double Welcome. A Poem to the Duke of Marlboro*. He even made a spiteful attack on the rival who had trodden the easy path to fame and fortune, without having suffered for his principles. He says of his own Muse:

> To truth and merit she was always true,
> She never could the flattering flight pursue,
> And never praised but William, Sir, and you.
> Let Addison our modern Virgil sing . . .
> Maecenas has his modest fancy strung
> And fixed his pension first or he had never sung.
> Envy and Party-spleen he hath never known
> No humbling jails has pulled his fancy down . . .

Defoe was still smarting over the lack of thanks he got for *The Shortest Way*, and he turns the poem to Marlborough into another attack on the High Church Tories:

> You're welcome, Sir, because you're wanted here
> We want you here to calm our wild debate
> And balance parties as you balance States . . .
> To calm the Church's sea and keep it still,
> And fix the nation's peace against her will.
> A Pulpit War whence should sedition come?
> Our soldiers fight abroad, our priests at home . . .
> Priests like the female sex when they engage,
> There's always something bloody in their rage.
> There famed Sacheverell leads the vast forlorn,
> By him the Party's Bloody Standard borne . . .
> High Church buffoon, the Oxford's stated jest,
> A noisy, saucy, swearing, drunken priest . . .

The High Church Tories in Parliament were just as determined as ever to take England out of the Grand Alliance, and late in 1704 they attempted to 'tack' the Occasional Conformity Bill on to voting supplies for Marlborough's army. The 'Tackers' effectively made the persecution of the Dissenters a prime condition of fighting the war against France. The 'Occasional Bill', as it was now derisively called, had failed two years earlier largely because of the ridicule heaped on it by Defoe. When the Bill came to the vote in the House of Commons on 8 November 1704, the 'Tackers' were outnumbered by moderate Tory 'Cheaters' (as they were dubbed by the Tackers), including Sir Simon Harcourt, the Solicitor-General who had prosecuted Defoe at the Old Bailey and even demanded a whipping sentence. When a modified Bill was passed by the House of Commons and went to the Lords, both Marlborough and Godolphin openly voted against it. Still more significantly, the Queen was present throughout the debate and let it be known that she now opposed the Occasional Conformity Bill, which was duly rejected by the Lords. Defoe, who only two years ago had complained that 'tis hard for a man to say, all the world is mistaken but himself', now saw the world accepting his views.

The conflict within the Tory party necessitated a General Election; the campaign began in February 1705, and polling took place in different parts of the country between April and June. The parliamentary electoral system at that time gave representation to the producers of wealth and payers of taxes, and did not substantially change until the Great Reform Bill of 1832. Property was the main qualification for the vote, and in most constituencies there was a very limited franchise. The exceptions were some of the populous areas of Greater London, notably Westminster and Middlesex, and counties like Kent with a broad land ownership. On the other hand, in many seats an MP was returned by only a handful of voters, who were virtually in the control of some rich grandee. In the *Tour* Defoe often rails at these 'rotten boroughs', as they came to be called.

The Tories and Whigs were not political parties in our sense, but loose coalitions based on economic interest, religion and, above all, hope of paid office. The trading class and Dissenters were almost all Whig. The landed gentry were on the whole Tory, though not all were 'High Fliers' in religion, or supporters of a Jacobite Succession. Although most regular readers of the *Review* were probably Whigs, Defoe was hoping to win over moderate Tories to support the war against France.

Historians of the period agree on the major part played by Defoe in helping the ruling triumvirate to beat the High Church Tories in the 1705 elections. 'Defoe's reports to Harley of his journeys through England were giving his patron a broader idea of English public opinion and of English interests than any that found its way to High Tory chiefs or Whig aristocrats,' says Trevelyan. His dossier on the views and characters of important men in the shires and boroughs was already proving useful in the handing out of office and patronage in the months before the election. Still more important was the extraordinary series of articles in the *Review* in the spring of 1705, which established Defoe as the most powerful journalist in the country.

It was on 17 April 1705 that Defoe published the first of his trenchant, witty and still very readable attacks on the High Church Tories, which doubled the circulation of the *Review* in spite of the temporary dropping of its most popular feature, 'Advice from the Scandalous Club'. Defoe announces that he had hitherto 'repulsed the invitations made him from sundry persons to meddle with the contending parties', but he had changed his mind on receiving a letter containing 'so many importunities' that he could hold out no longer. His enemies at the time claimed that the real inducement came from government money, and they were doubtless right, though we have no written evidence to confirm this. But whether or not he received payment from Harley, as well as from sales and advertisements in the *Review*, Defoe never tailored his views to suit a patron. In the very first article in this polemical series we hear his distinctive voice making a plea for peace:

> For this I freely expose myself to fines, gaols, pillories, and extortionate and unjust sentences. If the worse enemy to me, or my writing, will calmly prove I ever wrote anything that did not tend to peace, I'll explode it, and own myself in error; if anything I am yet upon, has any other end, I'll freely decline it, and if my silence would farther it, I'll never write more . . . They insult the Church in a most scandalous manner who say that peace and union can be prejudicial to her, and they give too much reputation to the Dissenters . . . who call the Queen Presbyterian, Whig and I know not what.

In spite of Defoe's appeals for PEACE, in capital letters, the election campaign was often fierce, especially in Coventry, where the *Review* described 'railing, envying, fighting and all sorts of violence; club-law has been the decider of controversies; these things are risen to that height that the parties draw up in little armies in the street, and fight with all the fury and animosity imaginable, 500 and some say 1000 of a side' (*Review*, 10 May). Defoe blamed the troubles of Coventry and much of England on magistrates, 'whose duty it is to suppress vice and immoralities', but are themselves flagrant offenders. In a recent 'Advice to the Scandalous Club' Defoe had recounted how two

Clerkenwell magistrates tried to force a butcher's wife into a drinking bout in a tavern and, when she refused them, called her a whore and threatened to send her to Bridewell.

Two days later, on 12 May, the *Review* warned that party strife in England was making the country vulnerable to invasion from France:

> But if we are embroiled here at home while we are at war abroad; if by putting gross and illegal affronts upon each other: if by the constitution jangling with itself we are disabled for the war, the Confederacy broken, the Dutch ruined and the French victorious, Pardon me Gentlemen, I won't answer for the people of England when universal monarchy is obtained and all Europe submits to the tyranny of the House of Bourbon, who are we to resist. What proportion can this little spot have to the triumphant power of Popery and French government?

Defoe then anticipates the argument that the country does not need its redcoats in Europe but can defend itself with the 'wooden walls' of the navy:

> These are arguments indeed, and talking big may be useful sometimes, but if the gentlemen were to ask the soldiers, they would tell them another tale: nay, even the admirals of our fleet would give another answer. A nation may be invaded in spite of a great fleet, and an enemy may land an army when our fleet is remote, land-locked, wind-bound, and a hundred things. Why do these gentlemen applaud the victory of Blenheim? Why call the Duke of Marlborough a hero if there is no need of an army, and if we are able to fight the whole world.

On 15 May the *Review* urges its readers not to be alarmed by the election of some 'Tackers' in certain parts of the country, but to look at Kent, where not one Tacker has been victorious: 'And they that have attempted it have been hissed off the place with the utmost contempt, both them and their adherents, a particular instance of the sense, courage and fidelity of the inhabitants of that populous, wealthy county, and in which they have set an example to the whole nation.' Defoe was no doubt thinking of the Kentish Petition of 1701, in which he took up the cause of the imprisoned leaders. He speaks warmly of Kent in the *Tour*, and frequently travelled there throughout his life.

On 19 May the *Review* warned the 'hot' or High Churchmen of the peril of allying themselves with the Papists:

> If a Hot Churchman, if a Tacker be set up for a Member of Parliament, on one side, and a moderate Churchman, Whig or call him what you will, stands on the other, on which side, shall the Papists, the Atheists, the drunken, swearing and most vicious of the people vote? . . . The Church of England and the Church of Rome are very direct opposites: the former is a schismatic separation from the latter, and their principles are directly contrary extremes; and as warm as you are, Gentlemen, against your Dissenting, Separating Brethren, this Church of England, in a few ages before ours, was called the hypocrite, her professors the Separatists, Schismatics, Fanatics, and all the rest of the invidious terms you now too plentifully bestow on others.

Among the *Review*'s advertisements in May 1705 we see: 'Just Published. *The Consolidator. Or Memoirs of Sundry Transactions in the World of the Moon*. By a Native of that Climate. Translated from the Lunar Language by the Author of *The True-Born Englishman*'. This was one of the lucrative verse satires Defoe continued to write on top of his articles, his work for Harley, and the enormous philosophical poem *Jure Divino*, which was to be published in 1706. He had already had a success with *The Dyet of Poland* (Diet or Parliament), purportedly printed in Danzig, in which his various enemies appear with the suffix *-ski* to their name, such as Finski for Daniel Finch, the Earl of Nottingham. The Occasional Conformity Bill figures large in the politics of Poland, as of the Moon, and we even find a reference to *The Shortest Way with the Cossacks*. Following the custom among journalists, Defoe's *Consolidator* was panned by his rivals, especially John Tutchin, the editor of the Whig *Observator*. In the *Review* of 31 May Defoe relaxes from politics to answer his critics; and, incidentally, to reveal his sense of social and educational inadequacy:

> He's no scholar, says one. That may be true. He was apprentice to an hosier, says another; that's false, and adds to the number of the intolerable liberties, Dr B and Mr Observator give themselves, he having never been a hosier or an apprentice.
>
> But he's been a trader, that's true; and therefore must know no Latin. Excellent logic this . . . I easily acknowledge myself

blockhead enough to have lost the fluency of expression in the Latin, and so far trade has been a prejudice to me; and yet I think I owe this justice to my ancient father, yet living, and on whose behalf I freely testify that if I am a blockhead, it was nobody's fault but my own; he having spared nothing in my education . . .

Defoe then turns all his fire on Tutchin. Their common suffering at the hands of the High Church Tories did nothing to bring these rivals together, since Defoe clearly resented Tutchin's claim to superior social class and education:

That I'll take any Latin author he shall name, and I'll translate these into English and after that retranslate them crosswise, the English into French, the French into Italian and the Italian into Latin; and this I challenge him to perform with him who does it soonest and best for £20 each book; and by this he shall have an opportunity to show the world how much De Foe the hosier, is inferior in learning to Mr Tutchin, the Gentleman.

Defoe then sees him off with a fable about a black dog that frequently barked at a brown dog, which 'took no notice of him a long time, but being once more than usually teased and provoked, he gravely turns about, smells at black, and finding him a currish, cowardly breed and not worth his notice, very soberly and unconcerned, he holds up a leg, pisses upon him, and goes about his business. And so do I.' Some *Review* readers may have recalled that this was the same Defoe who never wrote 'anything that did not tend to peace'.

After this squabble with 'Mr Observator' Defoe returned to bashing the High Church Tories. He seized on and reproduced a sermon preached at St Giles-in-the-Fields to show that much of the Church of England itself rejected Dr Sacheverell and his 'bloody flag of defiance'. The Revd Mr Knagg had begun by asking: 'O Holy Jesus, when was it ever thy command, that religion should be propagated by consecrated daggers? Or when didst thou ever bring men over to Christianity by barbarous and bloody means? While you hold up your differences, some for Toleration, some against Occasional Conformity, some promoting one opinion, some another, you catch at the shadow and lose the substance.'

With this and his own persistent argument for freedom of conscience in religion, Defoe appealed to the instinct and common sense of many English people, who wanted to put behind them the persecution and hatred of the seventeenth century. His message appealed to the voters in 1705, who greatly reduced the power of the High Church Tories and brought back the Whigs into a share of government. Trevelyan reminds us just how important this outcome proved to be: 'Before midsummer, the Grand National Pantomime of the General Election was over, but though it might seem mere clowning to an amused or cynical spectator, the election had decided the fate of Europe and of Britain. The new House of Commons was not only certain to push on the war in the manner that Marlborough wished, but it was capable of dealing wisely with the very dangerous question of the relation of England to Scotland.'

In mid July 1705, at Harley's behest, Defoe set off on his longest and most far-reaching trip through England, taking the southern route to Cornwall, then back up the north coast to Bath and Bristol, then skirting the Welsh border to Lancashire, crossing the Pennines to Yorkshire, then down through the East Midlands into East Anglia, returning to London on 6 November. The details of this journey are preserved partly because of the problems Defoe encountered in south-west England, the bailiwick of the High Church Tory, Sir Edward Seymour. On the day he set off for Cornwall Defoe wrote to Harley thanking him for his official pass, or letter, and assuring him that he would use it only in the last resort. His troubles began at Weymouth, in Dorset, where the letters he had sent ahead to a friend, Captain Turner, arrived instead at the house of a different Captain Turner, the commander of a Guernsey frigate. These were probably coded letters, for Defoe complains that 'the ignorant tar, when he found things written dark and unintelligible, shows them to all the town'. His reaction was understandable in time of war, when the south coast was on the alert for a French invasion or another rebellion like Monmouth's at Lyme or William's at Torbay. When the 'ignorant tar' quite rightly took the mysterious letter to the mayor, Defoe was obliged to explain himself.

Suspicion followed Defoe to Exeter, the political base of Sir Edward Seymour, the friend of Lord Nottingham and a constant butt of Defoe's satire. Here a complaint was made to Mr Justice Price that 'there are several seditious persons come down into the country, spreading libels etc and embroiling the people, and advises the Justices to apprehend them'. At Taunton, according to Defoe, one of the aldermen 'blustered that he was sorry that he did not take me up and list me for a soldier' – that is, conscript him into the army. At Crediton, Defoe reported to Harley, a country justice granted 'the enclosed warrant against me, and searched the town with constables, and particularly the Dissenting Minister's house. But I was then at Liskeard in Cornwall.' Returning through Bideford, Defoe was again apprehended and 'for the first and last time showed your pass'. He later sent a stiff letter to the authorities in Devon, complaining of their 'injustice-like and ungentlemanlike warrant'. It is easy to understand why Defoe caused suspicion in a part of the country still overshadowed by Monmouth's rebellion: he talked politics and was heard to complain of the laziness and stupidity of the Tory MPs: he befriended Dissenting ministers, and denounced the Occasional Conformity Bill; he was known to Sir Edward Seymour – and maybe to some of his magistrates – as Daniel Defoe, a survivor of Sedgemoor, the author of *The Shortest Way*, who had recently been in Newgate and the pillory. For this particular Daniel, Devonshire was a true lion's den.

Defoe sent Harley progress reports on the dossier he was compiling on the English governing class. From the West Country he claimed to have 'a perfect skeleton of this part of England, and a settled correspondence in every town and part of it'. He found Lyme (Regis) 'a town completely united and the Church men very moderate and very well affected.' At Exeter he claimed to have 'a list of all the parties exactly, and a model of how Sir Ed Seymour may be thrown out against another election, without any difficulty at all'. Of Taunton and Bridgwater he had 'an exact account', and likewise of Tewkesbury, 'a quiet, trading, drunken town, a Whig bayly and all well'.

From Leeds, Wakefield and Sheffield, which he had visited between 23 and 26 September, Defoe reported: 'Here I have made useful remarks on trade, and observe that frequent elections having no influence here to divide the people, they live in much more peace with one another than in other parts.' From Lutterworth, in Leicestershire, he reports: 'Here Justice Bradgate rode horseback into the meeting-house [of Dissenters] and told the parson as he was preaching, he lied.'* In Coventry he met the correspondent who gave the *Review* its story on the election riots in May. From Cambridge on 26 October Defoe

---

* Defoe mentions Lutterworth in the *Tour* as the home of one of his heroes, John Wyclif, the fourteenth-century religious reformer. He no doubt regarded Justice Bradgate as a successor to Wyclif's enemies.

wrote 'Done before', meaning that he had been there the previous year. Presumably he told Harley in person how in the recent elections Isaac Newton, the scientist and Whig candidate, was shouted down by High Church students saying 'No Fanatic!' From Cambridge Defoe started to describe some of his overall impressions:

> In all parts the greatest hindrance to the forming the people with moderation and union amongst themselves, next to the clergy, are the justices. Wherever there happens to be moderate justices, the people live easy and the parsons have then less influence, but the conduct of the justices in most parts is intolerably scandalous, especially in Wilts, Lancashire, in Nottingham, Leicester, Warwick, Northampton, Suffolk, Essex and Middlesex ...

The secret intelligence mission of 1705 provided Defoe with some of the richest material for his *Tour*, written and published twenty years later. Meanwhile it gave Harley the edge in plotting not only against the High Church Tories, but also against his government colleagues, who now were inclined to the Whigs. When Defoe first started working for Harley in 1704, he urged him to bring back the Whig Lord Somers, who had written the draft for the Declaration of Rights and later became Lord Chancellor under William III. Defoe added a personal memoir:

> I remember when I had the honour to serve the late King William in a kind like this [as adviser], and which his Majesty had the kindness to accept, and over value by far, expressing some concern at the clamour and power of the party ... Your Majesty must face about, oblige your friends to be content to be laid [aside], and put in your enemies; put them into those posts in which they may seem to be employed; and therefore take off the edge and divide the party.

Defoe's suggestion of giving a share of power to the Whigs was acceptable to Godolphin and Marlborough, but not to his own patron Harley or to the Queen herself. During the course of 1706 a rift began to appear: on the one side there was Harley and Anne; on the other, Godolphin, Marlborough and Whigs such as Lord Somers and Lord Wharton. The quarrel grew worse when Harley's cousin Mrs Masham supplanted the Whig Duchess of Marlborough as Anne's favourite. Already, in the autumn of 1705, the balance of power had shifted so far towards the Whigs that Tory pamphleteers like the poet Ned Ward were made to stand in the pillory.

During the parliamentary session of 1705–6 the Whigs helped to bring in the Regency Act, settling the Succession on the Protestant House of Hanover, whose members were descendants of James I, through Elizabeth of Bohemia. By a process of polarization, the High Church Tories such as Sir Edward Seymour were edging towards their later support for the Jacobites. Party allegiance increasingly came to govern attitudes to the Duke of Marlborough, who opened his summer campaign in Flanders in May 1706. The Whigs were keen to pursue the war for maritime and commercial advantage, while the Tories increasingly favoured peace with France, the protector of the Stuart Pretender. Although neither Whig nor Tory, Defoe supported the war against France as conceived by William III and now furthered by his new hero, the Duke of Marlborough. However, in the *Review* of 18 May 1706 he saw no hope of Marlborough achieving a quick victory in the Netherlands:

> No man in the world has a greater opinion than I of the conduct of the Duke of Marlborough, and that he is cut out for uncommon designs; nor do I doubt but that had his Grace a full liberty of action, something extraordinary and suitable to his character in the world would be undertaken. But to exalt his power to impossibilities, and make him more than a man ... that is making a satyr upon the Duke of Marlborough's discretion, lampooning his judgment and exposing our own ignorance ... The prospect of the campaign is nowhere promising, except in Spain.

On the day this was published the news reached England of Marlborough's comprehensive victory at Ramillies, followed soon afterwards by the expulsion of Louis XIV's armies from the Netherlands and Italy. The Grand Alliance achieved its war aims everywhere except in Spain, whose people would not accept the king imposed on them by Austria and repulsed an English invasion of Catalonia. To Defoe's credit, he freely admitted and even rejoiced in his wrong predictions, writing on 21 May:

> I cannot but acknowledge the last Review a little wide of the state of things ... being printed the very day that the Express arrived of the glorious Victory obtained by the Duke of

Marlborough at Ramillies, the paper seemed like a son born out of season.

> But who dreamt of a victory, and that too, before we thought all the troops were even together? The Duke of Marlborough, born to surprise the world, makes all our diviners mad, out-runs our conjectures, and brings action in the stage of the world, that the most penetrating head never entertained or thought of.

In this commentary on the Duke of Marlborough Defoe also reveals himself as a very great journalist, who recognized the importance of the events through which he lived. He had understood from the start that the Duke was a military genius, who almost alone was capable of beating the armies of France. In the same way Defoe always understood the higher significance of the Glorious Revolution, religious toleration, the Union with Scotland, the Protestant Succession, and all the other causes for which he campaigned with his pen. Aware that he was living through events that would shape the future of Britain and Europe, he tried to catch these events on the wing. Reading Defoe's *Review* through nine and a half years and twenty-two volumes of wise and witty commentary, one comes to accept his claim to be 'writing history by inches'. In his comment on Ramillies, for example, he had guessed wrong on the details, but he knew that Marlborough was a man who brought 'actions in the stage of the world, that the most penetrating head never entertained or thought of'. He also knew that Marl-borough's victories in Europe depended on peace at home and per-ceived the link between Ramillies and the Occasional Conformity Bill.

In 1706, the year of England's greatest triumph in Europe, Defoe completed and published *Jure Divino. A Satyr upon Tyranny and Passive Obedience*, for which he had long sought subscribers through advertise-ments in the *Review*. He had begun this book in the reign of William III, writing most of it in Newgate Prison, as a philosophical counter-blast to the Divine Right of Kings. Even in 1706, when the question of the Succession was in everyone's mind, *Jure Divino* never enjoyed the popularity of more frivolous works like *The True-Born Englishman*. Perhaps Defoe wanted to prove his scholarship, as he had when he challenged Tutchin to a translation contest. Perhaps, like many a toiler in Grub Street, he wanted to prove he was 'not just a journalist'.

In May 1706, two and a half years after leaving Newgate Prison, Defoe was once more faced with disaster, this time from creditors of the 1692 bankruptcy. On 6 May he wrote in despair to Harley: 'Sir, My case being come to that crisis, that without some powerful aid, or some miracle, which I ought not to expect, I shall soon be rendered entirely useless, both to the public and myself.' He saw only two ways of escape from his predicament:

> 1st, Sir, that I may be assisted as far as 2 or 3 hundred pounds will do it, to free myself of the immediate fury of 5 or 6 unreasonable creditors; after which I shall by my own strength work through the rest in time.
>
> 2dly Or Sir, that according to your kind promise which I cannot but claim, you will please to send me somewhere abroad, out of the reach of their hands, and that her Majesty's bounty may be some way applied to the support of my family.

Although on 21 August 1706 Defoe managed to fend off his 'most furious, subtil and malicious pursuers' in court, Harley had already agreed to the second of his suggestions by dispatching him to the still foreign country of Scotland.

6

The Birth of Great Britain: 1706–10

DEFOE'S HERO William of Orange is still often blamed for the never-ending feud between England and Ireland; yet he is never given credit for the equally long and enduring peace between England and Scotland. King William regarded the Irish, the Scots and the English with equal coldness, if not dislike, but he wanted to see them united against the French. He had invaded Ireland, not for the sake of the people who now call themselves Orangemen, but to crush a rebellion by James II, backed by the army of Louis XIV. When he lay on his death-bed in February 1702, William urged Parliament to press ahead for a Union with Scotland because he feared that France might also try to invade that country on behalf of James's son, the Pretender.

As an accidental result of William's invasion of England in 1688, the Roman Catholic Irish are still at odds with the English and with the Ulster Presbyterians, while the Scots are at peace with the English and with each other. Yet in the years that followed William's death it seemed to Defoe and many Englishmen that Scotland rather than Ireland threatened the peace and prosperity of the British Isles. Relations between the English and the Scots had never been worse than during the years before the Act of Union of 1707. According to Trevelyan, the English writers on Scotland were, 'with the signal exception of Defoe', overwhelmingly hostile and contemptuous. Defoe himself remarked in *An Essay at Removing National Prejudice against Union with Scotland*, one of many he published in 1706, that the English seemed unable to tell their friends from their enemies:

> It is too long a work here to say why the wild, ungoverned Irish, that mortally hate the very name of an Englishman and have often, with the utmost barbarity, murdered thousands of our people in cold blood, are less hated by us than the Dutch

... why the French between whom and this nation frequent terrible, and bloody wars have often happened, are more respected than the Scotch, who inhabit the same Terra Firma ...

During his years as a propagandist for Union Defoe gained a huge knowledge and understanding of Scottish history, economics, social life and religious attitudes. Much of this learning appeared in his semi-official *History of the Union of Great Britain*, published in 1709 and dedicated to Anne, who received Defoe and gave him her hand to kiss – a further sign of forgiveness for the author of *The Shortest Way with Dissenters*. Defoe later wrote a delightful account of Scotland in the final volume of his *Tour*, and brought the country into two of his novels, *Colonel Jack* and *The Memoirs of a Cavalier*.

Since Defoe was writing largely for English readers, he always took pains to expound and emphasize the Scottish side of any issue between the two countries. This no doubt came easily to him, for though a patriotic and even chauvinistic Englishman, he sympathized with the Presbyterian Scots in their politics and their religion, for most regarded themselves as 'Whigs' and were anti-Jacobite. And although he was often exasperated, baffled and even scared by the fury of Scottish quarrels, he clearly enjoyed and was proud of his work on behalf of the Union. Since most of what he wrote about Scotland now seems wise, prophetic and (with hindsight) obvious, the reader can only regret that Defoe never turned his mind to the question of Ireland.

Throughout his writing on the Union Defoe constantly harks back to the 'mutual, barbarous, cruel and unjust executions' that characterized the border conflict, especially the crimes of the English kings. In the *Review* of 29 October 1706 he reminds his English readers of 'the case of the brave Wallis, and the barbaric and dishonourable murder of the sons of the Scots governor of Berwick, only because he would not basely deliver up his charge, which he defended like a man of honour, the worst blot on the otherwise most glorious prince, Edward III'. The name of Wallace, now once more popularized by Hollywood, struck terror throughout the northern counties of England as late as the Act of Union, and again during the Jacobite risings of 1715 and 1745. Moreover, the Scots were in a position to seize the coalfields of Durham and Northumberland, on which the commercial life of London depended.

However, Defoe reminded the Scots that if it came to a war with

England: '1. You must at last most certainly have the worst of it. 2. If you are beaten you would be ruined. 3. If you were not conquered you would be quite undone' (*Review*, 19 July 1707). The Scots must lose because they have not got England's money, 'and nobody will debate with me, I am sure, the way of fighting being with the longest purse, not the longest sword'. If the Scots were beaten, they would be ruined:

> Your trade, your lands, your corn, your manufacture, all would be over-run, and that loss that in England might be retrieved . . . would to you be irreparable.
>
> Your country could not bear the destruction of a harvest, the poor would perish for want of bread . . . the destroying the corn in the field in the south part of Scotland would ruin the whole country.

The Scots could only get the better of England by putting themselves in the power of France: 'It is too evident, nothing could protect them from French power but by English power; and how is it, Gentlemen in Scotland, that you had rather be ours by conquest than by Union?'

Defoe broods on the absurdity of the Scots having fought on the side of the French against the army of Henry V, and praises Henry VII as a pioneer of Union. He skates over the still sensitive topic of Mary, Queen of Scots, who was sent to the block through the guile of Sir Francis Walsingham. However, in one of his pamphlets (*An Essay at Removing National Prejudice*) Defoe blames Mary's son, King James VI of Scotland and James I of England, for failing to build on the union of crowns, and 'forgetting the true interest of his country instead of gratifying the Scots with what might have been for the general good of the kingdom, only brought a long train of them hither, who gaping for preferment, and equally neglecting their own country, served only to make the English jealous'.

Scots troops formed the elite of the army of King Gustavus Adolphus of Sweden: in a footnote to his poem *Caledonia* Defoe explains how during the Battle of Leipzig: 'The Scots were ever seen to fire with their ranks closed forward, and their pieces closed over one another's shoulders, or as we call it, kneel stop and stand'. As a result:

> Gustavus saw how fury-like they fought,
> And better witness never soldier sought.

Defoe wanted to see still more of these Scottish soldiers fighting in Marlborough's army against the French.

In his *Memoirs of a Cavalier* Defoe tells the story of the ill-judged war on the Scots waged by Charles I in 1639 in an attempt to make them accept the English Prayer Book. He argues cogently that Oliver Cromwell understood the need for a Union between England and Scotland, but does not explain why he failed to achieve it by force. Cromwell himself and most of his army were religious Independents, rather than Presbyterians like most of the Scots and some of the English Puritans, including Defoe. Quite apart from their different brand of Calvinism, Cromwell's troopers were rude and arrogant to the Scots, and mocked them by sitting on their stools of repentance, which were to be found in every parish church.

The Scots Presbyterians at first welcomed the Restoration, but soon suffered the horror of the thumbscrew and the 'boot' in the Privy Council torture chamber in Edinburgh. Defoe often refers to the persecution of Covenanters in south-west Scotland. The Scots Presbyterians, who numbered perhaps two thirds of the nation, welcomed the Glorious Revolution of 1688 and made a hero of 'King Willy', though not to the same extent as their fellows in Ulster. From then on their Kirk was the established Church of Scotland; the Episcopalians were the Dissenters. Many Episcopalians joined the Catholic Highlanders in a Jacobite rebellion in 1688–90, trouncing the Presbyterians at the Battle of Killiecrankie. Later the largely Presbyterian Campbells regained ascendancy over the smaller Highland clans despite bringing disgrace on their name with the Glencoe massacre. The Duke of Argyll, the head of the Campbell clan, was later a moving force in the Act of Union.

During the reign of William Scotland recovered its Parliament and its Presbyterian Church, but in material wealth it was falling further behind its English neighbour. Indeed, as Defoe pointed out in the *Review* (25 October 1709), Scotland's agriculture was poorer than that of Ireland, with its 'rich and fruitful soil'. Most of the Scottish peasants lived in feudal dependence on their lairds, to whom they paid rent in kind from their meagre supply of chickens, oats, barley or peat. In the countryside all the children and most of the adults went barefoot, lived huddled together in damp, smoky cabins; and worshipped in thatched churches, resembling barns, or out on the open moors.

As Dr Johnson remarked in 1775, most Scottish farmland was naked of trees for shelter or hedges to keep in the cattle; indeed, it was largely due to Johnson's raillery on the subject in his and Boswell's account of their trip to the Highlands in 1773 that Scotland's lairds were shamed into planting more than two million trees. At the time of the Act of Union Scotland's exports consisted of little but coal, salt, salmon and herrings, though most of the last were taken by Dutch boats. Its second city and future industrial centre, Glasgow, was still merely a pretty town of 12,000 inhabitants. There were small universities at Glasgow, Edinburgh, Aberdeen and St Andrews, but no intimation as yet of the intellectual Renaissance that was to come with Adam Smith, David Hume, Robert Burns, Sir Walter Scott and the *Edinburgh Review*.

As we know from the banter of Dr Johnson, the Act of Union led to a big emigration south: 'Sir, it is not so much to be lamented that Old England is lost, as that the Scotch have found it.' It is hard to grasp that before the Union England was more alien to Scotsmen than most of the rest of Europe. Scots Jacobites went into exile in Italy or France; Presbyterian soldiers and traders sought their fortunes in Holland, Germany or Scandinavia; Edinburgh advocates finished their education by studying Roman law at Leiden.

Thinking Scotsmen understood that the only way to escape from isolation and poverty was to share in England's commerce with its expanding overseas empire. Scotland's exclusion from this was a cause of resentment and envy, which drove the Scots into mounting the ill-fated Darien expedition. This began in 1698 when a group of Scottish entrepreneurs founded a 'Company for trading with Africa and the Indies', whose very title presented a challenge to London's Africa and East India companies. However, the Scottish promoters elected instead to establish a colony on the Darien Isthmus, in what is now Panama, with access to the Atlantic and the Pacific. It was a crack-brained venture from the start, for the Spanish, who ruled all Central America, had zealously kept out intruders, from Sir Francis Drake onwards, and would no more welcome the Scots than the English. Yellow fever and malaria made Central America dangerous for traders and soldiers, but altogether unsuitable for a European settlement. Moreover, King William could not support this enterprise without enraging the City of London, on which he largely depended for his revenue.

The collapse of the Darien venture in 1700, coming on top of successive bad harvests, still further exacerbated Scottish resentment of England, yet at the same time highlighted the advantage of Union.

The Scots would be called upon to give up their Parliament and their independence; the English to admit the Scots to their jealously guarded overseas trade. The disaster at Darien seems to have brought home to both parties the churlishness of their former behaviour, for after the Act of Union the new British government reimbursed the Scottish investors with all the money they had lost.

The Darien venture seems to have whetted Defoe's lifelong enthusiasm for colonization and trade in Spain's American territories. He later wrote a short biography of Sir Walter Raleigh, who had gone into Venezuela in search of the city of Eldorado. As we shall see, he was to propose to Harley the establishment of a British colony in Chile or Argentina; and later a plan for the South Sea Company, winning for Britain the South American slave trade. Perhaps accounts of the deaths of so many Scotsmen at Darien gave Defoe the idea for his manual on how to survive in the Tropics, *Robinson Crusoe*.

The issue of Union reached a crisis in March 1702, when Anne came to the throne and pledged herself to the Hanoverian Succession, as well as to the war against France. This announcement disappointed and angered the Jacobite Scots, who had hoped the Succession would go to Anne's brother, the Pretender. It also offended many Presbyterian Scots, who wanted a Protestant monarch – but one of their own Parliament's choosing. Anne herself was torn between High Church principles and the need to stay on the throne. As long as the war lasted, Louis XIV would be plotting a Jacobite–French invasion of Scotland in order to dethrone Anne in favour of the Pretender, at least in the northern kingdom. If she wanted to wage war in Europe, while remaining secure from attack in Britain, Anne had to rely on the Scottish Presbyterians, for they alone would resist a Jacobite–French invasion. And so, in her first speech to Parliament on 11 March 1702, Anne expressed her desire for a closer Union. 'Such a Union', Trevelyan explains, 'would not fail to guarantee the Presbyterian establishment in Scotland, ensure the accession of the House of Hanover in the whole island, and shatter all Jacobite hopes.'

The English High Church Tories, who in their hearts did not favour the Hanoverian Succession, therefore opposed the Act of Union. When Dr Sacheverell raised his 'bloody flag of defiance' against the Dissenters, and his followers in Parliament backed the Occasional Conformity Bill, the Scottish Presbyterians understandably took alarm. In 1703 the Scottish Parliament passed an Act of Security, giving itself the right to veto a monarch enthroned in England. The Westminster

Parliament replied with an Alien Act, in effect saying that if the Scots chose to become a separate kingdom, they would lose the right to live and trade in England and Ireland. Hostility between the two countries came close to war in April 1705, when an English merchant captain, Thomas Green, was hanged in Leith on a trumped-up charge of piracy off the coast of Madagascar.

Two months later the General Election in England brought in a moderate Tory and Whig administration, which favoured an Act of Union. They were joined by some of the Scottish Whig and Presbyterian noblemen, including the Duke of Argyll, the head of the Campbell clan. The Queen appointed two Commissions – one English, one Scottish – made up of statesmen, religious leaders and lawyers, who, during the summer of 1706, would sit in separate but simultaneous meetings in London to work out the terms for a Treaty of Union, which would then have to be approved by the separate Parliaments. On 22 July 1706 the treaty was signed by all but six of the sixty Commissioners, and was carried by them to the Queen in St James's Palace. 'It was the other great moment in her reign, beside the receipt of the news of Blenheim,' Trevelyan writes in *Ramillies and the Union with Scotland*. The Scottish Commissioners then set off north for the next and much more difficult task of making the treaty acceptable to their Parliament and people.

Defoe's interest in Scotland went back many years, and he may well have discussed with William III the means of achieving a closer Union. Almost alone among English journalists and pamphleteers, he did not join in the outcry against the Scots over the Act of Security of 1703 or the lynching of Green, the English merchant captain, two years later. In his six-volume poem *Jure Divino* he prophesies correctly that the Act of Security, in spite of its hostile tone, will have the effect of drawing the countries together:

> And all the threatening clouds of Northern Night
> Assist to make that Union still more bright . . .

In his references to the hanging of Green, he points out that the other two victims were Scotsmen.

Defoe had made the acquaintance in London of George Scott, a merchant who was in favour of the Union, and whose brother was the Professor of Philosophy at Edinburgh University. When the Scottish Commission came to London in 1706 to draw up the Treaty of Union,

Scott introduced Defoe to some of its prominent members. Following this, Scott scribbled a note to his brother on 14 May:

> I must tell you that having the Honr: to converse with some of our great folks viz: Lord Stairs, Lord President, Sir Dav. Dalrymple, Lord Roseberry & others, I did bring them acquainted with one Mr Deffoe who seeing to understand trade & the interests of nations very well, he was the person that wrote the pamphlet cal'd the shortest way with the dissenters & for which he was pilloryed . . . at our request he has wrote an essay at removing national prejudices against a union with Scotland, it is very well done & is only the introduction to more books he designs upon the Union before the Commissioners have done . . .

Through Sir David Dalrymple and his two brothers Defoe became friends with another Scottish Commissioner, John Clerk, the Duke of Queensberry's son-in-law and an expert on economics. On 13 July Clerk wrote enthusiastically to his father to say that Defoe was going to Scotland and should be of great assistance. These letters, discovered in Edinburgh by Paula Backscheider, suggest that it was the Scottish supporters of Union, rather than Harley, who had first encouraged Defoe to make the journey north.

Although Harley was the Secretary of State with responsibility for Scotland, he always affected not to understand the country, telling Parliament that he knew 'no more of Scottish business than of Japan' and 'avoided even the conversation of those of that country'. When Defoe first started working for him in 1704, he wrote to him in a memorandum: 'A settled intelligence in Scotland, a thing strangely neglected there, is without doubt the principal occasion of the present misunderstanding between the two countries.' In fact Harley already employed a network of agents in Scotland, from William Greg, who later spied for the French, to some of the greatest men in the country. Among them was William Carstares, the wisest of the Presbyterian divines, who had been William III's adviser on Scottish affairs; the economist William Paterson, to whom Defoe had written from Newgate Prison; and the Earl of Seafield, the Scottish Chancellor and one of the principal architects of the Act of Union. The historian W. T. Morgan says in *English Political Parties and Leaders in the Reign of Queen Anne* that Harley was very knowledgeable about Scotland and its legislators:

No secretary of state could have been better served by agents, spies and informers than he, because few secret service men have ever displayed such genius for work of this sort as did Defoe and his companions ... William Paterson kept him in touch with the economic side of the negotiations, Seafield informed him on all political developments, while the versatile author of *Robinson Crusoe* attended to both sides of the question in a sympathetic, thoroughgoing and impartial manner.

In a letter to Harley just before leaving for Scotland Defoe set down what he saw as the tasks of his mission. These were to identify the parties opposed to Union and to undermine them; to dispose people to Union through conversation; to answer through pamphlets and the *Review* 'any objections, libels or reflections on the Union'; and to dissipate fears about secret designs against the Kirk, the established Presbyterian Church of Scotland. The difference between Defoe and what would today be called a lobbyist or public relations consultant is simply that he believed in the cause he advocated. He asked Harley for money – on this occasion £25 for a pair of horses and harness – because he was left with nothing by his creditors. At the end of the same letter he gives a gentle reminder to Harley that 'you have a widow and seven children on your hands', meaning Defoe's own family.

From Leicester Defoe wrote to Harley to say he had been 'locked up by a rain of 48 hours', but he also seems to have made a detour to see the annual market at Stourbridge, outside Cambridge, the largest fair in Europe, which he describes with gusto in the *Tour*. At Newcastle upon Tyne he met John Bell, the government's northern agent and paymaster, who in turn reported to Harley: 'I have had the favour of [Defoe's] conversation for two or three days and find him to be a very ingenious man.' Defoe had written to Harley from Newcastle, the first of many complaints about being left in the dark: 'I am your messenger without an errand, your ambassador without instructions, your servant without orders.'

This prodded Harley into writing a letter back, telling Defoe to conceal his government work and let it be known that he went to Scotland 'upon your own business and out of love of the country ... You may completely assure those you converse with that the Queen and all who have credit with her, are sincere and hearty for the Union.' Defoe should also warn the Scots that this was their best chance of a

Laudatur et Alget
Juven. Sat. I.

As a man pursued by creditors and political enemies, Defoe avoided having
his likeness portrayed. This rare engraving by Michiel van der Gucht is after
a painting by Jeremiah Taverner, 1706.

Left Charles II's illegitimate son, the Duke of Monmouth, led the revolt in 1688 against his uncle, the Roman Catholic James II. Defoe joined Monmouth's army and almost certainly fought in the losing battle of Sedgemoor; he remained loyal to the memory of Monmouth, who was captured by James's soldiers and later beheaded.

Right George Jeffreys, first Baron of Wem, who, as Judge of the Bloody Assizes in 1685, condemned to death many of Defoe's fellow rebels.

In the image above, a scroll reads: *Wilhelm III von Oranien und Maria Stuart, seine Gemahlin, von groß Britanien, Frankreich und Irlandt.*

William and Mary on the occasion of taking the oath to preserve the Protestant religion, soon after their accession in 1689.

Left Charles II's mistress, the Duchess of Portsmouth (*detail*), by Kneller. Defoe mentions in the *Tour* that Queen Mary had the painting removed from her apartment at Windsor.

Below In Dissenting chapels, 'popish' statues and decorations had been replaced by austere reproductions of the Ten Commandments.

Above One of Defoe's few successful business enterprises was his brickyard at Tilbury in Essex, which also produced pantiles. Defoe's bricks were carried across the Thames to Greenwich and used in the construction of Sir Christopher Wren's Naval Hospital.

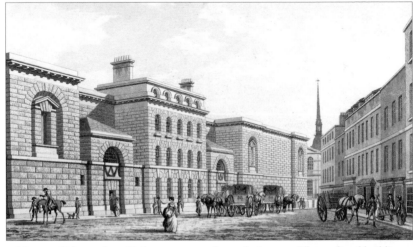

Newgate Prison, where Defoe spent several months in 1703. The medieval building had burned down in the Great Fire of 1666. It was rebuilt in 1672, and lasted into the nineteenth century, when Elizabeth Fry exposed the appalling condition of female prisoners.

In 1703 Queen Anne had Defoe brought to Windsor Castle, to question him on his real or imagined associates in writing *The Shortest Way with Dissenters*. She later sprang him from prison and gave financial help to his wife and children.

Whether under attack from the Tories, as in this 1711 print, or from the rival Whigs, Defoe was often shown as a friend of the Pope and the Devil.

Opposite above Here he is shown in the stocks (detail).

A Deformed head in the Pillory.

What awkard ill-look'd Fellow's y? | With blobber Lips, & Lockram Jaws,
He has an ugly frightfull Phys; | Warts, Wrinkles, Wens, & other Flaws:
And sure as black his conscience is? | With nitty beard, & Neck that's scabby,
Cadaverous, black, blue, and green, | And in a dress, that's very shabby,
Not fit in publick to be seen. | Who this should be I do not know,
With dirt besmear'd, & goggle-ey'd | Unless a Whig? I guess he's so,
With a long Nose, & Mouth as wide; | If I am right, pray take a Throw.

During the Nonconformist revival of the mid-nineteenth century, Defoe and John
Bunyan, the author of *Pilgrim's Progress*, were held up as martyrs for their Dissenting
faith. This illustration from George Lee's flattering biography suggests that Defoe, in
the pillory in 1702, was pelted with flowers rather than brickbats.

To The Queens Most Excellent Majesty

The Humble Peticion of Daniel de Foe

295

Sheweth

That yor Peticoner wth a sincere design to Propogate The Intrest of The Hannover Succession and to Animate The people against The designs of the Pretender who he allways look'd on as an Enemy to yor Majties Sacred Person and Government did Publish severall Pamphlets Perticularly One Intituled Reasons against The Hannover Succession, what if The Pretender should come. and Others

In all which books Altho' The Titles seemed to look as if written in Favour of the Pretender and sundry Expressions, as in all Ironicall writing it Must be, May be Wrested Against The True Design of the whole; and Turned to a Meaning quite different From ye Intencon of the Author: yet yor Peticoner Humbly Assures yor Majtie in The Solemnest Manner Possible, That his True and Onely Design in all ye said books was by An Ironicall Discourse of recommending The Pretender, In The strongest and Most forcible Manner to Expose his designs, and The ruinous Consequences of his Succeeding Therein.

And yor Peticoner Humbly hopes The Truth of this will appear to yor Majties Satisfaction, by The books Themselves where The Following Expressions are Very plain (Viz) That The Pretender is recommended as a Person proper to Amass The English liberty into his Own Soveraignty; Supply Them wth The priviledge of wearing Wooden shoes, easing Them of The Trouble of Choosing Parliaments, and The Gentry and Nobillity of The hazard and Expence of Winter Journeys; By Governing them in that More Righteous Method of his Absolute will, and Enforcing his Laws by a Glorious standing Army, Paying all The Nacons Debts at Once, by stopping the Funds, and Shutting up the Exchequer: easing and quieting Their Differences in Religion, by bringing them to The Union of Popery Or leaving Them at liberty to have no Religion at all: and The like

These May it please yor Majtie are some of the Very Expressions in ye said Books, wch yor Peticor Sincerely desired to Expose and Oppose as far as in him lyes The Intrest of the Pretender: and with No Other Intencon; Nevertheless yor Peticoner to his great Surprize has been Misrepresented, and ye said Book Misconstrued, as if written in Favor of the Pretender, and yor Peticoner is Now Under Prosecucon for The same, wch Prosecution if farther Carryed On will be The Utter Ruine of your Peticoner, and his Numerous Family.

Wherefore yor Peticoner Humbly Assureing yor Majtie of the Innocence of his Design as aforesaid; Flyes to yor Majties Clemency, and Most Humbly Implores yor Majties Most Gracious, and Free Pardon.

and yor Peticon shall ever Pray &c.

On two separate occasions, in 1703 and here in 1712, Defoe petitioned Queen Anne to explain that a seemingly seditious pamphlet was intended ironically.

favourable Union with England but that such an opportunity 'once lost or neglected is not again to be recovered'. Harley further instructed Defoe to write to him at least once a week, care of Mrs Collins at the Posthouse, Middle Temple, or Michael Read, in York Buildings, Harley's porter, who was once described by Swift as 'an old Scotch fanatick and the damndest liar in his office altogether'.

Edinburgh was infamous as the fiercest, most turbulent city in Europe, whose mob only the previous year had threatened to slaughter the Privy Council if Thomas Green, the English merchant skipper accused of piracy, was reprieved. Now, in October 1706, the mob was just as enraged against the Commissioners of the Treaty of Union, or 'traiters', as they were called in the local pronunciation. As Scotland's old Parliament met for the last time to debate an Act which would abolish its own existence, the nobles, barons and burgesses streamed into the capital from all corners of the country, often accompanied by gangs of excited supporters. Soon after arriving, Defoe witnessed the savagery of an anti-Union mob. He wrote to Harley on 24 October: 'I was warned that night that I should take care of myself and not appear in the street, which indeed for the last five days, I had done very little, having been confined by a violent cold. However I went up the street in a friend's coach in the evening ... and some of the mob were heard to say when I went into a house, There was one of the English dogs etc.' In his *History of the Union of Great Britain* Defoe explains that the mob were determined to kill Sir Patrick Johnson, one of the Treaters:

First they assaulted his lodgings with stones and sticks and curses not a few; but his windows being too high, they came up the stairs to his door, and fell to work at it with sledges, or great hammers; and, had they broke it open in the first fury, he had without doubt been torn to pieces without mercy, and this only because he was a Treater in the Commission to England, for before that no man was so well beloved, over the whole city. His lady, in the utmost despair with this fright, came to the window with two candles in her hand, that she might be known, and cried out, for GODS sake to call the Guard; an honest apothecary in the town, who knew her voice and saw the distress she was in, and to whom the family, under GOD, is obliged, for that deliverance, ran immediately down to the Town Guard.

The Town Guard rescued the Johnsons, but this did not stop the turmoil, for the rabble were now 'prodigiously increased': 'They put out the lights that they might not be discerned, and the author of this had one great stone thrown at him, for but looking out of a window ... The city was now in a terrible fright ... the rabble went raving about the streets till midnight, frequently beating drums and raising more people.'

Defoe adds that 'the author of this had his share of the danger, and though unknown to him, was watched and set by the mob in order to know where to find him ... but by God's Providence, he escaped.' In this book, published in 1709, and in several letters to Harley written some time after the riots, Defoe harps on about the risks he ran on his secret mission to Scotland, but during the early months he clearly revelled in the excitement. Through the Scottish friends he had made in London, Defoe attended debates in the Scottish Parliament, and sat on committees to work out some of the technical problems of Union, especially referring to weights and measures, customs and excise. He joined the inner circle of the Commission of the General Assembly of the Church of Scotland, which some regarded as more influential than Parliament itself. Within weeks Defoe knew most of the churchmen and statesmen frequenting Fortune's coffee house, generally known as Sue's because it had been the home of Susannah, Countess of Eglinton.

For once in his life Defoe discovered his name and his reputation to be an advantage. As the man who had stood in the pillory on behalf of the English Nonconformists, he already commanded respect in the Presbyterian Church of Scotland. The Commissioners he had met in London, such as Dalrymple and Clerk, spoke well of his writing and introduced him to everyone of importance in Edinburgh. His cover story, that he was fleeing from enemies in England and hoped to settle in Scotland, was all the better because it was largely true.

Defoe boasted to Harley on 2 November that he had convinced the Scots that he was a friend of their country; once again, this was very largely true. For the first time in his life Defoe, the English Dissenter and outsider, had a sense of being part of the Church and the political establishment. He met and was accepted by such revered divines as William Carstares, who had endured the thumbscrew and the boot under Charles I and Charles II, before becoming Chaplain to William III. Having seen *The Shortest Way with Dissenters* condemned to be burnt by the English House of Commons, it was gratifying to hear his pamphlets on Union praised by the Scottish statesmen.

The social climate of Scotland was probably more to Defoe's liking than that of England. Although he always insisted on being a 'gentleman', he was aware that his education at Dorking and Dr Morton's Academy was lacking; that his former employment as a hosiery merchant did not make him acceptable to fellow authors like Addison, Steele and Swift. Scotland was both more feudal and more democratic than eighteenth-century England, especially in its Church and education. The Presbyterian lairds and even noblemen attended the same kirk as their tenants and sent their children to local schools, for there was then no Scottish version of Eton, Winchester or Westminster. Presbyterian leaders like Carstares had not sullied the purity of their faith for the sake of power and wealth, in the fashion of English Dissenters like Edwin and Abney. If, as is likely, Defoe spoke with an accent and choice of words that marked him out in England as a Dissenter and tradesman, the Scots would not have discerned these nuances in what to them was alien speech.

Defoe was having the time of his life in Scotland, as can be seen from the boastful letter he sent to Harley on 26 November:

> I have compassed my first and main step happily enough, in that I am perfectly unsuspected as corresponding with anybody in England. I converse with a Presbyterian, Episcopal-Dissenter, papist and non-juror, and I hope with equal circumspection ... I have faithful emissaries in every company and I talk to everybody in their own way. To the merchants I am about to settle here in trade, building ships etc. With the lawyers I want to purchase a house and land to bring my family & live upon it (God knows where the money is to pay for it). Today I am going into a partnership with a member of Parliament in a glass house, tomorrow with another in a salt work. With the Glasgow mutineers I am to be a fish merchant, with the Aberdeen men a woolen and with the Perth and western men a linen manufacturer ... Again, I am in the morning at the Committee [of Parliament], in the afternoon in the Assembly [of the Kirk], I am privy to all their folly, I wish I could not call it knavery, and am entirely confided in.

This bragging is merely the prelude to an appeal for more money to meet the cost of 'this sharping, dear place', but even so one is struck by the folly of writing such a letter, which might well have fallen into the hands of an enemy of the Union. Many years later his Scottish friend Clerk wrote of Defoe: 'He was a spy among us, but not known to be such, otherwise the mob of Edinburgh had pulled him to pieces.' Clerk himself and other supporters of the Union probably knew or guessed that Defoe had the confidence of the English government, and considered this useful to their cause. But Clerk would have been aghast to learn that Defoe was boasting to Harley about how he had duped all parties in Scotland and, what is more, talking of the folly and knavery of the Kirk. Defoe was putting the Act of Union at risk, just for the sake of blowing his own trumpet.

This reckless letter, followed by others like it over the next twelve months, confirms the idea that Defoe enjoyed living dangerously, even if he did not actually court destruction. During the first six months of 1703, when he was on the run, he had written and published a criminal libel against some of the men who would soon be his judges; now, in a daredevil spirit, he made fun of the Scots among whom he was mingling as an English spy. It is stranger still to find that Harley failed to rebuke Defoe for his indiscretion, indeed sometimes replied in the same jokey style. This was before Harley's first fall from power, early in 1708, and before he came close to being implicated in Greg's treason. When he came to power once more in 1711, he had apparently learnt his lesson, for most of Defoe's letters to him from Scotland were now written in a disguised hand, under a false name, as well as in code.

Defoe's folly in writing that letter of 26 November was all the greater because of the mounting fury in Scotland over the Act of Union. On 30 November he wrote to warn Harley that war had already begun in the west, meaning that hundreds of Covenanters had taken up arms. A fortnight earlier he had described the throng of Highlanders parading in the streets of Edinburgh as 'formidable fellows, and I only wish Her Majesty had 25,000 of them in Spain, a nation equally proud and barbarous as themselves'.

As well as attending Parliament and the Kirk Assembly Defoe was promoting the Union in his *Review*, in numerous pamphlets and even poems. The series in the *Review*, which he must have started writing even before he left for the North, was aimed at allaying the doubts of both Scots and Englishmen about every aspect of Union. For instance, on 26 December 1706 he deals with the Scots' objection that Union would bring them under the influence of 'a wicked, unreformed nation, full of innumerable, open and tolerated vices'. He argues that England, 'bad as she is', has made more progress in reformation than any country in the world. Anybody who doubts this should look back to the days of Charles II, 'when rampant vice over-ran the court, when all sorts of lewdness spread the face of authority'. He reminds the Scots of 'the late royal pair of King William and Queen Mary, how vice learnt to blush, and virtue and good manners became the mode there.'

In his poem *Caledonia* Defoe praises the Scots for their martial valour but chides them for not exploiting the wealth of the sea and rivers. Like many visiting Englishmen, he could not understand why even the poorest Scotsmen refused to eat salmon every day, and noted that the Dutch were catching most of the North Sea herrings.

> If they reject the bounty of the sea,
> Bid 'em complain no more of poverty . . .
> When Caledonians, when will you be wise,
> And search for certain wealth in native seas?

Defoe used verse satire to answer a famous speech against the Union by Lord Belhaven, a Presbyterian but also a fiery Scottish nationalist. According to Trevelyan, 'Lord Belhaven's emotional oratory had great vogue when he printed it for consumption out of doors, but it aroused only laughter in the Parliament House, as delivered by the "rough, fat, black, noisy man, more like a butcher than a lord".' Belhaven's speech was a vision of Scotland's betrayal: 'I think I see our ancient mother Caledonia, like Caesar sitting in the midst of our Senate, ruefully looking about her, covering herself with her royal garments attending the fatal blow . . . I see our ancient mother Caledonia, breathing out her last . . .' Defoe laughed off this rhetoric with a comic ditty:

> Here's a Lord in the North
> Near Edinburgh Firth . . .
> He's seen such a vision, no mortal can read it,
> I challenge the clan of Egyptians to match it . . .

Harley approved of this deflation of Belhaven: 'The ballad is the best answer to that stuff.'

In January 1707, Presbyterian prudence triumphed over Jacobite romanticism as Scotland's last Parliament gave its consent to the Treaty of Union, creating Great Britain on 1 May that same year. Although he reported to Harley on 16 January that 'a universal joy of the friends of both countries' was running through Edinburgh, Defoe was downhearted. He had recently received the news of the death of his father and of his youngest child, born when he was in Newgate

Prison. Moreover, his contract with Harley extended only until the Scottish Parliament gave its consent to the Treaty of Union. From now on he worked on a less certain basis, and his letters to Harley alternate between pleading, complaint and extravagant boasts.

Early in January he claims to have been 'a true spy to you' in meeting some Jacobite followers of the Duke of Gordon, but immediately afterwards voices discouragement over the lack of news from Harley. On 27 January 1707 he tells him: 'I have hitherto kept myself unsuspected, have whispered and caused it to be spread that I am fled hither for debt and can not return . . .' But Harley knew that this was to some extent true. A few days later Defoe is reminding him of his promise to ask the Queen for a pension for his family. We do not know if Harley kept this promise, or whether he wanted to hold Defoe in a state of dependency.

On hearing that Harley has been unwell, Defoe urges him not to work too hard and rather pointedly cites his own recent experience, 'who having despised sleep, hours and rules, have broke in upon a perfectly established health, which no distress, disasters, jails or melancholy could ever hurt before . . .' In the spring he is once more boasting about his secret work, but points out that it entails expenses:

> In my management here I am a perfect emissary. I act the old part of Cardinal Richelieu. I have my spies and my pensioners in every place, and I confess 'tis the easiest thing in the world to hire people here to betray their friends [18 March 1707].

> I am spending your money a little freer than ordinary on the occasion of the Assembly [of the Church of Scotland], but tis from the sense of the danger if it miscarries, and I have some engine at work among the ministers. In short money will do anything here [3 April 1707].

By September 1707 Defoe is feeling sorry for himself, and even accuses Harley of ingratitude:

> I faithfully served, I baulked no cases, I appeared in print when others dared not to open their mouths, and without boasting I ran as much risk in my life as a grenadier in storming a counterscarp . . . Tis true I spent a large sum . . . If you were to see me now, entertained of courtesy, almost grown shabby in clothes, dejected etc, what I care not to mention, you would

be moved to haste my relief, in a manner suitable to that regard
you were always pleased to show me ...

Both Harley and Godolphin valued Defoe's work in Scotland and
wanted to offer him a salaried post there, perhaps in the Customs; but
the advancement of Englishmen caused envy and even suspicion among
the Scots now jostling for preferment in the British administration. If
Defoe was only a part-time government agent, he could never be idle.
He was doing research for his *History of the Union*, writing pamphlets
on trade and religious questions, and helping to form the Edinburgh
Society for the Promotion of Christian Knowledge, whose principal
field of missionary work was the pagan or Papist Highlands. Defoe
travelled in the west and north-east of Scotland, though not perhaps
as extensively as he pretends in the *Tour*.

During his first two years in Scotland Defoe also returned to what
he called his 'whore' – trade. Forgetting the disaster of the 1680s and
1690s, he went back into the business of wholesale wine, especially
canary and claret. He dealt in horses, in which he always fancied
himself an expert. Moreover, he joined with a Scottish master weaver
in manufacturing tablecloths. Just as he once claimed to employ 100
poor families at his Tilbury brickyard, so now he boasted of giving
work to 'above 100 poor families' in Edinburgh. He made a present
to Harley of one of his Scottish tablecloths.

As well as conducting his business ventures, reporting to Harley,
and putting together his *History of the Union*, Defoe continued to bring
out the paper, whose title was changed on 8 March 1707 to a *Review
of the State of the British Nation*. Although for a time the *Review* was
printed in Edinburgh as well as in London, the distance between them
meant that copy had to be written well before the publication date.
Defoe insisted that he had 'never purported to turn the Review into
a News-Paper' (27 March 1708), but living in Edinburgh left him no
choice but to make it a timeless journal of comment. Even after the
new Great Britain came into being on 1 May 1707, he continued to
write on the issues dividing the English and Scots, especially the schism
among the Protestants. Whereas the established Church of England
was Episcopalian – that is, governed by bishops – and the majority of
the Dissenters were Presbyterian Calvinists, in Scotland the very
reverse was true. The Church of Scotland, established by William III,
was Calvinist in religion and governed by synods answerable to the
congregations, while members of the much smaller Episcopalian

Church were Dissenters. In Scotland, even more than in England, the differences between the Protestants were political as well as religious, and centred on the Succession to Queen Anne. Many ministers of the Scottish Episcopalian Church were Jacobites, loyal to the Pretender.

Since 1685, when he joined the Monmouth Rebellion, Defoe had fought, argued, written, stood in the pillory, gone to prison and ceaselessly prayed for religious toleration and the Protestant Succession. These twin issues had dominated politics in England between 1702 and 1705; they dominated Defoe's stay in Scotland between 1706 and 1709; and they would dominate British politics from 1710 until the Accession of George I in 1714. In the looking-glass world of Scottish religion Defoe had to defend the established Church from accusations of cruelty to Dissenters. As he admits in a pamphlet,* many English Dissenters believed these accusations, saying, 'I wish the Scots would use the Episcopalian Party more gently', or 'I am afraid there is some truth in it'.

Defoe constantly argued that the Scottish Episcopalians abused their religious freedom to further the Jacobite cause. 'Their meetings dispersed over Scotland are everywhere as they please, open and undisturbed,' he wrote in the *Review* (29 November 1707), 'and fifteen of them in particular in the city of Edinburgh.' But many of their ministers refuse to take the loyal oath, reject the government, 'pray not for the Queen ... and plainly pray for the usurping Pretender'. He tells his readers that if they were on the spot they would see 'that really the Episcopalian people persecute the Church, and not the Church them' (17 December 1707). This was certainly true of north-east Scotland, where Episcopalian Jacobites far outnumbered the Presbyterians. The *Review* carried a hair-raising report of what happened in June that year when the Presbyterians tried to hold a synod at Dingwall: they were soon besieged inside the manse by an angry rabble:

> And then Isbel Macka, a scandalous person, as being a common notorious whore and vagabond came into the room, and after she had expressed herself very profoundly, she addressed all

---

* Defoe's pamphlet, published in Edinburgh in 1707, has the ironic title: *An Historical Account of the Bitter Sufferings and Melancholy Circumstances of the Episcopal Church in Scotland, under the Barbarous Usage and Bloody Persecution of the Presbyterian Church Government*. When writing of Scotland in the *Tour* almost twenty years later, Defoe admits that in Glasgow at least, the Episcopalians had to abandon church attendance because of the persecution by Presbyterian rabblers.

the ministers and told them before the sheriff principal and
bailiffs of the burgh, that she came in as an ambassadress (as
she worded it) that she had about 300 under her command,
most part of them women and the rest of them in women's
clothes, and that she and they desired us to go back, else if we
should attempt to go to the church, and preach there, that she
and they would all oppose us, and that we might all be sure
to be beat and knocked down [14 August 1707].

An official report the following year described what happened later:

Thereafter, a multitude of women . . . came with battons, and
stones and clods, and surrounding the ministers' chamber
made the outer door fast with nails . . . And such was the
barbarity of the Women-Rabblers, that they were heard to say
that all the [Presbyterian] women that came to the worship
would be ravished, and the men-rabblers lie with them. And
further, these rabblers cried out loudly and frequently, King
Willie is dead, and that their king was alive, but that King
Willie is dead [*Review*, 6 November 1708].

At the time he published his first report on the women-rabblers, Defoe
wrote to Harley: 'I must confess I never saw a nation so universally
wild and so readily embracing everything that may exasperate them.
They are ripe for every mischief, and if some general step to their
satisfaction is not taken, . . . they will certainly precipitate themselves
into some violent thing or other . . .' (9 August 1707).

In his preface to the fifth bound volume of the *Review* (March 1708)
Defoe has to acknowledge that some of his readers are bored with
Scotland: 'People would take up the paper and read two or three lines
in it, and find it related to Scotland and the Union, and throw it away;
Union, Union! This fellow can talk of nothing but Union – I think
he will never have done with the Union. He's grown mightily dull of
late.' But even in 1707, the year in which Great Britain came into
being, Defoe kept an eye on the war in Europe, and warned his readers,
correctly as it turned out, not to expect a triumph from the Allied
siege of Toulon that summer. As in the first *Review*s of 1704, Defoe
upset some of his readers by praising the French, who on this occasion
were holding 'a solemn fast, a day of humiliation and sorrow, a day
of repentance, of sack-cloth and mourning, to appease the wrath of
heaven'. He points out that on 'the same day the general humiliation

was observed in France, and the whole kingdom was praying against an English invasion, which was the judgment they feared; that very day the Confederation [Allied] fleet was driven back into Torbay by contrary winds, lay there wind-bound about 14 weeks till the season of action was over' (*Review*, 8 July 1707).

Defoe's praise for the piety of the Roman Catholic enemy was typical of his independence of mind and his originality. The *Review* was quirky. For example, in his frequent articles on the war in north-east Europe Defoe always referred to Sweden as S — because, as his readers knew, the Swedish envoy in London had tried to have him imprisoned for writing about the Swedish King. Defoe was a pioneer of the journalistic joke of referring to people by circumlocution – for instance, 'a Church of England parson not above 150 miles from Exeter' (26 June 1707), i.e. an Exeter parson.

To entertain readers bored with the Union, Defoe discoursed on a recent plague of flies in London, suggesting that they were really ants, like those he had seen from his brickworks at Tilbury: 'I once knew a flight of these ants come over the marshes in Essex, in a most prodigious quantity, black like a cloud ... I had two servants rowing a small boat over the river just at the time, and I believe near two pecks of them fell into the boat; they fell so thick that I believe my hatful came down the funnel of two chimneys in my house, which stood near the river's edge' (*Review*, 16 August 1707).

In almost every issue of the *Review*, whose 7,000 smudged facsimile pages fill twenty-two volumes, there is more entertainment, surprise and intellectual stimulation to be found than in most modern newspapers. Defoe was conscious of writing 'history in inches'; moreover, like many people steeped in the past, he was often correct in his prophecies for the future. One exception to this was his vision of British North America in two consecutive articles in December 1707. Having explained how the Act of Union would make Scotland rich and therefore bind it to England, Defoe went on to propound a view of Britain's relationship with its overseas colonies: 'I am in this part of my work proving that, were our colonies in America put in the greatest posture of strength and opulence imaginable, it would be so far from prompting them to an independency upon England, that it would conform and secure their dependence upon us for ever, past any possibility of breaking off.'

Defoe had dropped the 'Scandalous Club' for a 'Miscellanea', in which he expressed his own puritanical views on manners and morals.

To a reader's question, 'What is the worst sort of husband a sober woman can Marry?' (4 October 1707), Defoe kicks off with, 'the drunken husband, his drunken passions, his drunken humours, his drunken smell, his drunk bedfellowship . . .' Next on the list, before the Fighting or the Extravagant Husband (in which category Defoe put himself), he castigates the Debauched Husband, who 'having a sober, pleasant and beautiful wife, slights and abandons her to take up with an ugly, a tawdry, a nasty and noisome strumpet . . . This sort of wretch has but one act of kindness to his wife . . . that coming home laden with vice and rotteness, he gives his wife an ill disease that lifts her out of the world, putting her out of his reach, and out of her torment altogether.' This fearsome article helps to explain why Defoe's *Review* always carried at least one advertisement such as this: 'Anti-venereal pills, which perfectly carry off the infection of a clap, or running of the reins, and complete the cure in a few days time, without any hindrance of business. They free the body of the remains of any ill-cured pox or clap, and of mercury (unskillfully given).'

In another 'Miscellanea' column Defoe replies to a reader who asked him to comment upon a recent trial for sodomy, a crime which then carried the death penalty. Sodomites, he says, should be tried and punished as secretly as possible, for publication of the evidence 'serves but to excite and gratify the corrupted appetites of the vicious' (*Review*, 27 November 1707). Moreover, he continues:

> The public prosecution and punishment of these hellish crea-
> tures makes it but too public, that there are such monsters
> among us; O tell it not in Gath, publish it not in Ascalon;
> smother the crime and the criminals too in the dark; and let
> the world hear no more of it . . . As for the persons, I leave
> them to justice. I believe, every good man loathes and pities
> them at the same time; and as they are monuments of what
> human Nature abandoned of Divine Grace may be left to do –
> so in their case they ought to be abhorred of their neighbours,
> spewed out of society and sent expressly out of the world as
> secretly and as privately as may consist with justice and the
> laws.

The 'Miscellanea' column also ran the *Review*'s obituary for the editor of the rival *Observator*, John Tutchin, who had been beaten to death by a gang of thugs, presumably in the pay of the High Church Tories. An anonymous reader, no doubt recalling the war of words in

1705 when Defoe had challenged Tutchin to a translation competition, wrote on 15 November 1707: 'Mr Review: Well, now your constant plague is removed, the Observator is dead and I congratulate your deliverance for he was ever abusing you. Have you no leisure to do yourself justice on his memory and give us a taste of your lash, on a character that gave you so much reason for it ... Your Friend and Servant etc.' Although it is probable that Defoe himself had composed this letter, he answers in a tone of surprise and hurt: 'Now really, this is either a man that is laying a snare for me, or else he is a very indifferent Christian. The author of the Observator is dead; and if he was my friend, this gentleman cannot expect me to gratify his desire; if he was my enemy, it would be ungenerous to insult his ashes, and trample on him when he is dead, and I assure him, I have it neither in my education or my temper.'

Defoe must have been aware of how closely Tutchin and he resembled each other in background, career and quarrelsome nature. Tutchin was born about 1661 into a Nonconformist family in the City of London, his father, grandfather and uncle all having been Puritan ministers. He joined the Monmouth Rebellion of 1685 and was afterwards caught and tried at Dorchester Assizes, where Judge Jeffreys told him: 'You are a rebel and all your family have been rebels since Adam. They tell me you are a poet. I'll cap verses with you.' When Jeffreys ordered him to be flogged each year through every market town in Dorset, Tutchin appealed to King James, in vain, to commute the sentence to one of death. Later Jeffreys was bribed into releasing Tutchin, who went to Holland and came back with William in 1688. Tutchin was given a clerkship in William's government, but left after accusing his superiors of corruption. He turned against William and his Dutch cronies, writing *The Foreigners. A Poem* in August 1700, to which Defoe replied with *The True-Born Englishman*. Although Tutchin supported Defoe in his trouble over *The Shortest Way*, he later regarded him, rightly, as an instrument of the moderate Tory triumvirate of Harley, Godolphin and Marlborough. Although the *Observator* was Whig, its editor Tutchin was by temperament a democrat, or what would later be called a socialist. He ferreted out and exposed corruption in high places and, though always in debt, refused to be bought off with government money. However, Defoe suggests at the start of his obituary that Tutchin was somehow compromised:

That he was a man of misfortune, that he had run through infinite difficulties; this may call him unhappy, but not dishonest and will not entitle him to the epithets the Party [High Church] bestow on him; a man may be an honest man, and not be able to [capable of] every honest thing he would do; he may be just in design, though he cannot be in practice, and I sincerely believe that Mr Tutchin owes all that reproach to his own disasters, not to his inclinations; he may be an honest man that cannot pay his debts, but he cannot be honest that can and will not. And this he is not charged with.

Here Defoe is writing of Tutchin what he would like to have written about himself and the compromises he had to make following his own disasters. He is generous, too, in his praise of Tutchin's courage and constancy in defence of the cause they had in common:

I believe none of his enemies will say he was a fool, and I shall take none of my time up to suggest a defence of his wit; let his answers to his High Church enemies and their baffled arguments speak for him, in which especially when he answered calmly, he was generally too hard for them.

Well Gentlemen, Mr Tutchin not being fool, knave or vicious person, what is next upon him – If you will say he was an enemy to persecution, to Jacobites and HighFlyers; I believe if he could convey his mind to us, at the distance he now is, he would desire to have it written upon his tomb – He was indeed an enemy to all these, and GOD made him a wall of brass against them; he was neither to be silenced by the noise; nor terrified by their figure; he stood out the battle to the last gasp.

Defoe refers briefly to Tutchin's weaknesses, such as his boastful claim to scholarship:

He had a competent stock of learning . . . With this he had a zeal against tyranny, uncommon and perhaps rather too warm, especially for his own safety. This ran him into arms against King James, whose resentment he escaped by that famous act of his not often imitated, of petitioning him to turn a barbarous punishment into that of the gallows; by the Revolution he gained his liberty coming over with the glorious King William. After that he met with hardships not a few of which perhaps might help to sour his temper, and turn him against, not so much the camp he had espoused, so much as the person ... He was led into his reflections on mismanagement and representing persons too much by the contrivance of his enemies, who took advantage of his temper ... Tis true he had his passions and want of temper was his capital error – And where is the man that under his pressure may not be embittered and lose himself sometimes among the crowd of his own provoking misfortunes.

As to his treatment of me, which I suppose this gentleman [the letter writer] expects would move me to speak ill of him, I am persuaded he was moved to it not by inclination, so much as by solicitation, joined with the repeated mis-information of a treacherous friend, and waspish, implacable enemy, and who is safe or proof against the insinuations of such? – I forgive it heartily even to his memory – and shall sum up his character in this, that had his circumstances been easy, had he been unpersecuted by insulting enemies and unmerciful creditors, that his temper had not been ruffled and irritated beyond his own government, he had appeared in a more agreeable shape, and abstracted from them, was really a very valuable person.

After more than a year in Scotland Defoe wrote to Harley giving his 'humble opinion that the best way to make me truly useful in this affair I am upon, is to have me 8 months here and 3 months in London each year, with the one month travelling in between, going various roads ...' (31 October 1708). Harley approved and sent Defoe £100 to travel south, by one of the 'various roads' he took to frequent himself with different parts of the North and Midlands. Over the next four years, up until his last report from Scotland in 1711, Defoe would travel continually between the two countries, increasingly spending more of his time in England.

Not only did Defoe want to be with his wife, whom he had not seen since the death of their youngest child; he was probably eager to hear the political gossip of London, especially as this might affect his work on behalf of the government. As previously mentioned, during the course of 1707 a rift had appeared in the leadership of the nation – Harley and the Queen on one side, and Godolphin and Marlborough on the other. The so-called Junto Whigs, who had joined Godolphin after the 1705 election, were distrustful of Harley, who in turn wanted

to bring back some of the High Church Tories. But these Tory equiva-
lents of the Junto Whigs still detested Godolphin and Marlborough
for having opposed the Occasional Conformity Bill. The battle for
power was fought in the open on matters as various as the appointment
of bishops, the Allied failure to take Toulon, and maladministration
in the Admiralty. In private Harley had gained an important advantage
when Mrs Abigail Masham, his cousin, supplanted the Duchess of
Marlborough as Anne's favourite.

With Anne on Harley's side, the Duke of Marlborough and Godolphin were now obliged to break up the moderate coalition and turn
it into a Whig party government. In spite of his plotting with Mrs
Masham, Harley was forced to resign in February 1708, when he was
also threatened by the treachery of his clerk William Greg, who had
sold state secrets to the French. The intrigues of Harley and Mrs
Masham contributed to the development of the party political system,
as Trevelyan explains in *Ramillies and the Union with Scotland*: 'Because
Abigail encouraged the Queen to assert herself against the Churchills,
the Crown ceased to hold the balance between parties and became the
instrument of party Ministries, alternately Whig and Tory. No one
of the persons whom this busy woman set by the ears – neither Anne
nor Harley, neither Godolphin nor Marlborough – got what they
wished out of the quarrel.'

The fall of his patron Harley did not mean that Defoe was out of
a job, for Godolphin admired his reports from Scotland, calling them
'serious and deserving reflection', and had also contributed to his salary.
Early in 1708 Defoe called on Godolphin, who received him politely
and introduced him to the Queen, 'for the second time', as Defoe later
wrote in a published memoir. Defoe was politically closer to Godolphin
than to Harley, especially in his attitude to the High Church Tories, but
he remained devoted to Harley as the man who had saved him from
Newgate Prison. Although Harley seems to have been distrusted by most
politicians, who called him 'Robin the Trickster', the literary men be
befriended, such as Defoe, Swift, Addison, Pope and Matthew Prior,
were unanimous in their praise for his kindness, courage and piety.

Defoe was in London in March 1708, when the Pretender made an
abortive effort to land a French and Jacobite army in the Firth of
Forth. This venture, which Defoe describes in his novel *Colonel Jack*,
was defeated more by the North Sea gales than by the British navy.
Before leaving for Scotland to report on public opinion there, Defoe
wrote an article on the Jacobite danger which clearly foresees the

risings of 1715 and 1745. He warns his English readers that Britain will never be safe as long as the largely Jacobite Highlanders are permitted to carry arms, a right denied to the Presbyterian Lowlanders:

> Our disaster in Scotland lies on two accounts. Those we may trust we will not; those we wish we could trust, we cannot. Were the Highlanders of Scotland universally affected to, and zealous for the government, the King of France would as soon attempt the City of London as the Firth or any other part of Scotland; you needed no other army, no other militia, they are able at the suddenest notice, and with the least disciplining, to form the best body of raw men in the world; they are all provided with arms and understand them; they are entirely under subordination to their superiors ... But on the other hand, these people are not generally speaking your friends, that is, indeed their lairds and superiors espouse a wrong interest, and the poor people are under that entire bondage to the commands of their lairds ...
>
> As to the army of the other party [the Presbyterians], I know the alarm will be great here, and yet I must tell you, this must be done, let your jealousies be what they will.
>
> Arm Presbyterians! ... Well, if you won't do this, what will you do? Will you have a standing army to keep you safe, numerous garrisons, strong fortifications and the like?
>
> It is a bad case, gentlemen, that you will not trust the Presbyterians with the power of defending themselves, and yet you will trust the barbarous, uncultivated mountaineers with fire-arms, and all sorts of weapons on every occasion to cut their throats.
>
> O but these Presbyterians declare against you, or in common style, are against the Union.
>
> I pray gentlemen, will you distinguish between dissatisfaction and disaffection; the Presbyterians (indeed that is many of them), are dissatisfied; but the Highland Jacobites and Episcopalians are disaffected; these decline uniting with you, but those abhor your very constitution; the one do not like us but the other hate us (*Review*, 3 April 1708).

Reading that article, at once so sensible, clear and prophetic, one wishes again that Defoe had turned his mind to the problems and future of Ireland. But on that subject the English listened to his rival

Swift. And whereas Defoe understood and admired the Scots after only a year's acquaintance, Swift loathed and despised the Irish, with whom he spent his life.

In March, when the invasion was feared, the authorities had arrested many political suspects and later examined them for evidence of complicity. In several May issues of the *Review* Defoe pleads for fairness to the imprisoned men, and says he is fully persuaded that most of the Roman Catholics are innocent of conspiracy, being 'men of honour, estates, experience and sense' (*Review*, 6 May 1708). He insists that although many Presbyterians were opposed to the Union, 'not one of them was concerned in the invasion'. He was probably thinking of Lord Belhaven, whom he had ridiculed back in 1706, and who was now in Edinburgh Castle. At Lord Belhaven's request, Defoe paid him a prison visit, as he describes in a charming obituary notice (*Review*, 10 July 1708):

> Tho I was remote from hence when it happened, and therefore it came out late, yet I cannot help setting pen to paper upon the melancholy subject of the death of my Lord Belhaven.
>
> And let no man wonder that this should come from me, who perhaps as warmly as anybody, thwarted this noble person in the opposition he made to the Union, and perhaps used him with freedom enough; but let such people understand from this noble person, that it is easy for men of honour to distinguish between difference in argument and personal difference, and I count it my honour to say, that though in debating these matters, I never slacked my hand in opposing his Lordship's opinion, yet his Lordship knew how to differ in opinion without personal resentment ... I think it due to his memory, to set his character right ... To make way for this, I cannot but reprint two passages in the first letter I had the honour to receive from ... the noble person. His Lordship's words were: 'I confess I thought you gave yourself too much liberty in bantering me and my speech in your writings ... yet by what I have seen of your other writing, you are of the same sentiments with me as to government & except in the matter of Union, you are a man after my own heart ... And I am so well pleased with some of your later Reviews with relation to the affairs of Scotland ... that I freely forgive you all your sins of ignorance ...'

In my last progress to Edinburgh, I arrived a few days after his Lordship was confined to the Castle, whither I went to wait on him; I found him very much concerned at his confinement, and the more so, to use his Lordship's own expression – that he should be confined as suspected in a cause he had always abhorred . . . In another of his Lordship's letters to me before I came to Scotland, his Lordship used this expression: 'Tis now 27 years since I had the honour to be a prisoner in this very place, for opposing a Popish succession in the Parliament [of] 1681; when the Successor himself was on the throne representing his brother' . . . He had opposed tyranny and K. James both in the Court and in the field, had assisted to depose him, and assisted to keep him out at the hazard of his life, having commanded the cavalry at the Battle of Killycrankie.

It is curious to observe that although Defoe had met Lord Belhaven, he quotes directly only from his letters, putting his spoken words into indirect speech. It was not until the end of the nineteenth century that people in public life gave interviews to the Press for direct quotation, and not until the end of the twentieth century that people stopped writing letters, or trying to express themselves on paper.

Defoe observed the Scottish end of the first British General Election in 1708, and in his reports to Godolphin and the *Review* condemned the fraud and venality of the politicians and place-seekers. A few years later he advised against the appointment of a Scottish Secretary of State, as the office would be 'the centre of the hungry solicitation natural to this country'. Besides, he added, 'Scotland no more requires a Secretary than Yorkshire or Wales'. Defoe admired the puritanical side of the Scots, which other Englishmen disliked. In a grim, even revolting 'Miscellanea' Defoe praises the Scots because they hang people for three other crimes besides treason, murder, piracy, felony, burglary, rape, sodomy, clipping [coins], 'or any of the sorts for which men are usually put to death in our country' (*Review*, 31 August 1708). After telling his English readers that the Scots still execute forgers, adulterers and atheists, he exclaims, 'O necessary severity!' Defoe meant no irony; he is writing in earnest, as in his article on sodomites. He hated forgers because he always suspected that his creditors from the bankruptcy had been tampering with the bills. He was equally harsh against the other two crimes, 'which in England they make nothing of, nay commit in the face of the sun, boast of, and insult others with it, namely adultery and atheism'.

In Scotland in 1693 'an obstinate atheist was executed for openly denying God, his name was Akenhead, and at the very gallows he persisted in it and pretended to deny his Maker. But his eyes opened just as they were to be shut for ever, and he died in the utmost confusion; a terrible spectacle and example to all the wretched crew of miserable [people] who say in their hearts there is no God.' A few years after the execution of Akenhead 'two men and a woman made their exit by the halter at the Cross of Edinburgh, for that most fashionable crime of adultery.' Defoe complains that in England 'men may deny God, insult their neighbour, debauch the virtuous, delude the simple, and rage in unrestrained lusts, while the silent law puts neither fetters upon the crime nor upon the criminal.' Here he harks back to Oliver Cromwell's time, when adultery was punishable by death, in England as well as in Scotland. However, it has to be pointed out that if the law had persisted Defoe's two most popular heroines, Moll Flanders and Roxana, could not have survived for fifty pages.

During his first year in Scotland Defoe had been too remote from the field of action to comment more than occasionally on the war in Europe, although in the summer of 1707 he once again warned readers of the *Review* against complacency with regard to the fighting power of the French. In the following year the Duke of Marlborough won the third of his major victories, the Battle of Oudenarde, and went on to occupy all the Spanish Netherlands and even the city of Lille in France. At the beginning of 1709 the war against France had been won; but peace did not come until four years later.

On top of its defeat on the battlefield, France suffered more than any country in Europe from what was known as the 'Russian winter' of 1708–9. When the 'Great Frost' struck London on Christmas Eve, the heartier citizens attended an Ice Fair on the Thames, regaling themselves with hot punch and roast beef cooked on an open fire. But when the relentless cold was followed by rain, producing a poor harvest in south-east England, most people never wanted to see a 'Great Frost' again. Merely a nuisance in England, the Russian winter was cata-strophic for France, destroying cornfields and vineyards, killing mil-lions of sheep, cattle and poultry, and forcing hundreds of thousands of famished peasants to beg for food in the towns.

Louis XIV, who had rejected calls for negotiations in November

1708, now sent an envoy to The Hague to sue for peace with Holland, England and Austria. He agreed to surrender the whole Spanish empire outside Spain itself to Charles III of Austria, who was the claimant to the throne. He offered to give up all his remaining fortresses in the Netherlands, and even the French cities of Lille and Strasbourg. He promised to smash the fortifications of Dunkirk, the port harbouring the privateers which had tormented England's merchant fleet. He agreed to try to coerce his grandson Philip to give up the throne of Spain, which had been the *casus belli* of the War of the Spanish Succession.

But Louis would not and could not agree to hand over Spain itself to Charles III of Austria. For although the three main Allies had won the war against France, they had lost the war in Spain, as Trevelyan notes in *Ramillies*:

> The net result of the five years' fighting in the Peninsula had been to attach the Spanish people to Philip V, no longer as the French candidate but as the Spanish king. In 1702 Louis could have withdrawn his grandson from Spain by a word . . . But in 1707, and still more in 1709, no orders from Versailles would have sufficed to make Philip abdicate, and all Europe could not compel the Spaniards to accept King Charles. The reason why the negotiations for European peace broke down in 1709 was that the Allies refused to admit these facts, and still insisted, several years after it had ceased to be possible, in trying to dispose of the throne of Spain by a treaty with France alone. Louis knew he could not deliver the goods in that form, and he said so. The war was therefore allowed to proceed on its aimless, endless way, until a revolution in English politics placed in power the Tory party, whose chiefs had already in November 1708, been privately writing to each other, 'For God's sake let us be once out of Spain!'

During the peace negotiations of the spring of 1709 Godolphin, Marlborough and the Whigs were committed to the slogan of 'No Peace without Spain'. The City, which largely financed the war, expected a share of the Spanish empire – not least the Asiento, or African slave trade, which France had seized from Spain in 1702. When Louis XIV failed to meet the Allied demands in June 1709 and resigned himself to a last-ditch defence of his country, Richard Steele's new *Tatler* joined in gloating over the Sun King's forthcoming eclipse. But

Defoe had already warned the British in 1702 and once again in 1707 that they should not underestimate the courage, skill and endurance of the French. During the spring and summer of 1709 the King and his popular marshal, the Duc de Villars, transformed a beaten rabble into a proud and devoted army. The King ordered provincial governors to furnish the army with bread, at the expense of everyone else, and Villars gave his regiment food every day they were on the march. When news that the army were eating spread through the countryside, thousands of peasants volunteered for the colours. Louis XIV ignored advice urging him to recall the States General, the Parliament of France whose time would come in the Revolution of 1789, but for once he stooped to explain to his subjects why they must make a new effort – because 'the immense concessions I was ready to grant prove useless for the re-establishment of peace'. Rather as Stalin rallied the Russians during the Second World War the despotic Louis appealed to the French people during this year of common danger.

By the end of June the French had assembled 80,000 men on the plain of Lille to meet the advance of an army half as big again, under Marlborough and Prince Eugene of Austria. Villars understood the danger of meeting Marlborough in open battle, even on equal terms, but knew that he had to stop an advance on Paris. He therefore resorted to the defensive warfare favoured by France in the seventeenth century. He extended the system of mines and tunnels protecting the fortress of Tournai, at the same time ordering the construction of a forty-mile length of earthworks, supplementing the natural obstacles of forest and marshland. This was the type of warfare that Laurence Sterne's Uncle Toby remembered from King William's campaigns in the 1690s: 'If the French have the advantage of a wood, or you give them a moment's time to entrench themselves, they are a nation which will pop and pop for ever at you.'

For the first time in the War of the Spanish Succession, a French general was doing as Defoe had advised in *A Hymn to Victory* on using 'surprises'. The siege of Tournai offered many surprises to madden the English. Its elaborate defensive system of mines and tunnels obliged the attackers to fight in the dark, facing unknown terrors. 'Our miners', wrote Marlborough, 'have discovered one of their galleries at each attack, but dare not advance to make the proper use of this discovery, because of the enemy's continual fire of small shot under ground.' When the siege of Tournai began in June, the Allies had hoped to take it in a month, but the town and citadel did not fall until 3 September, by which time the attackers had suffered 5,000 casualties, including a large proportion of British.

It was not until 11 September 1709 that Marlborough attacked the heavily fortified French positions at Malplaquet, in the fourth and last great battle of his career. It ended in victory, in the sense that the Allies forced the French to withdraw, with the loss of all their cannon and many prisoners. However, the Allies suffered between 16,000 and 18,000 casualties; their opponents only 11,000. The makeshift French army left the field with their heads held high; the Allies had missed the chance to take Paris; and France deservedly claimed a moral and diplomatic victory.

In England the Whigs hailed Malplaquet as a triumph, and wrongly predicted the imminent fall of Paris. One of their ballad-mongers warned Louis XIV to recall his grandson Philip, Duke of Anjou, from his throne in Madrid:

> Monsieur, monsieur, leave off Spain,
> To think to hold it is in vain,
> Thy warriors are too few.
> Then without more ado
> Be wise and strait call home little Anjou.

The author cannot have heard the news from Spain, where the Allies were on the run, and only Catalonia still adhered to the Austrian candidate Charles III. The City financiers were just as blindly committed to 'No Peace without Spain', as Godolphin complained in a letter to Marlborough:

Sir Gilbert Heatcote, who is Governor [of the Bank of England] said to me, 'Pray my Lord, don't let's have a rotten peace'. 'Pray tell me,' I answered, 'what do you call a rotten peace.' 'I call anything a rotten peace,' he said, 'unless we have Spain.' 'But Sir Gilbert,' I said, 'I want you a little to consider the circumstances of the Duke of Marlborough and me; we are railed at every day for having a mind, as they call it, to perpetuate the war.' He replied very quick, 'They are a company of rotten rogues: I'll warrant you, we'll stand by you.'

With the encouragement of this bloodthirsty banker, not to mention £600,000 in Exchequer bills, Godolphin and the Junto Whigs increased the pressure on France to hand over Spain to the Allies. In order to buy the support of the war-weary Dutch, in the autumn of 1709 the

Whigs agreed to a 'Barrier Treaty', giving Holland all the fortresses in what is now Belgium that served as a barrier to attack from France. Through the same Barrier Treaty the Whigs hoped to ensure Dutch military support if the Jacobites challenged the Hanoverian Succession. Just as the Whigs had allied themselves with the Dutch, so the Tories like Harley, over the next few years, would be driven into alliance with the French, and therefore the Jacobites.

During the summer and autumn of 1709, public opinion in Britain was turning against the war and the politicians who wished to prolong it. The Tories, predictably, seized on the casualty list from Malplaquet and talked of Marlborough's 'butcher's bill', but this time much of the country agreed with them. The press-ganging of unemployed men for the army revived the old Tory dislike of redcoats in general, and Marlborough in particular. Defoe did not report to Godolphin, as he had formerly done to Harley, the rude things said of him by the ordinary people of England, but the *Review* of that year reflects some of their grievances – over the Palatine refugees and the high price of corn, for example.

Between May and October 1709 about 14,000 Lutherans from the Rhineland Palatinate arrived in England, complaining of persecution by England's ally Austria. Defoe, who had recently gone to live for the first time in the road that is now Stoke Newington Church Street, persuaded the local parish 'to settle four families of the Palatines, to the number not exceeding twenty persons, at the rate of five pounds per head'. There is still a Palatine Avenue at the end of the present Defoe Street. In keeping with the views he expressed in *The True-Born Englishman*, Defoe stood up for the Palatines in numerous issues of the *Review*, and suggested settling them on 'unemployed land', meaning one of the old Royal Forests. About 2,000 of the Palatines proved to be Roman Catholics and were packed off back to Germany. More were sent to Ireland, did not like it, and also went home. The remaining Palatines were targets of popular xenophobia, now inflamed by dislike of the war. The Church of England called them Dissenters; the country people believed that they carried the Plague; and the poor, as always, set up the complaint that 'charity begins at home'.

As already mentioned, the 'Russian winter' and rainy spring of 1708–9 produced a bad harvest in parts of England, which in turn was blamed for doubling the price of corn in London. In late summer that year Defoe was on his way up to Scotland, and saw the result of the harvest in different parts of the country. He later explained to *Review* readers why the price of corn had increased in what was a truly bumper year:

> I went out of London just as the harvest was beginning in Hertfordshire; here I observed the oats and barley very good, but the wheat was not as good, and indeed the meanest I saw in the south of England and backward, and this being near London, I doubt not has filled the mouth of our meal-men with the noise of scarcity, and encouraged the husbandmen to lay by their corn for a market, as they call it – I was no sooner come to Bedfordshire, and open corn country, but the case was very altered; the corn was good, the crop was well.

Northamptonshire had never enjoyed a better harvest, Defoe reports, and because of the high price of corn in London all the local farmers would be rich by the end of the year. Nottinghamshire and Leicestershire had not known a better harvest in 100 years: 'And though the poor manufacturing and labouring people will suffer by it, the farmers no doubt will triumph – and hurry their corn down the Trent to Gainsborough, or Hull, and from thence to London by sea.' Defoe concludes that, far from a scarcity, there is ample corn in Britain to feed the island for three years.

However, all Defoe's skills as a journalist could not allay the discontent in Britain over the price of bread, the Palatine refugees, the press-ganging of soldiers and all the other grievances people had come to blame on the war. During the winter of 1709–10 the grumbling turned into a Tory revolt against the war, the Whigs, the Dissenters and even the Hanoverian Succession. Over the next five years of uproar, before the country became settled under George I, Defoe was the foremost writer in Britain, as usual calling for peace and moderation, as usual abused and hated by both rival parties. He was to be once more ruined, twice jailed, and in the end driven out of journalism and politics to start a new career as a writer of books.

As if to prepare himself for the coming ordeal, in November 1709 Defoe devoted two issues of the *Review* to a statement of his political and religious principles. The first of these was his annual hymn of praise to William of Orange, 'the thunderbolt that split all the mighty work, that blew up the foundations of the Devil's kingdom in Europe ... His perils have been our safety, his labours our ease, his cares our comfort, his continued harassing and fatiguing, our continued calm and tranquillity' (5 November). Three days later he explains that he cannot belong to the Church of England because it is not entirely reformed: 'And for this reason I DISSENT; believing every Christian to be obliged to worship God in that manner or form he finds most agreeable to the will of God declared in the Scriptures, and to join in Communion with those that he thinks do so – and upon these reasons I SEPARATE.' However, he goes on to say that his dissenting and separating in no way lessens his charity and reverence for those 'who in the honesty of their hearts and with simple uncorrupted alms, adhere to the dictates of their conscience, join with the Church of England'.

Defoe then renews his attack on those Church of England clergymen who disgrace the cloth by swearing, drunkenness and lewd behaviour. The most famous of these, Defoe's old enemy Dr Henry Sacheverell, had just delivered a sermon which would cause even more political fury in 1710 than the one he delivered at Oxford in 1702; and once again Defoe was the doctor's main antagonist. Sacheverell's sermon and subsequent trial by the House of Commons in front of the Lords opened the final act of the drama of the reign of Queen Anne.

The Return of Dr Sacheverell:
1709–11

SINCE THE SERMON at Oxford in 1702, when he had hung out the 'bloody flag of defiance', Dr Sacheverell had grown still angrier with the Dissenters, the Whigs, the Low Church bishops and moderate Tories. In December 1705 he had preached a violent sermon at Oxford, to the applause of his university colleagues but not of the nation at large, which had just voted against the High Church Tories. Now, in the autumn of 1709, when public feeling was high against the war, the Whigs and moderate Tories such as Godolphin and Marlborough, the choleric priest delivered another tirade, this time in front of the Lord Mayor of London at St Paul's Cathedral on 5 November. This was not only Guy Fawkes Day, when Protestants burned the effigy of the Popish plotter, but twenty-one years since the landing of William of Orange. If Dr Sacheverell had spoken on some more appropriate date, such as the anniversary of Charles I's execution or Charles II's restoration, his rhetoric might have passed unnoticed. On 5 November his insults to the Dissenters, as well as his advocacy of Non-Resistance to the crown, were rightly seen as Jacobite provocation.*

Moreover, the doctor's abuse of 'Volpone', the nickname commonly given Godolphin (after the 'Fox' in Ben Jonson's play), pricked the thin skin of the haughty Lord Treasurer. Acting from what Swift described as 'foolish, passionate pique', Godolphin ordered Sacheverell to be impeached by the House of Commons in front of the Lords, in a trial to be held in the Great Hall of Westminster. In this awesome building, which still survives from the reign of William II, Sir Chris-

---

* Defoe's long poem *Jure Divino* was a theological attack on the High Church doctrine of 'Non-Resistance' to the monarch.

topher Wren erected scaffolding for the extra seats needed to hold a crowd expected to be as large as the ones that witnessed the condemnation to death of Sir Thomas More in 1535, Queen Anne Boleyn in 1536, Guy Fawkes in 1606, and the Earl of Strafford in 1641. As the Whigs prepared their indictment of Sacheverell, the Tories chose as the doctor's defence counsel Sir Simon Harcourt, who had prosecuted Defoe at the Old Bailey in 1703.

Defoe had reason to see the Sacheverell trial as a chance for personal vindication. Seven years earlier he had been forced to go into hiding because of this man, and later to suffer the pillory and Newgate Prison. Now Sacheverell had resumed his attacks on everything that Defoe held dear, choosing 5 November, the sacred day of Parliament and the Glorious Revolution. Defoe must have found it especially wounding that Dr Sacheverell should air his views at St Paul's, which he describes so splendidly in the *Tour*.

In spite of his own strong feelings about Sacheverell, Defoe thought it best to ignore his provocations, and he let more than a month pass by before he referred to the sermon in the *Review*, and then with mockery rather than indignation. In the first of two dazzling metaphors from the animal kingdom, he advises his readers to treat Dr Sacheverell

> as we do a hot horse – when he first frets and pulls, keep a stiff rein, and hold him in if you can; but if he grows mad and fumes, slack your hand, clap your heels to him, give him his belly full of it – Away goes the beast like a fury, over hedge and ditch, till he runs himself off his mettle, perhaps bogs himself and then grows quiet of course ... Now, Gentlemen, this wild man, unweighed, hot and furious, see how he flies, champs, foams and stinks; he begins with the Dissenters, do but spur him, he'll run over everybody that stands in his way, bishops, magistrates, parliaments, Queen, hedge and ditch, till he'd run himself out of breath ... and then he'll be as tame as a lamb [*Review*, 8 December 1709].

In the same *Review* he compares Dr Sacheverell to a huge black mastiff in a kennel 'about the size of a pulpit', who rushed at a good old lady and frightened her almost to death, 'but however he beat and roared and flew about to get at her, he was fast to his kennel'. At which the old lady said: 'Ah, thou art a terrible beast, but thank God, like Satan, thou art chained.' Defoe then remarks on the nature of angry dogs: 'If you pass by and take no notice, they will yelp and make a noise, and perhaps run a little after; but go but on and mind them not and they give over again; but turn back, offer to strike them, or throw stones at them, and you'll never have done, nay you'll raise all the dogs in the parish upon you.'

It was good, homely advice but, as so often, Defoe himself was unable to heed it. As the High Church horse continued to champ, foam and stink, and the dogs of the Tory Press once more started to bark at Defoe's *Review*, he grew angry and bitter, especially against the Dissenters. He had complained of them in a letter from Newgate Prison in 1703. Seven years later he scolds them again for failing to heed his warnings: 'And now, Gentlemen Dissenters, do you think I can forbear to throw The Shortest Way in your faces upon this occasion, and make myself a little amends upon you? Was the author guilty of injuring the [High Church] Party, when he represented them sending all the Dissenters to the gallows and the galleys?' (*Review*, 27 December 1709). Defoe recalls how 'wise Sir S[imon] H[arcour]t' had bullied him in the Old Bailey dock, and had tried to suggest that he, Defoe, was persecuting Dissenters. Defoe rubs in the fact that 'the good Sir S—, whose honesty and modesty were born together', is shortly to be the counsel for Dr Sacheverell, who in his St Paul's sermon doomed the Dissenters 'to the Devil and all his angels', declared that they ought to be prosecuted for high treason, and roared that 'every Dissenter from the Church is a traitor to the State'.

Defoe reminds the Dissenters that he had warned them of their danger, 'even at the price of my own destitution', quoting from his *Hymn to the Pillory*. Again he reminds the Dissenters of what he endured on their behalf:

> I suffered the overthrow of my fortune and family, and under the weight of which I remain as a banished man ... No fear has deterred me, though often threatened, bullied and insulted. No favour has withdrawn me, though often caressed and tempted with wheedles and promises ... I am to this day ruffled by your enemies, insulted by those that hate you, threatened and maltreated for the little endeavours I use to serve you – And by yourselves! I am used – How! Just as you know and I expected – and who am I to repine? ... No, no, he that will serve you must be hated and neglected by you, must starve and hang for you, and must yet serve you. And thus I do.

This harangue, with its shrill self-justification, its boastfulness and its maddening air of 'I told you so', is sure to have made Defoe still more unpopular with Dissenters. However, once again he seems to have relished playing the role of Cassandra and clearly enjoyed his lonely position, just as Robinson Crusoe was proud of having survived on a desert island. Even the Old Testament hero from whom he took his Christian name was famous as much for his strength of mind as for venturing into the lion's den.

The trial of Dr Sacheverell and his transformation into a popular hero represented the last hurrah of the old Tory England, before the long ascendancy of the Whigs. The doctor went on trial because, by preaching the doctrines of Passive Obedience and Non-Resistance, he challenged the legitimacy of the Revolution of 1688, and therefore the Protestant Succession. Although he would not admit it in public, Sacheverell was a Jacobite. Thanks to his lawyer Sir Simon Harcourt, the doctor evaded the real charge against him, and turned his defence case into a fresh attack on Dissenters, especially their schools and seminaries. Indeed, Sacheverell's speech in Westminster Hall inspired the Tories to pass the Schism Act of 1714, which banned Dissenting colleges such as Dr Morton's Academy.

The Sacheverell trial attracted a crowd of the highest in the land, among whom the ladies, including the Queen herself, were ostentatiously on the doctor's side. The Lords, who heard the trial of Sacheverell by the House of Commons, arrived at a popular verdict by finding him guilty but passing a sentence of no more than a three-year ban on preaching. The trial took place in a national mood of intense and sometimes violent excitement, which lasted until the Tory election triumph in October. On every day of the trial Sacheverell's coach from the City to Westminster was surrounded by a cheering multitude, armed with bludgeons or drawn swords. In the first days of March the London mob pillaged the meeting houses and even the homes of Dissenters. After his trial Sacheverell set forth on a journey through England which soon became a triumphal procession, like Monmouth's thirty years earlier. The gentlemen of each county rode in troops behind his carriage, the church bells pealed, and each town greeted him with banquets and addresses.

Six weeks before the start of the trial Defoe had urged Parliament to 'declare it a crime for any man to assert, that the subjects of Britain are obliged to an absolute, unconditional obedience to the prince' (*Review*, 1 January 1710). Two days before the great event he seems to have understood that the trial might go in Sacheverell's favour:

'Well, Gentlemen, to speak a little allegorically, on Monday the 27th Instant, Madam Revolution is to be tried for her life – God send her a good deliverance – If she is condemned we are all in a fine pickle' (*Review*, 25 February). A few days later he warned that the High Church faction was using the London mob to intimidate Parliament: 'Dr Sacheverell in his passing and repassing has been huzza'd by the canaille, the rabble ... There is no doubt that when the House of Commons comes to hear how the mob have cried Hosannah to this elevated saint, they will not dare to proceed any further against him ...' (*Review*, 2 March 1710). Two days later he tells how the mob

> went to the Dissenting meeting-house, and pulling down the pulpits, pews, galleries, windows, and everything they could demolish, carried them out into the streets and burned them; besides this they broke open and rifled the homes of two Dissenting ministers ... carried away or destroyed their goods, books etc ...
>
> And now, Gentlemen, you see, what The Shortest Way with the Dissenters so long ago warned you of, was here in another exemplification of Dr Sacheverell's Bloody Flag – The Dissenters and Low Churchmen ... may in this miniature see plainly what they were to expect, and what the meaning of the non-resistance doctrine is. Blinded Nation! Will you now open your eyes?

The attacks on the Dissenters did not worry Defoe so much as did the feeble prosecution of Dr Sacheverell. On 8 March he wrote a letter to General John Stanhope, a Whig MP and one of the Managers of Impeachment, offering him assistance in the Sacheverell affair:

> I was moved to give you this trouble, Sir, upon my being informed you had sent for some *Review*s [i.e., back numbers] to furnish something of the Doctor's character ... Nothing, Sir, has withheld me from blackening and exposing this insolent priest but a nicety of honour, that I thought it dishonourable to strike him when he was down, or to fall on when he had other enemies to engage. But since his defence is made of false suggestion as to his being for the Revolution and his character is part of his applause among this rabble ... I find it necessary to represent him right to those who are his judges.

Defoe offers Stanhope the names of two MPs who can testify to

Sacheverell's drunkenness. 'Then, Sir, as to favouring the Revolution, that he has drunk King James's health upon his knees', Defoe offers the name of Samuel Eberall of Birmingham, who had heard Sacheverell say that he hoped King William would be 'De-Witted' – that is, killed by a mob like Cornelius De Wett in Holland in 1672. Trevelyan thinks this letter 'more injurious to Defoe than to Dr Sacheverell', but Defoe says nothing to Stanhope that he has not already said in print. Moreover, he took a risk in attacking Sacheverell. His printer at this time was frequently threatened by High Tory roughs, and eventually kidnapped. The *Review* ran an advertisement to say that 'whereas great industry has been used to suppress this paper . . . by which art the publication of it has been stopped, that none has been had either by hawkers, or shops where other such papers are sold . . .' (21 March) But copies of the *Review* could still be obtained at 'Nathaniel Cliff's bookseller in Cheapside, and at Mrs Pike at the sign of the Golden Perriwig at Charing Cross'.

Except when it came to scolding Dissenters, Defoe remained calm throughout the Sacheverell affair. After the sentence was passed he remarked that both sides seemed disappointed, but he himself was content: 'From the beginning I said, let the Parliament but censure the crime, let them but put a stop to the running plague sore . . . and I care not how lightly they dropped the man. Tis a moderate sentence. Thus the world sees the glorious spirit of moderation, that according to the blessed dealing of our Maker with us, punishes the highest insults with gentleness and compassion' (*Review*, 28 March). In the next *Review* (30 March) Defoe publishes, 'for the benefit of the female reader', this anagram:

> O Henry Sacheverell
> He cars on [travels to] very Hell

During the first few days of the Sacheverell trial Defoe remarked that 'the ladies begin to talk of falling in love with him', and he later suggested facetiously that they now were running the Tory party: 'The women lay aside their tea and chocolate, leave off visiting after dinner, and forming themselves into cabal, turn Privy Councillors and settle the state; the men leave off smoking, learn plain work, and to knit knots . . . and leave the more weighty affairs of the nation to the newly assuming sex' (*Review*, 9 May 1710). He even suggests that ladies were keeping female secretaries: 'There is a sad cry already among the waiting women; since none of them will be entertained [employed] by a lady of quality, but such as can speak French, Dutch and what is worse Latin . . .' He concludes that 'tyranny is government, and Non-Resistance in subjects are doctrines more taking and more suitable to the women than to the men'. A few days later he is telling his readers what kind of people in London are supporters of Dr Sacheverell: 'Among the ladies – show me a virago, a termagant, a stride-rider, that loves her cold tea, and swears at her maid; that plays all night and drinks chocolate in her bed; I'll hold five to one, she's for the Doctor.'

Contemporary readers may have thought that Defoe was having a dig at Mrs Masham, the Queen's new favourite and the head of her petticoat government. The crafty Abigail was busy throughout the summer of 1710 getting rid of Godolphin and the Whigs to replace them with her kinsman Harley and the Tories. Indeed, Defoe's articles could be construed as a reference to Queen Anne herself, who admired Dr Sacheverell, and was widely known to indulge in 'cold tea', the euphemism for brandy. However, the Queen was certainly not a termagant or virago, and was much too frail to get on a horse, let alone to sit it astride. Moreover, even a man as rash as Defoe would not have been foolish enough to offend the Queen, or even Mrs Masham, when he was just about to apply for work from Harley.

Defoe had stayed calm when the mob attacked the Dissenters in London in March 1710. Later he laughed at the Tory hysteria of the summer: 'The triumph of Dr Sacheverell; the face which he makes; his cavalcade through the country; and his public entry into the towns; the vanity with which he pleases himself at the huzza of the mob; his giving his hand to kiss to the rabble, who, in a few months, after they have been glutted with their folly, will be as pleased, and shout as heartily, if they were to see him hanged' (*Review*, 15 July).

Having travelled extensively round England, Defoe understood where Sacheverell found his supporters: 'Take a country town – Go among the clergy . . . Is there a swearing parson that rides a hunting with the young gentry, and gets drunk with the old; that debauches his neighbours first and then their wives . . . Go among the tradesmen. Is there an ale-house keeper that dare not offend the Justice, for fear of his licence, or a vintner for fear of losing his custom?' (*Review*, 18 May). In several *Review*s and in a pamphlet entitled *A New Test of the Sence of the Nation* Defoe makes fun of those High Church Tories throughout the country who sent addresses to the Queen, declaring 'Unlimited Obedience' and thanking her for their liberties and their franchise: 'Alas! When obedience is to be unlimited, farewell liberties, farewell franchise ... The words cannot stand together – Tis to say, dry water or cold fire.' Long before Orwell, Defoe was explaining how politicians – in this case Jacobites – corrupt the language in order to hide from others, and even themselves, the truth about their beliefs and intentions:

> It would be endless to go through with all the nonsense and inconsistency, that the gentlemen fill up these things called addresses with. The great use I shall make of them is that you may see the doctrine of Non-Resistance is in itself so ridiculous, so self-contradicting, so inconsistent, that the wisest men in the country cannot put it together, so as to speak sense. They that in other cases speak clear and explicit, that are masters of the tongue, and other tongues too; that write a fluent, easy, copious style, strong in sense, flowery in eloquence, and rich in the beauties of conception, when they come to this, when they have these incongruities to put together, how they do chew it and mumble it like an ass upon thistles, and when it is digested with all the art and cunning they can employ upon it, behold it comes out incomprehensible nonsense ...

The Sacheverell affair and the surge of Tory emotion throughout the country emboldened Queen Anne to rid herself of Godolphin's ministry and to bring in a government willing to make peace. Since the Whigs were still the largest party in both houses of Parliament, the Queen was obliged to make the change by a gradual process of sackings and new appointments that went on from April until September 1710. She was advised throughout by Mrs Masham and two of the statesmen she wanted to head her new administration, the Duke of Shrewsbury and Robert Harley. The palace revolution began on 6 April, when the Duchess of Marlborough was finally banished, in tears, from the friendship and confidence of the Queen. Ten days later the Whig Lord Chamberlain was offered a dukedom to make him resign, and was then replaced by the Duke of Shrewsbury, a nominal Whig but in fact a man without political affiliation. In June the plotters persuaded the Queen to dismiss the Earl of Sunderland, a Junto Whig who had frequently asked Defoe for information on Scotland. It appears that these services had been well rewarded, for Defoe later referred to 'my Lord Sunderland, to whose goodness I had many years ago to be obliged, when I was in a Secret Commission sent to Scotland' (letter to Charles de la Fay, 26 April 1718).

When Sunderland was dismissed, the *Review* praised him for turning down a pension of £3,000 for life: 'A sum which if his Lordship should live 40 years, as he may very well do, might have brought £120,000 to the family. A sum nothing but a soul untainted with covetousness could resist – But his Lordship has refused it, not in disrespect to the Queen, but in regard to his country, already burdened by a heavy war' (22 June 1710). Did Sunderland pay Defoe for singing his praises, as the Duchess of Marlborough had done for the *Hymn to Victory* in 1704? We do not know. But when the Whigs were back in power during the reign of George I, Sunderland helped Defoe to find employment.

Since Sunderland was married to the Duke of Marlborough's daughter, his dismissal was a portent of the coming end of the war, as well as the Ministry. It was on 8 August 1710 that the Queen dismissed Godolphin, the man who had governed England over the last eight years. At first Tory, then neutral and finally Whig, Godolphin's Ministry had broken the power of France, united Scotland with England, and shown Great Britain the way to its future glory. As Trevelyan sadly records, Godolphin got no thanks from the Queen he had served so faithfully: 'Anne treated Godolphin even worse at parting than Victoria treated Gladstone. She refused to see him at all; she sent him no message of kindness or gratitude, but merely an order to break the white staff of his office ... Queen Anne was quite as ungrateful as any of her Stuart ancestry who have been charged with that fault.'

On 10 August Harley succeeded Godolphin, first with the title of Chancellor of the Exchequer, and then as Lord Treasurer. By the end of the year virtually all the senior government posts were held by Tories, though Harley shielded the Civil Service and most of the country's magistrates from party careerists. Three weeks before he took office Harley had heard once more from Defoe:

I cannot but hope that Heaven has yet reserved you to be the restorer of your country by yet bringing exasperated madmen to their political senses ... If I can be useful to so good a work, without the least view of party advantage, I should be very glad, and for this reason I presume to renew the liberty of writing to you ... PS. If I may have the honour of a line or any order by your servant, be pleased to direct it to A. Goldsmith as usual [letter, 17 July 1710].

Defoe, aka Goldsmith, wrote again on 12 August to congratulate Harley on his return to power: 'It was always with regret that when you met with ill treatment I found myself left and obliged by circumstances to continue in the service of your enemies.' There is no reason to doubt Defoe's sincerity, for he was always loyal to Harley, in good times and bad. In a pamphlet entitled *The Conduct of the Parties* (1712) he expresses his feelings about the quarrel within the triumvirate in 1708: 'When the late Tr[easure]r [Godolphin] and the D— of M—gh thought necessary for the support of their interest to break with Mr H—ley, they did it in the most uncourtly, unpolitick way imaginable . . . far from dropping him easy, or letting him fall, as a man might say, on his feet . . . they flung him from them as a stone out of a sling, or as a glass or cup dashed to the ground.' Defoe disapproved of Godolphin's manners, rather than his politics, and refused to join with the Tory Press in accusing him of corruption. Moreover, Defoe had supported Godolphin against Dr Sacheverell, even though he considered the prosecution ill-advised.

Although he appears to have done little Secret Service work for Godolphin since his trip to Scotland in the spring of 1708, Defoe had remained on the government payroll, receiving at least £400 a year, according to the researches of Paula Backscheider. However, it is clear from a letter he wrote to Harley on 2 September 1710 that he was hoping for an official salary or pension, if not anything like the £3,000 per annum offered to the Earl of Sunderland: 'I will say nothing of being capable of serving, willing, faithfully and in the affair of the Union, successfully; I leave that, Sir, to your kindness in recommending; if I would move her Majesty in any part of it, twould be of a wife and six children, almost grown up, and perfectly unprovided for, after having been stripped naked in the jail from which you Sir, were once pleased to redeem me.' Here, once again, one has the suspicion that Harley never approached the Queen on Defoe's behalf, or even reminded her of his existence, let alone introduced him, as even Godolphin had done. Harley kept him in the shadows, and paid him out of the Secret Service fund.

Harley had to conceal all knowledge of Defoe from his Cabinet colleagues, many of whom were High Church Tories, or even crypto-Jacobites. The most brilliant of them was Henry St John, the Viscount Bolingbroke, who later quarrelled with Harley and joined the Pretender in Paris. Both Harley and St John dined once a week with Sir Simon Harcourt, who had prosecuted Defoe and later defended Dr

Sacheverell. Defoe was equally anxious to keep secret his links with Harley, and usually called on him after dark at the tradesmen's entrance.

Defoe's Secret Service work became even more dangerous, as English politics polarized to the point of civil war. The General Election of October 1710 was more than usually corrupt, boozy, violent and bitter. 'Drink! Horrid satisfaction, a draught of God's vengeance', proclaimed the *Review* of 7 October, putting the blame exclusively on the High Church Tories: 'Drink that the senses may be dozed, you may be capable of giving up liberty to French bondage, property to rapacious tyranny, chastity to tyrannous lust, religion to idolatry, your nation to God's enemies and your soul to the Devil.' The polling was followed by riots in Northampton, Whitchurch, Coventry, Norwich and, above all, London, where homes 'looked like bawdy houses, with their windows broken, their shutters daubed with dirt, and the balconies full of stones'. Defoe pointed out that both parties suffered from this alleged Tory mob: 'Let any man view the streets; are they all Whigs that dwell between Ludgate and Temple Bar?' The elections brought into Parliament a High Tory ginger group, the October Club, who were said to be Hanoverian when sober but Jacobite in their cups.

The October Club posed a problem to Harley, and was one of the regular targets of the *Review*. But Defoe's main service to Harley at first was as an adviser and writer on economic matters, especially the question of credit. Whereas Godolphin had been a financial wizard, Harley had no qualifications as Chancellor of the Exchequer. After eight years of war the nation was crushed by debt, and the Whig Bank of England was trying to bring down Harley by destroying financial credit. Defoe had remarked on this while Godolphin was still in office: 'If the very rumour of a Tory Party coming into the administration has sunk every person's personal estate by 14 or 15 per cent, what would the blow itself do?' (*Review*, 18 July 1710). At this time he was working for Godolphin and much admired his financial skill. He continued: 'If the King of France was to be asked who had done his affairs most harm, the Duke of Marlborough and Prince Eugene, or my Lord Treasurer, who would he lay it to? If the King of France had it in his offer to break our credit and destroy our funds, or to ruin the whole Confederate army and to have the Duke of Marlborough and Prince Eugene prisoners of war; which would he choose?'

When Godolphin fell and was replaced by Harley, Defoe took up the cause of credit, both for the sake of his patron and of his country in his *Essay on Publick Credit*. It starts by explaining that 'trade was derived by convenience from the profitable exchanges of goods from nation to nation, and from place to place, as people increasing, found their neighbours possessed of what they wanted, and themselves having to spare of what their neighbouring countries did not produce.' He then explains the function of credit in trade: 'Credit is a consequence, not a cause; the effect of a substance, not a substance; it's the sun-shine, not the sun; the quickening something, call it what you will, that gives life to trade, gives being to the branches, and moisture to the roots; tis the oil of the wheel, the marrow of the bone, the blood in the veins, and the spirit in the heart of all the trade, cash and commerce in the world.'

Defoe praises Godolphin, the last Lord Treasurer:

> But after this is said, credit, which has for some years been the nation's happy guest, by whose aid such mighty things have been done, cannot be said to be the whole property of My Lord Treasurer personally . . . Thus the honour, the probity, the exact punctual management, which has raised our credit to the pitch it is now arrived at, has not merely been the great wheel that turned about the treasure, but the great spring that turned about the wheel, and that is the Queen and Parliament.

This astonishing pamphlet went into many editions and had the desired effect of checking the run on credit. In a letter to Harley on 5 September Defoe claims that the essay 'has been successful and done more service than I expected, in which the town does me too much honour, in supposing it well enough done to be your own'.

Since Harley was an incoherent writer, few people can really have thought him the author, and yet his name appeared on the title page of later editions of *An Essay on Publick Credit*. It is even stranger to think that national faith in credit was saved by a bankrupt and chronic debtor, who had only recently used the *Review* (5 January 1712) to answer the accusation that no one would trust him with a shilling. But as we shall see, Defoe, the failed dealer in civet cats and diving bells, went on to be Harley's adviser on African trade, the South Sea Company, and the problem of the National Debt.

The October Club Tories were clamouring for a Schism Act to close down English Dissenting schools, and also a Toleration Act for the Scottish Episcopalians. Both these measures alarmed the Presbyterian Church of Scotland and gave fresh heart to the Jacobites there. At the end of October 1710 Harley decided to send Defoe to

Edinburgh to sound out opinion and to calm the fears of his Presbyterian friends. Whereas in 1706 Defoe had boasted to Harley of his
cleverness as a spy, he now took elaborate precautions to hide his
connection with Westminster. The *Review* was not a Tory paper, he
told its readers on 2 November: 'The rage with which I am daily
treated by the party testifying for me – Yet because I cannot run the
length that some of the other would have me – Now scandal fills their
mouths, and now they repeat I have gone over to the new ministry.'
His reports to Harley from Scotland this time are written in a disguised
hand, signed 'C. Guilot' – one of his pseudonyms – and even employ
a numerical code like the one used by Marlborough in his dispatches
from Flanders: thus 212 = Parliament, 233 = the Queen, 214 = the
Pretender, 288 = the Whigs, 116 = Scotland, 106 = the Dissenters,
109 = the Scottish Episcopalians, and 161 = the Jacobites. On 18
November 1710 'C. Guilot' reports that 161 believe that 233 is prepared to resign in favour of 214. A few days later he warns that if 109
are put in command of the military, it will give 214 possession of this
part of the island. In fact 'C. Guilot' was merely writing in code what
D. Defoe was writing in the *Review*: that the Jacobites would triumph
in Scotland unless arms were given to Presbyterians. Defoe was more
useful in giving Harley character sketches of Scottish politicians such
as the Marquis of Lothian, 'made odious by scandalous vice'.

On his return from Scotland early in 1711 Defoe discovered to his
chagrin that he did not have the easy access to Harley that he had
hitherto enjoyed. In an anxious letter from Newington on 13 February
he makes it clear that he would have preferred to give his report in
person, as he used to do in 'frequent and long audiences'. As Defoe
certainly understood, Harley still had plenty of time for conversation
with literary men, but he now preferred the company of Defoe's main
rivals, Matthew Prior and Jonathan Swift. In the words of one historian
of this period, I. S. Leadam: 'Both as a man of letters and a burrower
in unknown ways, Harley discovered the value of the press and was
the first statesman to enlist it in the regular service of a ministry.' At
about the same time as Defoe's services were re-enlisted, Harley had
taken on to the payroll Matthew Prior, who after the death of Dryden
in 1700 was widely seen as the foremost poet in England; he is now
chiefly remembered for some of his lighter verse:

> No, no, for my virginity,
> When I lose that, says Rose, I'll die;

> Behind the elms last night, says Dick,
> Rose, were you not extremely sick.

Prior, the son of a Dorset artisan, was taken up by a noble patron, educated at Oxford and found a job as a diplomat in the Paris embassy. On the accession of Anne he joined the Tory party and sang the praises of Marlborough for £400 a year. When the Whigs grew in influence in 1707, Prior lost his well-paid job as Commissioner for Trade, and angrily turned on his patron Marlborough. He was now writing in praise of Harley, and would soon be playing a major role in the peace talks with France.

The other resident literary man at the court of Robert Harley was the angry, neurotic clergyman Jonathan Swift, whose political satire *Gulliver's Travels* remains as famous as Defoe's *Robinson Crusoe*. The two greatest authors of the age both worked almost full time for Harley between 1710 and 1714, disliking each other without apparently ever meeting or even deigning to mention the other's name. All they had in common was a devotion to their employer, for as Leadam comments, 'Literary men were sensible of the fact that the condescension with which Marlborough and Godolphin dispensed their bounty was not the comradeship offered by Harley.'

Although Swift was born and spent most of his life in Ireland, he loathed the country, and craved the social success he enjoyed on his visits to London. With his satire *A Tale of a Tub*, published in 1704, Swift became for a time a literary lion to the aristocratic Whigs, but although he remained a friend of the Whig writers Addison and Steele, he turned on the party politicians for failing to give him preferment in the Church. On a visit to England in the autumn of 1710 Swift decided to offer his services to the new Tory government and obtained an introduction to Harley. The story of their first meeting and hundreds that followed is told in Swift's *Journal to Stella. 1710–1713*, a diary he kept to amuse Esther Johnson, his former pupil and later possibly his mistress or wife:

> 4 October 1710. And today I was brought to Mr Harley, who received me with the greatest respect and kindness imaginable . . .

> 7 October. Mr Harley came out to me, brought me in and presented me to his son-in-law Lord Doblane . . . and among others Will Penn, the Quaker. We sat two hours drinking as

good a wine as you do ... He told me he must bring Mr
St John and me acquainted, and spoke so many things of
personal kindness and esteem for me, that I am inclined to
believe what some friends have told me, that he would do
anything to bring me over.

By 19 February 1711 Swift was able to boast to his young friend in
Ireland: 'Mr Harley has invited me to dinner tomorrow, which is the
day of the week [Saturday] that Lord Keeper [Harcourt] and Secretary
St John, dine with him privately, and at last they have consented to
let me among them on that day.' On many occasions Matthew Prior
joined Swift at Harley's table, but more frequently they dined alone,
sometimes on seven days in a row. In the index of *Journal to Stella*
there are fifty-eight entries under: 'Harley, Robert, Chancellor of the
Exchequer; Swift dines with'. There is not one entry for Defoe, who
almost certainly never dined with Harley.

In his paper, the *Examiner*, Swift soon displayed the venom and fury
with which he later destroyed the Duke of Marlborough's reputation.
As early as 1710 the *Examiner* joined the rest of the Press in attacking
the *Review*, and since Swift had the cruel knack of finding an opponent's
sensitive spot, he called Defoe 'illiterate' and jeered at his education.
Such jibes must have hurt Defoe still more since they came from his
rival for Harley's favour.

Both Swift and Defoe, in their different ways, were horrified by an
attempt on Harley's life on 8 March 1711. A suspected French spy,
the Marquis de Guiscard, stabbed Harley with a pen-knife during his
questioning by the Cabinet Council. Although Harley recovered, and
indeed became for the first time hugely popular, receiving the title of
Earl of Oxford, for a few days he had been in danger of dying. Both
Swift and Prior immediately published tributes to the wounded statesman, and Swift at least was truly upset, as we see from this entry in
the *Journal to Stella* for 8 March, the day of the stabbing: 'O dear. my
heart is almost broken. I took a chair to Mr Harley, who was asleep,
and they hope he is in no danger; but he has been out of order, and
was so when he came abroad today, and it may put him in a fever. I
am in mortal pain for him – I now think of all his kindness to me –
the poor creature now lies stabbed in his bed by a desperate French
Popish villain.'

Defoe made no printed reference to the stabbing, except to compare
Count Guiscard to a member of the October Club. Unlike Swift, he

was not able to visit Harley on his sickbed, and does not appear to have seen him until about six weeks later. In a subsequent letter Defoe reveals his passionate conviction that Harley is doing God's work on earth:

> I am comforted with the sight of your personal safety, which no man has more reason to be thankful for than myself, yet when I see the wonders of Providence in your preservation, and reflect upon what depends on your life, I confess I am silent with astonishment . . . Why was he [de Guiscard] permitted to assault and not permitted to effect his design; what armour guards the precious part; what restrained the point; why directed just to the only little solid part that was in the wounded place, but to bear witness to this glorious truth, that verily there is a God that governs the earth, that the hairs on our head are numbered, and not a sparrow falls to the earth etc . . . But the why is the thing I dwell upon, why a life thus clothed with wonder and covered with mercy – But because the same hand that guards your life Sir from evil by its immediate power, has some great work for you to do . . . The subject Sir, is so moving, my weakness betrays itself, and I am forced to break off, only praying that the life thus saved by wonder may be dedicated to him that preserved it . . . that it may be employed for, blessed by and directed for himself, that Heaven may have the praise, the nation the benefit, and yourself the open comfortable reward of Him That Sees in Secret. Amen [25 April 1711].

Not content with employing Defoe, Swift, Prior and Dr John Arbuthnot, a genial Tory squire, who was both the Queen's physician and an amusing writer and the creator of John Bull, Harley tried but failed to enrol Joseph Addison and Richard Steele, the authors of the *Tatler* and the *Spectator*. Although the journals lasted only from 1709 to 1712, they set the tone and style of the English critical essay for at least the next two centuries. The two men were friends at Charterhouse School and Oxford, before moving by different paths into literary life and politics. Because they were Whigs, they both turned down at different times invitations from Harley, but got their reward during the reign of George I, when Harley was in the Tower.

Although neither journal acknowledged it, both the *Tatler* and the *Spectator* were partly modelled on Defoe's *Review*, especially its

'Scandalous Club' and 'Miscellanea', which dealt with questions of manners and morals. Just as Defoe's first *Review*s had campaigned against duelling, so Steele took up the same social problem in the first few *Tatler*s. Both Steele and Addison shared Defoe's concern with the legal and social position of women, and soon had a large female readership. They were both religious men who wished, like Defoe, to correct the vices and folly of the age. Like him, they wanted to reconcile the warring political parties, represented in the *Spectator* by Sir Roger de Coverley, a kind old Tory squire, and Sir Andrew Newport, a Whig and a wealthy merchant.

The difference between the *Review* and the two later journals was not in the message but in the style, for Defoe at his best could never compete with them in elegance, wit, erudition and polish. In his essay on Addison in *The Lives of the Poets* Dr Johnson explains why the *Tatler* and the *Spectator* were still obligatory reading in the second half of the eighteenth century:

> To minds heated with political contest, they supplied cooler and more inoffensive reflections; and it is said by Addison . . . that they had a perceptible influence on the conversation of that time, and taught the frolick and the gay to unite merriment with decency; an effect which they can never wholly lose, while they continue to be among the first books by which both sexes are initiated in the elegance of knowledge . . . They superadded literature and criticism, and sometimes towered far above their predecessors; and taught, with great justness of argument and dignity of language, the most important duties and sublime truths.

Far from resenting these brilliant rivals, Defoe's *Review* constantly praises the 'glorious Tatler' and the 'deservedly popular Spectator'. Defoe had been jealous of Addison's ode to Marlborough after the Battle of Blenheim, and later he quarrelled with Steele on politics, but he always remained a devotee of their journalistic art. Indeed he acknowledges, in the *Review* of 14 August 1711, that the *Tatler* and *Spectator* have made some of his own writing redundant:

> You have had so many authors of late to please you by their Speculation, and that fill you with their moral essays, as well as moral subjects to inform you, as on your follies to reprove you; that accordingly (as it is every man's duty that knows how

to speak, to know also how to hold his tongue) I have left off
meddling with, or so much as thinking, either to instruct or
improve. The Tatler and Spectator, that happy favourite of
the time, has pleased you all; indeed you were ashamed not
to be pleased with so much beauty, strength and clearness; so
much wit, so gentlemanly reproof; and such neat touches at
the vulgar errors of the time.

Defoe praises the wit but fears that mockery may not get rid of the
vice of the age: 'To tell people that swearing is ungentlemanly, and
grows out of fashion, was a pretty thought of the late Tatler . . . But
what said a proficient in that hellish science when he was reading the
Tatler on that subject? Swearing out of fashion! Senseless rascal! G–d
damn you to h—!' He refers to two recent attempts to make bad
language generally accepted, first by having it written in letters and
books, and then by having it used by women. He admits that a few
coarse women will sometimes swear, 'but there is something so harsh,
so rude in the thing itself, that shocks the very natural softness of the
sex, and it would never go down with them, no, not in the worst of
them today; drunkenness and swearing will never be called female
vices.'

Defoe was so much in awe of Addison and Steele that he seldom
ventured to cap their jokes or match their style, though he sometimes
corrected their errors of fact or offered a helpful suggestion. When
the *Spectator* published an essay on the Mohocks or Mohawks, the
aristocratic bully boys who were terrorizing London, Defoe harked
back to the Popish Plot of 1679, when people commonly carried flails.

Under the influence of the *Spectator* Defoe adorned the *Review* with
Latin quotations, and even devoted an issue to Boileau, written partly
in French. When the *Spectator* carried an essay on Milton, he replied
with a rare attempt at English literary criticism. He begins with a
curious story about the Plain of Mecca, whence, legend has it, Eve
departed after a quarrel with Adam, and there gave birth to twins, a
son and a daughter, and 'they being untainted with the sin of their
parents, which was committed after their conception, begat a most
holy, sanctified race, which Eve left behind her in her wandering
and from which came by a right lineal descent, the Holy Prophet
Mohammed'.

From the Plain of Mecca, a part of the world he mentions again in
the *Tour*, Defoe turns his attention to *Paradise Lost*, 'but I think all

comment upon this text is imperfect, and far from raising the rate of a poem above all praise, and sublime'. He then tackles what he sees as the difficult question of 'whether Adam knew his wife Eve before the Fall?' Defoe concludes that he did and, to prove it, cites the two most erotic passages in the poem, including the lines: 'To the nuptial bower/I led her, blushing like the morn . . .' and: 'But if the sense of touch whereof mankind/Is propagated, seem such dear delight . . .'

While Addison and Steele were reforming the nation's manners in the *Spectator*, Defoe was outlining his plans for the future British empire. In a series of articles, pamphlets and confidential letters to Harley he worked out a strategy for increasing African trade, annexing Canada, strengthening the colonies of Maryland and Virginia, and finally forming a South Sea Company to take over the Spanish American empire. Defoe seldom wrote of the East India Company, or what would later become the British Raj, but he must be accounted one of the prophets of empire in Africa and the New World.

Defoe regarded West African trade as 'the most profitable, honourable and most useful . . . of any branch of commerce, proportionate to its size' (*Review*, 27 June 1710), and warned of the danger to England's coastal forts from 'the encroaching Dutch and the invading French' (*Review*, 13 June 1710). He wrote enviously of a Dutch merchant ship that had recently come from Africa with a cargo worth £60,000 in gold and 'elephants teeth'. Robinson Crusoe starts his trading career in Africa, which Defoe seemed to regard as a practice ground for the challenge of the Americas. He insisted on a monopoly for the African Company, to guard the coastal trading forts and to guarantee a regular and cheap supply of slaves to the American colonies. He ridiculed those West Indian planters who wanted a free market slave trade: 'They must be madmen not planters, that petition to have Negroes dear, when they may have them cheap, to have but a few, when they may have many' (*Review*, 15 March 1711).

The role of the African Company is compared to that of the Chartered Company for the Virginia settlers, which built forts and castles against the 'perfidious savages'. Private traders could not have achieved this. As the colony prospered, the settlers 'scattered about in separate trade, unprotected by their forts and castles, what was the consequence? – the case is plain, upon a petty disgust among the natives, they fell upon the whole colony, the 22 March 1621, and destroyed almost all, they murthered near 2,000 of the poor separate trading partners, and in short ruined the whole colony' (*Review*, 15

March 1711). As Defoe explains in his novels *Moll Flanders* and *Colonel Jack*, Virginia was later populated and reinforced by tens of thousands of convicts, many of them from Newgate Prison.

Defoe also wanted to drive the French from Canada, correctly seeing their presence as a threat to the British settlements (*Review*, 31 January 1712):

> The French, by their possession of the great Gulf of St Laurence and the river of Canada, are thereby situated on the back of all our colonies in the continent of America, even for those of New England, to the southernmost part of Virginia; ... by this situation they not only proscribe our commerce, and straighten our people, but raise rebellions, wars and combinations against us among the Indians ... by whom, at the instigation of the French, frequent invasions and depredations, murthers, plunderings and all the violence of war are committed and the English exposed very often to the barbarities of the savage natives, who are supplied with arms and ammunitions by the French.

Not content with taking Canada from the French, as Wolfe succeeded in doing some fifty years later, Defoe dreamed of evicting the Spanish from Central and South America, the territory they had conquered more than two centuries earlier. This romantic vision, nurtured on stories of Drake, Raleigh and other Protestant heroes of the Spanish Main, inspired two of Defoe's most extraordinary inventions, the South Sea Company and the novel *Robinson Crusoe*. In 1711, when the first of these came into being, Defoe was economic adviser to Harley, as well as the country's leading writer on trade and industry. Thanks to his highly successful *Essay on Publick Credit*, the Bank of England had failed to create a crisis of confidence, yet the country was nevertheless sagging under its debts from the war. Soldiers, sailors and public servants went for months, even years, without receiving their pay. In one of his pamphlets, *An Essay on the South Sea Trade*, Defoe gave a breakdown of Britain's various debts – to the navy, the ordnance (artillery and munitions) and the Hanoverian government, for instance – adding them up to a grand total of £7,213,571. 10*s*. 11*d*. After recovering from the knife attack, Harley returned to the House of Commons in April 1711; before going up to the Lords as the Earl of Oxford, he decided to put the country's finances on to a more secure footing and to consolidate the floating debt by setting up a South Sea

Company, of which Harley himself became Governor. In the creation of this company, Defoe was Harley's chief adviser, if not inspirer.

The South Sea Company, when it was set up in 1711, was not the wild speculation that it became in the 'Bubble' of 1720, when £100 shares sold for £1,200. The original shareholders were creditors of the State for the various war loans, most of them bankers and joint stock companies rather than individual punters. The South Sea Company paid an assured 6 per cent annual interest. Although it later handled every kind of business, including a Greenland whaling fleet, its principal wealth was expected to come from the South and Central American trade that Britain intended to win from the peace talks. Thus the financial future of Britain was based on the assumption that the Asiento, or monopoly of the Spanish American slave trade, would be wrested from France, and none of it shared with Holland. Harley's South Sea Act committed the country to making peace with France, on terms unfavourable to the Allies.

Defoe's part in establishing the South Sea Company may not have been as great as Trevelyan suggests, but he had often dreamed of overthrowing the Spanish empire. In the *Review* of 20 January 1711 he talks of the plan he advanced to the late King William for sending a fleet to Havana in Cuba 'to seize the port and the island, in which it is situated, and from thence to seize and to secure the possession of, at least the coast, if not by consequence the terra firma of the empire of Mexico, and thereby entirely cut off the Spanish commerce and the return of their Plate [silver] Fleet; by the immense riches whereof . . . both France and Spain have been enabled to support the war.'

A few months later, when 'all eyes are bent upon the new undertaking of a trade to the South Seas', Defoe reminds his readers of what he had 'told the world in a late Review, long before the project was on foot' (28 June 1711). Like so many journalists, he loved to be able to say: 'You read it here first.' As he reminds the reader, he had advised King William of the need to bring the war to New Spain rather than Old Spain, 'which proposal, his Majesty approved of, and fully prepared to put into execution, had not death, to our unspeakable grief, prevented him; after this, I say, no man can expect that I should speak against setting a trade to the Spanish dominion.'

In his letters to Harley about the South Sea Company Defoe points unerringly to its major flaw: that whatever the terms of the peace agreement, the Spanish of Old Spain would never agree to foreigners sharing their South American trade. He advocates starting a British colony on the South American mainland, which would soon grow prosperous in a place where the Spanish would starve. He takes the example of Barbados, 'upon which there now subsist so many souls, which if it was in the government of the Spanish would eat up one another'. Although the Spanish would never open their ports to British traders, the British could open theirs to Spanish sellers, as happened already in Jamaica. Defoe suggested forming a colony in Chile, or possibly Patagonia, where the climate was suitable for English settlers: 'The natives are very numerous, hating the Spaniards, and willing to receive any nation that is willing to deliver them from slavery.' But all these plans for launching the South Sea Company, and acquiring control of the Asiento, waited upon the secret peace talks of the summer of 1711.

Peace and the Protestant Succession:
1711–14

IN THE LAST WEEK OF APRIL 1711 Louis XIV's minister the Marquis de Torcy sent to England a formal request that the two countries should make peace on the basis of Spain for Philip, the Bourbon Prince, a protective barrier for the Dutch, and a huge commercial advantage for Britain on both sides of the Atlantic. It was on this basis that Henry St John, later Lord Bolingbroke, negotiated a peace with England's enemy – to the detriment of its allies, the Dutch, the Austrians and some of the German Protestant states, including Hanover. Thus the peace achieved at Utrecht in April 1713 became involved with the rival claims to the English throne of George, the Elector of Hanover, and James Stuart, the Roman Catholic and French-supported 'Old Pretender', who may or may not have been the legitimate son of James II.

Although Bolingbroke was a leading Jacobite, and later went into exile at the Old Pretender's court, his colleague and rival Harley, Lord Oxford, was just as deeply committed to the new friendship with France. Almost as soon as he regained power in August 1710, Harley began top secret negotiations with France through Torcy's agent in London, the Abbé Gaultier, and Gaultier's friend, the Tory-Jacobite Earl of Jersey. According to G. M. Trevelyan, who based his account of the peace talks on extensive research in French as well as in British archives:

> Ever since August 1710, when Jersey first got into touch with Torcy through Gaultier, Holland was spoken of by the negotiators as their common enemy, or at least as their destined dupe. It was not St John but Jersey who first based the policy of the new ministers on close friendship with France at the

expense of Holland and the German princes; and it was Jersey who first offered the French Minister security for the continuance of that friendship by indicating the readiness of the Tory chiefs to restore James III on Anne's death. The responsibility for the basic terms of the Treaty of Utrecht and for the policy of an exclusive friendship with France, does not lie with St John in the first instance. It lies with Jersey, and with Harley who left him in charge of the negotiations from August 1710 to April 1711.

In that month when Torcy made his formal request for peace talks, almost nobody in the Cabinet knew of Lord Jersey's negotiations, let alone the commitment to James III. Neither Defoe nor Swift ever learned the full extent of their patron Harley's link with the Jacobite cause, which they both – for different reasons – detested.

However, in April 1711, when France made Britain a formal offer of talks, Harley was still recovering from his stab wound, and so the management of the negotiations fell to his colleague St John, who spoke fluent French and whose convictions led him to favour the change of alliance. In particular, St John shared to the full the traditional Tory dislike of the Dutch, and delighted in doing them out of the Mediterranean trade and their share of the Asiento. After three months of negotiation through Abbé Gaultier, the priestly spy, St John dispatched the poet Matthew Prior to Paris to meet De Torcy in person. A better choice could not have been made, since Prior was witty, fluent in French and well known in Paris, where he had served as a diplomat for King William. Although he was now a Tory, Prior was almost as loyal as Defoe to William's memory, and always resisted French efforts to draw him into the Jacobite schemes in which his political masters were embroiled. But in spite of his loyalty to the Protestant Succession, Prior went to prison early in George I's reign.

As the peace talks progressed in the summer of 1711, Defoe – and probably Swift as well – was kept as much in the dark as the general public. In August, when Defoe presented Harley with his plan for a British colony on the South American continent, he could not know that Harley had long since renounced all territorial claims in return for control of the Asiento. He certainly did not know that Harley had long since agreed that Philip should keep the Spanish throne, when he wrote in the *Review* of 1 September 1711: 'To give up Spain to the House of Bourbon is a thing so absurd, so ridiculous, you ought as soon think of giving up Ireland to them.' But later that month, and shortly before the news of the peace talks astonished the British public and infuriated the Dutch, the newly ennobled Lord Oxford seems to have warned Defoe of the forthcoming change of alliance. While Defoe was given the difficult task of making the peace terms agreeable to his paper's largely Whig readership, his rival Swift was chosen to put the government's case in his anti-Dutch diatribe, *The Conduct of the Allies.* Oxford and St John both admired Swift's genius, but knew they could use it best by exploiting his vanity. He was invited to Windsor, provided with access to secret information, and even promised an interview with the Queen, although, unknown to Swift, his sovereign detested him. Both Oxford and St John were careful to hide from Swift their own partial commitment to the Pretender, whom all Irish Protestants feared and loathed. One can see from the *Journal to Stella* how Swift savoured the taste of power as much as the food and drink of the Green Cloth, Queen Anne's table for guests at Windsor:

> Windsor. Wednesday 28 September. I came here a day sooner than ordinary at Mr Secretary's [St John's] desire, and supped with him and Prior, and two private ministers of France, and a French priest. I know not the two ministers' names but they are come about the peace . . . We have already settled all things with France, and very much to the honour and advantage of England: and the Queen is in mighty good humour. All this news is a mighty secret; the people in general know that peace is forwarding. The Earl of Strafford is to go soon to Holland, to let them know what we have done: and then there will be the devil and all to pay; but we'll make them swallow it with a pox.

> 29 September. Lord Treasurer [Oxford] came tonight as usual at half an hour after eight, as dark as pitch. I am weary of chiding him, so I commended him for observing his friend's advice and coming so early &. I then supped with Lord Treasurer after dining at the Green Cloth . . . It is much the best table in England and costs the Queen a thousand pounds a month.

Although in the summer of 1711 Oxford and St John were already showing signs of the rivalry that would turn three years later into loathing, they joined in forming a Tory club, 'The Brothers', to rival the Kit-Cat Club of the Whigs. Besides the two statesmen, 'The Brothers' included Swift, Prior and John Arbuthnot. Needless to say, only one of the Ministry's writing team was not invited to join the Brothers or to dine at the Green Cloth in Windsor. 'To get service out of Swift he must be treated as an equal,' Trevelyan remarks, 'not as poor Defoe was always used.' Such was the flattery heaped on Swift that we find him boasting to Stella of how he had intervened with one of the secretaries of State in the case of a man condemned to hang for raping his mistress. Characteristically, Swift uses all his powers of persuasion *against* a pardon, although, as he laughingly writes to Stella, the man had lain with the woman 100 times before.

Meanwhile Defoe was addressing the forthcoming peace talks in pamphlets as well as the tri-weekly *Review*. His journalistic rivals at the time and for many years to come claimed that he was writing on the instructions of Oxford, or anyone else they disliked, such as the Whigs, the Dutch, the French or even the Old Pretender. One of the many libels and lampoons that were hawked around depicts Defoe standing between two friends, the Pope and the Devil. Almost three centuries later he appears in a far more admirable light, indeed as a journalist and pamphleteer of prophetic vision, a harbinger of the future greatness of Britain. On every topic he discussed during the next three years, whether it was peace, the dismissal of Marlborough, the renewed attack on Dissenters, the Union with Scotland, the relationship with Holland, or the Succession, Defoe was proved right. In the midst of the political and religious rage of those last three years before the Hanoverians, he was almost the only public man who belonged to no party, and wrote for no interest other than truth.

Although he wanted an end to the war, Defoe was always critical of the peace terms obtained by St John, especially the shabby treatment of Holland. When the Whigs were in power in 1709, they had bribed the Dutch to continue fighting with the Barrier Treaty, virtually giving them the Spanish Netherlands. Now, under the terms of the peace between France and England, most of this region, the present Belgium, would go instead to the Austrian empire to compensate for the loss of Spain. Moreover, the Dutch were facing a blow to their Mediterranean trade through Britain's acquisition from Spain of Gibraltar and Menorca. As a crowning insult, the Dutch would get no share of the Asiento, which was all reserved for Britain.

Swift relished the prospect of forcing these terms on the Dutch – 'We'll make them swallow it with a pox' – but Defoe resented the treatment of this Protestant ally, the nation of William of Orange. 'For my part', he wrote in the *Review* (9 October 1711), 'I cannot but think if an unfair step is taken, the Dutch whose vigilance to their own safety and interest has been always a great share of their true character, will be none of the last to complain.' He called it 'a kind of satire', or bad joke on the Dutch, that they learnt the terms of the treaty only after the English newspapers did.

On the question of Spain Defoe was obliged to do a little back-tracking. He was now content that a Bourbon king should sit on the throne of Spain as long as he did not keep all its foreign possessions; he thought that Spain under the Austrian Habsburgs would pose an even greater threat to the peace of Europe: 'Is not Spain in the hands of King Philip with a considerable possession freely given us in Peru and Chile, a trade to the rest of America, and a tariff to the Old Spain, better for us than Spain in the hands of King Charles [of Austria] entirely resigned, without any of the advantages?' *(Reasons why the Nation should put a speedy end to this Expensive War*, 1711).

To support this argument, Defoe revived the memories of Habsburg tyranny and Croat crimes that he had first referred to in 1704, and also raked up stories from the Thirty Years War: 'Let any man read a book called *The Lamentations of Germany* ... the miseries of that flourishing country, especially the Protestant part ... occasioned by the cruelty and fury of the Emperor Ferdinand II; when mothers eat their own children, and the merciless soldiers, nay the German Crabats, in many cases, killing men, women and child, and eat and devour the children they murdered' *(Review*, 22 November 1711).

In 1709, when the high cost of the war first roused discontent in the British people, Defoe was in the employ of a Whig and pro-war Ministry, and did not play up stories of economic misery. As we have seen, he had even written a series of articles in the *Review* to prove that the high price of corn was not the result of famine. Two years later, under a Ministry dedicated to peace, Defoe felt free to complain of the mounting cost of the war. In the country at large, he wrote, one only needed to ask the manufacturers if the poor were employed and the wool was consumed to get an idea of the economic stag-nation. In London, one only needed to see how trade was replaced by trivia:

Tis a true observation that men grow shabbily gay as they grow poor, not as they grow rich; the reason is because pride is oftener the companion of poverty than of wealth; mark then in the chief trading streets of this great city, and see how trumpery and gaudy trifles fill up the vacancies, the gaps and the intervals, from whence your departed substance of trade is fled ... there's the fine and famous street of Cornhill, since I remember, filled with whole-sale men, and rich shopkeepers, if I mistake not, two or three most famous perriwig-makers, five or six spacious coffee-shops, three or four illustrious cake-shops and pastry men, one or two brandy-shops and the like ... the alleys where the small places were full of Notary Publics, offices of Assurance ... now are crowded with stock-jobbing brokers, buying and selling of bearskins, and tricking and sharping to get estates ...

From thence go into Cheapside and Fleet Street, Paternoster Row and St Paul's Churchyard; looking-glass shops, leather guilders, take up the great shops of the woolen-drapers; ale-houses, cooks, cheese-mongers, head dressers and pamphlet shops [to replace] the mercers in Paternoster Row [*Review*, 12 January 1712].

While Defoe argued for peace in a spirit of reason and moderation, in late November 1711 his rival Swift published his savage pamphlet *The Conduct of the Allies*, denouncing the Austrian empire, the Dutch, the Whigs and, above all, the Duke of Marlborough. Within a month of its publication the pamphlet had sold 11,000 copies – 'a great number', Dr Johnson observed, 'at that time, when we were not yet a nation of readers'. With typical ice-cold fury, Swift overwhelmingly made the case for 'Peace without Spain'. He exposed the enormous cost, in money and lives, of refusing Louis's offer of peace in 1709–10, and the foolishness of British conduct in the Peninsula, which Marlborough and the Whigs considered a major diplomatic objective but could not win by force of arms. Swift reminded his readers of the terms of William's Treaty of Grand Alliance more than in 1701, including its war aims; St John was now boasting that he had more than fulfilled these aims ten years later. In that treaty, Swift pointed out, 'not a syllable' was said about driving Philip from Spain.

If Swift had confined himself to attacking the Whig politicians of 1709, he might have produced a cogent and helpful pamphlet. But, probably under instructions from St John, he went on to suggest that the war had been futile from the beginning, and that Britain had all along served as a tool of Austria and Holland. According to Swift, the British should have allowed the Germans and Dutch to defend themselves as best they could against Louis XIV's aggression, rather than sending in an army. And here Swift unleashed his venom against the Duke of Marlborough, preparing the way for his dismissal, and the subsequent charges of graft, incompetence, treason and even cowardice. Swift's mentor St John knew that these accusations were unfair, for he himself had begun his career as Marlborough's aide. 'But in 1711', Trevelyan argues, 'it was his cue to make his country forget all that they owed to Marlborough, and to turn the current of public antipathy away from France into hatred of Austria and Holland. In this, with Swift's help, he largely succeeded, and so, by a false and ungrateful reading of the past, helped to secure a satisfactory liquidation of the future.'

Defoe replied with another pamphlet – *A Defence of the Allies and the late Ministry, or Remarks on the Tories New Idol, Being a Detection of the Manifest Frauds and Falsities in a late Pamphlet, entitled, The Conduct of the Allies* . . . This was not his first published attack on the man who had supplanted him in Oxford's favour. In the *Review* he had replied to the taunts of the *Examiner*, and he had satirized Swift in a pamphlet, *The Secret History of the October Club*, which purported to be written by a member. In the second part of this pamphlet Defoe suggests that the High Tory October Club is looking about for a 'scribbler' to abuse the administration. The club decides to employ the author of the *Examiner*: 'a smooth, nothing-saying jingler, he is necessary to amuse the vulgar, because the common people always take for granted, there is a great deal of meaning to everything that they cannot understand . . . for unintelligible jingle, fine-spun emptiness and long-winded repetition, without truth, without evidence and without meaning, the *Examiner* was listed . . .'

For all his brilliance, Swift laid himself open to all these charges in writing *The Conduct of the Allies*. In his answering pamphlet Defoe tears to shreds Swift's argument that 'the Dutch are principals in the war and we are only auxilliaries' and exposes Swift's ignorance of commercial matters, adding that some of these errors might have been avoided if 'he had read Defoe's Reviews upon trade'. *The Conduct of the Allies*, he claims, is marred throughout by '1. Gross ignorance of the facts, and 2. a strenuous soliciting the Papal and French interest.' Defoe may well have been jealous of Swift's intimacy with Oxford, but he truly deplored the other man's bitter and confrontational style. Defoe always inclined to moderation, tolerance and compromise, three qualities never found in Swift. Moreover, as is evident from Defoe's generous praise for Addison and Steele, he was not by nature envious of his more polished competitors.

Swift's *The Conduct of the Allies* had the effect of fatally antagonizing the Whigs, the Dutch, the Austrians and, most important of all, the Elector of Hanover, George, the future King of England. George's belief that the Tory Ministry had betrayed the Alliance, of which his country formed part, reinforced his anger against them as crypto-Jacobites. In turn, his hostility to their foreign policy persuaded the Tory politicians that their careers would be finished as soon as he came to the throne, and therefore encouraged them to work for a Stuart Restoration. For much the same reasons, the Whigs favoured continuing the war in order to please their future master.

When Parliament met in December 1711, the Whig leaders at first attempted to lure Lord Treasurer Oxford, the moderate Tory, into an all-party coalition, excluding St John and his October Club supporters. They hoped that Oxford would then hold out for peace terms more favourable to the Allies. But he truly believed that the terms obtained were the best possible for Britain and Europe. Moreover, he had secretly offered a hostage to fortune and France by pledging his Ministry's loyalty to the Pretender.

When the Whigs could not detach Oxford from St John, they turned instead to a much less likely ally, Lord Nottingham, or 'Dismal', the High Church Tory who had pursued Defoe in 1703 and later tried to make him denounce his friends. Soon after Defoe's release from Newgate Nottingham had quarrelled with the moderate triumvirate, and devoted himself to Defoe's old bugbear, the Occasional Conformity Bill. Yet his decision to throw in his lot with the Whigs was not as strange as it might at first appear for, although a High Church Tory, he wanted a Hanoverian, not a Stuart Succession; moreover, from the outset of the war he had supported Austria's claim to the Spanish throne. In return for 'Dismal's support in opposing the peace terms, the Whigs agreed to dish the Dissenters by voting for the Occasional Conformity Bill.

Swift expressed the rage of the High Church Tories at what they considered selling out to the Whigs:

> An orator dismal of Nottinghamshire
> Who has forty years let out his conscience to hire . . .

The Whigs for their part praised Nottingham's patriotism, and drank his health in these words: 'It is Dismal will save England at last.' Thanks to the Whig support, the Occasional Conformity Bill went through the House of Lords as well as the House of Commons, only to be abandoned under George I. Still more momentously, the Lords voted against 'Peace without Spain'. Queen Anne replied with the unprecedented measure of creating twelve new peers to outvote the Whigs, and the Ministry then showed a touch of menace by jailing on a corruption charge the Whig politician Robert Walpole, who was to be the long-serving Prime Minister during the next two reigns.

Although he wrote in a pamphlet many years later that Walpole was innocent of the charges of graft, Defoe at this time was understandably furious with the Whigs. Having campaigned so steadfastly against the Occasional Conformity Bill, having suffered the pillory and Newgate Prison, he now saw the Whigs betraying their most loyal supporters, the Nonconformists. As usual, Defoe was angriest with the Dissenters themselves for once more putting their trust in princes and politicians. 'Unhappy credulity! Supine negligence!' he railed in the *Review* of 4 March 1712. Once more he reminds the Dissenters of how they swallowed the bait set for them by James II in 1688, and how as a young man he had warned them against it. He predicts – correctly – that the 'Occasional Bill' would be followed by a Schism Act, obliging Dissenters to send their children to Scotland to get an education. Defoe poured out his sorrow and disappointment to Lord Treasurer Oxford, who, though he was now a convert to Anglicanism, shared his Puritan beliefs. In a letter dated 20 December 1711 Defoe expresses a bitter joy at seeing how the Whigs, whom the Dissenters had so admired, had sold them into 'perpetual Tory bondage: But my Lord, this joy is like singing a psalm at a funeral, too sad to be sonorous.'

In order to ensure the success of the peace talks due to begin at Utrecht in January 1712, St John and Oxford knew that they must get rid of the Duke of Marlborough, whose presence at the head of the Allied army still gave hope to the European war-mongers. As recently as March 1711 Oxford had tried to persuade the Duke to detach himself from the Whigs and support the Tory peace. For his part, Marlborough detested both 'those vile enormous factions', and his loyalty lay with the Queen and her chosen successor, George, for although he kept in touch with the Jacobites, he had committed himself to the House of Hanover. When George, as a member of the Alliance, denounced 'Peace without Spain' in October 1711, Marlborough had no choice but to follow suit. He may also have hoped to take Paris during the year's campaign. From then on, Oxford and St John resolved to replace a superb fighting general, Marlborough, with the less talented but more amenable Jacobite, the Duke of Ormonde. But they dared not remove such an honoured and popular figure until they had first blackened his character with the same sort of corruption charges used against Walpole. This was later followed by a campaign of vilification under the willing leadership of Swift.

Two main charges were brought against the Duke in the House of Commons. Sir Solomon Medina, the contractor for bread to the Allied armies, testified that between 1702 and 1711 he had paid Marlborough over £63,000 in commissions. The second charge was that the Duke had taken 2½ per cent, amounting to £280,000, from the pay of the foreign troops in English employ. Marlborough answered that it was customary for the Commander-in-Chief to take a commission to pay for his secret intelligence, and that in the case of the 2½ per cent, he had a document to prove it, signed by the Queen. As to the smaller amount from Medina, Marlborough had no proof of how the money was spent except the famed efficiency of his spies. It was common knowledge at the time that statesmen and generals took commissions, but seldom repaid it with such good measure as Marlborough did. The Duke's principal accuser, St John, had only a few months earlier lined his pockets out of commissions for an expedition to Canada, without employing a secret service or, indeed, taking Quebec.

As soon as the charges were made against Marlborough, the Queen sent him a letter of dismissal, couched in language so ungracious that he flung it on the fire. The nation at large showed more gratitude than the Queen, and the Duke was wildly cheered on his every public appearance. Within a few days of his dismissal his friend and comrade-in-arms, the Austrian Prince Eugene, came to England to argue against a Peace without Spain. 'The mob', wrote a lady living in St James's Square, 'are so fond of Prince Eugene that his coach can hardly go about, and he is in some danger of being killed with good cheer.' The Whigs, of course, were delighted by this show of support from the friend of their martyred hero; and the Tories made the best of it by portraying Eugene as a greater general and nobler man than Marlborough. Sir Roger de Coverley, in the *Spectator*, came all the way down from Worcestershire to see 'Prince Eugenio' and 'stand in some convenient place, where he might have full sight of this extraordinary man'.

Later in 1712 the Duke of Marlborough went into semi-exile in Holland, where he was honoured by the Dutch, and still revered by the Allied armies he had once led. Before leaving England, the Duke attended the deathbed of his closest friend and political ally, Godolphin, another victim of Anne's ingratitude. Now, out of the old triumvirate who had conducted the War of the Spanish Succession with such success, only Harley, the Earl of Oxford, remained in office. Just as Marlborough had fought the war and Godolphin had financed it, so 'Robin the Trickster' was bringing it to a conclusion.

Even before his dismissal the Duke of Marlborough became the butt of the most successful smear campaign in English history, orchestrated and largely penned by Swift. Even as a young man, John Churchill had been the subject of gossip because of his skill at using women to further his career. Although his marriage to Sarah put an end to these sexual adventures, Churchill was always equivocal in his politics. While serving with William's army in the war against France, he kept in touch with James II at Saint-Germains, and was widely accused of warning the French of a British attack on Brest or Dunkirk. Although William personally chose and groomed Marlborough to lead the Allied armies in the War of the Spanish Succession, slander maintained that he got the job through his wife's control of Queen Anne. Even after the triumphs of Blenheim and Ramillies, slander accused the Duke of ambition, avarice and uxoriousness, of which last he was indisputably guilty, for he adored the termagant Sarah. Slander even accused him of petty faults such as poor spelling and having once admitted that his only knowledge of English history came from Shakespeare's plays.

All these accusations, and more, were regurgitated by Swift in the *Examiner*, *The Conduct of the Allies* and a misleadingly titled book, *The History of the Four Last Years of the Queen*, which was written in 1712 but not published until after Swift's death. In this vile and almost demented piece of character assassination Swift claims that Marlborough's courage had never been tested, since he avoided action. Of the Duchess of Marlborough he says: 'Three furies raged in her breast, the most mortal enemies of all softer passions, which were sordid avarice, disdainful pride, and ungovernable rage.' He even suggests that Prince Eugene had come to England that year to murder the Earl of Oxford. Thanks to his fame as the author of *Gulliver's Travels*, many generations came to accept his judgement on the character of the Duke of Marlborough. It colours Thackeray's novel *Henry Esmond*, and even affected the Whig historian Lord Macaulay, who accepted his view of the Duke as a man interested only in money. It was not until the 1930s that Macaulay's great-nephew, George Macaulay Trevelyan, corrected this view of Marlborough in his three-volume history, *England under Queen Anne*. At about the same time Winston Churchill was writing a four-volume life of his ancestor, *Marlborough*, to which he brought his own vast knowledge of war and politics.

Almost everything written in Marlborough's defence by Churchill and Trevelyan was said at the time by Defoe in pamphlets and the *Review*, often in direct reply to the accusations of Swift. As so often when dealing with a contentious subject, Defoe considered the Duke's dismissal from many points of view, and without partisanship. When writing for the *Review*, with its mainly Whig readership, he speaks of Marlborough with detached respect: 'Though I was never for making man an idol . . . yet as I was forward in his praise which I thought just, and I am sure far from flattery, having never made any court to him for a reward I shall be the last man to detract from the merit' (*Review*, 22 January 1712). Defoe is careful to say that he did not court a reward for the *Hymn to Victory*, for he later received a gift in cash from the Duchess of Marlborough. Although he praises the Duke for his past achievements, Defoe also suggests that he has grown too powerful in relationship to the monarch, comparing his downfall with that of Thomas Cromwell in the reign of Henry VIII or the Earl of Essex under Elizabeth. He makes the same point in a pamphlet entitled *No Queen or No General*, approving Marlborough's dismissal but not the corruption charges; these, he suggests, should be left to Parliament. In another pamphlet approving the Duke's dismissal, *The Conduct of the Parties in England, more especially those Whigs, who now appear against a new Ministry and a Treaty of Peace*, Defoe reproaches Marlborough and Godolphin for their shabby treatment of Harley, now Lord Oxford, in 1707–8. He goes on to remind the Whigs that it was they, in the early years of the war, who first accused Marlborough of 'embezzling the public money and cheating the poor soldiers'.

Defoe argued convincingly that Marlborough's dismissal was necessary in bringing an end to the war, and to that extent he agreed with Oxford, St John and even Swift. But his whole being revolted against the attempt to destroy Marlborough's character. He expressed his feelings in a superb pamphlet called *A Short Narrative of the Life and Actions of his Grace John, Duke of Marlborough*, purporting to be written 'By an Old Officer in the Army'. Defoe assumes the character of a bluff, simple gentlemen, perhaps a Sir Roger de Coverley, who had served under Marlborough in William III's war with France. 'The first time I had the honour to see him', it begins, 'was at a place called Tuidigne in Brabant [where] an English column was relieved by my Lord in person, who ordered the retreat to such an advantage, that he flanked the enemy with perfect fire.' Here Defoe is defending the Duke against Swift's outrageous accusations of cowardice. He was in a good position to make this defence, for he had been in action with the Duke at Sedgemoor, although on the other side. The 'Old Officer' goes on to defend the Duke against the charge of betraying Dunkirk to the French. The 'Old Officer' argues that neither William nor Anne believed these stories, or they would not have given Marlborough another command. Oddly enough, the same charge of betraying the country to France was soon to be made against Marlborough's accusers, Oxford and St John, this time with justification.

The officer then tackles the question of Marlborough's correspondence with the exiled James II and his dubious loyalty to William. He dismisses the story that once, when William 'was troubled by long spitting from a consumptive cough', Marlborough had wished that the fit would kill him. He reminds his readers how, near to the end of William's reign:

> My Lord was brought again to the King's nearer conversation, and after the last peace, as his Majesty found himself decaying in health . . . he chose him again his General and Ambassador to the States [Holland] that he might be instructed in all the necessary offices of both nations, he recommended him to his successor, our most gracious Queen, as the only fit person whose spirit might encounter the genius of France.

The officer then takes to task 'an author called the Examiner' – that is Swift – who has written of 'great profits' made by Marlborough out of the army: 'What the Queen is pleased to allow the Duke for the Secret Service, because his ears and his eyes must be in all secret cabinets (and without doubt his intelligence must be very good) it is not for me or the Examiner to know.' Defoe may be thinking of Swift's wining and dining with the Brothers and at the Queen's Green Cloth, when he calls the Duke 'temperate in meat and drink, as a good commander needs to be'. Though 'stricken in years, the Duke has to endure sieges, bad weather and daily exposure to danger and death'. Perhaps thinking again of Swift, that most unchristian clergyman, Defoe points out that 'the service of God according to the order of our church, is strictly enjoined by the Duke's special care, and in all fixed camps, every day, morning and evening, there are prayers'.

Defoe, aka the 'Old Officer', ends by expressing what was without doubt the British army's opinion of Marlborough:

> As our Commander indeed is known to the world, or at least to the greater part of it, to be temperate, sober, careful, coura- geous, politick, skilful, so he is courteous, mild, affable, humble and condescending to people of the meanest rank. And as tis said of Moses, the Great the valiant Captain-General of Almighty God, for an immortal title of honour, that he was one of the meekest men upon earth, so without doubt, our Captain-General John Duke of Marlborough has a good share of it.

It is a sad reflection on the British that they have so long accepted Swift's libels against a national hero, ignoring the wiser, nobler judge- ment of Defoe.

With the Duke of Marlborough out of the way, Oxford and St John went ahead with their plan to withdraw the British army from Europe and, in effect, make a separate peace with France. Through this bold and unscrupulous volte face England would eventually force the Allies to accept the terms of the Peace of Utrecht, but at the cost of political turmoil at home. From May 1712 until the accession of George I in August 1714 the country came, in the words of Defoe, as close to civil war as is possible without the shedding of blood. Although he remained loyal to Oxford to the end, in spite of much doubt and anguish, Defoe never realized how close his patron had come to being a Jacobite and a traitor.

When the peace talks began at Utrecht in January 1712, all the Allies disliked the terms proposed by Britain and France. In particular, Austria still demanded the throne of Spain, and the Dutch wanted the forts and the trading rights promised to them by the Whigs in 1709. St John did something to salve the pride of the Habsburg empire by forcing Philip of Spain, Louis XIV's grandson, to renounce his claim to the throne of France as well. But St John refused to placate the Dutch, and even said he preferred to make peace without them. 'Doesn't it make your blood curdle', he wrote to a friend, 'to hear it solemnly contested in Holland, whether Britain shall enjoy the

Asiento?' Trevelyan thinks that St John 'had come to believe the things that Swift and Arbuthnot wrote at his instigation about Holland for the delighted and self-righteous English public'.

St John and Oxford maintained that nothing would make the Allies agree to peace except the withdrawal of British troops from the field. If they had done this openly, giving their Allies due warning and without acting in concert with the enemy, this might have been acceptable to the Dutch, the Austrians and, perhaps most important of all, to their future King, the Elector of Hanover. Instead they agreed with the French to issue what came to be called 'restraining orders' to Ormonde, the British commander, telling him not to engage the enemy, and to treat with suspicion his ally, Eugene. Since the 'restraining orders' were also made known to Villars, the French commander, they gave him the chance to destroy Eugene's army. Indeed, on the day that Anne signed the 'restraining orders', the Abbé Gaultier wrote to Torcy: 'I asked Mr St John what Mons de Villars should do if Prince Eugene took the offensive with the Dutch. He replied there would be nothing to do but fall on him and cut him to pieces, him and his army.' To compound this treachery to the gallant 'Prince Eugenio', whom all England had welcomed at the beginning of the year, Oxford and St John sent word to Torcy through Gaultier on 29 October 'that they had been informed this morning by a courier that Prince Eugene has resolved to surprise Nieuport or Furnes. This advice has been given by a spy they have about the Prince, whose services he is to use on the expedition.' Fortunately for Oxford and Bolingbroke, this shameful document lay unseen in the French archives until it was found by Trevelyan two centuries later. Had its contents been known to George I when he came to the throne just two years later, both Oxford and Bolingbroke could have lost their heads.

For the first few weeks of the summer campaign the Duke of Ormonde commanded an army he was not allowed to send into battle. Then, at the end of June, the Queen ordered the withdrawal of all British troops as well as the foreign regiments paid for jointly with Holland. Fury raged through the Allied camp, and most of the foreign soldiers in Ormonde's army sacrificed half their pay to remain with their comrades under the Allied command. Characteristically, St John made this another grievance against the Dutch and Prince Eugene, 'a beggarly German general' who had bribed British troops to desert. Many British soldiers wept with shame at their country's dishonour, and harked back longingly to the days of the 'Old Corporal', the Duke of Marlborough. Most of the British public, however, were glad to see the end of the war, and as a reward for his efforts St John was made Viscount Bolingbroke, though not, to his fury, an earl like Oxford.

Defoe was convinced of the need for peace, but remained unhappy about the way it had been achieved and the motives of some of the Tories who supported it. 'If they argue for peace', he wrote in the *Review* of 8 April 1712, 'they make no scruple to give Spain and the Indies to France, and insult the Dutch as treacherous confederates ... I do not enquire what Jacobite principle or what else moves them.' On 28 June he is denouncing those who say that 'the peace is for the Pretender', and once more proclaims his hatred of Jacobitism. He warns once again that the High Church Tories are equivocal on the Succession, and illustrates this with a curious anecdote in the *Review* of 19 June 1712: a man living 'not a hundred miles from the city of Worcester' swore that when his wife gave birth he would call the child Sacheverell, whether it was a boy or a girl:

> It pleased Heaven to deliver this man from the burden of his vow ... for that the poor woman, when her time came, brought forth neither a son nor a daughter, but an odious hermaphrodite creature, with a conjunction of sexes, and other parts unfit to name ... so that it now may be said, there has been more than one monster of that name in the world ... A man who in a solemn oath swears allegiance to her Majesty and abjures the Pretender, but at the same time in his heart retains allegiance to the Pretender, is he not a hermaphrodite in religion?

As a writer in favour of peace but against the Pretender, Defoe was increasingly hated by both the Whigs and the Tories. He had long been accustomed to printed abuse, and had once had a bottle hurled at his head in the dark, but he was now receiving death threats, as he explains to his readers:

> It was but two days ago that I received at one and the same time, a letter from a passionate Whig and another from a furious Jacobite; the one threatening me with the gallows, when their party gets up again; and the other with murther and assassination, after the manner of John Tutchin – and how can they agree? The one charges me with writing for the Party that would bring in the Pretender, and the other with abusing the Pretender ... Now in what case is a man who dare speak

truth to two such enraged parties? How is it possible that these
two parties can be in the right? Nay what can more testify to
me that I am in the right, that the mad men on both sides are
thus enraged? [*Review*, 10 July 1712].

Defoe publishes both the letters – the Jacobite writing in French to
remind him how Tutchin was beaten to death for his 'infames libelles',
and the other in English, assuring him that 'Tyburn will be worse
than the pillory'. This Whig fanatic accuses Defoe of seeking a war
with Holland, when in fact he had long opposed it. Indeed, his articles
and a pamphlet on Holland reveal Defoe at his brilliant best in the
war of words against Swift.

After the British had left the field in July 1712, the Dutch and the
Austrians fought on against France in the hope of obtaining better
terms at Utrecht. Since Britain was now the friend, and in all but name
the ally, of France, there was real danger of war being waged against
Holland. Some of the more violent Tories, like Swift, appeared to
relish the prospect, as did some of the Whigs – except that *they* hoped
the Dutch would win. Defoe denounces the Whig as well as the Tory
hot-heads in one of his best-argued pamphlets, *An Enquiry into the
Danger and Consequences of a War with the Dutch*:

I cannot say I am of the number of those who will, that if we
have a war with the Dutch they may beat us, because it has
something in it so unnatural for an Englishman or a Briton
to rejoice in the destruction of his own country, and in the
triumph of our neighbours of any kind over us, that he cannot
see it without horror and aversion: yet I cannot but say that I
will those, who talk with so much satisfaction of a war with
the Dutch, would look a little into the certain consequence of
such a war, whether victory or disadvantage on our side shall
attend it.

In this pamphlet, as in many *Reviews*, Defoe predicts that war with
the Dutch would 'bring the Pretender upon us' and lead to a civil war
in Britain. However, he thinks that the Dutch are too shrewd to risk
such a war:

The Dutch may, and they are in the right of it, put themselves
into such a posture as to let the French king see it is worth
his while to make larger offers; but to say they will push on
the war with France, recover Spain, and do all the mighty

things the [Austrian] Imperial generals talk of, you may talk
as you think fit, and please yourselves with vain schemes, but
the Dutch know too well the effects of pushing things that
length; they know that Britain now holds the balance and will
turn the scale, and that which side pushes to extremity, must
split upon this rock . . . It is not that I desire it, but the nature
of the thing is such, it cannot be otherwise [*Review*, 12 July
1712].

This article was as prescient as it was wise, for the Dutch withdrew
from the war as soon as it started to go against them. Yet although
he was on the side of the Dutch, and hotly against the Pretender, all
Defoe's articles on these subjects angered the Whigs as much as the
High-Flying Tories:

If I talk for the Protestant interest and the Protestant Succession, and against the Jacobites, and for keeping the peace
with the Dutch, in their own way [i.e., the Whig way], then
I am a Whig, but though I talk for the same thing as zealously,
as sincerely, as rationally, and perhaps a little too un-
answerably, yet if it is not the peculiar dialect of the day, if it
be not with a certain turn upon the Court, upon the Ministry,
and upon the Queen, against the Peace and for giving all to
the [Austrian] Empire, then I am a Tory.

In modern parlance, Defoe refused to accept a package or menu of
opinions.

Unlike other journalists who wrote about Holland, Defoe understood that war would be an economic disaster. In the pamphlet already
quoted he points out that most of the warmongering Tories 'are landed
men, and fancy they are in no way dependent on trade'. However,
they forget it was trade that put up the price of their land, 'so the
decay and ruin of trade' will once more lower its value. He explains
how the Dutch, if it came to a war, would seize British corn-ships and
Newcastle colliers: 'It is needless to enlarge on how much dearer it
will make all such goods as are wrought by fire, and how severely it
will pinch the middling families or our tradesmen and the poor, who
have no relief in the case of cold weather.'

Here Defoe is putting the case of the traders against the country
squires, who of course burnt wood to keep warm in winter. Yet on
other occasions he put the case of the landed class against those, like

the *Spectator*, who said it was only trade that mattered: 'I find the opinion of some gentlemen runs so highly against land, that they will have trade to be the only agent of wealth, depreciating the *terra firma* of England to that degree that the soil is rendered a perfect wilderness.' He refers to a recent issue of the *Spectator* that called this country 'a barren, uncomfortable spot, and that no fruit grows originally among us, besides hips and haws, acorns and pig-nuts'. Defoe gently corrects an author 'I so exceedingly esteem', explaining why England is rich in fruit, and why cherries and strawberries grow wild in Scotland. The soil and climate of England are especially good for sheep and therefore wool:

> Bring foreign sheep hither with wool like dog's hair, matted and coarse, I'll undertake how to make their wool fine, the staple large, and the fleece heavy, and that without mixing the breed. Carry English sheep abroad into most countries, I think I may say all Spain excepted, though when they were here their wool was rich, large and fine, it shall degenerate, grow coarse, short and thin; no soil, no climate but this shall uphold them [*Review*, 28 June 1711].

A week later Defoe explains that the English soil and climate are equally good for the horse, the bull, the dog and the hound:

> The best pack of hounds in England carried abroad, lose their nose in 2 or 3 years, and their breed in two or three removes are good for nothing; the best English bulldog carried abroad, loses his courage, and their produce know not a bull from a hedgehog; the generous racer, fleet as the wind, yet strong as the charger, that at Newmarket Heath flies over the four mile course at the rate of a 1000 guineas a heat, send him abroad, and he loses his spirit and his swiftness.

When replying to Whigs like Steele and Addison, Defoe often sounds like a John Bull patriot. He finds it unnatural that an Englishman should side with the Dutch and 'rejoice in the destruction of his own country'. He did not like to see the *Spectator* decry even the soil and climate of England. He would soon attack Steele for what he considered an unpatriotic and even treacherous pamphlet. Just as Burke would denounce the British dupes of the French Revolution, and Orwell the British dupes of the Soviet Union, Defoe distrusted 'the friends of every country but their own'.

In an attempt to silence his Whig opponents, Bolingbroke brought in a Stamp Tax, at the rate of a penny a sheet on pamphlets and newspapers, as well as a shilling on every advertisement in the public prints. It came into force at the start of August 1712, and by the seventh Swift was writing to Stella: 'Do you know that Grub Street is dead and gone last week.' However, the Whigs continued to publish, and soon Swift was complaining: 'These devils in Grub Street are not to be silent . . . They are always mauling Lord Treasurer, Lord Bolingbroke and me.' We do not know if the government paid Defoe the cost of the Stamp Tax, although the Whigs thought so, and on 2 August he brought out a two-page instead of a four-page *Review*, but promised his readers 'to take more heed, to avoid trifling'.

Defoe had considered shutting down the *Review*, 'that after eight years struggling with the enemies of the nation's peace, to have enjoyed some peace myself, to have dropped insensibly out of the public broil, and have laboured as much as possible to be forgotten among you'. However, the crisis facing the country was too pressing 'for any man that has spoken at all, now to hold his peace'. In a preface to the eighth bound volume of the *Review* he complains of ill health, the vengefulness of his enemies and the ingratitude of his friends. Lord Treasurer Oxford was one of the readers who sent his commiserations, to which Defoe replied on 19 August: 'The notice you were pleased to take of my melancholy case . . . and the goodness wherewith you were pleased to express it to me, made deep impressions on a mind fixed to your Lordship by so many obligations.' Although Oxford was now giving all his time and attention to Swift and the Brothers, Defoe retained what he valued most, his freedom of conscience:

> Your Lordship has always acted with me on such foundations
> of mere abstracted bounty and goodness, that it has not so
> much as suggested the least expectation on your part that I
> should act this way or that, leaving me at full liberty to pursue
> my own reason and principle; and above all enabling me to
> declare my innocence in the black charge of bribery . . . What-
> ever your Lordship has done for me, you never so much as
> intimated (although ever so remotely) that you expected from
> me the least bias in what I should write or that her Majesty's
> bounty to me was intended to guide the opinion.

He then mentions that his physician has recommended a trip to Derbyshire to take the medicinal waters there, and offers to do some government service 'in counteracting the measures taken to disturb the country, and calming and quieting the minds of the poor prepossessed people'. The journey he made that autumn resulted in one of the most delightful passages in the *Tour*, as well as the last of his Secret Service reports. He first visits Stourbridge Fair, then proceeds 'incognito' to Lynn, the Parliamentary seat of the Whig leader Walpole, just released from the Tower of London: 'Here, my Lord (asking your licence to jest a little with what is indeed the nation's disaster) I found myself out of her Majesty's dominion in the capital city of the territories of King Walpole.' In a letter from Newcastle, dated 3 October, he tells how he has tried to calm the people and scotch some of the wildest rumours: 'If I ventured to say that the Queen was not a Jacobite or that the Ministry were Protestants, that the Pretender was not just coming ashore and the like, tis hardly possible to tell your Lordship how the people listened with a kind of amazement, which testifies to how glad they are to hear it so, and how they wonder at the delusions they have been under before.'

Here Defoe once more assumes the trouble-shooting role he had played in England in 1704–5, and in Scotland during the passage of the Union. Yet in spite of his confident manner and jokes about Walpole, one senses that he has lost his rapport with Oxford. He makes fun of the rumours that the Ministry are Jacobites, but he himself must have worried about their dealings with the French; he must have known that Bolingbroke was moving towards the Pretender. He was well aware that he did not enjoy the old understanding with Oxford, as we can see from this letter of 15 January 1713: 'I humbly ask leave to claim your Lordship's promise to me, made long ago that if in anything I incurred your dislike or displeased you, I should know it from yourself.'

After his long absence in Derbyshire Defoe explains to *Review* readers on 3 January 1713 that 'the interruptions of this paper have been occasioned by a dangerous illness the author has been under for some time, and at a great distance, which, Blessed be God, being somewhat recovered from, he hopes there will be no more stop to the paper'. But Defoe's ill-health was not the *Review*'s only problem. Its many readers in commerce had always especially enjoyed Defoe's observations on trade, his favourite subject. For several months now he had been saying how much the country would benefit from the trading agreement with France and Spain following the Peace of Utrecht; as he often reminded his readers, he had always campaigned for trade with France, even in wartime. But many readers no longer believed in Defoe's independence of mind, as is shown in a letter he published on 16 January 1713:

> You are a Damned Rascal; do you think to persuade us that you are not writing for the Ministry because you are writing about Trade? Don't you know it is in the Ministry's interest to have the people persuaded that Trade shall flourish and increase after the Peace? I tell you, it is in the interest of every honest man to ruin trade, and to hasten things on to that confusion, which is now our only remedy, and that the great maxim of our circumstance at this time is the worse the better . . . Nothing can save us now but the Pretender and he by this one thing; that his coming will set us all together by the ears; and then we shall beat this new gang of rogues, not only out of their seats, but out of this world too; and you shall be sure to be hanged, you Dog you. (Signed) Cicero.

Defoe was in a dilemma: he understood that the trade terms won by Bolingbroke were generally in Britain's favour, but because most of the trading class were Whigs, they refused to accept a peace won for them by the Tories. They even preferred war, like 'Cicero'. Sometimes, as if in despair of his readers, Defoe offers them non-controversial topics like this (31 January 1713): 'Why are women fatter than was known in former times? One would have it that men are better husbands than their ancestors . . . Another will have it that they drink freer than their grandmothers did . . . Some will have it be chocolate in bed, Bohea [tea] and bread and butter, some hot tea, some cold [i.e., brandy]; and these being modern drinks which our ancestors never had, I incline to think there may be something in that . . .'

While Defoe chattered away about the drinking habits of women, his enemies were plotting his destruction. In the party rage before and during April 1713, when the statesmen of Europe signed the Treaty of Utrecht, Defoe was twice landed in prison, once openly by the Whigs and once by a creditor, probably acting on behalf of the Whigs. Besides the *Review* Defoe was at this time writing pamphlets on the Succession, with eye-catching titles like *What if the Queen Should Die?* One of these was a light-hearted satire, *And What if the Pretender should come, or some Consideration of the Advantages and Real Consequences of the Pretender's Possessing the Crown of Great Britain.* If any Jacobite bought this pamphlet, hoping to find his opinion strengthened, he would quickly have found it a spoof. Defoe argues that, with the accession of the Pretender, Britain would have no more disputes with France, but instead would share the advantages now enjoyed by the French:

> We see France entirely united as one man; no virulent scribbler there dare affront the government; no impertinent Parliament there disturbs the monarch with their addresses and representations . . .
>
> The French are as well satisfied when they have wrought hard 20 or 30 years to get a little money for the king to take away, as we are to get it for our wives and children . . . The badge of their poverty which we make such a noise of, and insult them about so much, viz. their wooden shoes, their peasants make nothing of it . . . In the happy circumstances of the demise of [our] Parliament, this country will be eased of the intolerable burden of travelling to elections, sometimes in the depth of winter, sometimes in the middle of the harvest . . . Pamphleteers shall then not be whipped and pilloried but hanged . . .

Defoe must have thought that the satire was broad enough to prevent people from taking it seriously, as they had *The Shortest Way with Dissenters.* The blow, when it came, was all the more shocking because he was then already in trouble over another misfortune. Among his letters to Oxford is a note dated 1 April 1713 to say he has been detained on proceedings brought by a person from Yarmouth, his most vindictive creditor from the bankruptcy. Defoe is apparently writing from jail, for he adds at the end of the note: 'The youth that brings this is my son, and shall attend you if your Lordship please to permit it.' It seems that Lord Oxford gave the boy money to get his father out of prison, or to pay the people who afterwards offered to put up bail, for a few days later Defoe wrote to thank him: 'This my Lord, is the third time I am rescued from misery and a jail by your Lordship's generous and uncommon goodness.' We can only assume that this unnamed Yarmouth man or woman had sold one of Defoe's IOUs to some political enemy. Yet only a few days later Defoe was once more back in prison – this time Newgate, where he had languished ten years earlier.

Defoe described his experiences to the readers of the *Review*, beginning on 16 April 1713:

I doubt not but the Town has been amused for some days, with an account of the author of this paper being informed against, as the author of several treasonable pamphlets, one entitled *Reasons against the Succession of the House of Hanover*, another *What if the Pretender should come*. That I should be put to trouble, prosecuted and taken up is no surprise to me at all, who have so many enemies, who are ready to take everything I write by the wrong handle; and to construct things piecemeal, without their connection with and relations to the subsequent parts of them; a method by which one may indict the Apostle St Paul of writing blasphemy and King David of denying the being of God ... However that it should be possible for men of sense and impartiality to believe of anything I have written that it should be in favour of the Pretender, or against the succession of Hanover, this I confess, is surprising to me.

In subsequent *Review*s Defoe explains that the people who had him arrested were Whig pamphleteers or journalists, themselves awaiting trial for what they had written. They had denounced his pamphlets in order to try to prove that the government would not prosecute one of its supporters. On about 6 April two of these journalists had called on Defoe's printer and bullied him into admitting the authorship of the pamphlets, under threat of being arraigned for high treason. One of the printer's servants was then commanded to take the Chief Justice's tipstaff to confront Defoe at his home in Newington. Defoe let the servant into the house, but the tipstaff stayed outside the door: 'But it was apparent afterwards, the design was to bespeak constables, and people to make a Cavalcade the next day, and do the thing with as much malice and clamour as possible.'

One of the journalists in the plot, George Ridpath of the anti-government *Flying Post*, claimed that constables had to be called since Defoe had strengthened his house in order to resist arrest. To this Defoe replied in the *Review* of 18 April: 'I say if thou, Mr George Ridpath, art the author of the Flying Post, thou hast published a lie! ... all who know my house, know there is not a lock, bolt or bar in it, more than when I came first to it, except a stair-head door to keep down thieves.' The Chief Justice's tipstaff, the constables and a curious throng arrived next morning to take Defoe to a jail in London, almost certainly Newgate. Since it was a Saturday, he had to remain there until Monday before obtaining bail.

Defoe's main accuser, the Scots Presbyterian Ridpath, failed to convince the court that the pamphlets were seditious. However, when Ridpath's own trial was about to be heard in May 1713, he skipped bail and fled the country, which gave Defoe the excuse to indulge in one of his outbursts of self-justification. But before we laugh at Defoe for so loudly blowing his own trumpet, we should consider that he was on his own, without a party, a claque or even a coterie of important friends. On the contrary, he was an outsider, hated and vilified by the rest of Grub Street. Who can blame him for answering back occasionally? His revenge against Ridpath was all the more sweet since only a few weeks earlier, when he was in prison following the accusations of his Yarmouth creditor, the *Flying Post* had maliciously printed the names of the friends who had stood bail. Defoe kicks off with this in his diatribe in the *Review* (7 May 1713):

> To see a person, who when I lately fell into public trouble, basely expose in print the names of such friends as had been bail for me – I say, to see him first expose my bail, and then run away from his own!
>
> To see a person, who in print gave an account with all possible exaggeration of my latest disaster, in falling into the displeasure of a Court of Justice, himself not dare to appear before the same Court of Justice but fly the country for fear of the punishment, which his own conscience gave him reason to expect!
>
> To see a person who had frequently reproached me with suffering the indignity of the Pillory, though in a cause he pretends to espouse, run away from his friends, and his cause too, for fear of the Pillory!

And here Defoe reminds his readers of how he had been in Ridpath's position ten years earlier, because of his pamphlet, *The Shortest Way with Dissenters*:

> I remember a time when in much a juster cause ... though on behalf of the same people, my case was not the same only, but much worse than Mr Ridpath's now is, for I had not only the whole weight of the incensed government upon me, but two other weights which he knows nothing of (viz.) 1. The resentment of some in power, because I would not answer base ends; and 2. The resentment of the then ignorant blinded

Dissenters and Whigs, who were enraged at me, as if I had written The Shortest Way directly for their destruction.

He is pointing out to his readers that the Earl of Nottingham, or 'Dismal', who tried to make him betray the Whigs and Dissenters 'for base ends', is now allied with the Whigs against the Dissenters. He then gives an account, for which we have only his word, of how he was offered the chance to skip bail before being put on trial in 1703:

> My friends were so apprehensive for me, and for my family, that they earnestly pressed me to go away; and offered to give it me under their hands that they had given me their free consent [i.e., to sign a statement, releasing Defoe from his obligation to stand trial]; but the honour and justice of the cause I was embarked on, the character of the good people I was embarked for; the reputation of my own integrity, and the reproach of running from my bail; These outvoted fear, and outvoted compassion of my friends, and resolved me to bear the utmost indignities, rather than quit the cause I had undertaken.

Defoe heaps scorn on Ridpath and his associates for their lack of 'passive courage' – by which he means patience and doggedness, as opposed to active courage such as a soldier feels in the heat of battle:

> Is their passive courage equal to their clamorous fury? No, no, they fly from the fiery trial, disgrace the cause they appear for, dare not look the laws in the face; for there can be no courage in suffering, without innocence of design in acting: Nothing but truth can make men bold, nothing but suffering for truth can make us look upon the World with contempt, or to Heaven with confidence; Guilt is the shame of punishment, as sin is the sting of death.
>
> If a man is not sure his cause is right, his pursuit of it just, his design honest, his principle clear, no wonder he flies; But if Truth be his foundation ... gaols, pillories, gibbets and death have nothing in them to terrify him.
>
> I bless God, I can say this was my case, and therefore when danger threatened, friends exhorted, and bail consented, Nehemiah's words followed me, Shall such a man as I flee? I considered it would reproach the cause I suffered in; that many thousands would hear I had run from my bail, to a few that

would know my Bail gave me their consent; that it would be remembered to posterity that I had left my bail, when it would be forgotten that they gave me leave: That it would reproach my principle, my friends, my children, and my Party [i.e., the Dissenters]; and upon these considerations I resolved to hazard all rather than fly, and suffered the utmost accordingly.

During the first weeks of April 1713, as Defoe was in and out of jail in London, at Utrecht the plenipotentiaries of Britain and France had at last concluded a peace between their two countries. This was not quite the end of the War of the Spanish Succession, for in the summer Austria mounted a last feeble campaign, and in Spain itself the Catalans refused to submit to the Bourbon King Philip. The betrayal of the Catalans was a blot on Britain's conduct during the war: having encouraged them to declare for the Austrian King Charles, it then abandoned them to their fate. Indeed, when the armies of Spain and France besieged Barcelona in 1714, the British navy blockaded the port of its former ally.

The cost of fighting the war meant the end of Holland's role as one of the great powers of Europe. Yet neither the Dutch nor any of the Allies except the Catalans did badly out of the Peace of Utrecht: Austria had obtained the Spanish Netherlands and Italian possessions. France, though no longer a threat to the rest of Europe, was neither bitter nor bent on revenge. In *The Peace and the Protestant Succession* Trevelyan claims that Britain in 1713 was relatively more important in the world than in 1815, after the wars with Napoleon, or in 1919, after the First World War, since no country save France was a match for its greatness. He goes on to say: 'Bolingbroke settled the terms of Utrecht to a far greater degree than Castlereagh those of Vienna, or Lloyd George those of Versailles. But whereas Lloyd George negotiated the peace with his allies and dictated it to the enemy, Bolingbroke negotiated it with the enemy and dictated it to his allies.' While Bolingbroke's peace lasted, with minor interruptions, until the Napoleonic Wars, and Castlereagh's into the twentieth century, Lloyd George's peace was expiring at the time Trevelyan wrote. The Allies who dictated peace to Germany after the Second World War were soon close to fighting each other.

The end of the War of the Spanish Succession in April 1713 signalled the end of Defoe's career as a journalist and secret agent. Although the *Review* lingered on into June, and Defoe remained in Oxford's employ until the end of July, the following year, there was no longer a role in British politics for men of an independent mind. During the final year of the Stuart dynasty the voices of reason were drowned by the clamour about the Succession. Not only were Whigs and Tories at each other's throats; the Ministry was also split between Oxford and Bolingbroke. Defoe, along with his rival Swift, stood glumly by as the two statesmen went squabbling to their ruin.

Defoe had set up the *Review* in February 1704 with a series of articles warning the English against complacency in the coming struggle with France, and the war was the *leitmotiv* of the paper throughout its existence. To a large extent, all Defoe's regular themes – trade, Dr Sacheverell, the Union with Scotland and public credit – were subordinate to that war. He made the *Review* the Protestant voice of the Glorious Revolution, whose leader William of Orange was honoured on every Guy Fawkes Day. Now, with the Peace of Utrecht and the humbling of France, Defoe must have known that William's work was completed, except for securing the Protestant Succession, and this was out of the hands of journalists and pamphleteers.

For a few weeks after the Peace of Utrecht the *Review* continued to support the trade agreements with France and Spain that Bolingbroke had won. But whatever the rights and wrongs of the matter, some of the terms were unpopular. Although much of the clamour came from the Whigs, there was real distress in businesses now open to French competition. Clothiers and silk-makers sent deputations to Parliament; traders with Italy, Turkey and Portugal saw themselves under threat; from now into the eighteenth century, port was the Whig drink, with claret for Tories. In one of the last *Review*s (19 May 1713), which also carries a letter from a distiller threatened with ruin, Defoe strikes an uncertain, even embarrassed note: 'It is plain that I am not the man I used to be, for I never used to refuse speaking my judgment, for the clamour and noise of any man or party of men, but really, gentlemen, it is otherwise with me now; I hear every day your terrible outcry against the articles published about trade with France; that the English interest is given up . . .' On 26 May he bemoans the fact that 'this new subject of the Treaty embroiled me with you'. On 6 June he says he cannot remember a time in history 'when such heats, such feuds, such rage of men among themselves, ever went off without blood'. On 9 June he once more chides the Dissenters, and on 11 June he says a wry farewell to his readers: 'Before I take my leave of you all, you must bear with my freedom a little, in reproaching one epidemic mischief which I see is growing among you all ... I observe you are all strongly addicted to the modish, abominable vice of MODERN WHORING.' One can just imagine the readers choking with wrath, before they continued reading and found that Defoe was teasing them; for the whores after which they lusted were power, money, politics or, in his own case, trade. He ends with the two words, 'Exit Review'.

Defoe continued to write on trade in a paper entitled *Mercator*, perhaps subsidized by the government, and he frequently joined in the pamphlet war, but the tone of debate had fallen since the Peace of Utrecht. All that mattered now to the politicians was whether George or James was to be the dispenser of power and riches. On this matter of the Succession Defoe was now in a hopeless dilemma. He was on the side of the Whigs in wholeheartedly supporting the claims of the House of Hanover, and yet he was loyal to Harley, the Earl of Oxford, who had on several occasions rescued him from prison and ruin. He therefore tried to convince himself that Oxford, too, favoured the House of Hanover – as in his heart he probably did. Defoe did not know and probably did not want to know how deeply his patron was compromised with France and the Pretender. Perhaps, in his muddled way, Oxford was trying to keep his options open. Like many Tories, he hoped that James the Pretender would change his religion in order to inherit the English throne. It was not until March 1714 that James finally made it clear from his court at Saint-Germains, in Paris, that he would not betray his Roman Catholic faith. It was only then that Oxford seems to have resigned himself to George's accession, with all the danger it meant for him.

Bolingbroke, on the other hand, was prepared to support a Roman Catholic James III – if necessary by force of arms. Indeed, in the last year of Anne's reign Bolingbroke constantly pressed for a purge of all Whigs from civil and military office, to be replaced by Jacobites. Oxford resisted this, and managed to hang on as Treasurer until shortly before the Queen's death. In the midst of the bitter and squalid wrangling, the Queen's favourite Mrs Masham deserted her cousin Oxford and took up the cause of Bolingbroke, for which she received a handsome share of the South Sea Company's Asiento trade.

If Defoe still trusted his patron Oxford, he certainly knew of Bolingbroke's Jacobite dealings, as we can see from the series of pamphlets, *The Secret History of the White Staff*, published after George's accession. His rival Swift, who was equally in favour of the Hanoverian dynasty, was stone-blind to the Jacobite side of both his friends Oxford and Bolingbroke. When he came back from Ireland in the autumn of 1713, he supported Bolingbroke in demanding a purge of the Whigs and could not see why Oxford objected. According to Swift, the Queen complained that towards the end of his time of office, Oxford 'neglected his business; that he was seldom to be understood; that he never came at the time appointed; that he often came drunk, that lastly he behaved himself toward her with ill manner, indecency and disrespect . . .'

During the twilight of Anne's reign Defoe, Swift and Steele became embroiled in a three-way quarrel that did little credit to any of their reputations. After editing the *Tatler* and the *Spectator* Steele had taken a post as Commissioner of Stamps, but had given it up to enter Parliament as a Whig. Early in 1714 he published *The Crisis*, a pamphlet on the danger to the Protestant Succession, which might have escaped notice if it had not been signed 'By Richard Steele Esq.' As Trevelyan dryly observes, 'That a member of Parliament should under his own name declare the succession not safe in the hands of Ministers, was unendurable, particularly as it was true.' Among those shocked by it was Defoe, who wrote to Oxford: 'If my Lord, the virulent writing of this man may not be voted sedition, none ever may, and if therefore he may be expelled it would suppress and discourage the [Whig] Party . . .' Defoe had good reason to dislike the Whigs, yet nevertheless this letter is rather sneaky.

Steele was duly expelled from Parliament, and then came under attack from his old friend Swift, with whom he had recently quarrelled. Swift, being even more blind than Defoe to the Jacobite leanings of Oxford and Bolingbroke, believed that *The Crisis* was just a Whig lie. His answering pamphlet, *The Public Spirit of the Whigs*, began by mocking Steele's self-important style, then turned into an attack on the Scottish peers, calling them beggars and parasites, foisted on England by an unwanted Union. At this, the Scots Lords called on the crown to have the author prosecuted for libel, which the Ministry refused to do because of the anonymity of the pamphlet. This excuse, of course, had not prevented the discovery of Defoe's authorship of *The Shortest Way* and his more recent pamphlets on the Succession.

Defoe now entered the fray with another anonymous pamphlet, *The Scots Nation and Union Vindicated from the Reflection cast upon them in an infamous Libel entitled The Publick Spirit of the Whigs*. He calls Swift a 'ravenous fury' and takes up his insolent challenge 'to name one single advantage that England could ever expect to get from such a Union'. When Swift compares the Union to an unhappy marriage, Defoe suggests that 'our author knows little of the laws of matrimony, perhaps he is under vows of priest's celibacy'; that is, he may be a Papist.

Defoe wrote of Scotland with sympathy and knowledge; Swift with malice and ignorance. Luckily for the sake of the Union, Oxford took his opinions on Scottish affairs from Defoe and his friend William Carstares, the wise Presbyterian divine. Indeed, Oxford, when he was writing to either man on Scottish matters, slipped easily into the language of his Nonconformist youth, as this letter to Carstares shows: 'My soul has been among lions, even the sons of men, whose teeth are spears and arrows, and their tongues sharp swords.' Oxford may have enjoyed the witty conversation of Swift, but he was nearer to Defoe in his religious belief. Knowing Oxford's sympathy for the Nonconformists, Bolingbroke and the High Church Tories tried to force him out of office by making him put through the Schism Act of 1714, banning Dissenting academies and schools.

To the delight of Swift, the Schism Act was even applied to the Irish Presbyterians, who then as now were concentrated in Ulster. It was during Queen Anne's reign that England neglected the chance to obtain for Ireland the same hope for the future that Union had brought to Scotland. Instead, the English politicians stepped up the persecution of Irish Roman Catholics, ruined the trade and industry of the Irish Protestants, and set Anglicans against Presbyterians through bigotry exemplified in the Schism Act. It was during Queen Anne's reign that the Scots Irish started to leave for America, carrying with them their grievances against England, which later helped to inspire the Declaration of Independence. Again, one can only regret that Defoe never turned his attention to Ireland. He sometimes mentioned the country in the *Review*, and promised to write of it in the future, but never went there and never even pretended he had been there.

Defoe's career in politics, which began with the Monmouth Rebellion in 1685, was brought to an end after thirty years when his patron Lord Oxford was sent to the Tower. From about March 1714, when Oxford realized that the Old Pretender would never convert to the Church of England, he held on to office in order to keep out Bolingbroke and the other determined Jacobites. He clung on until 27 July 1714, when he was told by the Queen of his dismissal, and then confronted Bolingbroke in the Privy Council, accusing him and Mrs Masham of graft. The Queen, who knew that Oxford had never enriched himself from the Treasury, took leave of him with more kindness and gratitude than she had shown to Godolphin or Marlborough. Nor did she give to Bolingbroke the Lord Treasurer's White Staff of office, although he was now the effective Prime Minister. But Bolingbroke did not enjoy power for long. On 29 July 1714 Anne had a stroke, and as she lay on her deathbed the senior Lords of the Privy Council sent word to George, Elector of Hanover, to prepare to accept the throne of England. Bolingbroke and the other Jacobite plotters saw there was no hope of a Stuart Restoration, and put their signatures on the welcome to George. Queen Anne died on the morning of Sunday 1 August, and George was proclaimed King that evening, to cheers from a vast crowd stretching from St James's Street, down the Mall and along the Strand. The Queen's death came on the very day that the Schism Act was due to come into force, and was therefore seen by Dissenters as an act of God. Although more than a century would pass before Nonconformists or Roman Catholics were admitted to Oxford and Cambridge, they were never again subjected to persecution.

The accession of George I brought in the rule of the Whigs, which lasted into the reign of his great-grandson, George III. The Prime Minister for much of the next three decades was Robert Walpole, whose 'kingdom' in Norfolk Defoe had described in a letter to Oxford in 1712. Joseph Addison was one of the Whig writers who shared in the spoils of office, becoming a Secretary of State with a pension of £16,000. His now estranged colleague Steele was given a knighthood, and bought a house on Haverstock Hill in Hampstead, over the road from the public house that bears his name, the Sir Richard Steele. Even Defoe's antagonist Ridpath was given a job by the Whigs on his return from Holland after skipping bail.

A very much worthier man, the Duke of Marlborough, also returned from Holland on the death of Queen Anne, and next month greeted King George when he landed at Greenwich. He had been re-appointed Captain-General, in case the Jacobites attempted an invasion, but soon retired to his palace at Blenheim. Most of the Tories dropped out of political life, but did not suffer for backing the losing side. Lord Oxford was impeached as a Jacobite in the House of Lords and spent two years in the Tower of London, before being released for want of evidence against him. His rival Bolingbroke fled to France, where he spent six months as Secretary of State to the Pretender. In 1723 he received permission to come back to England but not to his seat in the House of Lords. The poet Matthew Prior, who had helped to negotiate the Peace of Utrecht, was imprisoned for two years in the new reign, but his Tory friends helped to recoup his fortune by contributing handsomely to a folio edition of his works in 1719, to which Lord Oxford added a gift of £4,000 to buy an estate in Essex. Even the Tory club the Brothers reappeared in the form of the 'Scriblerus' or 'Scribblers' club, of which Oxford, Swift, Prior and Pope were members.

For Defoe, the only literary man of his age who was neither a Whig nor a Tory, the new reign brought isolation, financial disaster and threat of prosecution. The Whigs, who had tried to send him to jail the previous year and had threatened to have him hanged when they came to power, now thought they had Defoe at their mercy. His former protector, Lord Oxford, was himself about to be sent to the Tower. The only Tory now on good terms with the Whigs was Defoe's old enemy 'Dismal', the Earl of Nottingham, who had hunted him down in 1703. The Tory writers like Swift and Prior would not admit to the Scribblers Club a Dissenting tradesman and jailbird.

All the great causes for which Defoe had campaigned – the war against France, the Union, freedom of conscience for the Dissenters, and the Protestant Succession – were now achieved. During the last fifteen years of his life he was to write occasional political pamphlets and even undertake Secret Service work for the Whigs, though now of a mean nature, like spying on Jacobite newspapermen. But Defoe as a public figure was what we would now call 'marginalized' and he called 'silenced'.

Before he bowed out of public life and started to write the books which, centuries later, made him famous, he published two works of apology for his political career. The first was a series of three tracts, *The Secret History of the White Staff*, a defence of Robert Harley, Lord Oxford, during the last four years of Anne's reign. This was published anonymously, and its authorship was strongly denied by Defoe himself in the pamphlet he published under his own name in 1715, *An Appeal to Honour and Justice by Daniel Defoe. A True Account of his Conduct in Publick Affairs.* Needless to say, it is full of evasion and downright falsehood.

The first of these works was a sequence of three pamphlets under the full title, *The Secret History of the White Staff. Being an Account of Affairs under the Conduct of some late Ministers and of what might probably have happened if her Majesty had not died.* It begins, rather surprisingly, by blaming Godolphin's downfall on his decision to order the trial of Dr Sacheverell for his sermon at St Paul's. Defoe remarks that the sermon gave much offence, 'but no one ever expected the Ministry would trouble themselves in it'. This explains why the *Review* did not mention Sacheverell's sermon until more than a month after he preached it. Defoe believed that Godolphin had been needlessly confrontational. By contrast, he praises Lord Oxford, who tried to calm the hot-heads of both political factions. When Bolingbroke and the Jacobites wanted to 'give the Whigs the coup de grâce', Lord Oxford had told them: 'That they were to consider the Whigs as part of the Queen's subjects who, though they were to be restrained, were not to be oppressed, much less destroyed.'

The High Tories, according to Defoe, 'gave out among their own friends that the White-Staff was a Whig in his heart; that he was bred a fanatick and retains a warm side to the Dissenters ... That the Schism Act was a mine dug to blow up the White-Staff, is known to everyone that knows anything of publick matters.' He deplores the scheming of Mrs Masham during the last few months of the reign of Queen Anne: 'That female buzz which had, for many years past, too much indulgence in public management, began now to work, and men of station thought fit to plough with the heifer of the Court.' Defoe asserts that Oxford's attack on Bolingbroke at the last Privy Council so affected the Queen that it may have caused 'the sudden and dreadful stroke which in a very few days, or perhaps hours after, fell upon her Majesty's person'. He ends by saying that if the Queen had lived two months longer, James the Pretender would have arrived. Many readers of *The Secret History* took this to mean that Oxford had proof of Bolingbroke's dealings with the Pretender, which may have occasioned Bolingbroke's flight to France.

Defoe had written *The Secret History* in gratitude to his now fallen benefactor. He wrote *An Appeal to Honour and Justice* in self-justification, to show he had always been loyal to King William and then Queen Anne, and was not a paid apologist for Lord Oxford. It is a characteristic blend of truth, half-truth and untruth, leaving unanswered most of the riddles about Defoe's life, such as whether he actually fought at the Battle of Sedgemoor, whether he ever went abroad, and when he first started to work for William III. He describes his introduction to Queen Anne 'for the second time', but says nothing about the first time, which may have been when she questioned him as a prisoner.

An Appeal begins like a last will and testament: 'By the hints of mortality and by the infections of a life of sorrow and fatigue, I have reason to think I am not a great way off from, if not very near to the great ocean of eternity . . .' Defoe then looks back on some of the occasions when fatigue and sorrow weighed most heavily, starting with his bankruptcy: 'Misfortune in business having unhinged me from matters of trade, it was about the year 1694 when I was invited by some merchants . . . to settle in Cadiz, in Spain, at that with offers of a very good commission, but Providence, which had other work for me to do, placed a secret aversion in my mind to quitting England upon any account, and made me refuse the best offer of that kind.'

He goes on to explain how he came to write *The True-Born English-man* after reading 'a vile, abhorred pamphlet in very ill verse, written by Mr Tutchin and called *The Foreigners*, attacking the Dutch and King William himself'. The poem 'was the occasion of my being known to his Majesty, how I was afterwards received by him, and employed, and above my capacity rewarded.' If that is true, then Defoe did not know William and Mary early on in their reign, as he clearly implies in the *Tour* and sometimes in the *Review*. Perhaps he wanted to counter suggestions that William had paid him to write *The True-Born Englishman*. Or perhaps he was telling the truth here, but not in the *Tour*.

Defoe moves on to the summer of 1703, 'when I lay friendless and distressed in the prison of Newgate [and] a message was brought to me from a person who till that time I had never known: "Pray ask that gentleman what I can do for him."' (This pamphlet quotes direct speech – a rare occurrence outside Defoe's novels.) He goes on to say that Harley had put his case to the Queen who 'was pleased particularly to enquire into my circumstances and family and . . . to send a consider-able supply to my wife and family and to send me to the prison, money to pay my fine and the expenses of the discharge'. It sounds probable that a kind-hearted woman like Anne would think of the plight of Defoe's wife and children before releasing the man himself from jail. But Defoe also wanted to stress his gratitude to the sovereign as well as to her ministers: 'Being delivered from the distress I was in, her Majesty had the goodness to think of taking me into her service, and I had the honour to be employed in several honourable though secret services.'

When Harley fell from power in 1708, Defoe claims that at first he felt obliged to quit government service, but 'my generous benefactor told me that I should by no means do it'. He went to see the Lord Treasurer, Godolphin, who 'told me smiling he had not seen me a long while'. When Defoe asked if his obligation to Harley might be held against him, Godolphin replied: 'Not at all, Mr Defoe, I always think a man honest, till I find to the contrary.' On going to work for Godolphin, Defoe resolved to break off all correspondence with Harley. He then claims that Godolphin introduced him 'for the second time to her Majesty and to the honour of kissing her hand and obtained for me the continuance of an appointment [in Scotland] . . . in which I had run as much risk as a grenadier upon an escarpment'.

Defoe then sets out to defend himself from the charge 'that I have been employed by the Earl of O—d, the Lord Treasurer, in the late dispute about public affairs to write for him, or have written by his direction, taken the material from him, been dictated to or instructed by him. As for consideration, pension, gratification or reward, I declare to all the world I have had none.' The last four words are what Defoe sometimes called a FIBB. A few pages later he defends first himself and then Oxford against imputations of being a Jacobite:

> No man in this nation ever had a more revolted aversion to the Pretender than I, a man that had been in arms under the Duke of Monmouth against the cruelty and arbitrary government of his father . . . I ever believed [Lord Oxford] to have the true interest of the Protestant religion, and of his country, in his view . . . I have not received of the late Lord Treasurer or of anyone by his order, knowledge or direction, one farthing, or the value of a farthing, during the whole administration.

If, by 'the late dispute', he means his authorship of *The Secret History of the White Staff*, Defoe is probably telling the truth when he claims he had no instructions or payment. But to say that he had no payment 'during the whole administration' is simply untrue. According to Paula Backscheider, Defoe received £500 during the first half of 1714 and £100 from Oxford personally on his last day in office.

Towards the end of the pamphlet Defoe starts to ramble among his past triumphs and grievances. He recalls how, when the Whigs were attacking Marlborough and Godolphin: 'In this dispute, my lord Godolphin did me the honour to tell me I had served him and his Grace both faithfully and successfully.' He then lashes out at George Ridpath, the editor of the *Flying Post*, who had recently claimed that Defoe never paid for his children's education. The extraordinary pamphlet ends with what is supposed to be a 'Conclusion', written by the printer: 'While this was at the press, and copy thus far finished, the author was seized by a violent fit of an apoplexy ... It is the opinion of those who know him, that the troubles which he here complains of, and some others which he would have spoken of, have been the apparent cause of this.' Was Defoe really ill, or had he gone mad, or was he preparing to fake his own death to escape from creditors? Whatever its meaning, the printer's 'Conclusion' marks the end of Defoe as an influential journalist, and the start of his new career writing works of imagination.

The Emergence of the Author:
1714-25

DEFOE'S *Appeal to Honour and Justice* seems to announce the end of his long career as Britain's leading journalist, Secret Service agent and friend and adviser to some of the highest in the land. The report of his apoplexy, if not a suicide note, reveals the despair that came from chronic danger and indebtedness. Yet somehow Defoe's plight, for all its grimness and even tragedy, often puts one in mind of another famous debtor, Wilkins Micawber, in Dickens's *David Copperfield*, a character said to be based on the author's father.

Defoe, like Mr Micawber, had an irrepressible confidence in his business acumen, whether as wholesaler of stockings, trader in wine and tobacco, breeder of civet cats, promoter of diving bells, or maker of bricks and pantiles. In the same way Mr Micawber dealt in naval supplies and corn before he thought that 'there might be an opening for his talents in the Medway Coal Trade' and, when that failed, in Canterbury, 'on account of the great possibility of something turning up in a Cathedral town'. Like Mr Micawber, Defoe was aware of the hardships he was inflicting upon his family, reminding Harley, before setting off for Edinburgh, that 'you have a widow and seven children on your hands'. Yet almost as soon as he reached Scotland, he was seduced by his 'whore of trade' into buying and selling horses and manufacturing tablecloths. Defoe wore an extravagant wig and a diamond 'pinkie' on his finger, and yet he complained in Edinburgh of being so poor that he had 'grown shabby in clothes, dejected etc'. When Mr Micawber first met David Copperfield, 'His clothes were shabby but he had an imposing shirt-collar on. He carried a jaunty sort of a stick, with a large pair of rusting tassels to it; and a quizzing-glass hung outside his coat, for ornament, as he very seldom looked through it, and couldn't see anything when he did.'

Just as Mr Micawber was frequently 'crushed' or 'floored' by debt, and hinted at ending it all with a cut-throat razor, Defoe also talked of desperate measures, yet just as quickly recovered his spirits and even triumphed over his creditors, as Mr Micawber did over Uriah Heep. Instead of going to Cadiz in 1694, Defoe started his pantile works at Tilbury. In the summer of 1706, when he had just been pleading with Harley to send him abroad to escape his creditors, he triumphed in court and crowed over the downfall of his 'most furious, subtil and malicious pursuers'. At the beginning of April 1713 Defoe had been sent to prison and was once again in despair, yet within a few weeks he had routed his enemy George Ridpath, who had forfeited bail and escaped to Holland.

Just as Mr Micawber announced his ruin by farewell letters to his friends, so in *An Appeal to Honour and Justice* Defoe predicted his imminent death. This brings to mind the letter received by David Copperfield the morning after a jolly dinner at Canterbury: 'My dear young friend, The die is cast – all is over. Hiding the ravages of care with a sickly mask of mirth, I have not informed you this evening that there is no hope of a remittance! ... The result is destruction. The bolt is impending, and the tree must fall ... This is the last communication, my dear Copperfield, you will ever receive, from the Beggared Outcast, Wilkins Micawber.' David is so frightened by this letter that he runs to the inn to try to prevent a tragedy: 'But half-way there, I met the London coach with Mr and Mrs Micawber up behind; Mr Micawber, the very picture of tranquil enjoyment, smiling at Mrs Micawber's conversation, eating walnuts out of a paper bag, with a bottle sticking out of his breast pocket.'

Within days of the disaster brought about by Lord Oxford's sacking and then the death of Queen Anne Defoe responded in true Micawber fashion by moving into a larger house across the road. Perhaps he used the substantial cash sum given to him by Oxford to buy the lease on the three-storey building, which stood on what is the present Defoe Street. According to A. J. Shirren, the author of *Daniel Defoe in Stoke Newington*, one local resident called the house 'a poor specimen of Queen Anne's style', and said that without the wings, which Defoe himself added, 'it would look intolerably heavy'. Another visitor called the house 'a gloomy and irregular pile of red brick – remarkable for its number of doors with massive locks and bolts', and its walls were thick, 'having deep narrow window seats and curious cupboards in the recesses'. However, the property included a good stable and coach house, with four acres of land, on which Defoe created a garden and planted lime trees.*

Perhaps in this rustic retreat Defoe felt safe from the vilification and threats that were hurled at him after the fall of Lord Oxford, his friend and protector. The angry Whigs who had tried to put him in prison in April 1713 and warned him that when they came to power he would find 'Tyburn worse than the pillory' were now closing in for what they imagined would be the kill. Besides the usual accusations of being a turncoat, a political prostitute and a liar, his enemies printed items of ancient tittle-tattle – for instance, that he had once stolen a horse at Coventry, and impregnated the wife of Nathaniel Sammen, the Spitalfield weaver who had given him sanctuary when he was on the run in 1703.

Although his principal enemies were the Whigs, Defoe first ran into legal trouble during the reign of George I because of something he wrote against a Tory, Arthur Annesley, fifth Earl of Anglesey. When Defoe's antagonist George Ridpath jumped bail and fled the country in April 1713, the men he engaged to run his paper, the *Flying Post*, replaced his printer William Hunt with another. Unwilling to lose this source of income, Hunt decided to go on printing a separate *Flying Post*, and asked Defoe to provide him with copy. Although he was no longer a paid government agent, Defoe leapt at the chance to denounce the Jacobites and to get his own back on Ridpath. On 19 August 1714 Hurt's *Flying Post* published a letter that began:

> Sir, you cannot be ignorant of the late Journey of a No(ble)
> Pe–r to Ireland . . . part of the design of which we are assured
> was, to new model the Forces there, and particularly to break
> no less than 70 of the Honest Officers of the Army, and to
> fill up the Places with the Tools and Creatures of Con(stantine)
> Phi(pps), and such a rabble of cut-throats as were fit for the
> work that they had for them to do.

It was true that Lord Anglesey had gone to Ireland on the instruc-tions of Bolingbroke to help the Jacobite Phipps in crushing the Whig Corporation of Dublin. But since Anglesey was one of the Regents during the time between the death of Anne and George's arrival from

* Even today, I was told in a Stoke Newington Church Street wine bar: 'There isn't a mulberry tree anywhere near here that Defoe isn't said to have planted.'

Hanover, he could not lightly be accused of supporting the Old Pretender. The Ministry soon arrested Hurt and seized the original copy of the offending letter, unmistakably written by Defoe. On 3 September 1714 the Secretary of State, William Bromley, gave the Attorney General the depositions, and ordered him to prosecute Defoe in the name of the Regents. The indictment accused Defoe of being 'a seditious and malicious man and plotting and intending evil to the Queen ... and to scandalise and vilify the memory of the Queen ... and cause to be believed that she intended ... that wicked and dishonest reports' be spread concerning the Irish army. In July 1715 the jury found Defoe guilty of writing and causing publication of the *Flying Post* item about Lord Anglesey. Chief Justice Parker, a Whig, before whom Defoe had appeared in April 1713, deferred passing judgement until the autumn.

Defoe faced a heavy fine and perhaps a prison sentence as well. However, events that took place between his conviction and his sentence worked in his favour. In the Lords debate about the impeachment of Oxford and Bolingbroke the Earl of Anglesey made a speech betraying his Jacobite sympathies. Then, on 6 September 1715, the Jacobites raised the flag of revolt in Scotland, and twice tried to land on the Devonshire coast. Defoe used his knowledge of Scotland to write a series of pamphlets on the rebellion, giving advice on how to prevent a recurrence. He also joined in attacking English Jacobites like his old enemy Dr Sacheverell.

Chief Justice Parker, who had led the prosecution of Dr Sacheverell in 1710, was well aware of Defoe's abhorrence of Jacobitism, and may have suggested his recruitment as a government propagandist as a condition of his freedom. One of the Secretaries of State, Charles, Viscount Townshend, agreed to take Defoe into government service in order to neutralize the Tory opposition. Defoe would have to maintain the pose of a moderate Tory, loyal to the now imprisoned Robert Harley, Lord Oxford, and bitter against the Whigs. He was paid to start a moderate Tory monthly newspaper, *Mercurius Politicus*, and to infiltrate the extreme Tory, or Jacobite Press. He was once more back in the Secret Service, but now in the seedy role of nark and even *agent provocateur*. He no longer met and conversed with kings and Lord Treasurers, as he had done with William of Orange, Godolphin and Harley.

Although in *Mercurius Politicus* Defoe was able to write in the lively, intelligent style of the former *Review*, some of his government work was sordid and shameful. In the spring of 1717 he managed to infiltrate Nathaniel Mist's *Weekly Journal*, the most successful Tory paper in England. Mist himself was a wild, dangerous character, who probably did not trust Defoe but valued his flair for producing readable copy on every conceivable subject. As the circulation rose in 1718 to more than 10,000 Mist raised Defoe's wages from one to two pounds a week. Defoe nevertheless complained in a Secret Service report to Charles Delafaye, the Under-Secretary of State: 'I am Sir, for this service posted among Papists, Jacobites and enraged High Tories, a generation who I profess my very soul abhors: I am obliged to hear traitorous expressions and outrageous words against his Majesty's person, and government, and most faithful servants; and smile at it all as if I approved it.' The editor of Defoe's *Letters* comments: 'That Defoe was working for Mist's and other Tory publications was well enough known at the time, but that he was engaged to do so by the Whig Ministry was a secret so well kept that it did not become public knowledge until five letters to De la Faye were published in the *London Review* in 1864.'

Even without this written proof Defoe's contemporaries suspected what he was up to, as we see from this verse in Read's *Weekly Journal*, a rival of Mist's:

> *A fawning, canting, double hearted knave*
> Is the inscription fittest for his grave.
> Look there's the bribes with which this Wretch was paid
> When he his country and its right betrayed.
>
> Lo that false Vizard which the knave puts on,
> Wrote one day *Pro* and th'other day writ *Con*.
> There's no such Proteus to be found in story,
> One hour a Whig and the next hour a Tory.
> Sometimes Dissenter and sometimes High Church
> Strait turns his coat leaves both sides in the lurch.
> He wrote for all cause that did yield him most.

By the year of the publication of *Robinson Crusoe* – 1719, 'When not an old woman that can go the price of it, but buys thy Life and Adventures' – Defoe was writing anonymously for Mist's *Weekly Journal*, for his own Tory *Mercurius Politicus* and a Whig version, *Mercurius Britannicus*, for the extreme Tory *Dormer's Newsletter*, and his own Whig *White-Hall Evening Post*, which gave the programmes for

Newmarket races as well as extensive coverage of trials for piracy, robbery and murder. In 1720, the year of the South Sea Bubble, in which shares soared in price from £100 to £1200, before collapsing, Defoe used his financial expertise, first to cool the excitement, and afterwards to restore public confidence in the worth of the shares. In bolstering public credit in 1721, Defoe was rendering Walpole the same service that he had rendered Harley in 1710.

At the end of 1719 Defoe started two more papers, the *Manufacturer* and the *Daily Post*. By the start of 1721, according to Paula Backscheider's calculations, Defoe's eight periodicals together probably earned him as much as £1,200 a year, and she sees him transformed into 'a happy man going from coffeehouse to coffeehouse, mingling easily with the financiers at Jonathan's and Garraway's, with the churchmen at Child's, dropping in at the Temple coffeehouses and talking politics and economics, or exchanging jokes and good-natured gibes'. This sudden well-being, after the decades of solitude and want, appears to have gone to Defoe's head and sent him back to his 'whore of trade'.

On 6 August 1722 Defoe agreed to pay £1,000 to the Corporation of Colchester in Essex for a ninety-nine-year lease on several hundred acres of land. For an annual rent of £120 he acquired the right to 'fell, cut down and sell all manner of timber ... and log trees ... on any part of the premises'. He planned to use this rich farm land to breed cattle and raise corn, also selling cheese, butter, veal and beef. His timber could be sold to the naval yards at Chatham, if shipbuilding was stagnant at Ipswich and Harwich. He also hoped to produce and market pitch, tar, rosin and turpentine. Over the next few years he added honey and oysters to the goods he dispatched to market, and from Colchester he even sold metal buttons, tanned leather, cloth and imported anchovies. Most of the produce went to London, but Paula Backscheider claims that he was making sales as far away as Coventry and Lichfield in the West Midlands. The Colchester enterprise provided Defoe with the economic information in Letter One of the *Tour*, which starts in Essex in 1722.

Thanks to his many journals, his Colchester farm, and his Secret Service work for the Whigs, Defoe was as busy during the first ten years of the reign of George I as at any time in his life. He may even have come to hope that his greater earnings would last free him from his creditors. But he must also have felt that the purpose and pride had gone out of his work since the fall of Harley. For almost three decades, from 1685 until 1714, Defoe's career had been committed to principles, for which he had risked his liberty and even his life. He had fought at the Battle of Sedgemoor and published a pamphlet in 1688 denouncing James II, an act that could have brought him to trial before Judge Jeffreys. He had been a friend and adviser to his political hero William III. At the start of the reign of Queen Anne he had suffered the pillory and Newgate rather than compromise his principles. From 1704 to 1713 he had single-handedly written the *Review*, in which he could state his own opinion, free of pressure from either the Whigs or the Tories. With the same freedom of conscience he served the administration from 1704 until 1714, playing a major role in general elections, the Union with Scotland, winning the Peace, and frustrating the Jacobites.

For thirty years, until the accession of George I, Defoe had had reason to take pride in his career in politics and journalism. During the next decade his career was lucrative but ignoble. Instead of speaking his mind in his own *Review*, he now, when writing anonymously, had to disguise his voice in Whig or Tory journals. Instead of sounding out public opinion in England and Scotland, he descended to sneaking on Mist's *Weekly Journal*. Instead of addressing his mind to politics, trade and religion, he was listing the runners at Newmarket. Partly because he had lost his influence as a journalist, pamphleteer and secret adviser to statesmen, Defoe turned to writing books in order to express the thoughts and fantasies that teemed in his ever-active brain. This was in part a recycling into bound volumes of some of the millions of words from earlier pamphlets and the *Review*, and, of course, recycling the books into journalism in progress, such as *Mercurius Politicus* or the *White-Hall Evening Post*.

During the five years between the accession of George I and the publication of *Robinson Crusoe* in 1719 Defoe wrote lives of Peter the Great of Russia and Charles XII of Sweden, stories of pirates and murderers, bogus memoirs of soldiers and sailors, a history of the Church of Scotland, a manual of Christian family living, as well as dozens of short books and pamphlets. Defoe scholars still cannot agree on which of the hundreds of titles are really his. Occasionally one finds attributions that are inaccurate: the style is not Defoe's; but more often, he is indeed the author – as in the case of what seems an unlikely candidate, a book published in 1718 entitled *A Continuation of Letters written by a Turkish Spy at Paris. Giving an Impartial Account to the Diva at Constantinople of the most remarkable transactions of Europe, and discovering several Intrigues and Secrets of the Christian Courts, especially of that of Paris, continuous from the year 1687 to the year 1693. Written in Arabic, Translated into Italian, and from thence into English.* However, the account in 'Mohamed's' third letter of why Louis XIV in 1688 failed to stop a revolt by the 'malcontents' of England is pure Defoe in style and quotes one of his favourite maxims, comparing the French and English armies: '(viz.) that of the French, if the soldiers will but follow, the officers will always lead; and that of the English, if the officers will but lead, the soldiers will always follow'.

To modern readers, accustomed to thinking of books as either 'fiction' or 'non-fiction', it may seem odd that Defoe should pose as 'Mohamed', a Turkish spy at the court of Louis XIV. The preface to one edition of *A Journal of the Plague Year* denounces Defoe as a liar for his literary pretence. We like to make a distinction between what we think of as real and imagined, fact and fiction, true and false, news and propaganda. For Defoe the distinction was less clear cut. Just as his works of fiction, such as *Moll Flanders*, are based on fact, so his ostensibly factual *Tour* is full of amazing fibs and flights of imagination. As a journalist, Defoe used all the Fleet Street tricks and devices that were later to be satirized by Thackeray in *Pendennis* and Evelyn Waugh in *Scoop*. In his books, as in his journalism, he mixed fact with fiction in order to tell a better story and entertain the reader.

Defoe would not have agreed with, or even understood, the modern idea that fiction is a superior kind of writing to non-fiction, or even journalism. All the greatest authors of his age, notably Swift, Steele and Addison, were first and foremost journalists, and are nowadays so remembered. Swift's masterpiece *Gulliver's Travels* was a satire rather than an adventure story like *Robinson Crusoe*, but neither book is a novel in the modern sense of the term. The ambitious literary man in Defoe's age wanted to be a famous poet like Pope or Dryden, or a successful playwright like Addison, just as his modern counterpart dreams of winning the Booker Prize. Defoe himself achieved his greatest success with the verse satire *The True-Born Englishman*, but failed to win any plaudits for his serious five-volume poem *Jure Divino*. Although he continued to write occasional verses, he was honest enough to see that he was not a poet, or even an essayist in the class of Steele and Addison. He was a journeyman writer, or hack, to use the term in the sense that was then becoming accepted. He was, however, a hack of genius.

It is only at this late stage, when Defoe is nearing sixty and embarking on his great career as an author, that little by little we start to learn something about his private life and his family. We do not learn much, since almost nothing remains of his private correspondence. With Defoe, we face the problem that no contemporaries seem to have found him worthy of note. In all the letters and journals of prominent men and women of the early eighteenth century we look in vain for a mention of him. Even the hostile lampoonists, who vilified Defoe as a turncoat and devil, never ascribed to him any particular personal characteristic. From *The Lives of the Poets* we gain an intimate knowledge of Dryden, Addison, Steele, Prior, Pope and Richard Savage, but even if he had wished to, Dr Johnson could not have filled a page on the character of Defoe.

As a Dissenter from the trading class, Defoe may have felt an outsider even before his bankruptcy in 1692, but it was this that most probably turned him into a loner. Like all chronic debtors, Defoe was obliged to withdraw from the feasts and receptions of his liveried company, from his favourite coffee house or club, from the 'treats' of colleagues and even the dinner tables of friends and neighbours. He would not accept hospitality that he could not return. Jonathan Swift, who was a single man and never incurred any serious debt, complained of the cost of having to entertain the Brothers – the Tory statesmen, authors and lovers of good wine. Defoe could never have joined such a club. His bankruptcy could even have meant excommunication by the Presbyterian Church, which equated financial failure with sin.

Oddly enough, there is no record of where Defoe worshipped, though he probably went to the meeting house in Newington Green, which he knew from his years at Dr Morton's Academy. Nor do we know if he met his famous Dissenting neighbour Isaac Watts, who spent most of his life at the house of Defoe's old adversary, Sir Thomas Abney, in what is now Abney Park Cemetery, on the northern side of Stoke Newington Church Street. The parish records say that Defoe served for a year as Surveyor of Highways, which may explain the knowledge of roads he reveals in the *Tour*, but they also show that he paid £10 in 1721 to be excused the duties of overseer of the poor, and a churchwarden. This could have been an example of how some Church of England parish councils elected Dissenters to make them pay money in lieu of service. Defoe certainly thought so, as he explained in a subsequent pamphlet. However, the local historian A. J. Shirren thinks this did not apply in Defoe's case: 'The wording of the minutes rather suggests that Defoe himself had put forward the idea of paying a fine to be excused all offices, not only the ones to which he had been elected ... Further, when Sir John Hartopp, the leading local Nonconformist was elected Churchwarden, he was excused service without payment of a fine. The local vestry may very well have intended the election as a compliment to a well-known local resident.'

By 1724, when we get our first glimpse of Defoe's Stoke Newington home life, three of his six children had married and started families of their own. The elder son, Benjamin, first appeared in the story in 1709, when Defoe took him to Edinburgh to attend the university there, which, unlike Oxford and Cambridge, welcomed Dissenters. Benjamin did not finish his studies, and was soon employed by Defoe to sub-edit and work on his writing. He became so adept at re-cycling articles as books, and books as articles, that he soon became a journalist in his own right. During the South Sea Bubble year of 1720 Benjamin came up in court for attacking the Walpole administration which employed his father. Benjamin married and fathered no fewer than seventeen children – which contributed to his later financial problems. Defoe's younger son, Daniel, went into trade with more success than his father, and also seems to have made a happy marriage. The eldest daughter, Maria, married a suitable Nonconformist man, leaving the three other girls – Hannah, Henrietta and Sophia – still living at home in 1724. We have an account of them from a visitor called Henry Baker, the wooer and future husband of Sophia.

Henry Baker had been a bookseller's apprentice and had devised a method for teaching the deaf to read, write, lip-read and speak. In 1724, when he was twenty-six, he began to spend four days a week in Stoke Newington, where he was teaching a deaf pupil. He described this time in a later memoir, written in the third person:

> Among the first who desired his acquaintance there was Mr De Foe, a gentleman well known by his writings, who had newly built there, a very handsome house as a retirement from London and amused his time either in the cultivation of a large and pleasant garden, or in the pursuit of his studies, which he found means of making very profitable. He was now at least sixty years of age, afflicted with the gout and stone, but maintained all his mental faculties entire. Mr Baker readily accepted his invitation, and was so pleased with his conversation that he seldom came to Newington without paying a visit to Mr Defoe. He met usually at the tea table his three lovely daughters, who were admired for their beauty, their

education and their prudent conduct, and if sometimes Mr Defoe's disorders made company inconvenient, Mr Baker was entertained by them either singly or together, and that commonly in the garden when the weather was favourable.

Like many people who write of themselves in the third person singular, Baker was rather a pompous young man, who greatly upset Defoe by his subsequent haggling over Sophie's dowry. Nevertheless he remains the principal source of information about Defoe's final years, as told in the closing chapter of this book. Baker's account of Defoe and his daughters at home in 1724 is only a snapshot, and sadly does not include the elusive Mary Defoe. Yet Defoe himself, in some of his strangest and most unjustly neglected books, has painted a vivid picture of eighteenth-century family life in a household 'not 150 miles from Newington', as he would say. These books are the homilies or manuals on Christian family life, including advice on the bringing up of children, the choice of suitable marriage partners, and one of the first ever guides to a happy sex life. Defoe backs up his argument with moral tales, or what we would now call 'case studies', whose characters often develop a life and interest of their own, so that what began as a manual soon becomes a series of short stories, or even a novel. It is possible to see in Defoe's pious tracts the origin of the works of Samuel Richardson, Jane Austen, Anthony Trollope and the Brontës, in which the dominant theme is courtship and marriage. These manuals of family life and sexual behaviour also help us to understand some of his more famous books, such as *Robinson Crusoe*, *Moll Flanders* and *Roxana*.

The first of these manuals is *The Family Instructor*, published in 1715, and containing three parts: 'Fathers and Children', 'Masters and Servants', and 'Husbands and Wives'. A second volume was published in 1718 in two parts, the first relating to 'Family Breaches and their obstructing Religious Duties', the second to the 'Great Mistake of mixing the passions in the managing and correcting of Children'. The success of *The Family Instructor* encouraged Defoe to publish in 1722 *Religious Courtship. Being an Historical Discourse on the Necessity of Marrying Religious Husbands and Wives Only, as also of Husbands and Wives being of the same opinion in religion with one another*. Oddly enough, this sombre sounding book appeared at the same time as *Moll Flanders*, whose heroine chose her husbands on quite different principles. Defoe's pioneering sex guide was published in 1727 under the eye-catching title of *Conjugal Lewdness or Matrimonial Whoredom, A Treatise concerning the use and abuse of the Marriage Bed.* A fourth book on manners and morals, *The Compleat English Gentleman*, was found in draft form after Defoe's death, and was not published until 1890.

The whole of volume one of *The Family Instructor* concerns a middle-aged couple who try to enforce a stricter Christian observance on themselves, their children and servants. Although he insists that the story is based on fact, Defoe has made it a parable in order to disguise the identity of the characters. The family, he says, could be either Dissenter or Church of England, 'and no offence can be taken here on one side or the other'. Both the father and mother are shown as professing Christians who, 'acknowledging God in their mouths, yet take no effective care to honour him with their practice'. They have four almost grown-up children when they are blessed with an 'after-thought', an adored little boy called Tommy. As is sometimes the case in real life, but much more often in pious fiction, Tommy is an earnest, precocious child, who asks, for instance, why God has granted him the gift of speech, but denied it to dogs and cats. When the father tells him to pray, and to thank God for his creation and preservation, the child replies with this awkward question:

CHILD: Do you do so Father?
FATHER: Yes child.
CHILD: O, because I have never heard you do so father.

Little Tommy is gently reproving his father and mother for having abandoned communal family prayer. Most Anglicans at this time prayed together only in church or, if they could afford it, kept a chaplain to read the services for them. Defoe's patron Robert Harley was thought odd by his colleagues because he went home to family prayers each evening.

Although he is using little Tommy to preach a Christian message, Defoe also makes him ask some natural, childish questions:

CHILD: And must you die if you sin, Mother?
MOTHER: Yes my dear.
CHILD: But you never sinned I hope then.
MOTHER: Alas, my Dear, I am a great sinner.
CHILD: Why, you must not die Mother, you shall not die Mother, shall you?

(The Child weeps.)

Defoe understands that children of Tommy's age are often made miserable by the thought of their parents dying.

Under Tommy's influence his parents bring back family prayer and try to reform their older children. The mother resolves to stop her daughters playing at cards all night, going to theatres, wearing patches, reading foolish romances, singing idle songs, taking God's name in vain and going for walks on Sunday. She goes to her elder daughter's room and throws her novels and plays on the fire, leaving only the Bible and one sacred book. A furious row ensues and, as the mother tells her to keep the sabbath, the daughter 'turns away and with a kind of humming, low voice, sings the tune of a new play-house song', at which the mother strikes her, saying, 'Your contempt of your mother I place to my own account, but for your contempt for your maker, take that on God's account.'

The younger daughter complies because she has spent ten weeks at the home of an aunt, a pious Dissenter:

SECOND DAUGHTER: I thought I was in Heaven there, to what I am at home; everything there was so sober, so pretty, so grave, and yet so cheerful, so pleasant, so innocently merry.

THE MOTHER: Well my dear, how do they spend the Sabbath at your aunt? Not as we do, I dare say!

SD: No indeed, Mother, after quite another fashion: the young ladies are obliged to be down stairs half an hour after nine in the morning, ready dressed. Then my uncle calls to prayers, and soon after they all go away, either to the Church [the Uncle is Anglican] or to the Meeting House, but whichever it is, they are almost sure to meet together after the sermon, sometimes at the very door, and the children and servants, not one stirs from home: In the evening my Uncle calls them all together, reads to them in some good book, and then sings psalms, and goes to prayer; when that is over they go to supper, then they spend an hour or two in the most pleasant discourse imaginable; it is always about something religious.

The second son of the family also complies with his parents' wishes, but his elder brother defies their father: 'What, must I forsake all my mirth and good company, and turn hermit in my young days? I'll go to the galleys rather. I'll be content to go to the West Indies or be a Foot Soldier, or anything rather than be made such a recluse. Not go to the Park! Not see a play! Be as demure as a Quaker and set up for a saint!' He proceeds to buy a commission in the dragoons and goes off to war in Europe, much to the sorrow of his father, who swears he will never receive him again except as a penitent. The elder daughter is unwillingly sent to stay with the puritanical aunt, and eventually marries a pious cousin. She seems to be going back to her wicked ways, when she gets this alarming letter from her brother at Cambrai:

> My last gave an account of my being wounded at the siege of Douai, of which after a time I was cured; though I lay all the winter sick at Lille, now I am the miserablest creature in the world: I am taken prisoner-of-war last week and am brought to this place, having my right arm broken by a musket ball, and tomorrow it must be cut off. God is just, sister: I cut off my father's right arm when I broke from him in my violence, and went abroad without his consent, now I have lost my right arm by just retribution.

The father sends his eldest son the money to come back to England, but will not receive him in the home. The young man goes to stay with his married sister:

> After some time ... he grew melancholy and disturbed and offered two or three times to destroy himself; he removed from his sister, and God not being pleased to grant him either the Grace of repentance from his former sins, or to prevent future; he fell into an extravagant life, ill company, and drinking, and died in a miserable condition, atheistic and impenitent; having never seen his father, nor so much as desiring it, till on his deathbed, being delirious, he cried out for his father, his father: That he had abused his father! and begged to see his father! That he might ask his forgiveness! But he died before his father, who happened to be in the country, could be sent for.

In a preface to the second volume of *The Family Instructor* Defoe remarks on the common belief that sequels are never as good as the first book, citing the case of *Paradise Regained*. Moreover, he says, 'Mr Milton himself differed from the whole world in his opinion about it, affirmed that it was much the better poem, and gave this reason for the general dislike (viz) that people had a common sense of the loss of Paradise but not an equal gust [taste] for the regaining it.' In Defoe's second volume wicked and irreligious women appear as the culprits for family strife, although he denies prejudice against the sex. The opening story tells of a married couple, now scarcely on speaking terms because the wife refuses to join in family prayers. Their quarrel reaches a climax at the eclipse of the sun on 22 April 1715, 'the subject of all conversation at the time, having been as is well known so total, and the darkness so great, as that the like had not been known in that age'. The man rather unwisely quips that the moon is like a cross wife, that 'when she is out of temper could eclipse her husband'. His wife flies into a passion, 'and being of a sharp wit' answers, 'I warrant you that a wife, like the moon, has no light but what she borrows from her husband . . . [but] she can eclipse him when she pleases.' Having got the worst of this astronomical wrangle, the husband feebly retorts that 'the whole house is dark because of lack of family worship'.

Still smarting from the abuse of this clever, shrewish woman, the husband goes for sympathy to a friend who has also married an irreligious wife, but apparently for the sake of her money. It also appears that the friend is a Dissenter, and lives with his wife at the home of her High Tory brother, Sir Richard. The friend then relates how no grace was said at the very first meal he took with these irreligious in-laws: 'It happened at length we all sat down to table without a chaplain, and as Sir Richard made no offer to stand up, so no sooner was the dinner set [on the table] but my Lady had her knife in a boiled turkey, and we all fell to work as decently, and with as little respect to Him whose Hand fed us, as any pack of hounds in the country.'

When the husband expresses to his wife his astonishment at this omission, 'Phoo, says she, is that all? We never trouble our heads about those things . . . It's an odd thing for a gentleman to meddle with.' At dinner that evening the wife tries to embarrass her husband by making him repeat at the table what he had told her in private. She hopes to make him ashamed of his trading, Dissenter origins. The courteous Sir Richard refuses to be uncivil towards his brother-in-law, whereupon his sister loses her temper and flounces out of the room: 'Sir Richard, the best humoured man in the world, rose and took hold of her, swore she should not go, and dragged her back a good way, but she flung from him. I followed her, but she was too nimble for me and got into her room, and with flinging the door after her, and I too near her, struck me on the nose, as set me bleeding most violently.' When Sir Richard is told the cause of the row, he forthwith vows to say grace at all meals in future, at which his sister sobs and sulks for a further two hours.

The two husbands now resolve to defy their wives and insist on religious observance at home. They take as their inspiration Joshua's words to the people of Israel: 'As for me and my house we will serve the Lord.' Defoe also cites the example of his biblical namesake, 'Daniel, who would not, no not to avoid the being devoured by lions, omit his public and perhaps private worship ... Daniel might have satisfied himself with his private retirement and performed his private prayers in his closet, and this he might have done in safety.'

One of these irreligious women tries to tempt her husband to bed before he has made his public devotions. She then discovers that her own brother, Sir Richard, is falling under her husband's sway: 'Horrid brother! What's the matter with you all of a sudden, you are now turned so sober. This fit of religion will be over with you quickly ... If I were to see you and Sir Charles —, and Jack T— together at the Green Man, I should hear you damn and swear as fast as ever you did; and I warrant we shall have you come home as drunk as a wheel-barrow.' But Sir Richard has put his past behind him: 'I see it plainly now, sister; very plainly; a man once touched with a sense of duty to his maker, will like Daniel, die rather than omit it.'

In the second part of this volume, which deals with correcting children, Defoe once more shows a woman in the wrong. A story is again used to make his point that children should not be punished in anger; indeed, that often a true parent strikes his flesh and blood 'with more tears in his own eyes than he brings out in the eyes of the child'. He takes the case of a hot-tempered man, who one day is beating his son so hard that the neighbour knocks at the door to intervene, on the pretext of asking him out for a glass of wine. The father agrees, but says to his son: 'I'll give you your hire before I sleep, sirrah, I will so.'

At this point the governess, who has been watching from the stair-head, intervenes to protest at the breaking-off of the punishment. Described by Defoe as a gentlewoman, a relative of the boy's mother, and also hot-tempered, the governess now upbraids the father: 'Why don't you pay him? You haven't given him half enough. He'll never be good for anything if you don't pay him soundly!' Afterwards, over a glass of wine, the neighbour ventures to criticize the behaviour of the governess, to which the father replies, 'She is a good Christian.' But his companion is sceptical: 'If you had not said so, I should have believed quite otherwise of her ... It's a dangerous thing to trust the correction of children to those who want the bonds of nature.'

At the end of volume two of *The Family Instructor* we are introduced to the home of a man engaged in the shipping business, especially West Indian trade. He is a well-meaning but tipsy fellow, who lives in fear of a spiteful, irreligious wife. 'The Sabbath Day', we are told, 'was generally among them a day of company and diversion; after dinner the time was generally passed in drinking by the father; and either in sleep or in walking in the fields by the mother and daughter.' In addition to their almost grown-up children, the couple have an 'after thought', Jacky, the equivalent of Tommy in the earlier story. The mother delights in dressing him up as a clergyman in a cassock, scarf and bands, just in order to show her contempt for religion. When the husband objects, 'she rallies him with his drunkenness and the fits of repentance in between'.

A kindly sea captain discovers that one of the maidservants, Margaret, has been teaching Jacky about religion, and pays her two guineas towards his education. When Jacky is old enough to go to grammar school, he is given as his attendant a Negro boy of about fourteen called Toby. Soon Jacky is asking Toby about his earlier life in Barbados, and is shocked to hear that the black people are not allowed to be Christians:

JACKY: What do the black mans do?

TOBY: Make the sugar, make the grog [rum], much great work, weary work, all day.

JACKY: What, do they work on the Sabbath-Day?

TOBY: No, they sing, they dance, they sleep on Sunday.

JACKY: What do the white mans do then?

TOBY: They feast, they dine, they see folks home [go visiting].

JACKY: Why, do they not teach their servants to know God?

TOBY: No indeed. Negro man mustn't know white man's God. When Negro man know God, he go take the name [is baptized] and be free.

JACKY: So they won't let them know God, because they shall not be free mans, is that the reason Toby? They are very wicked mans, Toby, very cruel.

TOBY: Yes, very cruel, they beat the Negro mans very much cruel for go to church.

Jacky's mother scolds him for talking to Toby in this fashion: 'You fool, you, you'll put it into the boy's head to be baptised, and then he'll run away!' Here, the father takes Jacky's side in wanting to have Toby baptized:

FATHER: Must the boy be sent to the Devil for fear of running away! For my part, let him run away when he will, if he can be brought to be a true Christian.

MOTHER: Why need you care where anybody goes? You know well enough where you are going!

FATHER: To be sure, you act by the poor boy [Jacky] as I could not do by a stranger for all the world. You make me tremble to hear you!

MOTHER: Oh dear! You tremble! Tis because you haven't yet two bottles in your belly then; drunkards always shake till they have their dose.

Unlike most authors of pious tracts, Defoe had an ear for the language of ordinary sinners. He also tried to face up to some of the questions arising from slavery. When Jacky asks his father whether Toby has a soul, the answer is definite: 'Yes certainly child, for we all come from one original, old Adam.' To the subsequent question – why are some people black? – the father replies: 'Some say it was the effect of the curse of Cain . . . But we have natural reasons for it child, such as the violent heat of the climate . . . If a white man and woman were to go thither, and live by themselves, without mingling with the rest of the natives, yet in time their posterity would be black.' Defoe was wrong, for there are still white Barbadians to the present day, descendants of those transported during the seventeenth century. Yet his belief that Africans have souls, and descend from Adam, shows more respect for them than the Darwinite creed that they have no souls but descend from the apes.

While *The Family Instructor* brought in many topics and characters, Defoe's next moral tract, *Religious Courtship*, is solely concerned with one father's efforts to find suitable husbands for his daughters. It is tempting to see Defoe in this 'ancient, grave gentleman in a village near London', and his own three daughters in these 'very agreeable women, and what was still better . . . sober, modest, sensible and religious ladies'. But the gentleman in the story is rich enough to attract a host of suitors to the house, while, as we know from some of his final letters, Defoe struggled to find even £500 for his youngest daughter's dowry. The three fictional women are in a position to choose husbands not for their wealth, or even their charm, but for their religious principles. As one of them says, 'I would not marry a man that made no profession of religion, no, though he had ten thousand pounds a year, and I had but a hundred pounds to my portion.' However, Defoe explains at the start that he is not sectarian: 'I shall most carefully avoid giving any room here so much as to guess what opinion in religion they were bred up in, or whether the old Gentleman was a Churchman or a Dissenter.'

The book consists mostly of dialogue, and begins with the youngest sister telling the oldest why she cannot accept her present suitor:

> YOUNGEST SISTER: There's nothing of religion in him. No, I am not sure, but we have conversations this month now, and I never heard one word about it come out of his mouth, and if I speak a word he turns it off, and does it so cleverly, that I cannot put in another word for my life . . . Another time I asked if he was not a Papist. Immediately he fell to crossing of himself all over, and made himself and me so merry at it, that though I was really troubled about it, I could not for my life, get the least serious thing out of him.

The girl's father grows irate with what he regards as trivial objections:

> FATHER: I desire no reason, nor no discourse; answer me the question in short, whether you will have him or no; it will raise my passion less than your impertinent reasons.
>
> YD: If it must be so, Sir, without hearing any reasons, then my answer is no, no never while I live, and I leave my reasons for it to Him who judges rightful judgment.
>
> FATHER: Then from this time forward you are no relation of mine, any more than my cook-maid.

The father soon masters his temper, but then tries to persuade the eldest daughter to hear the suit of the son of a wealthy merchant, assuring her of his sober, religious character. But she, too, is reluctant:

> ELDEST DAUGHTER: I am in no haste, Sir, to marry. The times terrify me; the education, the manners, the conduct of gentlemen is now so universally loose, that I think for a young woman to marry, is like a horse running into battle; I have no courage so much as to think.
>
> FATHER: But there are a great many sober, civilized young Gentlemen in the world, tis hard to reproach them all because many of them are wicked.
>
> ED: Sir, it is those civilized people, which I speak of; for even

those who now pass for sober, are not like what it was formerly;
when you look narrowly among them, as there are in the gross
ten rakes to one sober man, so among the sober men, and whose
morals will bear any character, then are ten atheists to one
religious man; and which is worse than all the rest, if a woman
finds a religious man, it is three to one again whether he agrees
with her in principle [i.e. adheres to the same creed] and so she
is in danger of being undone even in the best.

FATHER: I never heard the like in my life! Why what are my
daughters made of! What, is nothing good enough in the world
for you?

Only the middle daughter of the three says she does not mind about
her suitor's religion, or whether indeed he has any. But the eldest
warns her at least not to marry a Quaker, or worse, 'that you may not
run into marriage blindfold, and make your marriage, as old Hobbes
said of his death, a leap in the dark'.* At this point the father introduces
a rich, charming suitor, a merchant from Leghorn, where there were
many Englishmen. Immediately the eldest daughter raises the question:

ED: All I desire to know is, that he is a Protestant. I hope you are
sure of this, Sir.

FATHER: Dear child what makes you talk so?

ED: He has been a long while in Italy, Sir, where they say they
are all Papists.

FATHER: Why so did I, child, when I was a young man, but never
turned Papist. I dare say he is a Protestant, I never heard anyone
suspect him before.

Some years have passed, and the middle sister has married the
Leghorn merchant. The father enquires about her from his youngest
daughter, now also married, and from the eldest daughter:

FATHER: Well Betty, you have been to visit your sister in her new
house, I find; how do you like the things?

YD: Sir, she is nobly married to be sure, she has a house like a
palace.

FATHER: He always had the finest collection of any merchant at
Leghorn.

ED: I like his fancy to pictures very well, but methinks I don't

---

* These were supposed to be the last words of the philosopher, Thomas Hobbes.

admire his having so many crucifixes and church-pieces among them.

FATHER: It is the custom in Italy, Child, all people have them.

ED: That is because they make a religious use of them, and then I observed he hangs them all just as they do; the crucifixes, Passion-Pictures hang just by the bedside, his Altar-piece just at the upper end of the room . . .

FATHER: Your sister is undone! . . . She is indeed undone! . . . And more than that, I have undone her; the man's a Papist (The father bursts into tears).

The father now discovers that his Leghorn son-in-law has an inner room, which he approaches through his closet. It is an oratory, a little convent chapel, 'and there stands an Altar and an Altar-piece over it, with a Crucifix and the Ascension above it'. The father blames himself bitterly for having assured his daughter that her suitor was a Protestant.

Eight years later the merchant from Leghorn dies, and the widow goes back to see her father and sisters, both of whom are now married. She explains the horror she felt on learning her husband's true religion. No kindness, no tenderness, no affection, she tells her sisters, can compensate for a difference in faiths. The youngest daughter cannot resist asking: 'Well Sister, and what became of your smart answers to my Sister . . . that if he was not of your opinion, you would be of his; that if he was a Christian Catholic, you were a Catholic Christian; and so you would have no difference about that . . .' The three young women in *Religious Courtship* are so different in character, so disputatious and so strong-minded, that it is not hard to see them as Defoe's own daughters – and very worthy chips off that cantankerous block. In the same way, *Conjugal Lewdness* probably tells us about the sexual life of Daniel and Mary Defoe.

In spite of its title, this is really a hymn to the joys of sex in marriage. The Puritans of Defoe's age, unlike the Victorian Nonconformists and Evangelicals, regarded sex as one of the God-given pleasures, like music, wine and tobacco. Although they abhorred blasphemous oaths or taking the name of the Lord in vain, they were not especially prudish in talking of bodily functions. The earthiness of the Puritans came from their Old Testament reading, especially the Book of Genesis. On the very first page of *Conjugal Lewdness* Defoe explains that we learn from Adam and Eve our sense of modesty in discourse, behaviour and 'in regard to sexes', for he used the word in its plural form. He reminds us, as he had done before in an article in the *Review*, that Milton in *Paradise Lost* not only approved but hymned the delights of sexual love, as in Book Four:

> Into their inmost bower
> Handed they went; and eased the putting off
> Their troublesome disguises which we wear,
> Strait side by side were laid, nor turned I ween
> Adam from his fair spouse; nor Eve the rites
> Mysterious of connubial love refused;
> Whatever hypocrites austerely talk
> Of purity and place and innocence
> Defaming as impure what God declares
> Pure, and commands to some, leaves free to all.

Defoe understood and enjoyed the seeming paradox that the Puritan Milton could write some of the most erotic and sensual poetry in the English language. Like Milton, Defoe believed that sex was only permissible in marriage:

> Hail wedded love, mysterious law, true source
> Of human offspring, sole proprietie
> In Paradise of all things common else.
> By thee adulterous lust was driven from men . . .

And also that the ecstasy of the marriage bed could not be found

> in the bought smile
> Of harlots, loveless, joyless, unindeared,
> Casual fruition, nor in Court Amours
> Mixt Dance, or wanton Mask, or Midnight Bal . . .

As we shall see, Defoe believed that a harlot like Moll Flanders, or a devotee of masked balls like Roxana, derived little or no pleasure from sex. However, he gives the impression in *Conjugal Lewdness* that most women are avid for the delights of the marriage bed, or what Lord Rochester called 'the frolic part', and goes so far as to say that some women are bent on having 'the frolic part' without the consequent chore of bearing and raising children:

For a young, handsome and agreeable lady, with all the blushes and modesty of her virgin years about her, and under the best of education, to marry, go naked to bed and receive the man as it were in her arms, and then say she hopes she shall have

no children . . . this is a laying [a proposition] I cannot understand; it will bear no modest construction in my thoughts, and
in a word, is neither more nor less than acknowledging that
she would have the pleasure of lying with a man, but would
not have the least interruption from her usual company keeping; the jollity and mirth of her younger days; that she would
not abate her pleasure, she would not be confined at home,
or loaded with the cares of being a mother . . .

According to Defoe, it is not his business to write of those 'unhappy
ladies who venture upon the dark doing, in pursuit of the wicked design
against child-bearing; they run great risk in taking such medicine; and
tis great odds but they ruin themselves by it.' He does not make clear
if this medicine is a contraceptive or an abortefact, but he roundly
condemns the quack who dispenses it as well as the wife who takes it:

But for an honest woman, openly and lawfully married! Whose
husband is publicly known; who lives well, and acknowledges
her to be his wife, and beds with her every night; for this
woman to desire to be barren, much more to endeavour to
prevent or, which is the same thing to destroy the conception,
blast the fruit of her own body, poison her blood and ruin
her constitution that she may have no children! this can have
nothing in it but witchcraft and the Devil; tis seeking the man
merely as such, merely for the frolic part, as my Lord Rochester puts it.

Defoe regards as 'conjugal lewdness' all sexual activity that cannot
result in childbirth. Intercourse when the wife is known to be pregnant
he calls 'an end so base, so mean, so absurd that no Christian man can
plead it in excuse'. He seems to believe that intercourse during the
woman's menstrual period results in children with scrofula, or 'scabs
and blisters upon their poor innocent lambs faces'. Once again, he airs
his view that sodomites should be tried and executed in secret, and
here presumably means those who use their wives in this fashion. He
also condemns husbands who demand their conjugal rights when their
wives are suffering 'woman's ailments', and wives who expect their
husbands to perform when stricken with palsy, epilepsy, dropsy, gall-
stones and gout. (Defoe himself suffered from these last two.) He
sometimes writes as if he believes that women are largely motivated
and even consumed by sexual desire long after their child-bearing days:

'If a woman of 55 years is asked why she married, she has nothing to say but to blush and look down, and to acknowledge that she did it to gratify (as the poet expresses it modestly) a frolic part.' It does not seem to occur to Defoe that a woman of fifty-five might marry for companionship.

In *Conjugal Lewdness* Defoe makes some interesting comments on the sexual life of royalty. He commends the Old Testament patriarchs for their practice of monogamy, but notes that 'the grosser use of women came in with David, as the setting up of a seraglio of whores did with King Solomon'. Coming down to more recent times, Defoe disapproves of marriages made for dynastic reasons, and claims that the happiest royal couples married for love:

> Such was the life of two glorious sisters, the late Queen Mary and Queen Anne, of whom it is said, and I never heard it contradicted, that they were entire mistresses of their Royal Consorts affection, Queens of their Hearts, enjoyed a complete conjugal felicity, and furnished back the same joy, making full return in kind.
>
> But then it may be added to both these happy couples, and yet which confirms what I am arguing upon, that they saw and loved before they married. They neither courted by pictures, or married by proxy; their Princes came over hither to view, choose and approve, and then married the persons they chose.

Defoe may have been praising Mary and Anne in order to condemn the private lives of the Hanoverian monarchs. When George I ascended the throne of England, he was without a queen, having divorced and incarcerated his wife for taking a lover, Königsmark, who later vanished in highly suspicious circumstances. Instead of a queen, George had brought over from Hanover two of his ageing mistresses, the bony Duchess of Kendal and the voluminous Countess of Darling-ton. George I's son, who came to the throne in 1727, the year *Conjugal Lewdness* was published, was said to be much in love with Caroline, his witty and beautiful wife, but nevertheless betrayed her with a suc-cession of mistresses. Both the first Hanoverian kings encouraged the theatre, masquerades and Italian opera, of which Defoe very much disapproved.

From *The Family Instructor*, *Religious Courtship* and *Conjugal Lewdness* we gain a vivid impression of Defoe's domestic life, not least of his love for Mary, the wife about whom so little is known. In the last of his moral tracts, *The Compleat English Gentleman*, Defoe lets us into the secrets of his manner of authorship. This unfinished work, which was kept in manuscript by his daughter's descendants and published only in 1890, recounts the attempts of a boorish squire to gain refinement and manners. The friend who has taken on this task tells the gentleman that he ought to have a library, whereupon the following dialogue ensues:

> G: I have no books. What should I do with them?
> F: But your father had a library, I don't doubt.
> G: Yes, a great Bible, the Ballad of Chevy Chase, set to very good music, with Robin Hood and some of the ancient heroes of that kind ... four or five folio books of Common Prayer and the old Book of Martyrs.
> F: I hope you have added to the stock since then.
> G: Not I! What should I do with books? I never read any. There's a heap of old journals and news-letters ... Those we have every week for the parson ...

Under the influence of his friend, the gentleman goes up to London to visit some of the bookshops in Paternoster Row, the street by St Paul's where Defoe's work was generally published and sold. The friend tries to dissuade the gentleman from buying whole shelves full of books, explaining that many of these are duplicates. At last the friend, who of course is really Defoe, explains how books can compensate for want of a proper education:

> If he [a gentleman] has not travelled in his youth, has not made the Grand Tour of Italy and France, he makes his tour of the world in books. He may make himself master of the geography of the universe in the maps, atlases and measurements of our mathematicians. He may travel by land with the historians, by sea with the navigators. He may go round the globe with Dampier and Rogers, and know a thousand times more in doing it than all those illiterate sailors.
>
> He may make all distant places near to him in his reviewing the voyages of those that saw them, and all the past and remote accounts present to him by the histories that they have written of them. The studious geographer and the well-read historian ... discovers America with Columbus, conquers it with the great Cortez, and re-plunders it with Sir Francis Drake.

That is the perfect cue to introduce the first and most famous of all Defoe's works of imagination, *Robinson Crusoe*, published in 1719. The next chapter will also examine two of the other novels still in print, *Captain Singleton* and *Colonel Jack* which, although they do not follow *Robinson Crusoe* chronologically, are also concerned with America and the South Sea Company. Chapter Eleven deals with Defoe's two most famous historical novels, *The Memoirs of a Cavalier* and *A Journal of the Plague Year*, published in 1720 and 1722 respectively. Chapter Twelve considers the two stories of wicked women, *Moll Flanders* (1722) and *Roxana* (1724). Chapters Thirteen, Fourteen and Fifteen follow Defoe through the three-volume *Tour of the Whole Island of Great Britain*, which many consider to be his finest achievement.

The Adventure Stories: *Robinson Crusoe, Captain Singleton* and *Colonel Jack*

DEFOE'S FIRST and most famous novel, *The Life and Strange Surprising Adventures of Robinson Crusoe*, was always said to be based on the story of Alexander Selkirk, a Scottish sailor from Largo in Fife. After getting into some scrapes at home, Selkirk joined an expedition of South Sea privateers against the Spanish, commanded by William Dampier, the author of *Voyage Round the World*. When they had turned the Horn and entered the eastern Pacific, Selkirk quarrelled with Dampier and in 1704, at his own request, was put ashore on the uninhabited, seldom visited island of Juan Fernandez. Five years later Captain Woodes Rogers, the leader of another privateering expedition, called at Juan Fernandez to pick up Selkirk, and eventually brought him to England in 1711. The story of Selkirk was mentioned in Rogers's own subsequent book, also called *Voyage Round the World*, and was written up by journalists such as Richard Steele. The poet William Cowper repeated the tale in verses supposedly written by Selkirk:

> I am monarch of all I survey,
>   My right there is none to dispute;
> From the centre all round to the sea
>   I am lord of the fowl and the brute.

Defoe certainly knew of Selkirk's adventure and, as we learn in *The Compleat English Gentleman*, he had studied the books of those two 'illiterate sailors', Dampier and Rogers. However, for several reasons Selkirk's story is not likely to have been the main or even a major inspiration for *Robinson Crusoe*. Throughout his life Defoe was an avid reader of tales of adventure in distant places, many involving shipwreck and marooning. In Dampier's *Voyage Round the World* he would have read how he and his crew were stranded on Ascension Island and lived for five weeks off goats and turtles. In 1705 Defoe spotted a story about a shipwreck off Madagascar, an island which features in many of his books.

It could be argued that other abandoned sailors had the company of their shipmates or learned to live with the natives, while only Selkirk was monarch of all he surveyed. But Selkirk was not in the strict sense marooned at all, having chosen to be put ashore on Juan Fernandez, an island occasionally visited by ships needing food or water – hence the abundance of cats, rats and goats. Even in *Robinson Crusoe* the hero's solitude takes up only a third of the story. Although we are told that Crusoe has spent twenty years on the island before the arrival of other humans, the time seems to pass in two or three. For at least two-thirds of the novel, Crusoe is not alone at all but rather trying to escape from his fellow human beings.

The theory that *Robinson Crusoe* was based on Selkirk starts to collapse as soon as we examine the geography of his island. Defoe was an expert on this subject and had even helped to prepare one of the best early atlases. He knew where Juan Fernandez lay in relation to South America, since he had once drawn up for Harley a detailed plan for the annexation of Chile. The adventures of Crusoe take place not in the realms of the imagination but in the very real world of the Spanish Main, in which Defoe had been interested for the last thirty years, and on which he had advised William III as well as Harley. The novel mentions the Asiento, which Britain still hoped to win for the South Sea Company. Moreover, Defoe pinpoints Crusoe's island as lying just north of the South American mainland, near the mouth of the Orinoco river, in what is now Venezuela but was then part of Guiana. It is close enough to the mainland to be reached by the natives in their canoes, but far enough to have escaped annexation by Spain. Defoe himself might have said that Robinson Crusoe's island was 'not 150 miles away from Trinidad and Tobago'.

The confirmation of this can be found in a pamphlet Defoe brought out in 1719, the same year as *Robinson Crusoe*, called *An Historical Account of the Voyages and Adventures of Sir Walter Raleigh*, which is dedicated to, or 'humbly proposed to', the South Sea Company. This pamphlet is in effect a suggestion that the South Sea Company should establish a British colony in that part of the continent that Raleigh had explored in his two expeditions up the Orinoco in search of the realm of El Dorado, the 'gilded man' who went about covered in gold-dust. Defoe does not announce his purpose from the start, but pretends he is only trying to clear the name of Raleigh, who had flourished under Elizabeth but was put in the Tower and later beheaded at the command of James I:

> The just resentment of the injustice done this Great Man, moved me to this work; in which I shall endeavour to supply defects of those who have gone before me, and give some more perfect account of the undertakings, discoveries, conquests, and improvements, which he made for the glory and interest of the sovereign, and of the country, not forgetting the immense wealth, commerce, power and excellence of empire which the British Crown now possesses, and the British Nation now enjoys in consequence of his immortal labour.

Defoe then claims 'the honour to be related to his blood' in order to impart some hitherto unknown information on Raleigh's youth – in particular how he read everything he could find on the explorations and conquests of Columbus, Cortés and Pizarro: 'I say, I can assure the world by family tradition, that these were the favourite histories that took up his early readings; and that on occasions were the subjects of his ordinary discourses while he was but a young man.' Apart from this titbit of family gossip Defoe has nothing new to say on Raleigh's career or the reasons for his downfall: 'Queen Elizabeth dying, the next reign was far more ignorant of the works of this man, and was therefore far more easily imposed upon by the Spaniards in the Popish conspiracy against Sir Walter Raleigh.' At the end of *An Historical Account* Defoe appends a 'Conclusion', addressed to the South Sea Company, and in effect suggesting that it should finish the work begun by Raleigh:

> I must say, it would be the glory of the Company to embark on such a discovery ... It seems worthy a Trading Company to attempt this part of the world, inhabited by millions of people, because numbers of people are the source of the trade, and they occasion the consumption of manufacture ... It seems a loud call to Great Britain to make such an attempt on Guiana and Peru, and as it cannot be done now but under that authority and by the permission of his Majesty's South-Sea-Company, the undertaking seems to be their due; their charter

begins at the River Oroonoque, and none can attempt it without this.

If the South Sea Company needed someone with expert knowledge to help them launch their expedition, Defoe can provide them with just the man: 'If they please to take such a proposition into consideration, the author of these sheets is ready to lay before them a plan or chart of the rivers and shores, the depths of the water, and all necessary instructions for the navigation with a scheme for the undertaking, which he had the honour about thirty years ago, to lay before King William . . .'

There is no point in trying to sort out fact from fantasy, since Defoe was never consistent in his stories. Here he talks of giving William charts of the Orinoco; on other occasions, the isthmus of Panama. Here, and in several other pieces, he claims to have known the King from 1689, or 'about thirty years ago', but in the fragment of autobiography under his own name he says he was first introduced after writing *The True-Born Englishman* in 1700. He never once mentions his ancestors, the Foes, yet here he boasts of his 'blood relations', the Raleighs.

But *An Historical Account* should not be written off as the harmless ramblings of an elderly journalist. Defoe was a distinguished writer on trade and finance, a former adviser to William III, and one of the men who had helped Robert Harley to set up the South Sea Company. He had warned from the start against letting the company fall prey to stock market gambling and 'bubbles', and had recommended that it should become involved in proper commercial ventures such as the African slave trade, whaling, plantations and, above all, the colonization of South America. Eight years before he put forward the Orinoco project Defoe had presented to Harley his plans for the annexation of Chile, Cuba and southern Argentina. We do not know if the South Sea Company, or a group of investors, paid Defoe to promote such a venture, first in *Raleigh* and then in *Robinson Crusoe*, but this may have contributed to the frenzy of speculation which culminated the following year in the South Sea Bubble.

Some modern critics have tried to 'deconstruct' *Robinson Crusoe* in search of its 'sub-text' or 'hidden agenda', without adding much to our understanding of it. Of course, *Robinson Crusoe*, like all his novels, reflects Defoe's preoccupations, especially his financial worries, but it is neither an autobiography nor an allegory of his own or the human predicament. Defoe doubtless tried to imagine himself in Crusoe's plight, just as we all do, and to that extent he may have revealed some of his own personality. He was well aware of the power of symbols, metaphor and allegory, having been brought up on the Old Testament stories and on the parables of Jesus Christ. He was deeply versed in Milton's great metaphysical poem *Paradise Lost*, and had almost certainly read John Bunyan's religious allegory *The Pilgrim's Progress*. He certainly read and enjoyed Cervantes' *Don Quixote*, which has allegorical undertones. But *Robinson Crusoe* is first and foremost an adventure story.

Robinson's father had come from Bremen to live in York, and had changed his name from Kreutznaer to Crusoe, giving rise to the theory that the Foes had come from the Netherlands and had once been called something else. In fact Crusoe was the surname of one of Defoe's contemporaries at Dr Morton's Academy who, like him, had joined Monmouth's Rebellion. Robinson Crusoe's father, like the father in *The Family Instructor*, is worried about the waywardness of his sons. Robinson's eldest brother has run off to join the army, and died in action at Dunkirk; the second has disappeared in a fashion not explained; the old man therefore implores the third boy, Robinson, to give up his plan for running away to sea: 'He told me it was for men of desperate fortunes on one hand, or of aspiring, superior fortunes on the other, who went abroad on adventure, to rise by enterprise and make themselves famous in undertakings out of the common road; that these things were all either too far above me, or too far below me; that mine was the middle state, or what might be called the upper state of low life . . .'

Robinson's father begs him to enter the law as a clerk to an attorney, but the young man, 'without asking God's blessing or his father's', joins the crew of a ship at Hull. During the first few days of the voyage to London Crusoe is seasick and full of remorse for disobeying his father, but as soon as he gets his sea-legs he forgets his good resolutions – like several characters in Defoe's novels. The ship is caught in a storm off the Norfolk coast and dashed ashore near Yarmouth, a town beautifully described by Defoe in the *Tour*. Here Crusoe is offered a new berth, either to London or back home in Yorkshire: 'Had I now had the sense to go back to Hull, and have gone home, I had been happy, and my father, an emblem of our blessed Saviour's parable, had even killed a fatted calf for me; for hearing the ship I went away in was cast away in the Yarmouth Road, it was a great while before he had any assurance that I was not drowned.' Robinson's father must now have thought that all his sons were dead.

Crusoe continues to London and from there to West Africa on a voyage that makes him both a sailor and a merchant, 'for I brought home five pounds, nine ounces of gold dust from my adventure, which yielded me at London on my return almost £300 and this filled me with those empty thoughts which since so completed my ruin'. This is the first of scores of accounts of fortunes won and lost which figure so large in all Defoe's novels. Before setting off on another African venture, Crusoe leaves £200 of his wealth with a widow in London, a sum she is destined to hold for him over the next thirty-five years. While heading for the Canary Islands, his ship is attacked by North African pirates and he is taken ashore as a slave of the Moors. After two years' captivity he escapes in a fishing boat with a Moorish lad, Xury, and sails down the coast to the land of the blacks – presumably Senegal or Gambia.

After encounters with lions and savages Crusoe hails a passing Portuguese ship, whose captain befriends him and takes him to Brazil. Here he most ungratefully sells Xury off as a slave, though on condition that he is freed after ten years if he has become a Christian. Crusoe becomes a sugar-cane and tobacco planter. He writes to the widow in London asking her to send out English cloth and baize, which fetch a large amount in Brazil: 'For the first thing I did I bought me a negro slave and a European servant also.'

If Crusoe had been content with his life as a planter, he could have followed his father's advice and lived in 'the upper state of low life'. But when talking about his adventures to friends in San Salvador, he mentions how easy it is in Africa to purchase 'negroes for the service of the Brazils in great numbers'. He explains to the Portuguese planters how they could gain a great advantage from the South Sea Company, although he does not mention it by name:

> They listened always very attentively to my discourse on these heads, but especially to that part which related to the buying of negroes; which was a trade at that time not only not far entered into, but, as far as it was, had been carried on by the *assiento*, or permission of the kings of Spain and Portugal, and engrossed to the public; so that few negroes were bought and those excessively dear.

Crusoe is now approached by a group of planters and merchants who want to enlist his help in obtaining contraband African slaves, in defiance of the Asiento:

> And after enjoining me to secrecy, they told me that they had in mind to fit out a ship to go to Guinea; that they all had plantations as well as I, and were straightened for nothing so much as servants; that as it was a trade that could not be carried on, because they could not publicly sell the negroes when they came home, so they desired to make but one voyage, to bring their negroes on shore privately, and divide them among their own plantations; and in a word, the question was, whether I would go [as] their supercargo in the ship to manage the trading part upon the coast of Guinea, and they offered me that I should have my equal share of the negroes, without providing any part of the stock.

Because of the euphemisms of 'servants' and 'negroes', as well as the incomprehensible Asiento 'engrossed to the public', few readers of *Robinson Crusoe* understand that its hero is a slave trader. And although it is on this slaving expedition that Crusoe is shipwrecked and marooned, Defoe at no point even suggests that this was a punishment for buying and selling his fellow men. Indeed, in a later novel, *Captain Singleton*, the hero succeeds in selling a cargo of Africans in Brazil. In Defoe's eyes, Crusoe is punished not for dealing in slaves, but for failing to be content with a quiet and modest life, and restlessly seeking adventure.

When Crusoe is shipwrecked, he comes to regret his lack of religious knowledge: 'What I had received by the good instruction of my father was then worn out by an uninterrupted series, for eight years of seafaring wickedness and a constant conversation with nothing but such as were like myself, wicked and profane to the last degree.' Defoe suggests subtly and with conviction that meditation and reading the Bible helped Crusoe to fight off loneliness and despair. However, at least one reader of *Robinson Crusoe*, Karl Marx, scoffed at these protestations of Christian hope and repentance. Surprisingly, in view of Defoe's strong religious convictions, this is the only novel in which he preaches at the reader.

The story of Crusoe's stay on the island has caught and held the imagination of all the world, and still lives on in an age when the power of the printed word is fading. One of the most popular radio programmes of all time, the BBC's 'Desert Island Discs', invited its guests to imagine themselves in Crusoe's plight, and then to choose for their comfort in solitude, eight pieces of music, one luxury item and one book, as well as the Bible and Shakespeare.

Defoe may have taken some of the details of Crusoe's island from Selkirk's account of his stay on Juan Fernandez – for instance, the plague of cats and the goatskin clothes. He probably learned even more from accounts of North America and the Caribbean islands, for although Crusoe appears as a castaway, he is also a colonist in Britain's expanding empire. Defoe's advice on planting corn, making a spade from iron wood, baking bread, fortifying one's home and building a dug-out canoe could serve as a manual for pioneers or mountain men in any part of America.

The twenty-eight years that Crusoe is said to have spent on the island is subtly compressed to avoid boring the reader. In fact Crusoe is only halfway through his adventures when he discovers that he is no longer alone. This is the terrifying and unforgettable moment when he sees a single footprint on the sand, a master-stroke of imagination which established Defoe as a genius*. For the reader, as much as for Crusoe, the island at once acquires a sinister new dimension:

> Sometimes I fancied it must be the devil; and reason joined with me in this supposition; for how should any other thing in human shape come into the place? Where was the vessel that brought them? What marks were there of any other foot-steps? ... Then I thought that the devil might have found an abundance of other ways to have terrified me than this of a single print of a foot ... in a place where twas ten thousand to one whether I should see it or not, and in the sand too, which the first surge of the sea upon a high wind would have defaced entirely ... I presently concluded that it must be some more dangerous creature, viz, that it must be some of the savages of the main-land over against me, who had wandered out to sea in their canoes ... Then terrible thoughts racked my imagination about their having found my boat, and that there were people; and that if so, I should certainly have them once again, in greater numbers and devour me.

* Robert Louis Stevenson called it one of the four supreme moments in imaginative literature (see p. ix).

Thus, with the *coup de théâtre* of a single footprint, Crusoe has changed from a solitary into a man living in terror of other human beings. He barricades himself in a fortress around the cave, never ventures out unless he is armed to the teeth, and searches the island for places to hide his valuables and his herd of goats. Two pages after the footprint – though we are meant to believe that two years have passed – Crusoe discovers the remnants of a cannibal feast; 'I turned away my face from the horrid spectacle; my stomach grew sick, and I was just at the point of fainting, when nature discharged the disorder of my stomach.'

A few years later Crusoe's initial revulsion has turned to rage, and to considering 'how I might destroy some of these monsters in their cruel bloody entertainment and, if possible, save the victims they should bring hither to destroy'. He plans to put gunpowder under their cooking fire, and blow up everyone near it: 'I then proposed that I would place myself in ambush, in some convenient place, with my three guns all double-loaded, and in the middle of their bloody cere-mony, let fly at them, when I should be sure to kill or wound perhaps two or three at every shot; and then falling in upon them with my three pistols and my sword, I made no doubt but that if there were twenty I should kill them all.'

Gripped by these murderous fantasies, Crusoe sets up an ambush at the beach, where the savages from the mainland come to devour their prisoners. But after a time his anger subsides and he starts to ask himself whether he has the right to be judge and executioner over these people: 'they do not know it to be an offence, and then commit it in defiance of divine justice, as we do in almost all the sins we commit. They think it no more a crime to kill a captive taken in war, than we do to kill an ox; nor to eat human flesh, than we do to eat mutton.' Here Defoe confronts a moral dilemma that troubled generations of British settlers in the Americas, Africa and later Australia. The argument runs through Hollywood's treatment of the American Indians – or Native Americans, as they are now called. Moreover, Crusoe wants to believe that the British are more humane than other Europeans, and says of his former plan to destroy the cannibals:

> That this would justify the conduct of the Spaniards in all their barbarities practised in America, and where they destroyed millions of these people, who, however they were idolaters, and barbarians, and had several and bloody and barbarous rites

in their customs, such as sacrificing human bodies to their idols, were yet, as to the Spanish, very innocent people; and that the rooting them out of the country is spoken of with the utmost abhorrence and detestation, by even the Spaniards themselves . . .

After another few pages, by which time Crusoe is said to have been on the island twenty-five years, a Spanish ship is wrecked on the reef, from which he salvages clothes, rum, gunpowder and, best of all, some pipes so that he can smoke the island's tobacco. Defoe cannot resist gloating over the ship's treasure, before writing it off as valueless:

Besides this, when I came to the till in the chest, I found there great bags of pieces of eight, which held about eleven hundred pieces in all; and in one of them, wrapped up in a paper, six doubloons of gold and some small bars or wedges of gold . . . I had no manner of service for it; twas to me the dirt under my feet; and I would have given it all for three or four pairs of English shoes and stockings.

That may well be true. However, a few lines later Crusoe admits that he lugged the money back to his cave, and laid it up with the treasure he saved from his own ship. Defoe cannot imagine life on a desert island without brooding over his debts.

Soon after the wreck of the Spanish vessel Crusoe resolves to capture one of the native visitors to the islands to teach him English and accompany him to the mainland. A few pages later he rescues from death the man he names Friday. He then rescues Friday's father and one of the seventeen Spaniards who had survived the wreck, later reminiscing, 'My island was now peopled, and I thought myself very rich in subjects. It was remarkable too . . . they were of three different religions. My man Friday was a Protestant, his father was a pagan and a cannibal, and the Spaniard was a Papist. However I allowed liberty of conscience throughout my dominion.'

The comings and goings on the island now become frantic. The Spaniard sails to the mainland with Friday's father to bring his ship-mates back to the island. No sooner have they gone than the island is visited by a party of mutineers from a British ship. Crusoe and Friday overpower the villains and hand back control of the ship to the captain. Crusoe is now the governor of a new British colony, which he hopes may become the base for the conquest of the mainland. He leaves on the island those mutineers he has spared from hanging, instructing them to expect the Spaniards from the mainland, and then departs for England as the guest of the grateful captain. Most readers remember Crusoe's words: 'When I took my leave of this island I carried on board for relics the great goat-skin cap I had made, my umbrella and my parrot.' But few remember how Crusoe continues: 'I forgot not to take the money, I formerly mentioned, which had lain by me so long useless that it was grown rusty, or tarnished, and could hardly pass for silver till it had been a little rubbed and handled; as also the money I found in the wreck of the Spanish ship.'

The remainder of the book describes how Crusoe regained and even augmented the fortune he lost through shipwreck. On returning to England in 1687, after an absence of thirty-five years, Crusoe revisits his 'faithful steward' the widow, and helps her in her financial straits. In Yorkshire he discovers that his family are dead, except for two sisters and two nephews. The owners of the ship he had rescued make him a present of £200, with which he sets off for Lisbon to find out what has happened to his estate in Brazil. Seven months later Crusoe receives a packet from his Brazilian partner containing a list of all the money owing to him in pieces of eight and gold moidores, besides a gift of seven leopard skins, five chests of sweetmeats, and 100 pieces of gold, uncoined, and not so large as moidores.

By the same fleet of ships to Lisbon Crusoe's trustees in Brazil send him 1,200 chests of sugar, 800 rolls of tobacco, and the rest of the whole account in gold. 'I was now master, all of a sudden', Crusoe reflects, 'of about £5000 sterling in money, and had an estate in the Brazils of about £1000 a year, as sure as an estate of land in England.' Here he faces a problem common to many of Defoe's protagonists: how to get his money safely back to London. Like most such passages, Crusoe's return from Lisbon has the quality of an anxiety dream, and expresses the torment Defoe must have endured as his trading ventures foundered before his bankruptcy of 1692. Crusoe at first feels 'a strange aversion to going by sea at that time', and his instinct is sound, for one of the ships he might have taken is seized by Algerian pirates, and the other is wrecked near Torbay in Devonshire, with the loss of all but three on board. He decides instead to carry his wealth overland through Spain, runs into a snowstorm at Pamplona, then has to fight off ravening wolves in the foothills of the Pyrenees. In the course of this long and bloodcurdling passage Man Friday demonstrates how to kill a bear by luring it up a tree.

Even when Crusoe arrives with his wealth in England, gets married and fathers three children, he is still obsessed with selling off his Brazilian plantation for 33,800 pieces of eight. After his wife's death he revisits his island, now a flourishing British colony, then returns once more to Brazil. At the end of the book he hints that 'of all these things, with some very surprising incidents and some new adventures of my own, for ten years more, I may perhaps give a further account hereafter'. This was a trailer for the *Further Adventures of Robinson Crusoe*, published in July 1719, only four months after its predecessor. One can admire the speed with which it was written but it is dull stuff. Crusoe revisits his island and Brazil, then wanders off round the Cape of Good Hope to India, Cambodia, Vietnam (Tonkin), China and returns home through Siberia. At Tobolsk he meets the political enemies exiled by Peter the Great, 'this being the country where the state criminals of Muscovy are all banished'.

The first edition of 1,000 copies of *Robinson Crusoe* appeared at the end of April 1719, a second of the same number on 9 May, and a third four weeks later. The fourth edition came out in August, shortly before the publication of the *Farther Adventures of Robinson Crusoe*, and both soon appeared in pirated and abridged editions. The publisher William Taylor took legal action against a rival who advertised *The Adventures and Surprising Deliverance of James Dubourdieu* as being 'very proper to be bound up with *Robinson Crusoe*'. By the end of the year *Crusoe* was published in French, German and Dutch translations.

The success of *Robinson Crusoe* and even the feeble *Farther Adventures* encouraged Defoe to dash off another sea-going story in 1719, *The King of Pirates; Being an Account of the famous Enterprises of Captain Avery, the mock King of Madagascar*. The following year he used some of the same material, and even the same 'Captain Avery', for one of his still enduring novels, *The Life, Adventures and Pyracies of the famous Captain Singleton*, with a long subtitle listing his travels in Africa and the West and East Indies.

Captain Bob, as Singleton later comes to be called, is kidnapped in Islington at the age of two and sold to a beggarwoman, who needs a pretty child to plead her case. When Bob is six, his 'good Gypsy mother, for some of her worthy actions, no doubt, happened in process of time to be hanged', and at twelve he embarks for Newfoundland under the care of a kind ship's captain. 'I tried well enough', he says, 'and pleased my master so well that he called me his own boy; and I would have called him Father, but he would not allow it, for he had children of his own.' It is a strangely touching and wistful remark from the otherwise oafish Bob.

Bob's travels take him to Lisbon, where he joins the crew of a Portuguese ship and, after an unsuccessful attempt at mutiny, is put ashore with some other sailors on Madagascar, a hide-out of pirates preying upon the East Indies trade. From Madagascar, Bob and his comrades sail to Africa, meaning to travel 'overland through the heart of the country from Mozambique in the east, over to the coast of Angola or Guinea, in the waters of the Atlantic ocean'. In the account of their journey Defoe displays his ignorance of central African vegetation and wild life. He describes in the central African jungle 'sand so deep, that it scalded our feet', and at night 'we began to hear the wolves howl, the lions bellow and a great many wild asses braying.' The natives had told Captain Bob to expect 'many great rivers, many lions and tigers, elephants and fierce wild cats (which in the end we found to be civet cats)'.

More than a century after the publication of *Captain Singleton* the British reading public would devour the books of African exploration by men such as Burton, Stanley and Livingstone; but theirs were factual accounts, not fantasy. In *Captain Singleton* and in other stories set in the tropics Defoe never once mentions malaria or the other fevers which carried off most Europeans. Captain Bob's journey does not grip the reader's interest until he reaches the Guinea coast, where he and his comrades sell the gold they have panned in the rivers of the interior. Here Bob is seized by Robinson Crusoe's terror of being unable to get his treasure back to London. He relates how one man in their party stayed some time with the Dutch at Cape Coast, in modern Ghana, 'and there died of grief, for he having sent a thousand pounds sterling over to England . . . the ship was taken by the French and the effects all lost'. This had been the fate of one of Defoe's cargoes in 1692. Captain Bob at last makes good his return to London, but lodges some of his money with a dishonest Rotherhithe inn-keeper, and squanders the rest in less than two years.

In 1686 Bob sails for Cadiz, where Defoe himself had thought of becoming a merchant, and begins a career as a pirate. He and some malcontents seize a ship, give themselves officer ranks – hence 'Captain Singleton' – and even start to drink wine with their meals, 'for we that were now all become gentlemen, scorned to drink the ship's beer'. They sail for the Canaries and then the Caribbean, making a base on Tobago, near Robinson Crusoe's island. Bob explains that when they captured a ship, they took its treasure, powder and bullets, small arms, 'and as for the men, we always took the surgeon and the carpenter, as persons who were of particular use to us; nor were they always unwilling to go with us, though for their own security, in case of accident, they might easily pretend they were carried away by force'. This heralds the introduction of William Walters, a rascally Quaker doctor on a ship from Pennsylvania, a comic figure who lifts the novel after a dull first half: 'He was a surgeon, and they called him doctor, but he was not employed in the sloop as a surgeon, but was going to Barbados to get a berth as the sailors call it . . . very good humoured and pleasant in his conversation.' Before joining the pirates, Walters asks the master of the ship to sign a statement that he and his surgical instruments had been taken off by force. He then explains to the pirate captain that, though he is willing to work for him, his conscience will not allow him to fight: 'No, no, says the captain, but you may meddle a little when we share out the money. Those things are useful to furnish a surgeon's chest, says William, and smiled. In short William was a most agreeable companion, but he had a better part of us . . . that if we were taken, we were sure to be hanged, and he was sure to escape.'

When the pirates engage a Portuguese naval ship, William's conscience does not allow him to fight, but he lashes the enemy rigging to the mainmast, and 'every now and then pulled a bottle out of his pocket and gave the men a dram to encourage them'. The pirates find a ship adrift with 600 Africans who have managed to overpower and kill their captors. Bob can hardly prevent his men from carrying out a massacre, but William gently explains to them that they would have done the same in the Negroes' position, 'and that the Negroes had really the highest injustice done to them, to be sold for slaves without their consent'. After this pious observation William escorts the Africans to Brazil, where he sells them secretly to the planters, thus completing the trading venture started by Robinson Crusoe. Defoe recognizes the hypocrisy of a Quaker slave trader, but never condemns the trade itself.

When Captain Singleton and his pirates decide to move from the West to the East Indies, William Walters is once again the brains of the operation. It is he who sells to some Japanese merchants the cloves, nutmeg, cinnamon, mace and silver robbed from a Chinese junk. When a number of the pirate band are murdered by the natives of Ceylon, the modern Sri Lanka, William quickly dissuades the survivors from seeking revenge: 'If I mistake not, your business is money. Now I desire to know, if you conquer and kill two or three thousand of these poor creatures, they have no money, what will you gain by them?' Defoe is of course making fun of Quaker pacificism.

William Walters now advises Captain Bob that the time has come to dispose of their loot and retire to enjoy the proceeds in England. They make their way to Surat on the west coast of India, where the English merchants had their principal trading post or 'factory', before moving south to Bombay. William knows that many employees of the East India Company also trade privately on the side, with very few questions asked. After making contact with some merchants and telling them he has goods for sale, William takes a sloop to a creek about six leagues from the factory. Here he receives, in exchange for the stolen merchandise, 'the whole parcel, amounting in money to about thirty five thousand Pieces of Eight, besides some goods which William was content to take, and two large diamonds, worth about three hundred thousand sterling'. When the East India men had paid the money, 'William invited them on board and the merry old Quaker diverted them exceedingly with his talk, and Thee'd them and Thou'd them till he made them so drunk that they could not go on shore for the night.'

Most of the pirates want to ply their trade from Madagascar, so William and Bob go off on their own to Persia, disguised as Armenian merchants, which heralds another anxiety dream about getting the money to safety. William has persuaded Bob to give up piracy by talking about his immortal soul, to more effect than he intended, for the new convert asks earnestly if God will allow them both to reach England with their ill-gotten wealth. William assures him that all will be well, provided they 'keep the money carefully together, with the resolution to do what right with it we are able'. The suddenly pious Bob now starts to talk in his sleep, crying out, 'I am a thief, a pirate, a murderer, and ought to be hanged'; William is terrified they will both be discovered. However, they leave Basra safely by taking a ship up the river Euphrates, crossing to Alexandria, and from there to Venice, 'with such a cargo, take our goods and our money and our jewels together, as I believe was never brought into the city by two single men, since the state of Venice had a being.' By now they are both terrified of being murdered for their money.

After spending two years in Venice the two men return to London, disguised as Greeks and swearing never to tell their true identities, except to William's sister whom Bob eventually marries. However, there is a furtive note to the end of *Captain Singleton*: 'And now having so plainly told you, that I am come to England, after I have so boldly owned what life I have led abroad, tis time to leave off, and say no more for the present, lest some should be willing to investigate too nicely after, Your Old Friend, Captain Bob.'

Three years after *Robinson Crusoe*, and two after *Captain Singleton*, Defoe published a third book of Caribbean adventure. Since it was one of at least six books he scribbled down in 1722, *Colonel Jack* not surprisingly shows all the signs of haste – repetition, clumsy syntax, a haphazard plot, and inconsistency in the character of the hero. It is a rag-bag story, bringing in themes from the other novels – for instance, piracy in the Caribbean and South American trade from *Robinson Crusoe* and *Captain Singleton*, soldiering on the Continent from *The Memoirs of a Cavalier*, crime and Virginia from *Moll Flanders*, as well as a hint of the sexual naughtiness in *Roxana*. The most entertaining part of the novel is Colonel Jack's doleful account of his five, mostly disastrous marriages, two of them to the same woman. This book also brings in a guarded but unmistakable reference to Defoe's escape from the Battle of Sedgemoor in 1685.

Colonel Jack is the nickname given to one of the children of military officers, raised by a foster-mother in Stepney. Here, as in *Moll Flanders* and later *Roxana*, Defoe expresses his strong disapproval of parents who have the money to raise their children but will not accept this natural duty. When his kindly foster-mother dies, Jack is forced at the age of ten to become 'a beggar boy, a blackguard boy', who lives on the streets and sleeps at night in a bed of warm ash in the glass-works.

The young Colonel Jack is a tearful, wheedling boy who knows how to play on the heart-strings of soft-hearted grown-ups: 'I can remember the people would say, that boy has a good face; if he was washed and well-dressed, he would be a good pretty boy, do but look what eyes he has, what a smiling pleasant countenance.' He is always very aware that his father was a gentleman. When someone offers a £50 reward for the bills of exchange that Jack and his friends have picked from his pocket, Jack sells them back through a go-between, a kindly merchant who pities the boy and afterwards acts as a sort of guardian. When, as a young man, Jack takes part in mugging a widow from Camden Town, he later repents and gives back the money, as usual blubbing his eyes out. One critic has counted thirty-three weepings in *Colonel Jack*. These early chapters about a well-born boy living with a gang of thieves may have given Dickens the story of *Oliver Twist*, but if so, he did not acknowledge the debt.

The young Colonel Jack lives in terror of losing his treasure. He secretes his stolen money in shoes and the hollow trunk of a tree, and finally banks his capital with the merchant. Like Captain Singleton, Jack is frightened of talking in his sleep, in case he gives away secrets. Although he has never been caught or punished for his crimes, Jack leaves London for Stamford, then Wakefield, but finds that the people of Yorkshire 'have their eyes so about them, and are all so sharp they look upon everybody that comes near them to be a pickpocket'. He continues to Scotland, learns to read and write, signs on as a soldier, deserts, and is finally kidnapped and sold as a servant or slave to Virginia.

After spending a short time picking tobacco, Jack is appointed an overseer, with instructions to flog the Negroes under his charge. However, he argues, and is soon able to prove, that the blacks work better if they are treated with kindness rather than cruelty. His master gives him his freedom, as well as assistance in setting up his own plantation, so that soon Jack grows rich. He sails for England during the War of the Spanish Succession, is captured by the French, and embarks on a career in the army of Louis XIV, becoming at last a true Colonel Jacques. In 1708 he joins the French and the Old Pretender on the expedition to raise a rebellion in Scotland. After its failure Jack decides to enjoy a gentleman's life in London.

Jack's first wife plays hard to get in order to ensnare this wealthy Virginia planter, 'too cunning to let him perceive how easily she could be had', but Jack is still naïve. Immediately after the wedding his wife reveals herself as 'a wild, untamed colt and carefree to conceal any part, no not the worst of her conduct'. In vain Jack tries to curb her gambling, for 'no estate is big enough for a box and dice', and he also deplores her extravagance – she spends £136 for the lying-in of their baby. When their marriage breaks down, 'She demanded a separate maintenance at the rate of £300 a year, and I demanded security of her that she would not run into debt; she demanded the keeping of the child, with an allowance of £100 for that, and I demanding that I should be secured from being charged with any keeping she might have by someone else, as she had threatened me.' Jack proves as obstinate as a Californian lawyer. He refuses to pay his wife's bills and, when she gets pregnant, shows proof that the baby is not his and sues for divorce before the Ecclesiastical Court. She sends round a bully-boy to challenge him to a duel, but Jack has not yet learned sword-play. The first wife may have commissioned the thugs who set upon Jack, slit his nose and almost cut off an ear. However, he gets his divorce and leaves the country in disgust to fight for the French in Italy.

As a prisoner of the Austrians at Trento, an inebriated Jack is seduced by his burgher landlord's daughter, whom he marries and takes off to Paris, where she starts an affair with a marquis. Jack, having now learned to wield a sword, challenges and wounds his rival, but since Louis XIV has outlawed duels, Jack hurriedly leaves for England. On the way from Dover to London he falls in love with a beautiful widow, who proves an excellent wife until, after her third child, and possibly suffering from post-natal depression, she is tempted by her maid to try a strong drink:

> She first took this cordial, then that, till in short, she could not live without them, and from a drop to a sip, from a sip to a dram, from a dram to a glass, and from one to two, till at last she took, in short to what we call drinking . . . She grew a beast, a slave to strong liquor, and would be drunk at her own table, nay in her own closet by herself, till instead of a firm, well-made shape, she was as fat as an hostess; her fine face blotched and bloated.

She is not only drunk by eleven o'clock in the morning; she and her maid have acquired a fancy man, taking turns to make love with him in front of each other. When his wife at last dies of drink, Jack decides to revenge himself on the man who debauched her – a naval captain, so we are told. Jack confronts him in a field at Stepney, knocks him down and canes him: 'In this condition he at last begged for mercy, but I was deaf to all pity a great while, till he roared out like a boy soundly whipped; then I took his sword from him and broke it before his face and left him on the ground, giving him two or three kicks in the backside and bade him go and take the law of me if he thought fit . . .'

Colonel Jack goes to live in Lancashire, but still needs a woman to care for his children, so he resolves to marry an 'upper servant' or housekeeper: 'And if she be a slut and abuse me, as I see everybody else does, I'll kidnap her and send her to Virginia to my plantation there, and there she should work hard enough and fare hard enough to keep her character, I'll warrant.' In fact this 'moggy', or north country girl, turns out to be cheerful, fond of the children, and also a prudent housewife or 'family manager'. Unhappily, she and all but two of Jack's children perish from smallpox in 1715. Initially this is the reason Jack gives for returning to his Virginia plantations, but we later learn that when the Jacobite rebels came to Preston he joined their army, and is now on a list of wanted traitors, just as Defoe was thirty years earlier. On returning to his plantation, Jack hires as a servant one of the women convicts recently shipped from Bridewell, and finds to his astonishment that she is his first wife. She is now truly repentant and, when they marry once more, is as faithful and good as she was previously wild and wicked.

Jack tells her of his terror of being arrested as a Jacobite – he had galloped away from the battle, shot and buried his horse, then made his way home on foot, without arousing suspicion. However, a number of the Scots soldiers captured at Preston had recently arrived as convicts in Virginia, some of them at the neighbouring plantation, and Jack now lives in fear of being recognized and denounced. His wife puts it around that Jack is suffering from the gout and must stay in his room until he can sail for the West Indies to take the medicinal waters. She smuggles him on to a private ship bound for Antigua, where there are no Jacobite prisoners. Meanwhile she hears from a lawyer in London that all the rebels of 1715, except for a handful of ringleaders, have now received a royal pardon.

The novel might well have ended here, but perhaps the publisher needed to fill more pages. So from Antigua Colonel Jack tries to break into the Spanish American trade, a matter of constant concern to British merchants, which would later lead to the War of Jenkins's Ear in 1739. Just as Robinson Crusoe offered to bring in slaves for Brazilian planters, so Jack offers to run English cloth to the merchants of Cuba. On the second of these clandestine ventures he makes a profit of £20,000, but nevertheless returns to Cuba for one last orgy of buying, selling and the exchange of opulent gifts. In the course of the novel Jack has progressed from an East End pickpocket stashing his loot in a hollow treetrunk to a Cuban grandee, who orders his Negro servant to pile up 8,750 pieces of eight in a corner of his apartment; the cry-baby has been transformed into a ruthless man of action, the cuckold into a domestic autocrat.

Neither *Captain Singleton* nor *Colonel Jack* enjoyed the success of *Robinson Crusoe*, and probably would not still be in print if Defoe had not been the author. Apart from *Crusoe*, none of Defoe's fictional works were as popular during his lifetime, or for fifty years to come, as *The Family Instructor*, *Religious Courtship*, *The Complete English Trades-man* and, above all, the *Tour*, the most lucrative of all his works to judge by its many editions. It is important to remember what Pat Rogers says in *Defoe. The Critical Heritage*: 'Defoe the great novelist is an invention of the nineteenth century. During his lifetime he was chiefly known for satirical and polemic works such as *The True-Born Englishman* and the *Shortest Way with Dissenters*.' His authorship of *Robinson Crusoe* was publicized largely because of the many attacks and parodies it attracted from rival Grub Street hacks – for example, Charles Gildon's *The Life and Strange Surprising Adventures of Mr D. . . . . D. . . . of London, Hosier*.

It is unlikely that many people who were not engaged in the pub-lishing or bookselling business knew that Defoe was also the author of *Captain Singleton* or *Colonel Jack* or any other fictional works we now know to be his. The reviewing of novels did not begin until 1731, the year of Defoe's death, which saw the foundation of the *Gentleman's Magazine*, and it was not until the end of the eighteenth century that the reading public came to accept the novel as a distinctive genre, and to look out for the latest books by their favourite authors.

The Historical Fiction

ALTHOUGH *Robinson Crusoe*, *Captain Singleton* and *Colonel Jack* were all presented as genuine memoirs, few of the readers can have thought that their heroes really existed – any more than the heroines of *Moll Flanders* and *Roxana*. Their exploits are too fantastic, the sins of the women too flagrant to be believable. But in addition to these five obvious works of fiction, Defoe wrote a large number of memoirs, which readers were meant to accept as true. Although most of these bogus memoirs are set in the fairly recent past, the only two that remain in print, *The Memoirs of a Cavalier* and *A Journal of the Plague Year*, describe events that took place before and shortly after Defoe's birth in 1660.

Because they are set in the distant past, these books are sometimes called historical novels; however, they bear no relationship to the works of Sir Walter Scott, to Thackeray's *Henry Esmond*, or to the stirring romances of Charles Reade, Sir Arthur Conan Doyle and Patrick O'Brian. Neither of these two works has any plot or story other than war and the Plague of 1665; the peripheral characters make only an incidental appearance; and although the Cavalier comes across as a real and engaging person, 'H. F.', who supposedly keeps the journal, is no more than a chronicler, like Defoe himself in his book on the storm of 1703. But if these books are not adventure stories like *Robinson Crusoe* or primitive novels like *Roxana*, they are certainly fictional treatments of fact, like much of Defoe's work, including the *Tour* and many pamphlets – his life of Sir Walter Raleigh, for instance.

Defoe wrote for various kinds of readers, much as a Hollywood studio brings out films for different categories of audience. Just as *Robinson Crusoe* comes under the heading 'Adventure', *Moll Flanders* under 'Crime', *Roxana* under 'Melodrama', and *A Journal of the Plague Year* under 'Disaster', so *The Memoirs of a Cavalier* comes under the

popular label, 'War'. At the time it appeared, in 1720, the country was
enjoying a term of peace after eighty years of almost continual conflict,
first in the Civil War, then in two wars against the Dutch, followed
by William III's and Marlborough's wars against France. There was
not, in Defoe's time, any general revulsion against the horrors of war;
indeed, the merchant class in England tended to favour war as a means
of destroying commercial rivals, expanding the empire, and stimulating
the coal, iron, steel, shipbuilding and clothing industries, all of which
had flourished during the War of the Spanish Succession. The Whigs,
who were now in government, had campaigned against the Treaty of
Utrecht on the slogan, 'No Peace without Spain'. In the aftermath of
the war against France, and the prospect of further clashes with Spain,
the public was eager for military memoirs and even manuals of combat.
Then, as now, there were plenty of old soldiers eager to write their
stories, and those with a good narrative style were able to find a
publisher.

Two years before he began the *Cavalier*, Defoe had written *The
Memoirs of Major Ramkins, a Highland Officer now in Prison in Avignon*,
whose subtitle promises details of his 'Amours, Gallantry, Oeconomy
&'. In choosing to write of a Highland soldier, Defoe was exploiting
the English terror of the Scots, which followed the Jacobite rising of
1715 and persisted until after the second rebellion of 1745. Ramkins
had first heard the call to arms in 1689, when the clans rose to the
defence of James II of England and VII of Scotland. Then a stripling
of seventeen at Aberdeen University, he had sold off his books and
furniture to equip himself for the fight. After the Jacobite defeat
Ramkins travels to Holland and then to Paris where, like Colonel Jack,
he fights an illegal duel. He sails to Ireland to join James II's army at
Cork, and is afterwards taken prisoner at the Battle of the Boyne,
giving Defoe a chance to praise his hero William of Orange. Like
Colonel Jack, Major Ramkins loses faith in the Jacobite cause, and
because of this, as well as his ill-judged amours, he is writing the
memoir from prison. It is a short and rather tentative essay in military
autobiography.

Ten years after the Ramkins book, in 1728, Defoe wrote the more
successful *Memoirs of an English Officer*, purporting to be by Captain
George Carleton, who is said to have gone to Spain with the Earl of
Peterborough's expedition in 1705. Captain Carleton starts out as a
naval officer in 1672, then, two years later, travels to Holland to serve
in the army of William of Orange. Here Defoe inserts a further tribute

to the courage of the man he had first met forty years earlier: 'I remember the Prince of Orange during the siege [of Maastricht] received a shot through the arm, which giving an immediate alarm to the troops under his command, he took his hat off his head with the wounded arm, and smiling waved it, to show that there was no danger.' In 1685 Carleton is ordered to London to guard the capital against the threat of Monmouth's rebellion, and is camped on Hounslow Heath.

Most of *The Memoirs of an English Officer* concerns the Spanish campaign which began with the capture of Barcelona and then pushed south to Valencia. Defoe, through Captain Carleton, says of Peterborough, who had been his commander in the militia in 1689: 'He was extremely well beloved, his affable behaviour exacted as much from all; and he preserved such a good correspondence with the priests and the ladies, that he never failed of the most early and best intelligence, a thing ... commendable and necessary in a general with so small an army, at open war, and in the heart of his enemy's country.' Captain Carleton is wounded and spends three years in 'Sainte Clemente de la Mancha, rendered famous by Cervantes', which enables Defoe to air his views on *Don Quixote* as well as on bull-fighting, nunneries and many other aspects of Spanish life. He says that the gentlemen of La Mancha are 'the least priest-ridden or sons of bigotry, of any that I have met with in all Spain' but that the enforcers of the Inquisition are active in every town and 'are more to be avoided than the rattle-snake'.

Defoe's *Memoirs of an English Officer* fooled even Dr Johnson, who prided himself on detecting literary forgers, such as James Macpherson, the author of bogus translations from the Gaelic. On Sunday 27 June 1784 Boswell and Johnson dined at Sir Joshua Reynolds's home in the company of Lord Eliot, whose tutor had also instructed the family of Lord Peterborough. Boswell records that Johnson asked Eliot:

> 'Pray, my Lord, do you recollect any particulars that he told you of Lord Peterborough? He is a favourite of mine, and is not enough known; his character has been only ventilated in party pamphlets.' Lord Eliot said, if Dr Johnson would be so good as to ask him any questions, he would tell what he could recollect. Accordingly some things were mentioned. 'But, (said his Lordship) the best account of Lord Peterborough that I have happened to meet with, is in *Captain Carleton's Memoirs*.

Carleton was descended of an ancestor who had distinguished himself at the siege of Derry.'

The editor of this 1887 edition of Boswell's *Life of Johnson*, George Birkbeck Hill, adds a puzzled footnote on Lord Eliot's remarks: 'Carleton, according to the *Memoirs*, made his first service in the navy in 1672 – seventeen years before the siege of Derry. There is no mention of the siege in the book.' Defoe's authorship of the book was not revealed until the twentieth century.

Lord Eliot had obviously not questioned the authenticity of the *Memoirs*, and nor, as we now discover, had Johnson, for Boswell's account continues: 'Johnson said he had never heard of the book. Lord Eliot had it at Port Eliot; but, after a good deal of enquiry, procured a copy in London, and sent it to Johnson, who told Sir Joshua Reynolds that he was going to bed when it came, but was so much pleased with it, that he sat up till he had read it through, and found in it such an air of truth, that he could not doubt of its authenticity . . .'

By an odd coincidence, it was during the same year, 1784, in which Johnson was taken in by 'Captain Carleton's' memoirs, that Defoe's name was first attached to *The Memoirs of a Cavalier*: it appeared on the title-page of the sixth edition, published by Francis Noble, though it was left unclear whether Defoe was the author or merely the editor of the work. It claimed that the 'Memoirs, Travels and Adventures of a Cavalier' were 'First published from the original manuscript by the late Mr Daniel Defoe, Author of the Adventures of Robinson Crusoe, And many other books of entertainment'. Defoe's name on a book was now considered more likely to sell copies than that of the unknown Cavalier.

The Cavalier was born in 1608, the second son of a rich country gentleman in Shropshire, a background that helps to explain his later choice of allegiance in the Civil War, since Wales and the border counties were Royalist strongholds. At the end of his studies at Oxford the hero requests his father's permission to make a tour of the Continent. 'In what capacity would you go there?' his father asks. 'You may go abroad either as a private gentleman, as a scholar, or as a soldier . . . but I see no war abroad at this time worth while for a man to appear in.' The Cavalier and an Oxford friend set sail from Dover to Calais on 22 April 1630; Defoe often uses specific dates to add verisimilitude, or because the narrator gives them a special significance. As we shall see, the Cavalier is obsessed by the coincidence of dates.

During his first year on the Grand Tour the Cavalier reacts in a typically bluff and English way to the foibles and vices of foreigners. In France he encounters thieves, rogues, persecuted Huguenots and, in Lyons, a mob of seditious rebels protesting about the price of bread: 'I confess this little adventure gave me an aversion to tumults all my life after, and if nothing else had been the cause, would have biassed me to espouse the king's party in England, when our popular heats carried all before it at home.' The Cavalier and his friend find that the English are very unpopular in France, so they pass themselves off as Scotsmen: 'Nothing was so much caressed as the Scots and a man had no more to do in France, if he wanted to be well received there, than to say he was a Scotsman.' In Savoy the Cavalier catches the plague, but 'it pleased God that the distemper gathered in my neck, swelled and then broke ... and the prodigious collection of matter which this swelling discharged, gave me immediate relief...' Defoe would return to this topic two years later.

In Rome the Cavalier is bored by the ancient remains, and takes a robust Protestant view of this Papist capital:

> As for what is modern, I saw nothing but lewdness, private murders, stabbing men at the corner of the street, or in the dark, hiring of bravoes, and the like; all the diversions here ended in whoring, gaming and sodomy ... I observed the people degenerated from the ancient, glorious inhabitants, who were a generous, brave, and the most valiant of nations, to a vicious baseness of soul, barbarous, treacherous, jealous and revengeful, lewd and cowardly, intolerably proud and haughty, bigotted to blind, incoherent devotion, and the grossest of idolatry.

After this thundering anathema against the Italian nation Defoe gives a richly comic account of a young man who visits a prostitute but loses his nerve or his potency at the crucial moment: 'At a certain town in Italy, which shall be nameless ... I was prevailed upon rather than tempted, *a la Courtezan*,' the Cavalier tells us. On entering her apartment, he is so overcome by the opulence of the jewellery, silver plate and furniture that he takes her at first for a lady of quality, 'but when after some conversation I found that it was really nothing but a Courtezan, in English, a common street whore, a punk of the trade, I was amazed, and my inclination to her person began to cool.' He is charmed by her conversation, 'but when the vicious part came on the stage, I blush to relate the confusion I was in, and when she made a certain motion by which I understood she might be made use of, either as a lady, or as —, I was quite thunderstruck, all the vicious part of my thoughts vanished, the place filled me with horror, and I was all over disorder, and distraction.'

In this Italian interlude Defoe reveals himself as the ancestor of the modern tabloid journalist, playing on popular xenophobia, sanctimoniousness, envy and salaciousness, even throwing in a prurient hint of sexual perversion. It used to be a feature of such newspaper reports that when the woman 'made a certain suggestion', the journalist 'made an excuse and left the room'. But the Cavalier in Defoe's story finds this difficult:

> I began however to recollect where I was, and that in this country there were people not to be affronted; and though she easily saw the disorder I was in, she turned it off with amiable dexterity, began to talk again *a la gallant*, received me as a visitant, offered me sweetmeats and some wine. Here I began to be in more confusion than before, for I concluded she would neither offer me to eat or drink now *without poison* and I was very shy of tasting her treat.

The young Cavalier at last makes good his escape and soon afterwards leaves for Germany to study the art of soldiering. In this year, 1631, there had been a renewal of conflict in what later came to be known as the Thirty Years War. Although the quarrel involved dynastic rivalry and the balance of power, it was also a confrontation between Protestant northern Europe and the Roman Catholic Church under the leadership of the Austrian Habsburg Emperor. The Cavalier arrives just in time for the epic contest between the imperial General Jan Tilly and the Protestant champion, King Gustavus Adolphus of Sweden. The Cavalier witnesses the capture of Magdeburg: 'the Austrians entered with such terrible fury, that without respect to age or condition, they put all the garrison and inhabitants, man, woman and child, to the sword, plundered the city, and when they had done this, set it on fire ... This was a sad welcome into the army for me and gave me a horror and aversion to the Emperor's people.'

This is the cue for the Cavalier to move from Tilly's camp to that of Gustavus Adolphus, Defoe's idol and the true hero of this novel, although he is shortly afterwards killed. The young Cavalier is struck by the discipline of the Swedish troops, whose camp resembles a well-ordered city: 'The meanest country woman with her market ware was as safe from violence as in the streets of Vienna; there was no regiments of whores and rags as followed the Imperialists; nor any woman in the camp, but such as being known to the provosts to be the wives of the soldiers, who were necessary for washing linen, taking care of the soldiers clothes, and dressing their victuals.'

In the preface to the *Cavalier* Defoe proclaims that the many accounts of battles, sieges and actions both in Germany and Britain can all be confirmed by the history books – not surprisingly, for they have almost all been plagiarized from such standard works as William Watt's life of Gustavus Adolphus or Lord Clarendon's *History of the Rebellion*. Defoe prided himself on his military expertise, so the *Memoirs* are full of redoubts, ravelins, horn-works, traverses and counterscarps. Thanks to the Scottish officers in Gustavus's army, the young Cavalier is able to meet the King, who gives him the chance to 'trail a pike' as an infantryman at the Battle of Leipzig, in which he serves with distinction.

Like all Defoe's characters, the Cavalier is obsessed by money and treasure, in this case the loot from the enemy dead, wounded and prisoners – 'a bundle of some linen, 13 or 14 pieces of plate, and in a small cup three rings, a fine necklace of pearls, and the value of 100 Rix-dollars in money'. Defoe insists that the Protestant soldiers did not steal from German civilians but rather retrieved the booty already plundered by the imperial troops, above all the Croats, or 'Crabats', whom he had so often attacked in the *Review*. The Cavalier's first spoils of war came from a Crabat running away with the bundle under his arm. The inhabitants had fled from Nuremberg with some of their goods, 'and what was left the hungry Crabats devoured, or set on fire, but sometimes they were met with by our own men, who often paid them home for it'. A few pages later 'we fell foul with 200 Crabats who had been upon the plundering account: we made ourselves some amends upon them for our former loss, for we showed them no mercy'. On his return to England the Cavalier reflects that he had seen 'the most flourishing provinces of Germany reduced to perfect deserts, and the voracious Crabats, with inhuman barbarity, quenching the fires of the plundered villages with the blood of the inhabitants'.

When Gustavus Adolphus is killed, riding almost alone into a squadron of Croats, two-thirds of Germany went into mourning, according to the Cavalier:

When the ministers mentioned him in their sermons or prayers, whole congregations burst out into tears: the Elector of Saxony was utterly inconsolable, and would for several days walk about his palace like a distracted man, crying the saviour of Germany was lost, the refuge of abused princes was gone; the soul of the war was dead, and from that hour was so hopeless of outliving the war, that he sought to make peace with the Emperor.

After a few more years with the Protestant armies in Germany the Cavalier comes back to England and kisses the hand of King Charles I, who 'was pleased to receive me well, and to say a great many obliging things to my father on my account'. During the winter of 1638–9 the Scots revolt against the attempt by William Laud, the Archbishop of Canterbury, to make them use the Book of Common Prayer; and the Cavalier, on joining the King's army at York, finds the camp and court full of parsons, 'for this was a church war in particular'. Defoe here uses the Cavalier to voice his own disapproval of Charles's policy.

The Cavalier goes as an emissary to the Scottish camp and gives a vivid description of the Highland troops which Defoe himself had observed in 1706, parading through Edinburgh:

> They were generally tall, swinging fellows; their swords were extravagantly, and I think insignificantly broad, and they carried great wooden targets large enough to cover the upper parts of their bodies. Their dress was as antique as the rest; a cap on their heads, called by them a bonnet, long hanging sleeves behind, and their doublets, breeches and stockings, of a stuff they called plaid, striped a-cross red and yellow, with short cloaks of the same ... They are in companies all of a name, and therefore call one another only by their Christian names, as Jemy, Jocky, that is John; and Sawny, that is, Alexander, and the like. And they scorn to be commanded but by one of their own clan or family. They are all gentlemen, and proud enough to be kings. The meanest fellow among them is as tenacious of his honour, as the best nobleman in the country, and they will fight, and cut one another's throats for every trifling affront.

His failure in Scotland obliges King Charles to recall Parliament and to face the discontent of his English subjects. When the Civil War follows, the Cavalier sees action at Worcester, Edgehill, Roundway Down and Marston Moor, among other famous battles, putting most of the blame for defeat on the King's advisers and on his headstrong commander, Prince Rupert. The Cavalier has witnessed the horrors of war in Germany, 'but I found a strange, secret and unaccountable sadness upon my spirit to see this acting in my own native country'. He is appalled to hear a man asking for quarter in English, 'and when I heard a soldier cry, *O God I am shot*, I looked behind me to see which of my own troop was fallen'.

However, Defoe maintains that the Civil War was in one way more merciful than the war in Germany, for it consisted of pitched battles rather than drawn-out campaigns and sieges: 'Twas the general maxim of the war, where is the enemy? Let us go and fight them: Or on the other hand, if the enemy was coming, what was to be done? . . . Draw out into the fields and fight them.' The Cavalier explains that the King might have won more battles if he had shown more prudence: 'And I shall remark several times, when the eagerness of fighting was the worst counsel and proved our loss. This benefit however happened in general to the country, that it made a quick though bloody end of the war, which otherwise had lasted till it might have ruined the nation.'

After the Roundhead victory at the Battle of Marston Moor the Cavalier escapes from Yorkshire dressed as a peasant, with a white cap on his head and a pitchfork on his shoulder, while his companions pose as a cripple and a woman. He is stopped by a suspicious local: 'Hark thee, friend, says he in a broad north country tone, whar hast thou thilk horse?' A fight ensues, in which the Cavalier pitchforks the Yorkshireman's horse in order to bring him down. It is the kind of unpleasant detail that is omitted from romantic historical novels, though Conan Doyle described the suffering of horses during the Hundred Years War. In another grim episode the Cavalier justifies killing some Leicester women 'who fired upon our men out of their windows, and from the tops of their houses, and threw tiles upon our heads'.

The Cavalier speaks with awe of a man who, even eighty years later, was still widely detested: 'About this time it was that we first began to hear of one Oliver Cromwell, who, like a little cloud, rose out of the east, and spread first into the north, till it shed down a flood that overwhelmed the three kingdoms.' When the Cavalier at last surrenders, in Cornwall, it is to Thomas, Lord Fairfax, a Parliamentary general untainted by regicide, and like Defoe a Presbyterian, not an Independent:

> I never saw a man of more pleasant, calm, courteous, down-right honest behaviour in my life ... No man in the world had more fire and fury in him while in action, or more temper and softness out of it. In short, and I cannot do him greater honour, he exceedingly came near the character of my foreign hero Gustavus Adolphus, and in my account is, of all the soldiers of Europe, the fittest to be reckoned in the second place of honour to him ... but I observed if at any time my civilities extended to commendations of his own actions, and especially to comparing him to Gustavus Adolphus, he would blush like a woman, and be uneasy, declining the discourse, and in this he was still more like him.

The *Memoirs* are shot through with sadness and even perplexity, as though the Cavalier has started to wonder whether his fighting career had served any purpose. Throughout the book the hero comes across as a man who is brave and honest but unreflecting, credulous and even a little stupid. As an epilogue to his *Memoirs*, the Cavalier offers a list of strange coincidences relating to the Civil War: for instance, Charles I was taken prisoner by the Scots on the same day – 10 May – that, six years earlier, 'against his conscience and promise, he passed the Bill of Attainder against the loyal noble Earl of Strafford'. On 6 April 1641 Parliament voted to raise an army against the King, and on the same day in 1648 Cromwell evicted Parliament.

One might accuse Defoe of padding out the book with some of the titbits of information published in almanacs along with horoscopes, interpretations of dreams, and stories of second sight and mental tele-pathy. Or perhaps he is simply rounding off the character of the Cava-lier by depicting him as the kind of former military man who in France would be reading Nostradamus, or in modern times would be fascinated by corn circles or UFOs. One can almost hear the sighs and groans in the club or coffee house as the old cavalier asks the assembled company if they knew that on the same day, 13 October, that Parliament recognized Cromwell in 1654, Parliament was itself dissolved five years later.

Early in 1722 the news reached London that the Plague, which had broken out in Marseilles about eighteen months earlier, was now spreading northwards, prompting Defoe to write *A Journal of the Plague Year*. This was not, as some have suggested, a hasty cobbling together of stories about the Great Plague in order to exploit public anxiety, since Defoe had for many years studied and written about the disaster of 1665. During the rainy summer of 1709, which followed the 'Russian winter', he reported in the *Review* on the famine and pestilence in northern and eastern Europe. Again, on 19 August 1712, he published in the *Review* the sort of article that came to be known in Fleet Street as 'A Doctor Writes':

> I shall close this paper with a short piece of advice to the publick good. I am no professed [professional] physician and I resolve never to commence quack doctor; but by a very experienced physician and for the general good of mankind, as well enemies as friends, I am desired to signify a piece of advice to all those who have been touched with the new and unaccountable distemper, a thing which though, God be praised, with a gentle and merciful, yet with an almost universal shock, has affected not only this nation, but France, Ireland, Holland and Flanders, the advice is that they should take care, by some gentle purge, such as salt of Epsom, mineral waters, or any such common methods, he prescribes not particulars, to cleanse and cool their bodies, after the distemper is over, and other applications at an end – He gives this caution with it, that it should by no means be any strong purge and that as they find their constitution will bear it they would let blood after the Dog-days* are over and before Michaelmas. This he proposes as a general necessary method to restore the constitution and prevent autumnal fever *which he expects will be very mortal, and, as he doubts, contagious* [italics added].

It was the last twelve words that upset many readers, as is clear from the next *Review* of 23 August 1712. It appears that Defoe was then staying in company somewhere outside London, possibly Epsom or Tunbridge Wells but more probably one of the spas in Derbyshire, where he spent a part of that autumn.

---

* The Romans called the hottest weeks of the year the dog-days, *caniculares dies*. Their theory was that the dog-star, Sirius, rising with the sun, added to its heat, and the dog-days (approximately 3–11 July) bore the combined heat of both (*Brewer's Dictionary of Phrase and Fable*).

It is not unknown to you all, that a light distemper or indisposition, has generally touched the whole nation; and I believe few families, from even her Majesty's household to the meanest subjects, have been free of it, and that not only here but in France, Ireland, Holland, Flanders and all this part of Europe.

I had not said anything more to it . . . if I had not found all the notices which have been taken of it, and the thing itself also, turned into ridicule and banter by the people of this age; not less than by three different companies was I accosted in this manner in the one day . . .

Are you one of the fools that make such an outcry, said the first to me, about this little sickness the people have had among them? What, do you not know it is the Dog-days, and faint weather, and that we have always something they call the New Distemper at this time of the year. And thus they went on until they thought they had jested it quite off with me.

I had scarce been a quarter of an hour gone from those, but I met with another – What have you heard the Dog star bark, says he, and has it frighted you into a fit? Prithee Daniel, what dost ail? What is the matter that you make such an ado about a little summer sickness, and disorder the people with melancholy notions of the plague? You are much in the wrong, and it may be of ill consequence; I wonder the government does not take notice of you for it.

In the evening of the same day, coming into some very grave company, they were pleased to tell me, I had got the hyppo [hypochondria]; and what is the matter with you says one, old enough to have had more wit; you have dreamed of nothing, I warrant you but of grave and sepulchre this fortnight – I warrant you, you have brought two or three bottles of Plague water to carry into the country with you – I expected you would not have come abroad without a sprig of RUE in your mouth? And then he went on, till at last, as all the company knows, he grew offensively profane.

Obviously hurt by the charges of being a scaremonger or hypochondriac, Defoe suggests that his critics are wilfully blind to the danger, or merely cynical, like an unnamed 'eminent physician who said publicly some time since, that if we could have the plague here, they should have fine sport'. He promises to return to the subject in future issues of the *Review*, meanwhile reaffirming his reasons for being apprehensive: 'I will not say, nor do I remember what some affirm viz. that we had a shock like this [the distemper] before the last dreadful Plague. I will not undertake to say positively in this paper ... that the Plague shall certainly reach hither next year though I assuredly expect and believe it ...' The Plague has for eight years past 'taken a gradual course, or kind of circuit through a great part of Europe' from Bulgaria up to Sweden, 'and every year it has come a step nearer and nearer to this country'. Defoe also claims that the affected countries, including Hungary and Poland, were 'visited with such a distemper as this, the very year before they had the Plague'.

In the *Review* of 26 August Defoe published a 'Bill of Mortality' for the week of 12–19 September 1665, when the Great Plague was at its worst. These weekly 'Bills of Mortality' were first compiled in the sixteenth century by the London Company of Parish Clerks. They were put together by 'searchers', most of them elderly women, who inspected all corpses in their parish, determined the cause of death, and sent a report to the parish clerk. According to Christopher Wills, the author of *Plagues*, although the searchers knew little of medicine, by long familiarity with their parishes they could distinguish a hundred or more causes of death. These Bills of Mortality, he says, 'were consulted like traffic reports by the privileged who used them to calculate when they should flee the city'. Here is the Bill, showing causes of death, that Defoe offered his readers to remind them of the Plague Year:

Abortive 5, Aged 43, Ague 2, Apoplexies and Suddenly 2, Bleeding 2, Burnt in his bed at St Giles Cripplegate 1, Canker [cancer] 1, Childbed 42, Chrisoms [a child which died in the first month of life, still wearing its baptismal chrisom-cloth] 18, Consumption 134, Convulsion 64, Cough, 2, Dropsie 33, Fever 309, Flox and smallpox 5, Frighted 3, Gout 1, Grief 3, Gripes in the guts 51, Jaundices 5, Imposthume 11, Infants 16, Killed by a fall from the Bellfrey at Allhallows the Great 1, King's Evil 2, Lethargy 1, Palsie 1, Plague 7165, Rickets 17, Rising of the lights 11, Scowring [diarrhoea] 5, Scurvy 1, Spotted Fever 101, Stillborn 17, Stone and Strangury 3, Stoppage of the stomach 9, Surfeit 49, Teeth 121, Thrush 5, Tympany 1, Tissick [phthisic, a lung or throat disease] 11, Vomitting 3, Wind 3, Worms 3.

Beneath this Bill of Mortality for a week in September 1665 Defoe added certain observations, perhaps to forestall complaints from *Review* readers of squeamish disposition:

> I shall spend none of your time in commenting on so melan-
> choly a subject; you may guess a little of it from two small
> articles in the Bill of Mortality abovesaid, and of which tis
> observed, some are in every Bill of that year, viz. Frighted 3,
> Grief 3.
>
> I think no one can call this terrifying to people; I think the
> thing a little too much forgotten among us; but if ye think
> otherwise, I will terrify you no longer, this may be sufficient
> for those that make a mock of the present circumstances, to
> let them see what kind of a thing a plague is in this City, and
> what it may be if it comes again; those who think we are in
> no danger of it, need be under no concern at this account,
> and those who think we are, will make a good use of it . . .

With the benefit of hindsight we can say that Defoe was causing needless terror. After the Plague Year the number of victims dropped to less than 2,000 in 1666, when the Great Fire occurred, to thirty-five in 1667, to fourteen in 1668, then slowly diminished until 1679, when the last two deaths were recorded. Christopher Wills offers an explanation for this:

> Is it too much to suppose that before the Great Fire there
> was some kind of focus of the plague, perhaps lurking in the
> sewage-filled alleys and tottering houses of Pudding Lane or
> nearby Thames Street, with its rotting wharves? . . . The
> nature of the focus can only be speculated about. Perhaps it
> was a particularly crowded population of rats and their fleas
> . . . The Great Fire, widely regarded as a disaster, seems instead
> to have been a much-needed prophylaxis, burning out a canker
> in the heart of the city. And once that canker disappeared, the
> cycle of the plague bacillus was broken as well.

Even without a Great Fire, the Plague was disappearing on the Continent as well. There was an outbreak at Amiens in 1667–8 but not in the much more crowded city of Paris. The flare-up in Marseilles, which began in 1720 and seemed to be spreading north, was in fact the last occurrence of plague in Western Europe, though neither Defoe nor anyone else at the time could have been expected to know this.

Indeed, by the beginning of 1722 the threat of the Plague spreading north from Marseilles was taken so seriously by the British government that the nation was close to a state of emergency. Before writing *A Journal of the Plague Year*, Defoe had brought out another book on the subject, *Due Preparations for the Plague*, also published in 1722, along with *Moll Flanders*, *Religious Courtship* and *Colonel Jack*. Although *Due Preparations* is not quite as long as the others, comprising about 65,000 words, this demonstrates the fertility of Defoe's brain as well as the physical strength of his writing hand.

The book's full title was *Due Preparations for the Plague. As well for Soul and Body. Being some seasonable thoughts upon the Visible Approach of the present dreadful Contagion in France, the properest means to prevent it, and the great work of submitting to it.* Defoe begins by saying that he does not wish to cause alarm, but points out that the disease has spread 100 miles in the last eight months. Moreover, the British government has already issued proclamations regarding the quarantine of ships and the airing of goods from suspect places, while Parliament has enacted laws to deal with another disaster: 'Can any man say that the government has not had occasion for such measures? Let such look to what has been done in Holland, where they not only burned two ships but hanged a man for attempting to save some goods out of the wreck of one ship that was cast away and which otherwise should have been burned.'

Besides approving the government's measure Defoe recommends that if the Plague returns to London all vagrants should be expelled from the city, all those in prison for debt moved at least fifteen miles away, and 'all criminals, felons and murderers should be forthwith tried, and such as are not sentenced to die, should be immediately transported or let out, on condition of going 40 miles from the City, not to return on pain of death'. He advises all those living in London to send their children into the country, and those who live on the outskirts to keep an eye on the weathercock, so that 'if the wind blows from the city towards them, let them for a time keep their windows shut on that side'.

As promised in the title, Defoe recommends due preparation 'as well for Soul as Body', and tells how during the Plague Year of 1665 one gentleman of his acquaintance – perhaps his father – held family prayers three times a day. In *Due Preparations*, as in *A Journal of the Plague Year*, Defoe sees the pestilence as a warning from Heaven:

Nay, the cry of the Nation's follies grows louder and louder every day, and so far we are from considering that when God's judgements are abroad on the earth, the inhabitants should learn righteousness; that we are rather learning to be more superstitiously wicked than ever; witness the increase of plays and playhouses, one being now building, though so many already in use; witness the public trading and stockjobbing on the Sabbath Day.

Although the author of *Moll Flanders* tactfully refrains from mentioning the vogue for saucy novels, he may be right to see in the reign of George I a return to the bad old ways of Charles II, thereby inviting punishment.

In *A Journal of the Plague Year*, as in his book on the Great Storm, Defoe moves gently into the action rather than giving the reader harrowing descriptions right from the start. The first two victims of the Plague died in December 1664 at the upper end of Drury Lane in the parish of St Giles-in-the-Fields, and there were no further deaths until February – again in the region of Holborn and Covent Garden. It was not until June 1665 that contagion spread from these western suburbs into the City of London, including Aldgate, where 'H. F.', the narrator, is said to live.

As alarm increases, Defoe tackles the question that must have been uppermost in the minds of all Londoners in 1722: whether to stay in a plague-ridden city or flee to the countryside. The narrator, a single man but with responsibilities for his servants and workmen, decides to keep going his wholesale saddlery business rather than seeking refuge with his relatives in Northamptonshire, 'whence our family first came from' – a hint that 'H. F.' may be Defoe's uncle Henry Foe. Throughout his journal he praises the mayor and officers of the City of London, as well as those doctors and ministers of religion who felt it their duty to stay. On several occasions he attacks King Charles II's decision to move his Court to Oxford, and also suggests that many clergymen of the Church of England abandoned their flocks. The vacant pulpits, he says, were frequently filled by the same Dissenting ministers who had been disbarred and even imprisoned under the Act of Uniformity three years earlier.

A few months before the outbreak of plague, as in 1666, a few months before the Great Fire, a comet passed over London, causing alarm among old women 'and the phlegmatic, hypochondriac part of the other sex, who I could also call old women'. People pointed out 'that the comet before the pestilence was of a faint, dull languid colour and its motion very heavy, solemn and slow; but that the comet before the fire was bright and sparkling, or, as others said, flaming, and its motion swift and furious . . .' Defoe, through his narrator, does not dismiss these portents: 'I saw both these stars, and, I must confess, had so much of the common notion of such things in my head, that I was apt to look upon them as the forerunners and warnings of God's judgments; and especially when, after the plague had followed the first, I yet saw another of the like kind, I could but say God had not yet sufficiently scourged the city.' But he does scoff at the rash of printed prophecies, dreams, astrological conjurations and old wives' tales which appeared during that summer of 1665 – *Poor Robin's Almanack*, *Godbury's Astrological Predictions* and the pseudo-religious *Come out of her, my People, Lest you be partakers of her Plagues*, for example. He puts his faith in the words of the Ninety-First Psalm, bidding us not to be afraid 'for the pestilence that walketh in darkness, nor for the destruction that wasteth at noonday'.

As the Plague takes hold in Shoreditch, Stepney, Whitechapel and Bishopsgate, the narrator notes with grim approval the disappearance of much of the vice and frivolity which had afflicted London since the Restoration, five years earlier:

> All the plays and interludes which, after the manner of the French court, had been set up, and begun to increase among us, were forbid to act; the gaming-tables, public dancing-rooms, and music houses, which multiplied and began to debauch the manners of the people, were shut up and suppressed; and the jack-puddings, merry-andrews, puppet-shows, rope-dancers, and such-like doings which had bewitched the poor common people, shut up their shops, finding indeed no trade.

The ignorant turned instead to quacks and peddlers of 'Sovereign cordials against the corruption of the air', or 'the only true plague water', or squandered their money on charms, philtres and amulets, which Defoe regarded as Papist trash. His narrator remarks 'how the poor people found the insufficiency of these things, and how many of them were afterwards carried away in the dead-carts and thrown into the common graves of every parish with these hellish charms and trumpery hanging about their necks, remains to be spoken of as we go along.'

Defoe praises the work of the Lord Mayor and Corporation, assisted by the College of Physicians, in planning ahead to contain the Plague, by shutting up the infected houses, appointing inspectors, watchmen and nurses, and digging the mass graves which, sure enough, were needed for the 100,000 or so who had died by the end of the year. The narrator visits one of these ghastly pits, into which the dead were nightly taken on carts. He observes a man who has buried his wife and children, and now is overwhelmed by grief, 'but with a kind of masculine grief that could not give vent to itself in tears'. He follows this man to a nearby inn and sees him taunted by blasphemers, who laugh at his sorrow for his wife and children and 'his want of courage to leap into the great pit and go to heaven, as they jeeringly expressed it . . .' Defoe does not mince his words in describing the pain and horror of the disease itself:

> The swellings, which were generally in the neck or groin, when they grew hard and would not break, grew so painful that it was equal to the most exquisite torture; and some, not able to bear the torment, threw themselves out at windows or shot themselves, or otherwise made themselves away, and I saw several dismal objects of that kind. Others, unable to contain themselves, vented their pain by incessant roarings, and such loud and lamentable cries were to be heard as we walked along the streets that would pierce the very heart to think of, especially when it was to be considered that the same dreadful scourge might be expected every moment to seize upon ourselves.

In one masterly passage, comparable to the description of Robinson Crusoe finding the single footprint in the sand, Defoe conveys how the terror of London in 1665 could suddenly break out in a quiet street:

> Passing through Tokenhouse Yard, in Lothbury, of a sudden a casement violently opened just over my head, and a woman gave three frightful screeches, and then cried, 'Oh! death, death death!' in a most inimitable tone, and which struck me with horror and a chillness in my very blood. There was nobody to be seen in the whole street, neither did any window

open, for people had no curiosity now in any case, nor could anybody help one another, so I went on to pass into Bell Lane.

Some of the Plague victims tried to pass the infection on to those who were healthy, and Defoe wonders if this is a symptom of the disease, as with rabid dogs, or simply a proof of man's fallen nature: one wild fellow, singing his way down Aldersgate, accosted a gentlewoman and asked for a kiss. She pushed him down to the ground,

> But very unhappily, she being so near, he caught hold of her, and pulled her down also, and getting up first, mastered her, and kissed her; and which was worst of all, when he had done, told her he had the plague, and why should not she have it as well? She was frightened enough as before, being young with child; but when she heard him say that he had the plague, she screamed out and fell down in a swoon, or in a fit, which though she recovered a little, yet killed her in a very few days, and I never heard whether she had the plague or no.

Although such ghastly anecdotes stick in the reader's mind, most of the *Journal* deals with how to survive a plague, just as *Robinson Crusoe* gave advice on how to survive on a desert island. The narrator explains how to disinfect a house with rosin, pitch, brimstone or gunpowder, and recommends a coal fire, even during the summer. He lists the amount of food that a household requires during a long isolation, and recommends poison to kill the rats – although he is unaware that they harbour the fleas which carry the Plague bacillus. He crosses the Thames to Greenwich and hears that virtually all the people who stayed in boats escaped infection.

The *Journal* contains a long subsidiary story of three men from Wapping who flee to Essex for safety. Because they know that the Epping people will not welcome them into the town, they pitch their tents in the woods outside. However, a delegation of townspeople approach and, from a discreet distance, tell them they are infected and cannot stay; at which one of the Londoners answers back:

> John argued very calmly with them a great while, and told them that London was the place by which they, that is, the townsmen of Epping and all the country round them subsisted; to whom they sold the produce of their lands, and out of whom they made the rent of their farms; and to be so cruel to the inhabitants of London, or to any of those by whom they gained

so much, was very hard, and they would be loth to have it remembered hereafter, and have it told how barbarous, how inhospitable, and how unkind they were to the people of London when they fled from the face of the most terrible enemy in the world; that it would be enough to make the name of an Epping man hateful through all the city, and to have the rabble stone them in the very streets whenever they came so much as to market.

Characteristically, Defoe is informative on how the Plague affected both foreign and domestic trade. He salutes the Lord Mayor and the guilds for keeping the markets open for bread, cheese and butter at normal prices, and fruit so cheap that some poor Londoners over-ate and suffered from colic. Although sales of manufactured goods were stagnant, clothiers kept their workers busy, 'believing that as soon as the sickness should abate, they would have a quick demand in proportion to the decay of their traffic at that time'. Defoe points out that the slump of the Plague Year was more than outweighed by the boom which followed the Great Fire the following year, 'when all the manufacturing hands in the nation were set to work' to supply the goods destroyed in the London warehouses.

Towards the end of 1665 the virulence of the Plague had weakened, and most of the sick recovered, whereupon they and those who had never caught the infection soon returned to their wicked ways. Defoe remarks bitterly on the renewed intolerance of the Church of England:

> The quarrel remained; the Church and the Presbyterians were incompatible. As soon as the plague had been removed, the Dissenting ousted ministers who had supplied the pulpits which were deserted by the incumbents retired; they could expect no other but that they should immediately fall upon them and harass them with their penal laws, accept their preaching when they were sick, and persecute them as soon as they were recovered again.

While naturally giving his own Dissenting opinion, Defoe pretends that 'H. F.', the narrator, is an Anglican: 'This [behaviour] even we that were of the Church thought was very hard, and could by no means approve of it.' In his *Tour* he also frequently praises Dissenters from the standpoint of an Anglican.

Although Defoe sees in the comets a sign of God's anger against the people of London, he loves the city too much to desire its utter destruction. He twice denounces the Quaker fanatic Solomon Eagle, 'who had predicted the plague as a judgment, and ran naked through the streets, telling the people that it was come upon them to punish them for their sins', only to see his own wife one of the first to be carried off in the Quaker dead-cart. At the end of the book Defoe compares the Londoners to the children of Israel, 'after their being delivered from the host of Pharaoh, when they passed the Red Sea and looked back, and saw the Egyptians overwhelmed in the water, viz. that they sang His praises, but they soon forgot His works.'

Moll Flanders and *Roxana*

IF *A Journal of the Plague Year* was meant for readers of horror and disaster stories, Defoe's more famous work of fiction from 1722 concerns the even more popular subjects of sex and crime, as we learn from the title, *The Fortunes and Misfortunes of the Famous Moll Flanders, Who was born in Newgate, and during a Life of continued Variety for Threescore Years beside her childhood, was twelve years a Whore, five times a Wife (whereof once to her own brother), twelve Years a Thief, Eight Years a transported Felon in Virginia, at last grew rich, lived honest and died a Penitent.* Although some modern critics have tried to re-interpret Moll as the victim of a repressive, uncaring and patriarchal society, Defoe clearly blames her as the author of her own misfortunes. She is greedy, selfish and callous, especially to her abandoned children, yet nevertheless a woman whom the reader has to admire for her candour, pluck and wit. The same combination of vices and virtues is found in that other great female rogue, Becky Sharp, in Thackeray's *Vanity Fair*. Defoe draws on his Newgate experiences to lead us into the underworld of pimps, prostitutes, pickpockets, muggers, forgers, fences, child-stealers, abortionists and highwaymen. He also gives an account of the transportation of convicts to America.

Unlike *A Journal of the Plague Year*, this scandalous story must have been treated as fiction by all but the most gullible readers. Nevertheless, Defoe begins with a preface in which he explains that the editor of the manuscript has toned down some of the Newgate language, and excised lewd and immodest ideas: 'In a word, the whole relation is carefully garbled of all the levity and looseness that was in it, so it is all applied, and with the utmost care, to virtuous and religious uses.' After this editorial humbug Moll herself tells how she was born in Newgate to a woman condemned to hang for petty theft, or rather for 'borrowing three pieces of cloth from a certain draper in Cheapside'.

Because of her pregnancy, Moll's mother was granted a stay of execution and sent instead to Virginia, though Moll does not know this until later.

Moll is taken to Colchester in Essex 'by those people they call gypsies, or Egyptians, but I believe it was but a little while that I had been among them, for I had not had my skin discoloured or blackened, as they do very young to all the children they carry about them'. Whether the gypsies left Moll at Colchester, or she left them, 'that is, that I hid myself, and would not go any further', she does not remember, but she is too young, at three, to do any work, and is taken into the care of the magistrates. She is 'nursed', or fostered by a sober, pious woman, who also runs a school, so Moll gets a better start in life than most orphans or children of convicts. At the age of eight she is horrified to be told that she must go into domestic service, perhaps to become 'a drudge to some cookmaid', so she begs her nurse to let her remain and earn her keep, 'for she had taught me to work with my needle and spin worsted, which is the chief trade of that city'. Her foster-mother tells her that her employers will not work her very hard. 'Yes they will,' answers Moll, 'and if I can't do it, they will beat me, and the maid will beat me to do great work, and I am but a little girl and can't do it.'

The old nurse grows angry and asks Moll why she is so determined not to go into service: 'What would you be – a gentlewoman?' Yes, says Moll, as she starts crying again. By gentlewoman, she means earning her keep at threepence for spinning and fourpence for needle-work. At length the old woman herself starts to weep, and then relents: '"Come" says she, "you shan't go into service; you shall live with me."' Defoe was in favour of small children earning their keep, and in his *Tour* praises the custom at Colchester, Taunton and in the West Riding. The Mayor of Colchester's wife and her two daughters come to see 'the little lass that intends to be a gentlewoman', and eventually, at the age of fourteen, Moll is taken into the family of a rich local merchant: 'Here I continued till I was between seventeen and eighteen years old, and here I knew all the advantages for my education that could be imagined; the lady had masters home to the house to teach her daughters to dance, and to speak French, and to write, and others to teach them music; and as I was always with them, I learned as fast as they.'

After this fortunate start in life Moll allows herself to be led astray by the two sons of the house, 'young gentlemen of very promising parts and of extraordinary behaviour'. The elder brother, employing flattery, kisses, and five guineas pressed into her hand, arouses Moll's ardour, although she later confesses: 'I was more confounded with the money, than I was before with the love, and began to be so elevated that I scarce knew the ground I stood on.' The same elder brother declares his intention of marrying her as soon as he comes into his inheritance, but meanwhile urges her to become his mistress. When she demurs,

> 'But what, my dear?' says he, 'I guess what you mean: what if you should be with child? Is not that it? Why, then', says he, 'I'll take care of you and provide for you, and the child too; and that you may see I am not in jest', says he, 'here's an earnest for you' and with that he pulls out a silk purse, with a hundred guineas in it, and gave it to me. 'And I'll give you such another,' says he, 'every year till I marry you.'

And so Moll loses her virginity. But meanwhile the younger son of the household has fallen in love with her and asks for her hand in marriage, which she refuses because of her secret relationship with his elder brother. The family are alarmed at the prospect of taking in a penniless foundling, and threaten to banish Moll from the house. At last the elder son cynically rids himself of his mistress by paying her £500 to marry his younger brother; and on the wedding night he gets the bridegroom 'so fuddled with drink when he went to bed, that he could not remember in the morning whether he had had any [sexual] conversation with me or no, and I was obliged to tell him he had, though in reality he had not.' Thus Moll conceals her lack of a maiden-head and becomes, in her own words, 'a whore to one brother and a wife to the other'.

Moll dismisses in one page the five years she spent with her first husband up until his early death. The two children she bore him are brought up by their grandparents. She has saved the money given her by the elder brother, and enters widowhood with about £1,200 in her pocket. She says of her first husband:

> I confess that I was not suitably affected with the loss of my husband, nor indeed can I say that I ever loved him as I ought to have done . . . and I was never in bed with my husband but I wished myself in the arms of his brother . . . in short, I committed adultery and incest with him every day in my

desires, which, without doubt, was as affectively criminal in the nature of the guilt, as if I had actually done it.

This is the first and last time that Moll admits to a sexual passion stronger than casual gratification after a good dinner and wine. It is money and security that she wants from men, throughout her adventures in London, Virginia, Bath, the North of England, London again, and finally Virginia as a transported thief. As we know from *Conjugal Lewdness,* Defoe believed that true sexual delight could only be found in the marriage bed. Moreover, he understood that sexual congress is seldom the ruling concern of human beings, even during their lusty youth, and normally matters no more than marriage, bringing up children, work, money, fame, power, adventure, war, politics and religion – in short, all the other subjects he discussed in his books.

As a wealthy widow, Moll receives offers of marriage from draper acquaintances of her husband in London, but although she is not averse to a tradesman, 'I would have a tradesman forsooth, that was something of a gentleman too; that when any husband had a need to carry me to court, or to the play, he might become a sword, and look as like a gentleman as another man; and not be one that had the mark of his apron-strings upon his coat, or the mark of his hat upon his periwig.' She gets what she asked for, and what she deserves, when she marries 'this land-water thing called a gentleman-trader', a spendthrift who runs through her money in little more than two years. When he flees to Paris, Moll has to escape from their creditors by going to live in another part of London, putting on widow's weeds and changing her name to Mrs Flanders. She makes friends with a sea-captain's widow, who like herself is hoping to find a husband to restore her fortune. In playing the marriage market, Moll has to conceal not only her want of a dowry but her incumbent husband; however, she finds a suitable man 'whose estate consisted of three plantations in Virginia, which brought him in a very good income, generally speaking, to the tune of £300 a year, but that if he was to live upon them, would bring him in four times as much'.

Moll sets her trap by telling the suitor that if she consents to marry him, she will on no account be 'transported' to the Americas, thus encouraging him to hope that she has money enough for them both to remain in England. Two days after the wedding she meekly owns up to her lack of a fortune, 'and I added that I was sensible that he had been disappointed in a wife . . . and I could do no less to make him amends, than tell him that I was very willing to go over to Virginia with him and live there.' This was exactly what she had planned to do in the first place.

She quickly adapts to plantation life on the York river, and gets on famously with her mother-in-law, 'a mighty cheerful, good-humoured old woman – I may call her old woman, for her son was about thirty'. The veteran settler is eager to tell the greenhorn how Virginia is run. Some of the colonists come as indentured servants, 'though they are more properly called slaves', and the rest are felons from Newgate and other prisons, whose death sentences have been commuted to transportation. When the servants and convicts arrive, 'we make no distinction between them, and they work together in the fields till their time is over'. Moll's mother-in-law goes on to explain with pride that some of the 'Newgate-birds' go on to become great men in Virginia, as justices of the peace and trainband captains; indeed, some of the magistrates have been 'burnt in the hand'.

At this point the gushing old lady admits that she too came to the colony as a felon, and takes off a glove to show Moll the brand on her palm. 'Depend upon it', she goes on, now warming to her story, 'there are more thieves and rogues made by that one prison at Newgate than by all the clubs and societies of villains in the nation; tis that cursed place that half peopled the colony . . .' As her mother-in-law prattles on, Moll 'began to be very uneasy; but coming to one particular, that required telling her name, I thought I should have sunk down in the place': Moll's mother-in-law proves to be her mother.

Moll is horrified: she refuses to sleep with her husband and soon announces a wish to return to England. When the bewildered man protests and then rages, Moll tells him the truth, at which he subsides into a state of melancholy. Defoe handles the dark subject of incest with delicacy and common sense. Instead of resolving the crisis by violent death, as Sophocles did in the Oedipus drama or Wagner in *Die Walküre*, Defoe lets Moll return quietly to England, taking with her a valuable cargo of tobacco.

Although it later emerges that Moll has had children by this incestuous marriage, she cares no more for them than for those by other marriages and affairs. She is more concerned at the damage done by a storm to her cargo of tobacco, now at Bristol. While attending to the business, she lodges at Bath and takes up with an unhappily married man, who gives her money but promises not to make any sexual demands, not even when they sleep together. Indeed it is Moll who, after a good dinner and 'after some other follies which I cannot name, and being clasped close in his arms, I told him (I repeat it with shame and horror of soul) that I could find in my heart to discharge him of his engagement for one night and no more'. The one night leads to six years and three children, but after a serious illness her lover, in a fit of remorse, returns to his wife. He takes care of the children and leaves Moll a generous settlement, which she invests with various goldsmiths and bankers. Her main trustee in this matter declares his love, but since he is married, albeit to a 'whore', Moll turns him down and goes to look for a husband in the North of England.

In Lancashire Moll has a whirlwind romance with a rich Irishman (or so she thinks), who marries her in a Roman Catholic ceremony but shortly afterwards disappears. Soon she finds out that her fourth husband is really a highwayman. He has also made her pregnant, so she returns to London to have the baby. Here Defoe gives a detailed and fascinating account of the business of 'Mother Midnight', who runs a maternity home, as well as being a procuress, a fence and abortionist. He even prints the tariffs of her three different grades of lying-in, from the thirteen-guinea economy to the luxury service at £53. 14. 0, including a private nurse for a month, the finest bed-linen, a minister to christen the baby, and even a festive supper – 'the gentlemen should send in the wine.'

Soon after bearing a boy to her highwayman husband Moll receives a letter from her previous admirer, the trustee. He has obtained a divorce from his faithless wife, and now offers marriage to Moll. She boards out her new-born baby, although on condition that she has visiting rights, for Moll has belatedly come to believe in the duties of motherhood: 'I wish all those women who consent to the disposing their children out of the way, as it is called, for decency's sake, would consider that tis only a contrived method for murder; that is to say, a-killing their children with safety ... Again, to give them up to be managed by those people who have none of that needful affection placed by nature in them, is to neglect them in the highest degree.'

After this sanctimonious twaddle, and having disposed of yet another child, Moll goes on to marry a fifth husband:

Then it occurred to me, 'What an abominable creature am I! and how is this innocent gentleman going to be abused by me! How little does he think, that having divorced a whore, he is

throwing himself into the arms of another! that he is going to
marry one who has lain with two brothers, and has had three
children by her own brother! one that was born in Newgate,
whose mother was a whore and is now a transported thief!
one that has lain with thirteen men, and has had a child since
he saw me! Poor gentleman,' said I, 'what is he going to do?'

He is going to marry Moll, of course, and make her rich.

For five years Moll lives quietly with her serious and hard-working
husband. 'I kept no company, made no visits; minded my family and
obliged my husband,' she says, having added two children to her enormous brood, 'when a sudden blow from an almost invisible hand
blasted all my happiness.' The bankruptcy of a partner fell heavily on
Moll's husband; 'he grew melancholy and disconsolate, and from
thence lethargic, and died.' Moll is now forty-eight and 'past the
flourishing time when I might expect to be courted for a mistress'.
She is scared, friendless and quickly running out of money, so that 'I
fancied every sixpence that I paid for a loaf of bread was the last that
I had in the world, and that tomorrow I was to fast, and be starved to
death'.

It is now that Moll turns to crime, for 'poverty is the worst of all
snares'. However, let modern critics be warned: when Defoe mentions
poverty he does not refer to the general social condition but to a
personal lack of money. He never suggests that the poor as a class are
driven to crime as a form of political protest; not having known any
other state, they are accustomed to poverty. It is the well-to-do, who
have known better things, who are most affected by friendlessness and
fear of want, as Defoe himself knew from his bankruptcy. At this point
in *Moll Flanders*, as previously in *Robinson Crusoe* and again in *Colonel
Jack*, Defoe quotes the saying, 'Give me not poverty lest I steal', a
paraphrase of *Proverbs* 30: 8, 9: 'Give me neither poverty nor riches;
feed me with food convenient for me: Lest I be full, and deny thee,
and say, who is the Lord? Or lest I be poor, and steal, and take the
name of my God in vain.' This passage explains Defoe's view of poverty
as a moral danger, affecting the individual, not as a social evil, as it is
understood today. Despite having spent her early years in Newgate,
Moll has never experienced hardship or hunger. But 'Give me not
poverty lest I steal,' she says, before snatching a bundle from an apothecary's shop in Leadenhall Street.

After the first theft Moll quickly acquires the arts and the whining self-righteousness of the criminal. When she robs a small girl of a necklace, she feels no guilt, 'as I did the child no harm, I only said to myself, I had given the parents a just reproof for their negligence in leaving the poor little lamb to come home by itself, and it would teach them to take more care of it another time.'

Under the tutelage of 'Mother Midnight' Moll becomes a nimble and versatile crook. At one Bartholomew Fair she picks up and 'rolls' a wealthy drunk, then, with the assistance of 'Mother Midnight', offers to sell back his watch and his valuables. 'This was an adventure indeed unlooked for . . . though I was not so past the merry part of life as to forget how to behave when a fop so blinded by his appetites, should not know an old woman from a young.' The poor gull is later so grateful for the return of his goods, and for the assurance that he has not been given the pox or, worse still, betrayed to his wife, that he starts to go back to Moll for further sexual encounters.

On one occasion Moll is recognized as a thief but charged with a crime that she has not committed; so, with the help of a rascally lawyer, she charges the trader with false arrest. With the £50 he agrees to pay her, Moll now has £700 in cash, besides clothes, rings, plate and two gold watches, yet still she persists in her life of crime. At last she is apprehended while emerging from a private house with a piece of silver plate. She is taken to Newgate, 'that horrid place, where so many of my comrades had been locked up, and from whence they went to the fatal tree [gallows]'. The other prisoners taunt her, drink to her health in brandy (at Moll's expense), and sing of St Sepulchre's bell which tolls on the execution day:

> If I swing by the string
> I shall hear the bell ring
> And then there's an end of poor Jenny.

In Newgate Moll meets her 'Lancashire husband' the highwayman, with whom she is joined in a tearful reunion. But thanks to a kindly prison chaplain, she is given a commuted sentence, and later her husband also escapes the rope and sails with her on a convict ship to Virginia.

Moll and her 'Lancashire husband' were not unusually lucky in having escaped the gallows. Sentences were often commuted at the time Defoe was writing in order to temper a savage penal code as well as to settle the North American colonies. As hanging was mandatory for even a trivial theft, both juries and witnesses were often reluctant to secure a guilty verdict unless they believed that the sentence would be commuted. The transportation of felons to Maryland and Virginia provided labour for the tobacco plantations, and later a stock of rugged settlers. While murderers and other serious criminals went to Tyburn, most of the petty thieves found themselves pioneers of the future United States. Since the climate was healthy and most of the convicts lived out their five or ten years of penal servitude, transportation to Maryland or Virginia was far less onerous a fate than that of the convicts sent to Australia in the nineteenth century, when Britain had lost its North American colonies. It was certainly mild compared to the horror endured by French convicts sent to the *bagne* of Guiana, including the fearsome Devil's Island, an institution that survived until after the Second World War. In *Moll Flanders* and once again in *Colonel Jack* Defoe suggests that transportation to Maryland and Virginia offered the chance to start a new life, as well as a blessed escape from the gallows.

Moll and her highwayman husband are living in fine style even before their transport ship has left Gravesend. With the help of the faithful 'Mother Midnight', Moll has exchanged some of her ill-gotten gains into goods and provisions for the future, including a bed, some furniture, tools for plantation work, plentiful food such as chickens, ten dozen bottles of good beer, wine and 'brandy, sugar, lemons etc. to make punch and to treat our benefactor, the captain'. For indeed Moll has so liberally greased the palms of the crew that she and her husband actually dine at the captain's table during the voyage to the Potomac river.

Within a day of landing in Virginia the couple have bought their freedom, and soon afterwards purchase a plantation in Maryland. Moll learns that her husband/brother is still alive but ill and feeble; her mother is dead but is said to have left her something in her will. Moll had described her earlier departure from Virginia with scarcely a mention of a child, or children, and certainly no word of regret. Now, catching a glimpse of her son Humphry, but not yet daring to reveal herself, she treats herself and the reader to an outburst of bogus emotion: 'Let any mother of children that reads this consider it, and but think with what anguish of mind I restrained myself; what yearnings of soul I had in me to embrace him, and weep over him; and how I thought all my entrails turned within me, that my very bowels moved, and I knew not what to do, as I now know not how to express these agonies!' But she is really after her mother's legacy.

In the second and larger of the houses in which he lived
on what is now Stoke Newington Church Street, Defoe
wrote most of his fictional works, as well as his semi-fictional
Tour Through the Whole Island of Great Britain.

In *A Journal of the Plague Year*, Defoe denounces Solomon Eagle, a Quaker fanatic who
went semi-naked through the London streets, with burning coals on his head 'telling
the people that the plague had come upon them as a punishment for their sins'.
Chalk drawing by E. M. Ward, 1848.

After Friday has been rescued by Robinson Crusoe, 'he came close to me, and then he kneeled down again, kissed the ground – and taking me by the foot, set my foot upon his head: this, it seems, was in token of swearing to be my slave for ever.'
Illustration to a French edition of 1786.

When Robert Louis Stevenson wished to illustrate the supreme moments in
imaginative literature, he instanced two from Homer, one from Defoe and one from
Defoe's fellow Puritan John Bunyan: 'Crusoe recoiling from the footprint; Achilles
shouting over against the Trojans; Ulysses bending the great bow; Christian running
with his fingers in his ears ... each has been painted on the mind's eye for ever.'
Illustration from 1790.

PORTRAIT *of the Celebrated* MOLL FLANDERS
Taken from Life in Newgate

The famous Moll Flanders, of beauty the boast,
Belov'd and distinguish'd, long flourish'd the toast,
But beauty is frail and soon comes to decay,
When shift and contrivance must enter in play;
Her arts of intrigue, as this book shall unfold,
Will keep you awake while her story is told.

Pub.ᵈ by C. Johnson.

Frontispiece to an early edition of *Moll Flanders*.

Defoe was contemptuous of old buildings like Westminster Hall (*above*, in *c.* 1720), which he saw as Gothic or 'popish' relics.

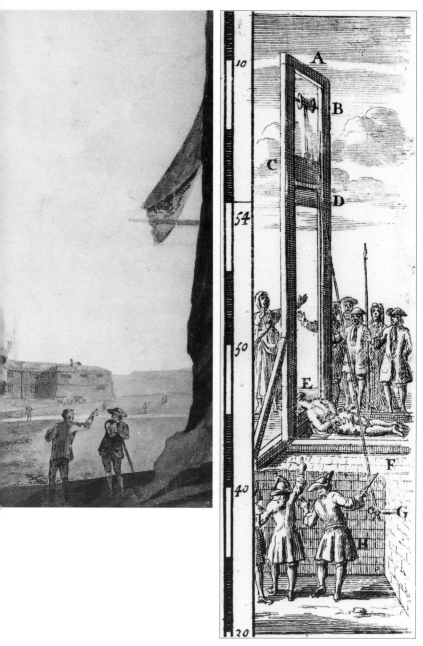

In his *Tour*, Defoe describes
at length this prototype of
the guillotine at Halifax, in
Yorkshire.

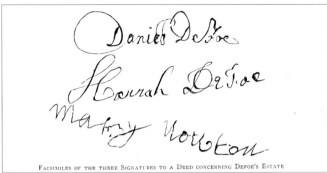

FACSIMILES OF THE THREE SIGNATURES TO A DEED CONCERNING DEFOE'S ESTATE

Top James Douglas, 2nd Duke of Queensberry, who worked with Defoe to bring about the Act of Union between England and Scotland. Defoe describes the Duke and his home Drumlanrig Castle in the *Tour*.

Above The three signatures to a deed concerning Defoe's Estate at Colchester.

Moll writes to her husband/brother, proclaiming her 'most passion-ate desire of once seeing my one and only child', apparently having forgotten the dozen or so by other husbands and lovers. Her son Humphry opens the letter (his father can no longer read) and rushes to greet his long-lost mother, with tears and embraces on both sides; after which Moll gives him a fine gold watch: 'I told him that I had nothing of any value to bestow but that, and I desired him he would now and then kiss it for my sake. I did not indeed tell him that I had stolen it from a gentlewoman's side, at a meeting-house in London. That's by the way.'

With her mother's inheritance, as well as the profits from the plan-tation, Moll buys her Lancashire husband 'all those things I knew he delighted to have; as two good long wigs, two silver-hilted swords, three or four fine fowling-pieces, a fine saddle with holsters and pistols very handsome, with a scarlet cloak; and in a word, everything I could think of to oblige him, and to make him appear as he really was, a very fine gentleman'. He in turn blesses the day he married Moll and a fortune in Lancashire. 'We are now grown old,' says Moll at the end; 'I am come back to England being almost seventy years of age, my husband sixty-eight, and we resolve to spend the remainder of our years in sincere penitence for the wicked lives we have led.' And so the brazen old scoundrel closes her tale.

Defoe's last work of fiction, *Roxana* or *The Fortunate Mistress*, published in 1724, is also the autobiography of a wanton woman, yet it is wholly unlike *Moll Flanders*. For one thing it is written with much greater care, both in its construction and in the attention to detail. Whereas *Moll Flanders*, and still more *Captain Singleton* and *Colonel Jack*, are picaresque tales of adventure, where anything may happen next, the events at the start of *Roxana* explain and even determine the later course of the action throughout the book. The other main characters engage our interest and sympathy, while Roxana herself remains true to her tortured and self-destructive nature. In this, unlike most of the other works, we get a sense of the passage of time, of how Roxana adapts to the onset of age. Whereas Moll Flanders ignores her children, except to extract some money out of her son in Virginia, Roxana is dogged to the end of the book by a daughter she had abandoned at the beginning. Because of its complex construction and the interplay of its characters, *Roxana* alone of Defoe's books can really be called a novel in the modern sense.

This is not to suggest that because *Roxana* is a novel, even arguably the first in the English language, it represents an advance on adventure stories like *Robinson Crusoe*, historical reconstruction such as *The Memoirs of a Cavalier*, or the picaresque *Moll Flanders*. The novel is not a better, merely a different genre. Moreover, like all pioneering efforts in literature, art, music or motion pictures, *Roxana* seems primitive by the standards of what came later. This is immediately apparent when we compare Defoe's story of an adulteress with those two great nineteenth-century novels, Gustave Flaubert's *Madame Bovary* and Leo Tolstoy's *Anna Karenina*.

If *Roxana* cannot compete with those two mighty successors, it is nevertheless a powerful and sometimes frightening book, which more than any other reveals the mind of its creator. While Moll Flanders is a light-hearted and cheeky rogue in a largely comic adventure story, Roxana is a tormented and tragic victim, first of misfortune and then of her own selfish ambition. Although he condemns Roxana's behaviour, Defoe makes it clear that her downfall is caused by her first profligate husband. The dread of financial ruin, as well as the sense of being pursued, which are minor themes of most of his earlier fiction, have taken command in *Roxana*, and give it an atmosphere of nightmarish terror.

Some modern critics suggest that Roxana suffers from manic depression or some other mental illness; yet her state of mind is much the same as Defoe's chronic misery and despair over his bankruptcy and incarceration. There are several apparent references in the book to its author's anguish and shame at having squandered his wife's inheritance, as well as his inability to provide his daughter Sophie's dowry. Those who have suffered prolonged financial worries will recognize in *Roxana* their own obsessive and frantic desperation.

The alluring woman portrayed in the frontispiece of the first edition is given the title, 'the person known by the name of the Lady Roxana in the time of King Charles II'. Yet in the opening sentence of the book the narrator informs us that she was born in Poitiers, 'from whence I was brought to England, about the year 1683, when the Protestants were banished from France by the cruelty of their persecutors'. This means that she was only a baby two years before Charles II's death. Defoe is giving the reader to understand that the grown-up courtesan of the story could have been Charles II's Nell Gwyn or one of the ladies at Court in 1720, and therefore the mistress of George I, or the Prince of Wales, the future George II.

When Roxana is fifteen (Defoe does not mention her original name), her rich Huguenot father gives her a dowry of £2,000 and marries her off to the son of a City brewer – 'pardon me if I conceal his name, for though he was the foundation of my ruin, I cannot take so severe a revenge upon him'. Roxana describes him with a controlled ferocity, as though through gritted teeth:

> With this thing called a husband, I lived eight years in good fashion, and for some part of the time kept a coach, that is to say a kind of mock-coach; for all the week the horses were kept at work in the dray-carts, but on Sunday I had the privilege to go abroad in my chariot, either to church, or otherways, as my husband and I could agree about it; which by the way was not very often ... He was a jolly, handsome fellow as any woman need wish for a companion ... he danced well, which I think was the first thing that brought us together. He had an old father who managed the business carefully, and he took the advantage of it, for he cared very little about it, but went abroad, kept company, hunted much, and loved it exceedingly.

When Roxana has been married for four years, her father dies, leaving her 5,000 livres, but since he distrusted her husband he has put the money in charge of her elder brother, who loses it all on a merchant venture similar to the ones that had ruined Defoe. Two years later Roxana's father-in-law also dies, leaving the brewery to her husband, who has no head for business. With his trade declining, he sells off the brewery, but very soon squanders the money he got for it: 'I was not wanting with all that persuasions and entreaties could perform, but it was all fruitless. Representing to him how fast our money wasted, and what would be our condition when it was gone, made no impression on him ... nor did he abate his horses or servants, even to the last, till he had not a hundred pounds left in the whole world.' After seven years of marriage all the money was spent on foolishness, for her husband 'kept no valuable company neither; but generally with huntsmen and horse-coursers, and men meaner than himself, which is another consequences of a man's being a fool, such as can never delight in men more wise and capable than themselves, and that make them converse with scoundrels, drink belch [bad beer] with porters, and keep company always below themselves.'

While Defoe neatly describes a wastrel husband, he must be aware that even a hard-working and sober man, such as himself, can bring his family into ruin by foolish ventures. He too had married a rich man's daughter and squandered her dowry, just as Roxana's brother squandered her inheritance.

The husband has talked of seeking his fortune 'somewhere or other', and early one morning gets out of bed, goes to the window overlooking the stable and sounds his French horn as a signal to his men to go hunting:

> It was about the latter end of August and so was light yet at five o'clock, and it was about that time that I heard him and his two men go out and shut the yard-gates after them. He said nothing to me more than as usual when he used to go out upon his sport; neither did I rise, or say anything to him that was material, but went to sleep again after he was gone, for two hours or thereabouts.

Roxana is slow to understand that her husband has deserted her. For the first night or two of his absence she does not worry, 'and also knowing that he had two servants and three horses with him, it would be the strangest thing in the world that anything could befall them all, but that I must some time or another hear of them'. However, as days run into weeks and then months, Roxana is faced with the problem of keeping her five children on £70 in cash and a few pieces of silver plate. She applies for help to her husband's family, but his sisters will not even ask her to sit down, while a kindly aunt-in-law is too poor to offer her more than a meal and sympathy.

Roxana's only support at this desperate time is Amy, her maid, who later becomes her closest friend, and even an *alter ego* or evil genius. Amy is young, artful, merry and quite without scruples, except with regard to Roxana. It is Amy who uses her wit and wiles to shame Roxana's in-laws into caring for the children. Although she is no longer paid her wages, Amy stays in the house 'that was before handsomely furnished with pictures and ornaments, cabinets, pier-glasses [large mirrors] ... now stripped and naked, most of the goods having been stripped by the landlord for rent, or sold to buy necessaries'. When Roxana and she grow hungry, Amy contrives to come up with 'a small breast of mutton, and two great bunches of turnips, which she intended to stew for our dinner'.

It is Amy who first urges Roxana to start an affair with the landlord – a rich City jeweller, living apart from his wife, who initially had ruthlessly stripped the house to recover his debts but comes to admire

Roxana and does not press for rent arrears. After two or three increasingly amiable visits the landlord arrives one day, announcing that he has come to dinner. The scene that follows is packed with delightful detail:

> So he called my maid Amy and sent her out to buy a joint of meat; he told her what she should buy, but naming two or three things, either of which she might take, the maid, a cunning wench and faithful to me as the skin to my back, did not buy anything outright, but brought the butcher along with her, with both the things she had chosen, for him to please himself, the one was a very good leg of veal, the other a piece of the fore-ribs of roast beef; he looked at them but bade me chaffer with the butcher for him, and I did so, and came back to him, and told him what the butcher demanded for either of them, and what each of them came to; so he pulls out 11s and 3d which they came to together, and bade me take them both, the rest, he said, would serve another time.

The landlord sends out for wine and beer, which neither Roxana nor Amy has tasted in months, then tells them to fill their glasses, before giving Roxana a hearty kiss. He continues to sing her praises, insisting that Amy should stay in the room, for 'I say all this, Madam, before your maid, because both she and you shall know that I have no ill designs, and that I have in mere kindness resolved to do something for you'. He then expresses his admiration for Amy as well, and asks her to join them at dinner. In the amorous parleys that take place over the next few days Roxana pretends to believe in the landlord's virtuous intentions, but Amy advises her to become his mistress: 'What, consent to lie with him for bread? Amy, said I, how can you talk so? Nay, Madam, says Amy, I don't think you would do it for anything else; it would not be lawful for anything else, but for bread Madam; why nobody can starve, there's no bearing that, I'm sure.'

When Roxana agrees to become the landlord's mistress, Amy is so delighted that she dances about the bedroom in her shift. The landlord signs a legal agreement to make provision for Roxana then, after a merry dinner, the laughing Amy puts the couple 'to-bed' by undressing Roxana and placing her under the sheet with the landlord: 'And thus in gratitude for the favour I received from a man, was all sense of religion, and duty to God, all regard to virtue and honour, given up at once, and we were to call one another husband and wife, who, in the sense of the laws, both of God and our country, were no more than two adulterers, in short a whore and a rogue.' Roxana insists that she does not sin for sexual pleasure, 'for I had nothing of the vice in my constitution; my spirits were far from being high; my blood had no fire in it, to kindle the flames of desire; but the kindness and good humour of the man, and the dread of my own circumstances concerted to bring me to the point.'

This lack of physical passion helps to explain the most puzzling episode in the novel, when Roxana urges her 'husband' to make love with Amy. Even to a modern reader, Roxana's behaviour appears shocking and even depraved. However, it was Amy who had first broached the idea at a time when Roxana was still unwilling to be the landlord's mistress, suggesting she do as Rachel did to Jacob, and 'when she could have no children, put her maid to bed with him'. When Roxana fails to conceive by her landlord 'husband', Amy returns to the same teasing suggestion: 'Law, Madam, what have you been doing? You have been married a year and a half ... I warrant you, Master would have got me with-child twice in that time.' Roxana replies that Amy is more than welcome to him: 'Nay, I'll put you to-bed to him one night or other, if you are willing.'

What had at first sounded like banter is now suggested in earnest by Roxana, as Amy prepares her for bed in front of the landlord:

> Then I began, and told him all that Amy had said about not being with-child, and of her being with-child twice in that time. Ay, Mrs Amy, says he, I believe so too, come hither and we'll try, but Amy did not go. Go, you fool, says I, can't you, I freely give you both leave; but my Amy would not go ... and with that I sat her down, pulled off her stockings and shoes, and all her clothes piece by piece, and led her to the bed with him. Here, says I, try what you can do with your maid, Amy. She pulled back a little, would not let me pull off her clothes at first, but it was hot weather, and she had not many clothes on, and particularly no stays on; and at last when she see I was in earnest, she let me do what I would; so I finally stripped her and then I threw up the bed and thrust her in.

Roxana tries to justify this outrageous behaviour: 'Had I looked upon myself as a wife, you cannot suppose I would have been willing to have let my husband lie with my maid, much less before my face, for

I stood by all the while, but as I thought myself a whore, I [thought] that my maid should be a whore too, and should not reproach me with it.'

As might be expected, the prank has an unhappy outcome, for Amy gets pregnant, and soon the landlord is angry both with her and with himself. The question remains whether this passage was simply pornographic, or whether Defoe intended to give it deeper significance. The fantasy of a man making love to one woman in front of another has cropped up in literature since Roman times, and was treated amusingly by Kingsley Amis in *The Green Man*. Defoe had already referred to it in *Colonel Jack*, where the hero's drunken third wife takes it in turns with her maid to perform with a naval captain. This, and the highly salacious account of Roxana undressing Amy, suggest that Defoe himself was excited by this fantasy. He may also be suggesting, as Amis does in *The Green Man*, that the two women fancy each other more than the man. On several occasions in the course of the book he mentions – for no obvious reason – that Amy and Roxana sleep in the same bed at night; we are told that Roxana does not enjoy sexual intercourse with men, though she does appear to enjoy undressing Amy. Perhaps Defoe is implying that Roxana's later feminist views are the product of lesbianism. He may be implying that Roxana is punishing Amy for having led her astray, or being 'the devil's engine', as she later calls her. Just as Amy is willing to give her body in the interests of her mistress, so she will later kill for her. Jungians might suggest that Amy is the dark or 'shadow' side of Roxana's personality, but, as Defoe often says when faced with an abstract proposition, that is for others to decide.

Roxana's landlord and lover, the jewel merchant, invites her to go with him on a business trip to Paris, which later develops into a longer residence, with Amy coming over from England to manage the household. One day the merchant is called to Versailles to discuss the sale of some jewels to a German prince in the service of France, with whom he has previously done business. Since he does not need to show him the merchandise and does not wish to take unnecessary risks, he leaves with Roxana his casket of jewels, as well as his gold watch and the diamond ring he wears on his finger (as did Defoe). Roxana is scared, 'for if you apprehend no danger, why do you use this caution', and later implores him not to go to Versailles: 'I stared at him as if I was frightened, for I thought all his face looked like a death's-head, and then immediately I thought I perceived his head all bloody.'

Roxana's premonition is soon fulfilled, as three highwaymen stop the coach on the road to Versailles and stab her lover to death, though getting away with only a few pistoles and livres in cash. Roxana is consumed by grief, but has the presence of mind to say that her 'husband' was carrying all his treasure with him, thus keeping it for herself, although she knows it belongs to his legal family. To complete the fraud, Roxana dresses in widow's weeds, which also happen to suit her complexion, for like Moll Flanders she takes pride in the fact that she does not need to 'paint', or put on make-up. Among those who come to pay their condolences to 'La Belle Veuve de Poictu', the Beautiful Widow from Poitiers, is the aide-de-camp to the German Prince, who intended to buy the jewels. A few days later his highness the Prince arrives in person and hears Roxana's pitiful story of how she had lost not only a husband but jewellery to the value of 100,000 livres. After a few more visits the Prince calls her the loveliest woman on earth, and the finest woman in France, and sets her up as his favourite mistress. Amy is useful for fending off snoopers, 'for you are to note that the people of Paris, especially the women, are the most busy and impertinent enquirers into the conduct of their neighbours, especially that of a single woman, that are in the world.' As a Huguenot, and therefore a 'Protestant whore' (as Nell Gwyn had once distinguished herself from the Duchess of Portsmouth, Charles II's 'Catholic whore'), Roxana does not have to confess to a priest, and can even keep secret the birth of a son to the Prince.

One morning at the Tuileries Roxana is devastated to see in the ranks of the Gensdarmes, or horse guards, 'Mr—, my first husband, the brewer'. In order to find out what he is doing without revealing her presence in France, Roxana dispatches Amy to meet him as though by accident. Amy spins him a yarn about Roxana's disappearance as well as her own distress, a tale she supports by much 'howling and snivelling'. The husband believes the story but asks for a loan of 150 livres, then gladly settles for one. However, Roxana is so alarmed at the thought that her husband might find and blackmail her that she hires a fulltime spy or private detective to make a weekly report on his movements. From these she concludes:

> The poor indolent wretch, who by his unactive temper had at
> first been my ruin ... was a meer motionless animal, of no
> consequence in the world; that he seemed to be one, who
> though he was indeed alive, had no manner of business in life

but . . . in short sauntered abroad, like one, that it was not two
livres value, whether he was alive or dead; that when he was
gone, would leave no remembrance behind that ever he was
here; that if ever he did anything in the world to be talked of
it was only to beget five beggars, and starve his wife . . . It
gave me most contemptible thoughts of him, and made me
often say, I was a warning for all the ladies in Europe, against
marrying of fools; a man of sense falls in the world, and gets
up again, and a woman has some chance for herself; but with
a fool, once fall, and ever undone; once in the ditch and die
in the ditch.

The Prince takes Roxana with him on a two-year mission to Italy,
providing her with a Turkish slave-girl, from whom she learns to dress,
sing and dance in the oriental style. Although Roxana likes Venice and
Naples, she does not think highly of the Eternal City:

The swarms of ecclesiastics of all kinds, the innumerable valets,
lackeys and other servants is such, that they used to say there
are very few of the common people in Rome, but who have
been footmen, or porters, or grooms to cardinals . . . In a word,
they have an air of sharping, cozening, quarrelling and scolding
. . . and when I was there the footmen made such a broil
between two great families in Rome about which of their
coaches should give way to the other, that there was above
thirty people wounded on both sides, five or six killed outright,
and both the ladies frighted almost to death.

Soon after returning to France the Prince learns that his wife, the
virtuous Princess, is dead, and in a fit of repentance he sadly renounces
Roxana. Although fond of the Prince and flattered by his attentions,
Roxana consoles herself with her wealth, which she now resolves to
take back to London. Having no friends in England, she asks the
advice of a Dutch merchant in Paris, who offers to give her bills of
exchange through his own business acquaintances in Holland. But first
he suggests that Roxana sells her jewels for cash in Paris, rather than
risk taking them with her to England. The Jewish dealer, who has
been called in to assess the value of the stones, immediately recognizes
them as the ones allegedly stolen by highwaymen on the road to
Versailles. Roxana could now be charged with murder and put on the

rack to force a confession unless she pays the Jew sufficient money to buy his silence.

Defoe superbly conveys the atmosphere of terror and menace during the next few days, until Roxana and Amy manage to slip out of Paris and carry the casket of jewels to Rouen, taking a ship for Rotterdam and the Dutch merchant's protection. Even after leaving the mouth of the Seine, the two women are not out of danger: shortly after they have passed the English coast at Dover, a storm arises. The crew of the ship fall on their knees in prayer, and barely manage to make the safety of Harwich. Amy is too frightened to put to sea again, but Roxana goes over to Rotterdam, where the story develops a new twist:

> I heard a noise of horses at the door ... which is not very common in a city where everyone passes by water ... and I looking towards the door, saw a gentleman alight ... it was the merchant from Paris, my benefactor and indeed my deliverance ... I confess it was an agreeable surprise to me, and I was exceedingly glad to see him, who was so honourable and kind to me, and who indeed had saved my life. As soon as he saw me, he ran to me, took me in his arms, and kissed me with a freedom that he never offered to take with me before: Dear Madam, says he, I am glad to see you safe in this country; if you had stayed two days longer in Paris, you had been undone. I was so glad to see him, that I could not speak a good while, and I burst out into tears, without speaking a word for a minute; but I soon recovered that disorder and said, the more, Sir, in my obligation to you that saved my life, and added that I may consider how to balance an account, in which I am so much your debtor.

From the outset it is clear that there is a serious misunderstanding that will later blight the happiness of the Dutchman as well as Roxana. She wants to express her gratitude by paying him money and, if he so wishes, by making love, but even though she believes, erroneously, that her own brewer husband is dead, she does not want to marry him. The widowed Dutchman, however, is deeply in love with Roxana; he does not want any money from her; moreover, he thinks it wrong to sleep with her except as a legal husband. This reversal of the sexual roles, and Roxana's justification of her behaviour, would appear more appropriately in a late twentieth-century novel, but few modern writers can match Defoe's wit and psychological insight. And although he brilliantly argues Roxana's case for sex outside marriage, he also explains why it may lead to misery.

At the start of his courtship the merchant tells Roxana, in a manner 'more polite and more courteous than is esteemed the ordinary usage of the Dutch', that he wants her to take the place of his late wife. She answers that she can deny him nothing except 'that thing only that I could not grant' – that is, her hand in marriage: 'He tried all the ways imaginable to bring his design to pass, but I was inflexible; at last he thought of a way, which he flattered himself, would not fail, nor would he have been mistaken perhaps, in any other woman in the world, but me; this was, to try if he could take me at an advantage, and get to bed with me; and then as was most rational to think, I should willingly enough marry him afterwards.'

Since he and Roxana live in the same house, the merchant soon gets her to bed. 'I made a show of resistance,' she says, 'but it was no more; for as above, I resolved from the beginning, he should lie with me, if he would . . .' Three nights later the merchant announces, 'I am ready to marry you, and desire you to let it be done tomorrow morning, and I will give you the same fair conditions of marriage as I would have done before.' To the merchant's astonishment, Roxana rejects him, apparently still thinking that he wants her money, although even on this matter he quickly disabuses her. The argument resumes again 'one morning, in the middle of our unlawful freedoms, that is to say, when we were in bed together', but Roxana repeats that she can deny him no favour, 'that of matrimony excepted'. She believes that 'a woman was a free agent, as well as a man, and was born free, and could she manage herself suitably, might enjoy that liberty to as much purpose as the men do . . .'

The Dutchman replies that although in some respects Roxana speaks truly, 'yet I ought to consider, that as an equivalent to this, the man has all the cares of things devolved upon him; that the weight of business lay upon his shoulders, and as he had the trust, so he had the toil of life upon him, his was the labour, his the anxiety of living; that the woman had nothing to do but to eat the fat, and drink the sweet; to sit still, and look around her; be waited on and made easy, especially if her husband acted as became him.' Roxana replies that while a woman was single, 'she was a masculine in her political capacity', that is to say, she had the same legal rights as a man:

I added, that whoever the woman was, that had an estate, and would give it up to be the slave of a great man, that woman was a fool, and must be fit for nothing but a beggar; that it was my opinion, a woman was as fit to govern and enjoy her own estate, without a man, as a man was, without a woman, and that if she had a mind to gratify herself as to sexes [i.e., have sexual intercourse], she might entertain a man, as a man does a mistress.

The merchant answers in the name of tradition and common sense, declaring that 'the other way was the ordinary method that the world was guided by'. He claims that true affection between a man and his wife silenced all Roxana's objections at becoming a slave, and where there was mutual love there could be no bondage. Roxana replies that, from her own experience (which she does not reveal to the merchant), a woman who allows herself to become 'the passive creature you spoke of' puts herself at the mercy of her husband, who may be a fool:

> Now often have I seen a woman living in all the splendour that a plentiful fortune ought to allow her, with her coaches and equipages; her family and rich furniture ... tomorrow surprised with disaster; turned out of all by a commission of bankrupt; stripped to the clothes on her back ... and she turned out into the street, and left to live on the charity of her friend, if she has any, or follow her husband, her monarch, into the Mint [a sanctuary for insolvent debtors in Southwark].

She describes 'crying myself to death, and how I nearly starved for almost two years together', which leaves the Dutchman mystified: 'He shook his head and said, where had I lived? and what dreadful families had I lived among, that had frighted me into such terrible apprehensions of things? that these things, indeed, might happen when men run into hazardous things in trade, and without prudence, or due consideration, launched their fortunes in degree beyond their strength, grasping at adventures beyond their stocks ...' One can sense the misery and the shame with which Defoe wrote these words, so exactly describing his own career as a businessman.

Roxana scorns the idea that a woman should marry a man because she has been to bed with him; on the contrary, she says, 'when a woman has been weak enough to yield up the last before, it would be adding one weakness to another, to take the man afterwards'. And unless that husband happens to be one man in 100,000, he will hold it against her afterwards, and if the children hear of it they will come to hate their mother. Even when she becomes pregnant by the Dutchman, Roxana refuses to marry him. He is horrified by her attitude, so 'contrary to the notions of all the world', and tells her of the unkindness she does to the unborn child, which 'must be branded from the cradle with a mark of infamy; be loaded with the crime and follies of its parents, and suffer for sins it never committed'.

Writing with hindsight, later in life, Roxana bemoans her folly: 'If ever a woman in her senses rejected a man of merit, on so trivial and frivolous a pretext, I am that woman ... and was ever woman so stupid to be a whore, where she might have been an honest wife? But infatuations are next to being possessed by the Devil; I was inflexible and pretended [ventured] to argue upon the point of Woman's Liberty.' The term 'Woman's Liberty' comes near to enraging even the long-suffering Dutchman:

> Dear Madam, you argue for liberty at the same time that you restrain yourself from that liberty [married love] which God and Nature has directed you to take; and to supply the deficiency, propose a vicious liberty, which is neither honourable or religious; will you propose liberty at the expense of modesty? ... He was astonished to think how I could satisfy myself to be so cruel to an innocent infant not yet born; professed he could neither bear the thought of, much less bear to see it ... and he could not stay to see me delivered.

And so the unhappy Dutchman despairs of winning her hand in marriage and leaves for Paris; while, as for Roxana: 'Having thus spent nine months in Holland, refused the best offer any woman in my circumstances had; parted unkindly, and indeed barbarously with the best friend and honestest man in the world; got all my money in my pocket, and a bastard in my belly, I took shipping at the Briel, in the packet-boat, and arrived safe at Harwich, where my woman Amy was come by my direction to meet me.'

After giving birth to the Dutchman's son and putting him into the care of foster parents, Roxana establishes herself in a Pall Mall mansion, overlooking St James's Park and near to the King, her intended lover. She entrusts her financial affairs to Sir Robert Clayton, the real-life merchant and politician who had been the adviser to Neil Gwyn during the reign of Charles II and probably sat on the bench at Defoe's Old

Bailey trial. Defoe had attacked Sir Robert in his *Reformation of Manners*; he died in 1707, but now comes back to life, advising Roxana to marry a merchant instead of a nobleman: 'A merchant in flush business, and a capital stock, is able to spend more money than a gentleman of £5,000 a year estate; that while a merchant spent, he only spent what he got, and not that; and that he laid up great sums every year. That an estate is a pond; but that a trade was a spring . . .'

However, Roxana does not intend to marry, and here Defoe punishes Clayton's ghost by forcing him to listen to her feminist harangue:

> My heart was bent on an independent fortune; and I told him, I knew no state of matrimony, but what was, at best, a state of inferiority, if not of bondage; that I had no notion of it; that I lived a life of absolute liberty now; was free as I was born; and having a plentiful fortune, I did not understand what coherence the words *honour* and *obey* had with the liberty of a free woman . . . and seeing liberty seemed to be the man's property, I would be a man-woman; for as I was born free, I would die so.

Although a mother of eight, and now in her forties, Roxana has kept her youthful looks, complexion and figure, and is soon the grand hostess of the 'Court end' of London. She holds gambling parties, balls and masquerades, taking handsome contributions in cash from her noble and royal guests. Occasionally, as the star turn of the evening, Roxana performs the eastern dance she learnt from the Turkish slave-girl, also wearing the costume bought at Leghorn:

> The robe was a fine Persia or India damask; the ground white, and the flowers blue and gold, and the train held five yards; the dress under it was a vest of the same, embroidered with gold, and set with some pearl in the work, and some turquoise stones; to the vest was a girdle five or six inches wide, after the Turkish mode; and on both ends where it joined, or hooked, was set with diamonds for eight inches either way, only they were not true diamonds; but nobody knew that but myself.

The costume and the exotic dance won her the name Roxana, which was then given to ladies from the mysterious east, like Mata Hari earlier in this century. The dress and the veil Roxana assumed as part of the masquerade were symbols of the depravity that Defoe deplored at the Court of Charles II and later of George I, who had a passion for eastern things and kept two Turkish servants. Defoe suggests that one of Roxana's lovers is the King himself, or another royal personage such as the Prince of Wales, the future George II. Although Roxana is now a royal mistress, as well as proprietress of an exclusive ballroom, salon and gambling club, she also sleeps with various wealthy noblemen. One of these lovers finds Roxana in bed with Amy and rudely lifts up her night-dress to make sure she is not a 'Mr Amy'. Defoe is once more pointing out that love and true sexual delight cannot be found in casual encounters.

Having spent eight years in England, Roxana is fifty and starting to ask herself: 'Why should I be a whore now?' She gives up her current noble lover and moves from her Pall Mall house to a cottage at Kensington Gravel Pits, at the north-west corner of Kensington Gardens, on what is now Bayswater Road. Even there she feels insufficiently far removed from the 'Court end' of London, and goes to live instead at Goodman's Fields in Whitechapel, near where Defoe was born and raised. She lodges with a Quaker widow and, in keeping with her new personality, puts on the sombre Quaker dress. She hopes she has now severed her ties with the 'Court end' and even the name Roxana:

> I was now in a perfect retreat indeed; remote from the eyes
> of all that ever had seen me, and as much out of the way of
> being ever seen or heard of by any of the old gang that used
> to follow me, as if I had been in the mountains in Lancashire;
> for when did a Blue Garter, or a Coach-and-six come into a
> little narrow passage in the Minories, or Goodman Fields. And
> as there was no fear of them, so really I had no desire to see
> them, or so much as to hear from them any more, as long as
> I lived.

Roxana finds out too late that she cannot escape reminders of her wicked past. First, the honest Dutch merchant comes to London and once more asks for her hand in marriage, promising to make her a lady in England and a countess in Holland. Roxana at first demurs, especially when Amy writes from Paris to say that her German Prince is also now ready to make her a princess. But the Prince is then hurt in a boar-hunt, and during his convalescence once more suffers religious remorse. 'Law, Madam', says Amy in her subsequent letter, 'you see he is gotten among the priests, and I suppose they saucily imposed some penance upon him; and it may be sent him of an errand bare-foot, to some Madonna or Nosterdame.' Amy advises Roxana that she would be better off as a lady in English, and countess in Dutch, than as a princess 'in the devil's language' of High-Dutch, or German.

Roxana's Nemesis takes the form of her second daughter Susan, one of the five children she bore to her first brewer husband but has never seen since. On first returning to England, Roxana had sent Amy to make enquiries about their situation and give secret financial support for their education and careers. While four of the children are quite content to accept this help from a mystery donor, Susan, now twenty-five, is a sad, neurotic woman, who has set her heart on finding and winning the love of her natural mother. By ill chance, Susan happens to have worked as a maid at Roxana's Pall Mall house at the time of the Turkish dances and royal affair. At first she thinks that Amy is her mother before she discovers a link to 'Roxana', whom she has never seen except in a veil.

The story builds towards its horrifying and nightmarish climax, when Roxana and the Dutchman she has now married go to dine aboard the ship that will shortly take them to Holland and find themselves in the company of the captain, his wife and her schoolfriend, Susan. As dinner progresses Susan becomes increasingly sure that this Dutch merchant's wife is 'Roxana' and also her mother. A few days later she calls at the house of the Quaker lady, where, to Roxana's mortification, she starts to talk of her life at the Pall Mall mansion, with the masquerades, Roxana's love affair with the King and, above all, the Turkish costume, which she describes in detail.

Now even the Quaker lady and, perhaps, her Dutch husband begin to suspect Roxana's past, and Susan has only to make the link with Amy to claim her natural mother's love. Roxana and Amy can now only meet in secret. Roxana takes refuge in Tunbridge (Wells) and, when Susan discovers her there, continues her flight to Woodford in Essex, where she is once more hunted to ground. Meanwhile Amy resolves to murder Susan to stop her tongue. She crosses the Thames with her from the Tower to Greenwich, but cannot entice her into the wilderness to the south of the park. At last the simple Quaker woman calls on Roxana to give her what she believes will be welcome news. Amy had told her that Susan would cause no more trouble, 'and after Amy had said so she had indeed, never heard any more of the girl'.

Roxana has understood the message, and calls Amy

a thousand devils and monsters and hard-hearted tigers . . . As for the poor girl herself, I saw her by night and by day; she haunted my imagination, if she did not haunt the house; my fancy showed her me in a hundred shapes and postures; sleeping or waking she was with me. Sometimes I thought her with her throat cut; sometimes with her head cut and her brains knocked out; other times hanged up upon a beam; another time drowned in the Great Pond at Camberwell.

After a month of this mental torment, which she tries to conceal from her honest husband, Roxana accompanies him to Holland; and soon she is joined there by Amy, her lifelong accomplice in whoring, and now in murder: 'Here, after some few years of flourishing and outwardly happy circumstances, I fell into a dreadful course of calamities, and Amy also, the very reverse of our former good days; the blast of Heaven seemed to follow the injury done the poor girl, by us both; and I was brought so low again, that my resistance seemed to be only the consequence of my misery, as my misery was of my crime.'

In this sombre, disturbing book we see into the depths of Defoe's shame and misery over his debt, the wrong done to his wife and later his daughter, Sophia, who may be the origin of the wretched 'Susan'. It was while he was writing *Roxana* that Defoe started off on his literary *Tour of the Whole Island of Great Britain*, almost certainly as an escape from his habitual worry and sadness. Its mood is as cheerful as that of *Roxana* is tragic, which helps to make it arguably the greatest of all his books.

13

The *Tour*: East Anglia and the South

Defoe's Tour of the Whole Island of Great Britain, published anonymously in three volumes between 1724 and 1726, is supposedly made in thirteen journeys, or 'circuits', each described in a letter to the reader. In the course of his lifetime Defoe had probably seen most of the places he claims to have visited in England and Scotland, if not in Wales, but while he was writing the *Tour* in his study at Newington it is doubtful whether he ventured further afield than London, Tunbridge Wells, where he took the waters, and Colchester, where he had a farm. At the very start of Letter One, 'Containing a description of the sea-coast of the Counties of Essex, Suffolk, Norfolk etc., and also parts of Cambridgeshire', Defoe mentions the date, 3 April 1722, when he rides over Bow Bridge into Essex. It is the first, and probably the last time in all three volumes of the *Tour* that Defoe describes an actual event in what is really a voyage through memory and imagination.

In the nearest Essex villages, such as Woodford, where Roxana sought refuge from her accusing daughter, Defoe found an enormous increase in the population, and houses of £20 to £60 a year, 'being chiefly for the habitation of the richer citizens such as either are able to keep two houses, one in the country and one in the city; or for such citizens as being rich, and having left off trade, live altogether in these neighbouring villages, for the pleasure and health of the latter part of their days'. As he passes through Essex, he is at pains to remind the reader 'how this whole kingdom, as well as the people, as the land, and even the sea, are employed to furnish the city of London with provisions . . . corn, flesh, fish, butter, cheese, salt, fuel, timber etc'. The Essex marshes also furnish London with teal, mallard and widgeon, although he remarks that sportsmen 'often return with an Essex ague on their backs, which they find a heavier load than the fowls they have shot'.

Such was the unhealthiness of the Essex marshes that in the region of Fobbing Defoe claims to have met with men who had had up to fourteen or fifteen wives. At nearby Canvey Island he was told of a farmer now on his twenty-fifth wife, while his son was on his fourteenth. He goes on to explain:

> The reasons, as a merry fellow told me, who said he had had about a dozen and a half of wives, (though I found afterwards he fibbed a little) was this: That they being bred in the marshes themselves, and seasoned to the place, did pretty well with it; but that they always went up into the hilly country, or to speak their own language into the uplands for a wife: that when they took the young lasses out of the wholesome and fresh air, they were healthy, fresh and clear, and well; but when they came out of their native air into the marshes among the fogs and damps, there they presently changed their complexion, got an ague or two, and seldom held it above half a year, or a year at most: and then, said he, we go to the uplands again, and fetch another; so that marrying of wives was reckoned a kind of good farm to them. It is true, the fellow told this in a kind of drollery, and mirth; but the fact, for all that, is certainly true; and that they have abundance of wives by that very means.

On his way through Essex Defoe speaks of the rich estates purchased by businessmen such as Mr Western, an iron merchant, and Mr Cresnor, a wholesale grocer, to show how 'the present increase of wealth in the city of London, spreads itself into the country and plants families and fortunes, who in another age will equal the families of the ancient gentry, who perhaps were bought out'. He recommends the cattle fed on Essex's marshland grass, and claims to have eaten 'part of a veal or calf ... the loin of which weighed over 30lbs and the flesh exceedingly white and fat'. He writes at length of Colchester, where he had a farm and where Moll Flanders started her wicked career. It was then a centre for making bays – or baize, as it came to be called – a woollen cloth that was used in Defoe's time for clothing, but later for linings, curtains and, more familiarly, as a dark green covering on tables and doors. Bays had been introduced in the sixteenth century by Protestant refugees from France and Holland, where it was known as *baais*, and Defoe was fond of quoting the couplet:

> Hops, Reformation, bays and beer
> Came to England all in a year.

Although Colchester was a Parliamentary town in the Civil War, it was captured by Royalists in the summer of 1648, and then besieged. Defoe quotes from a diary kept by a Cavalier, which he 'has no reason to question it being a true relation'. Whether a genuine document or one of Defoe's creations, like *A Journal of the Plague Year*, it shows that the Civil War was fought in a gentlemanly fashion. There were frequent parleys between the besieging Roundheads and the besieged Cavaliers, in which prisoners were exchanged and terms of surrender discussed. When the Royalists were accused of using poisoned bullets, they said that the claim had been made by two deserters, anxious to save their skins, 'but they added, that for shooting rough-cast slugs they must excuse themselves, as things stood with them at the time'. In other words, they were using dum-dum bullets because they had no proper ammunition. The Royalists were forced to capitulate because of the suffering of the townspeople – or rabble, as they are called by the diarist – 'who got together in a vast crowd about the Lord Goring's quarters, clamouring for a surrender, and they did this every evening, bringing women and children, who lay howling and crying on the ground for bread'. After Colchester's surrender the Parliamentarians spared all but two of the Cavaliers. Of Lord Goring's original 5,600 men, there were 3,513 survivors, an indication of how light the casualties were in comparison with wars on the Continent. Defoe adds that Colchester buried upwards of 5,259 people during the Plague Year of 1665, 'but the town was severely visited indeed, even more in proportion than any of its neighbours, or than the city of London'.

Defoe complains that the people of Harwich 'are far from being famed for good usage to strangers, but on the contrary are blamed for being extravagant in the public houses'. After the storm in *Roxana* the Harwich people taunted Amy with having in her terror confessed to all the men she had previously slept with. Now, in the *Tour*, he sneers: 'Harwich is a town of hurry and business, not much of gaiety and pleasure; yet the inhabitants seem warm in their nests; and some of them are very wealthy.' From Harwich he turns inland to mention the Essex town of Dunmow:

> I shall make the ladies laugh, at the famous old story of the
> Flitch of Bacon at Dunmow, which is this: One Robert Fitz-
> Walter, a powerful baron in this county, in the time of Henry

III, on some merry occasion ... instituted a custom in the
priory here; that whatever married man did not repent of his
being married, or quarrel, or differ and dispute with his wife,
within a year and a day after his marriage; and would swear
to the truth of it, kneeling upon two hard pointed stones in
the church yard: the prior and convent, and as many of the
town as would to be present: such person should have a flitch
of bacon. I do not remember to have read that anyone ever
came to demand it.

From Ipswich Defoe makes a detour to Hadley to see the place
where 'that famous martyr and pattern of charity and religious zeal in
Queen Mary's time, Dr Rowland Taylor, was put to death'. He prophesies that 'the memory of that good man will certainly never be out of
the poor people's minds, as long as the island shall retain the Protestant
religion among them; how long that may be as things are going, and
if the detestable conspiracy of the Papists now on foot should succeed,
I will not venture to say'. This is the first of many references to the
Jacobite plot discovered in 1722.

The *Tour* then continues to Bury St Edmunds, from where Defoe
had frequently written to Harley, using the name 'Alexander Goldsmith'. He calls it a town 'famed for its pleasant situation and wholesome air, the Montpelier of Suffolk, and perhaps of England'. Here
flourished the monastery of St Edmund the Martyr, the wealthiest in
this part of England, for the clergy always chose the best places in the
country to build their religious houses. For the same reason, Defoe
goes on, the monks brought to Bury the bones of St Edmund, which
soon increased the wealth of their house from pilgrims to his shrine.
He calls it a vulgar error that Edmund was murdered at Bury, rather
than Hoxne, to the north. For centuries it was thought that Defoe
was wrong, but a few years ago an amateur scholar, Margaret Carey,
turned up a document proving that Edmund was indeed killed at
Hoxne (pronounced 'Hoxon'). At the time Defoe was writing the *Tour*,
a recent crime had shocked Bury St Edmunds and 'made the place
less pleasant for some time than it used to be'.

Defoe then relates with grim relish the story of Arundel Coke, a
barrister from an ancient family, who hired an assassin to join him in
an attempt 'to murther in cold blood, and in the arms of hospitality,
Edward Crisp Esq, his brother-in-law, leading him out from his own
house, where he had invited him, his wife and children, to supper'.

Coke led his intended victim out into the night, on the pretence of going to visit a friend, then made a sign to the waiting desperado, who hacked Crisp with a bill-hook, then left him for dead: 'His head and face was so mangled, that it may be said to be next to a miracle that he was not quite killed: Yet so providence directed for the exemplary punishment of the assassins, that the gentleman recovered to detect them, who (though he outlived the assault) were both executed as they deserved, and Mr Crisp is yet alive.'

Here Defoe is not above the ancient journalist's trick of denouncing scandalous gossip, just in order to repeat it. He refers to a claim made in a recently published book, *Familiar Letters*, that many knights' daughters from Norfolk, Suffolk and Cambridgeshire came to Bury to market, to be bought or to buy:

> I shall believe nothing so scandalous of the ladies of this town and the country round it, as a late writer insinuates. That the ladies round the country appear mighty gay and agreeable at the time of the fair in this town, I acknowledge, but to suggest they come here as to a market is so coarse a jest that the gentlemen who wait on them hither, (for they rarely come but in good company) ought to resent and correct him for it.

He goes on to deny the imputation that all the women who go to the Bury '*assemblies*', the social gatherings fashionable at this time, 'go intriguing' late into the night: 'This is a terrible character for the ladies of Bury, and insinuates in short, that most of them are whores . . .' Having made a denial, Defoe then repeats the original accusation: 'Though it is far from true, that all that appear at *assemblies* are there for matches and intrigues . . . I do not doubt but that the scandalous liberty some take at these *assemblies*, will not bring them out of credit with the virtuous part of the sex here, as it has done already in Kent and other places.'

Defoe marvels at the decay of Dunwich, the once thriving herring port on the Suffolk coast, which was now mostly swallowed up by the sea. 'The ruins of Carthage, or the great city of Jerusalem, or of ancient Rome, are not so wonderful to me,' he exclaims, for the others were capitals of states, while Dunwich was a commercial town. After this rare meditation on time and destiny he returns to the mundane topic of modern Dunwich, in particular its trade in wheat, butter and 'coarse cheese, which as I mentioned before, is used chiefly for the king's ships'. The herring boats now went out from the estuary of the

Blythe between Southwold and Walberswick, hence the couplet:

> Swoul and Dunwich and Walderswick
> All go in at one lousie creek.

At Southwold, as on many occasions during the *Tour*, Defoe pretends to belong to the Church of England in order to praise his fellow Dissenters:

> There is but one church in this town, but it is a very large one and well-built, as most of the churches in this county are, and of impenetrable flint; indeed there is no occasion of its being so large, for staying here one Sabbath Day, I was surprised to see an extraordinarily large church, capable of receiving four or six thousand people, and but twenty-seven in it beside the parson and the clerk; but at the same time, the meeting-house of the Dissenters was full to the very doors, having as I guessed from 6 to 800 people in it.

According to Defoe, East Suffolk farmers were the first to raise sheep and cattle on turnips, a practice which later became the custom in most of southern England: 'And though some have objected against the goodness of the flesh thus fed with turnips, and have fancied it would taste of the root; yet upon experience tis found, that at market there is no difference, nor can they that buy, single out one joint of mutton from the other by the taste; so that the complaint which our nice palates at first made begins to cease of itself.' He marvels at the quantity of turkeys raised in Suffolk and the adjoining part of Norfolk, and cites an informant at Stratford Bridge, on the Stour between Suffolk and Essex, who in one year counted 300 droves of turkeys walking to London. Since each drove consisted of between 300 and 1,000 birds, he puts the total at 150,000 on just one route to the capital. Now geese were being driven to market as well: 'They begin to drive them generally in August, by which time the harvest is almost over, and the geese may feed in the stubble as they go. Thus they hold on to the end of October, when the roads begin to be too stiff and deep for their broad feet and short legs to march in.' The poultry breeders have also devised a system of carrying the birds on the back of a cart in four layers or storeys. To ensure a smooth ride the cart is drawn by two horses abreast: 'Changing horses, they travel night and day, so that they bring the fowls 70, 80 or 100 miles in two days and one night.'

Defoe says little of Norwich: he apparently never went there, for fear of meeting a creditor, yet he likes Yarmouth, the home of his most persistent tormentor. There he counted on one tide 'one hundred and ten barks and fishing vessels, coming up river, all loaden with herrings and all taken the night before'. Yarmouth was granted the right to try, condemn and execute malefactors without seeking a warrant from a higher authority, so that during the reign of Charles II a captain of one of the King's ships was hanged for murder there. Defoe approves of Yarmouth's summary justice, as well as its Puritan ways:

> I have nowhere in England observed the Sabbath-Day so exactly kept, or the breach so continually punished as in this place, which I name to their honour. Among all these regularities, it is no wonder if we do not find abundance of revelling, or that there is little encouragement to assemblies, plays and gaming-meetings at Yarmouth ... and yet I do not see that the ladies here come behind any of the neighbouring counties, either in beauty, breeding or behaviour.

Heading north from Yarmouth, Defoe remarks 'that the farmers and country people had scarce a barn, or a shed, or a stable, nay, not ... a hogsty, not a necessary house, but what was built of old plank, beams, wales and timber, the wrecks of ships, and ruins of mariners and merchants fortunes'. Robinson Crusoe suffered his first wreck off the Yarmouth coast, which Defoe in the *Tour* calls 'the most fatal to sailors in all England'. David Copperfield in Dickens's novel was born near by and reads *Robinson Crusoe* as a child. His friends, the Peggottys, live in an upturned boat on the shore at Yarmouth, and the novel reaches its climax with the shipwreck and drowning of Steerforth there.

Riding through Norfolk, Defoe is pleased by the great abundance of pheasants in the stubble, which he sees as a sign that the county possesses more tradesmen than gentlemen, since only gentlemen shoot for sport. He is so delighted with the idea that he goes on to say: 'Indeed this part is so entirely given up to industry, that what with the seafaring men on one side, and the manufacture on the other, we saw no idle hands here, but every man busy on the main affair of life, that is to say, getting money.' That last remark may be understood as expressing the 'Protestant work ethic', or even the ideology of 'early capitalism'; but Defoe was almost certainly pulling the reader's leg.

In northern Norfolk Defoe remarks on Houghton, the 'noble palace of Mr Walpole', now the country's first Prime Minister, but tactfully does not speculate on how he raised the money. He looks askance at the Marian shrine at Walsingham, and also at Ely Minster, the present cathedral, describing it as the only remarkable thing in the town: 'and of the Minster this is the most remarkable thing that I could hear, namely that some of it is so ancient, totters so much with any gust of wind, looks so much like a decay, and seems so near it, that whenever it does fall, all that is likely will be thought strange in it, will be that it did not fall a hundred years earlier.' Why did Defoe dislike this supremely beautiful church, which still survives nearly three centuries later? Part of the answer is there to see in the Lady Chapel, where at the time of the Reformation Thomas Cromwell's Puritans smashed the heads off every statue. A century later Oliver Cromwell worked as a tax collector in Ely, and after the start of the Civil War he ordered his troopers to stable their horses in Ely Minster, and even considered pulling it down. Defoe hoped it would fall of its own accord.

Defoe the Puritan disapproves of the betting and cheating at Newmarket races, where even the great nobility descend to 'picking one another's pockets, and biting one another as much as possible'. However, he clearly admires the skills of Sir R . . . Fagg at disguising the speed of his horses: 'If he was light as the wind and could fly like a meteor, he was sure to look as clumsy and as dirty, and as much like a cart-horse as all the cunning of his master and the grooms could make him; and just in this manner he bit some of the greatest gamesters in the field.'

Defoe gives less attention to Cambridge than to the annual fair at neighbouring Stourbridge, the largest in Britain or all the world, and also the model of Vanity Fair in Bunyan's *The Pilgrim's Progress*. From his many visits to Stourbridge Fair in August and September Defoe had acquired his prodigious knowledge of English trade, a subject he always discusses with lucidity and delight. At least fifty years before what we call the Industrial Revolution Defoe had spotted the great importance of cotton from Manchester, knives from Sheffield and brassware from Birmingham, sold at Stourbridge Fair in exchange for goods of London goldsmiths, drapers, milliners, mercers, hatters and pewterers. He explains the commercial value of hops, only recently introduced to Kent and Surrey but already considered essential by brewers all over the country.

On his way back to London through northern Essex Defoe stops at Wanstead to see Lord Castlemain's greenhouse, 'an excellent building, fit to entertain a prince'; its owner, he tells the reader, was one of the major losers from the South Sea Bubble: 'Pity and matter of grief it is to think that families, by estate, able to appear in such a glorious posture as this, should ever be vulnerable to such disaster as that of stock-jobbing ... and if my Lord Castlemain was wounded by that arrow shot in the dark, twas a misfortune: but tis so much a happiness, that it was not a mortal wound, as it was to some men ...' Defoe had warned against speculation during the frenzy of 1720, but after the bubble burst, he pointed out that the South Sea Company shares were still worth £400, compared to the opening price of £100 and the all-time high of £1,200.

Defoe starts Letter Two, 'Containing a description of the Sea-coast of Kent, Sussex, Hampshire and of part of Surrey', by taking a ferry from Tower Wharf to Greenwich. In *Roxana*, which came out the same year – 1724 – as volume one of the *Tour*, Amy crosses the Thames from Tower Quay with Susan but cannot entice her into the wilderness of Greenwich Park, where she means to murder her. In the *Tour* Defoe calls Greenwhich 'the most delightful spot of ground in Great Britain, pleasantest by situation, those pleasures enhanced by art, and all made completely agreeable by the accident of fine buildings, the continual passing of fleets of ships up and down the most beautiful river in Europe; the best air, best prospects and the best conversation in England'.

The Royal Naval Hospital for disabled seamen meets with Defoe's approval; in Greenwich there are 'several of the most active and useful gentlemen of the late armies, after having grown old in the service of their country, and covered with the honours of the field, are retired to enjoy the remainder of their time, and reflect with pleasure upon the dangers they have gone through, and the faithful service they have performed both abroad and at home.' Riding east past Blackheath, he writes of a 'hospital', or what we would call a retirement home, for 'decayed merchants ... to make their lives as comfortable as possible, and that, as they had lived like gentlemen, they might die so'. The founder of this hospital, Sir John Morden, a trader with Turkey, provided the old men with a chapel, a library, servants, coals, a cellar, beer and in 'each compartment a bed-chamber and a study, or large closet for their retreat and to divert themselves in with books'. It is sad to relate that, a few years after he wrote this, Defoe himself was living in or around Blackheath, not in a comfortable home for decayed merchants but on the run from his creditors.

At the Medway towns of Rochester and Chatham Defoe recalls how the Dutch made 'a memorable attempt upon the royal navy in this river (viz) on the 22nd of June in the year of 1667; for at that time all was left unguarded, and as it were, secure; there were but four guns that could be used at Upnore, and scarce as many at Gillingham, the carriages being rotten and broke, and in a word, everything conspiring to invite the enemy.' He continues to Faversham, where James II was apprehended by fishermen when he tried to escape in 1688, and from there to Maidstone, the county town, 'a very agreeable place to live and where a man of letters, and of manners, will always find suitable society, both to divert or improve himself'. Defoe had supported the Kentish Petition of 1701, and four years later, when Kent voted against the High Church Tories, he praised 'the sense, courage and fidelity of the inhabitants of that populous, wealthy county'. Kent, with its high proportion of yeoman farmers, enjoyed an unusually wide franchise.

At Canterbury, as at many stops on the *Tour*, Defoe insists that he does not want to write of 'antiquities', then launches into an anti-Papist history of the cathedral. He acknowledges that the first Bishop of Canterbury, St Augustine, was sent over by Gregory, Bishop of Rome, but adds a rider: 'This Gregory it seems was a true, primitive Christian Bishop of Rome; not such as since are called so; long before they assumed the title of popes, or that usurped honour of Universal Bishop.' He declares that Thomas Becket, 'or Thomas a Becket, as some call him, arch-bishop of this see, and several arch-bishops before him, plagued, insulted and tyrannised over the kings of England, their sovereigns, in an insufferable manner', until Becket, 'having made himself intolerable to King Henry II, by his obstinacy, pride and rebellion, was here murthered by the connivance, and as some say, by the express order of the king, and that they show his blood upon the pavement to this day'. Becket's canonization is described with scorn: his shrine was turned into 'the greatest idol of the world', with its steps worn away to a slope by the knees of 'pilgrims and ignorant people'.

Defoe goes on to say that 'the immense wealth offered by votaries and pilgrims, for several ages to the altar, or shrine of this mock saint, Thomas Becket, was such that Erasmus Roterdamus [the Dutch scholar, 1467–1536], who was in the repository and saw it, relates of it, that the whole place glittered and shone with gold and diamonds'. He then adds, with obvious approval, 'that all this immense treasure, with the lands and revenue of the whole monastery were seized upon, and taken away by King Henry VIII, at the general suppression of religious houses, except such as are annexed to the Dean and Chapter, and to the revenue of the arch-bishopric, which are not large'. Defoe notes, once more with approval, that underneath the cathedral at Canterbury is a French Protestant church, given first by Queen Elizabeth to the Walloon refugees from the Spanish Duke of Alba's persecution; its congregation was then augmented by Huguenots driven to Canterbury by 'the particular cruelty of Louis XIV'. Canterbury could not be called a populous town, according to Defoe, were it not for the 2,000 or 3,000 French Protestants.

Making his way round the coast to Romney Marsh, Defoe remarks on the size and excellence of the sheep but deplores the vulnerability of this coast to attack from the Continent. In William's reign a huge French fleet had appeared off Dungeness, but the English Admiral Herbert – with commendable prudence – would not engage it: 'According to all the rules of war, no admiral could justify the royal navy on such terms; and especially the circumstances of the time then considered, for the king was in Ireland, and King James ready in France . . . I have been told the king himself upon a full hearing justified the conduct of Admiral Herbert, and afterwards created him Earl of Torrington.'

Rye, which had stood on the sea in the Middle Ages, was now an inland port because of the silting up of the shore; ships of more than 200 tons no longer ventured to shelter there. Defoe complains that 'our merchant ships are often put to great extremity hereabout, for there is not one safe place for them to run into, between Portsmouth and the Downs; whereas in former times Rye-Bay was an asylum . . .' He mentions a recent Act of Parliament, voting money for the return of Rye port to its former state, but predicts, accurately, that this would not be put into effect.

From Romney Marsh Defoe turned north towards Tunbridge Wells, traversing 'the deep, dirty but rich part' of Sussex and Kent, where iron ore was smelted on charcoal fires. Here for the first time he joins in the long-running debate on the conservation of trees:

> The great foundaries, or iron-works . . . are carried on at such
> a prodigious expense of wood, that even in a country almost
> over-run with timber, they begin to complain of the consuming
> it for these furnaces, and leaving the next age to want timber
> for building their navies: I must own however, that I found

that complaint perfectly groundless, the three counties of Kent, Sussex and Hampshire . . . being one inexhaustible storehouse of timber never to be destroyed but by a general conflagration, and able at this time to rebuild all the royal navies of Europe, if they were all to be destroyed, and set about the building them together.

Defoe's views on timber were considered misguided by his own contemporaries, let alone by modern ecologists. It was during the reign of Henry VIII that the navy started to worry about the shortage of timber, especially oak. In the centuries since the Norman Conquest, four-fifths of the country's trees had been felled for agricultural land, building and smelting. The shortage of oak for the ever larger naval ships was growing acute in the counties of Kent, Sussex and Hampshire, near to shipyards like Portsmouth and Chatham. Felling increased after 1535, when Henry dissolved and started to plunder the monasteries, since oak was readily disposable.

Queen Elizabeth's first Parliament brought in laws on conservation, but later she sold off much of the Royal Forests for cash. Her chief minister, Lord Burleigh, attempted to check the decline by ordering thirteen acres of Cranbourne Walk in Windsor Park to be sown with acorns, creating a new plantation. Many private landlords resented the navy's constant demands for oak of between eighty and 120 years old. Either they sold them off young, to pay a pressing debt, or left them to die of old age for sentimental reasons. Elizabeth's successors, James I, Charles I and Oliver Cromwell, all plundered the Royal Forests in time of need.

After the Restoration the Navy Board in alarm and desperation appealed for advice to the newly formed Royal Society, which in turn commissioned a study by John Evelyn, who ranks with Pepys as one of the most readable diarists. Evelyn prepared a paper, published in 1664 as *Sylva: A Discourse of Forest Trees and the Propagation of Timber in his Majesty's Dominion*. This huge tome, crammed with classical references and practical advice, implored the landowning class to protect trees from 'the disproportionate spread of tillage' as well as from iron and glass manufacturers. Evelyn called for the restoration of those 'many goodly woods and forests which our ancestors left standing for the adornment and service of the country'. In a preface to the 1679 edition Evelyn boasts that the book had led to the planting of a million oaks.

In spite of Defoe's claim that Kent, Sussex and Hampshire had trees enough for all the navies of Europe, England was critically short of timber during the Seven Years War, the War of American Independence and the Napoleonic Wars. The matter obsessed Lord Nelson and still more Admiral Collingwood, who during his shore leaves always carried around a pocketful of acorns, ready to plant. Shortly after Napoleon's downfall the elder Disraeli wrote: 'Inquire at the Admiralty how the fleets of Nelson have been constructed, and they can tell you that it was with the oak that the genius of Evelyn planted.' The conversion to iron-clads during the nineteenth century eased the demand for timber, although this grew again during the U-Boat blockade of the First World War. In 1919 the government founded the Forestry Commission, charged with restoring woodlands and building a timber reserve sufficient for three years, in case of war. While Evelyn had recommended planting oaks for 'the ornament and service of the country', the Commissioners planted the ugly but fast-growing firs. It is only in recent years that public opinion has come to demand trees that are ornamental as well as useful.

At Tunbridge Wells, as at other fashionable spas, Defoe denounces the sins of the age: 'As for gaming, sharping, intrigues; as also fops, fools, beaus, and the like, Tunbridge is as full of them as can be desirable.' He happened to be there when 'His Royal Highness the Prince of Wales was there with abundance of the nobility and the gentry of the county.' Since Defoe disapproved of the Prince as much as his father the King, as he had clearly hinted in *Roxana*, his account of the visit is tight-lipped: 'The prince appeared upon the walks, went into the raffling shops [dicing dens] and to every public place, saw everything, and let everybody see him . . .'

Whether or not he saw the Prince, Defoe visited Tunbridge during the 1720s to take the waters for his gout and his gall-stone pains. He called the air 'excellent good', the country healthful, the markets abundant in turbot, mackerel, pheasant, partridge, woodcock, snipe, quail and 'a bird called a wheatear, or as we may call them, the English ortolans, the most delicious taste for a creature of one mouthful, for tis little more, that can be imagined'. He left Tunbridge 'for the same reason that others leave it when they are in my condition; namely that I found my money almost gone; and though I had bills of credit to supply myself in the course of my intended journey; yet I had none there; so I came away, or as they call it there, I retired; and came to Lewes.'

More probably Defoe retired and went back home to Stoke Newington. However, in the *Tour* he visits Lewes, Brighton, Chichester, Portsmouth and Southampton, before heading back to London. In his abuse of rotten boroughs, the parliamentary seats in the gift of the wealthy – which was a constant bugbear of his during the travels – Defoe comes down especially hard on Winchelsea – 'rather the skeleton of an ancient city than a real town' – and Bramber, also in Sussex, 'which hardly deserves the name of a town, having not many above fifteen or sixteen families in it, and of them not many above asking you an alms as you ride by: the chiefest house in the town is a tavern, and here, as I have been told, the vintner, or ale-house keeper rather ... boasted that upon an election, just then over, he had made £300 on one pipe of canary' (wine). It was easy to mock these rotten boroughs, yet their members often proved to be men of character and intelligence, who might not have got into Parliament through their party machine. One of the last MPs for Winchelsea was Henry Brougham, the mastermind of the Great Reform Bill, and therefore the man responsible for getting rid of the rotten boroughs. The long-time MP for Bramber was William Wilberforce, who led the campaign to abolish the slave trade.

Defoe enters Surrey at Farnham, 'the greatest corn market in England, London excepted', and makes his way north to Bagshot Heath. Here, for the first but by no means the last time in the *Tour*, he indulges his fictional urge by making the gentle and temperate British countryside sound as fearful and dangerous as the Himalayas or, in the case of Bagshot Heath, the imagined Plain of Mecca. He calls this part of Surrey

> a mark of the just resentment shew'd by Heaven upon the Englishman's pride; I mean the pride they shew in boasting of their country; its fruitfulness, pleasantness, richness, the fertility of the soil, whereas here is a vast tract of land, some of it within seventeen or eighteen miles of the capital city; which is not only poor, but even quite sterile, given up to barrenness, horrid and frightful to look on ... much of it in a sandy desert, and one may frequently be put in mind here of Arabia Deserta, where the winds raise the sands, so as to overwhelm whole caravans of cattle and people together; for in passing this heath, in a windy day, I was so far in danger of smothering with the clouds of sand which were raised by the storm, that I could not keep it out of my mouth, nose or eyes.

A few pages later, when making his way from Guildford, the county town, Defoe has another taste of the terrors of Surrey, on what is now known as the Hog's Back:

> The ridge of a high, chalky hill, so narrow that the breadth of the road takes up the breadth of the hill, and the declivity begins on either hand ... and is very steep, as well as very high ... This hill being all chalk, a traveller feels the effect of it on a hot summer's day, being scorched by the reflection of the sun from the chalk, so as to make the heat almost insupportable; and this I speak by my own experience.

Defoe revisits Dorking, where he went to school and goes back into Kent to take a look at Bromley, then famous for its hospital or retirement home for the widows of clergymen, 'a very noble foundation for one of the best charities in the world'. Turning west at Beckenham, Defoe remarks on the spas at Dulwich and Sydenham,

> where great crowds of people throng every summer from London to drink the waters, as at Epsom and Tunbridge; only with this difference, that as at Epsom and Tunbridge, they go more for the diversion of the season, for the mirth and the company; here they go for mere physic; and this causes another difference; namely that as the nobility and the gentry go to Tunbridge; the merchants and rich citizens to Epsom; so the common people go chiefly to Dulwich and Streatham; and the rather because it lies so near London that they can walk to it in the morning, and return at night; which abundance do; that is to say, especially of a Sunday, or on holidays, which makes the better sort also decline the place; the crowd on these days being both unruly and unmannerly.

In his tour of the southern fringes of London Defoe passes on gossip about the local celebrities, such as the dowager Lady Onslow, who drowned in a fish-pond at Croydon, though 'whether she did it herself, or whether by accident, or how, tis not the business of such a work as this to enquire'. Defoe was a master of scandalous innuendo. At Beddington he admires the orange trees of Sir Nicholas Carew – 'they having moving houses to cover them in the winter [and] they are loaded with fruit in the summer' – then adds that Sir Nicholas is lucky to have this property, which his father once lost on a throw of the dice. He commiserates with Sir John Fallows of Carshalton, 'late sub-governor of the South Sea Company . . . who lost all his unhappy wealth, and a good and honestly gotten estate of his own into the bargain'.

On his way to Epsom Defoe admires the racecourse on the nearby downs: 'When they are covered with coaches and ladies, and an innumerable company of horsemen . . . and then adding to the beauty of the sight, the racers flying over the course, as if they either touched not or felt not the ground they run upon; I think no sight, except that of a victorious army, under the command of a Protestant King of Great Britain, could exceed it.' From Defoe, that is praise indeed. He clearly approves of Epsom, which was patronized by his own people, 'the merchants and rich citizens'. He commends them especially for not talking shop or taking their business cares on holiday,

> for abating one unhappy stock jobbing year [the South Sea Bubble of 1720] when England took leave to act the frantick, for a little while; and when everybody's heads were turned with projects and stocks, I say, except this year, we see nothing of business in the whole conversation of Epsom; even the men of business, who are really so when in London; whether it be at the Exchange, the Alley or the Treasury-Offices, and the Court; yet here they look as if they had left all their London thoughts behind them, and had separated themselves to mirth and good company.

Since Epsom was then a collection of country houses, part of its charm was the air and freedom of movement after the clutter of London: 'Then you drink the water, or walk about as if you did; dance with the ladies, though it be in your gown and slippers; have music and company of what kind you like, for every man may suit himself as he pleases; the grave with the grave, and the gay with the gay, the bright and the wicked . . .' During the summer season many gentlemen of the 'grave' kind commuted each morning to London, rejoining their families only for supper. Defoe knew 'one citizen that practised it for several years together, and scarce ever lay at night in London during the whole season.' He himself may have visited Epsom while he was writing the *Tour*.

In the third and fourth letters of the *Tour* Defoe makes a journey to Land's End and back, beginning at Hampton Court and ending at Windsor, recalling his visits to these places during the reign of William and Mary. From Hampton Court, on the outward leg of the journey, he travels to Winchester and for once admires an ancient cathedral, finding it free from 'Popish' ornamentation:

> The outside of the church is as plain and coarse, as if the founders had abhorred ornaments, or that William of Wykeham had been a Quaker, or at least a Quietist: there is neither a statue, or a niche for a statue, to be seen on all the outside: no carved work, no spire, towers, pinnacles, balustrades, or anything but mere walls, buttresses, windows and coigns, necessary to the support and order of the building: it has no steeple but a short tower covered flat, as if the top of it had fallen down, and it had been covered in haste to keep the rain out, till they had time to build it up again.

Defoe praises William of Wykeham, the founder of Winchester College, who although 'he had no great share of learning, he was a great promoter of it, and a lover of learned men'. Before going to Winchester, William had been Secretary of State to Edward III, and is credited by Defoe with inventing the Order of the Garter, and prosecuting the Hundred Years War. Like many tourists in Winchester, Defoe is sceptical of the Round Table, said to have been King Arthur's, 'a piece of antiquity to the tune of 1,200 years, and has, as they pretend the names of his said knights in Saxon characters, and yet such as no man can read'. All this he believes 'to be no better than a FIBB'.

Riding west into Wiltshire, Defoe comes to a stretch of countryside he calls 'the most charming plain . . . in my opinion far excelling the plain of Mecca'. As we know from an article in the *Review* on *Paradise Lost*, Defoe apparently gave credit to the story that Eve, after a quarrel with Adam, had found her way to the plain of Mecca and there given birth to twins. Now in Wiltshire, Defoe appears to be telling his readers that he had actually seen the plain of Mecca, though he does not claim to have entered the Forbidden City.

From Salisbury, Defoe doubles back into Hampshire to see the New Forest and to air his contentious views on naval timber. In Letter Two he had claimed that, far from there being a shortage of trees, the New Forest is 'so overgrown with wood, and these woods so full of large grown timber, that it seemed as if they wanted sale for it . . . As I rode through the New Forest, I could see the ancient oaks of many hundred years standing, perishing with their withered tops advanced up in the

air, and grown white with age, and that could never yet get the favour
to be cut down, and made serviceable to the country'. It was here in
the New Forest, near Lyndhurst, that Defoe had wanted to build a
housing estate for Palatine refugees in 1709; in the *Tour* he reprints
his prospectus, including a map of the town. It looks suspiciously neat
and symmetrical. The land was not fertile – contrary to Defoe's claims
– so the Palatines probably had a lucky escape.

Defoe's hostility to the New Forest was partly ideological, for this
was the favourite hunting ground of William the Conqueror, whose
son William II was killed here during a chase. English resistance to
Norman forest law was later romanticized in the legend of Robin
Hood, but finds expression early on in the Anglo-Saxon Chronicles:

> He [William] made large forests for deer and enacted laws
> therewith so that whoever killed a hart or a hind should be
> blinded. As he forbade killing the deer, so also his boars, and he
> loved the tall stags as if he was their father. He also appointed
> concerning the hares that they should go free. The rich com-
> plained and the poor murmured, but he was so sturdy that he
> recked not of them.

It was part of the demonology of these Norman kings that in order
to guard the New Forest they drove out the peasants and razed more
than thirty towns and villages. Defoe in the *Tour* repeats this calumny
against that 'violent tyrant William the Conqueror', who 'unpeopled
the country, pulled down the houses, and which was worse the churches
of several parishes or towns, and of abundance of villages'. The wickedness of the forest law entered the Whig and Liberal history books, in
which monarchy is perceived to be at odds with Parliament and the
people. The last great historian of that old tradition, G. M. Trevelyan,
wrote in 1926 that in the Royal Forests 'the king's peace indeed
reigned, but in a form hateful to God and man'. He deplored the
alienation of so much wooded land, adding: 'The gradual deforestation
of district after district marked the economic and moral progress of
this country.'

The opposite point of view, that forests should be preserved, was
advanced in Defoe's time by Evelyn, and later by Dr Johnson, William
Wordsworth and, loudest of all, by the nineteenth-century radical
William Cobbett, whose *Rural Rides* cover much the same ground as
the *Tour* but preach a quite different message. Cobbett approved of
the Normans and pre-Reformation England, detested the Tudors and

still more William of Orange, claiming that most of our modern stock-jobbers arrived 'with the Dutch and the Devil'. Of the New Forest he wrote:

> If we had the same quantity of timber now that we had when the Protestant Reformation took place, or even when old Betsy [Elizabeth I] turned up her toes, we should be now more than millions of money richer than we are; not in bills; not in notes payable to bearer on demand; not in Scotch 'cash credit', not in lies, falseness, impudence, downright blackguard cheating and mining shares and the devil knows what.

Cobbett's pet scheme for the New Forest was the introduction of locust trees, the West Indian carob or false acacia; but, like Defoe's plan for the Palatine refugees, it was never implemented.

After passing through Christchurch – 'scarcely worth seeing, and less worth mentioning' – Defoe moves into Dorset, speaks well of the oysters at Poole and better still of the human beings at Dorchester:

> For though there are divisions and the people are not all of one mind either as to religion, or politics, yet they did not seem to separate with so much animosity as in other places. Here I saw the Church of England clergymen and the Dissenting minister or preacher drinking tea together, and conversing with civility and good neighbourhood, like Catholic Christians and men of a catholic and extensive charity.

This was no doubt what he reported to Harley in 1705. It was on that same mission that Defoe was arrested – when his letter of introduction went to the wrong captain at Weymouth – but does not hold it against that 'sweet, clean agreeable town'.

At Yeovil in Somerset Defoe remarks for the first time in his *Tour* on a local dialect of the English language, here called 'jouring'. He explains that the difference is largely in the abridgement of words, as he found when he went to visit a school at Martock kept by a relative:

> I went into his school to beg his boys a play day, as is usual in such cases; I should have said to beg the master a play day, but that by the way; coming into the school, I observed one of the lowest scholars was reading his lesson to the usher, which lesson it seems was a chapter in the Bible . . . I observed the boy reading a little oddly in the tone of the country, which

made me the more attentive, because on enquiry, I found that
the words were the same as in all our Bibles. I observed that
the boy read it out with his eyes still on the book, and his
head like a mere boy moving from side to side, as the lines
moved across the columns of the book; his lesson was in the
Canticles [Song of Solomon] 5.3. of which the words are these

'I have put off my coat, how shall I put it on, I have washed
my feet, how shall I defile them?'

The boy read thus, with his eyes, as I say, full on the text.

'Chav a doffed my coat, how shall I don't, chav a wash'd
my veet, how shall I moil 'em?'

How the dexterous dunce could form his mouth to express
so readily the words, (which stood right printed in the book)
in his country jargon, I could not but admire.

As another example of 'jouring', Defoe tells a story from Yeovil itself;

There lived a good substantial family in the town not far from
the Angel Inn. This family had a dog, which among his other
good qualities, for which they kept him (for he was a rare
hound dog) had this bad one, that he was a most notorious
thief . . . It happened that the good wife, or mistress at the
Angel Inn, had frequently missed several pieces of meat out
of the pail, as they say, or powdering tub, as we call it . . . It
happened at last, as with most thieves it does, that the inn-
keeper was too cunning for him, and the poor dog was nabbed,
taken in the fact and could make no defence . . .

Having found the thief, the master of the house, a good-
humoured fellow . . . cut off both his ears, and then bringing
him to the threshold, he chopped off his tail; and having thus
effectively dishonoured the poor cur among his neighbours,
he tied a piece of string about his neck and a piece of paper
to the string directed to his master, and with these witty west
country verses on it:

Hail master a cham a'com hoam.
So cut as an ape, a tail have I noan.
But stealing of beef, and pork out of the pail,
For thease they've cut my ears, for th' wother my tail
Nea measter, and tell us thee more nor that
And's come there again, my brains will be flat.

In Devonshire, as in Norfolk, Defoe is especially interested in the manufacture of woollen cloth, but he mentions first the 20,000 hogsheads of cider said to be shipped each year from Mary St Ottery up to London, 'and which is still worse, that it is most of it brought there by the merchants to mix with their wines, which if true, is not much to the reputation of London vintners . . .' Defoe heads his list of worthy sons of Devon with Sir Francis Drake and Sir Walter Raleigh: 'Of both of them I need say nothing: fame publishes their merit upon every mention of their names.' He had written a life of Raleigh and even claimed him as a relative. Among the other Devonians on his list are Sir Thomas Bodley, the founder of the 'best library in England which is now at Oxford'; the theologian Richard Hooker and, more to Defoe's taste, Dr John Moreman of Southold, for 'being the first clergyman of England, who ventured to teach his parishioners the Lord's Prayer, Creed and Ten Commandments in the English tongue, and reading them so publicly in the parish church of Mayenhennet, in this county'.

At Totnes Defoe watches the fishermen catch young salmon, or peal, with the help of a dog to drive them into the nets. Going further down river to Dartmouth, he spots a number of small fish skipping upon the surface, and points this out to a friend in the boat, whereupon one of the rowers, 'throwing his arms abroad, as if he had been bewitched, cried out as loud as he could bawl, "A school, a school."' Defoe's friend says that if he had had a day or two's warning he could have caught 200 tons of these pilchards, swimming into the harbour with the tide. As it was, the one small vessel that reached the shoal caught 40,000. That evening Defoe, his friend and a servant gorge themselves on pilchards broiled with pepper and salt which, together with wine or beer, cost just three farthings for all of them.

Defoe pays his respects to Brixham, in Torbay, where William of Orange came ashore on 5 November 1688. Brixham is apparently full of Dissenters, 'and a very large meeting-house they have here; how they act with respect to the great dispute about the doctrine of the Trinity, which has caused such a breach among these people at Exeter, and other parts of the country, I cannot give any account of.' Pretending to be an Anglican, Defoe keeps rather aloof from 'these people'.

At Plymouth Defoe recalls the Great Storm of 1703, which destroyed the newly erected Eddystone lighthouse, then tells of

another he witnessed in August 1705, when he was in the West
Country on a mission for Harley:

> It was at Plymouth, and walking on the Hoo [Hoe], which is
> a plain on the edge of the sea, looking to the road, I observed
> the evening so calm, so bright and the sea so smooth, that a
> finer sight, I think, I never saw; there was very little wind, but
> what was, seemed to be westerly; and about an hour after, it
> blew a little breeze at south west, with which wind there came
> into the Sound, that night, and the next morning, a fleet of
> fourteen sail of ships, from Barbados, richly laden for London.

This is the gentle preamble to one of Defoe's stories of death and
disaster at sea, here described from the shore. The next day, he says,
the wind started to freshen, and blow very hard:

> About midnight the noise indeed was very dreadful, what with
> the roaring of the sea, and of the wind, intermixed with the
> firing of guns for help from the ships, the cries of the seamen
> and people on shore, and, which was worse, the cries of those,
> which were driven on shore by the tempest, and dashed in
> pieces. In a word, all the fleet, except three, or thereabouts
> were dashed to pieces against the rocks, and sunk in the sea,
> most of the men being drowned . . .
>
>   This was a melancholy morning indeed; nothing was to be
> seen but wrecks of the ships, and a foaming, furious sea, in
> that very place where they rode all day in joy and triumph . . .
> The captains, passengers and officers who were gone off shore,
> between the joy of saving their lives, and the affliction of
> having lost their ships, their cargoes and their friends, were
> objects indeed worthy our compassion and observation; and
> there was a great variety of the passions to be observed in
> them; now lamenting their losses with violent excesses of grief;
> then giving thanks for their lives . . .

In this account of Plymouth in 1705 we find the raw material for the
storm scenes in *Robinson Crusoe* and *Roxana*, and for Moll Flanders's
grief over her damaged tobacco. Defoe never wrote a shipwreck scene
as melodramatic as Dickens's account of the storm at Yarmouth; but
if Dickens can wring our hearts over death and bereavement, Defoe
is there to remind us of our baser responses to disaster: thankfulness
for our own lives saved, and misery over our own riches lost.

At Land's End Defoe admits that he has not visited 'those ex-crescences of the island, viz. the rocks of Scilly', but mentions the efforts to salvage some of the wrecks there with various kinds of diving machine. However, he says, thinking gloomily back to his own failed venture of 1692, 'we could not learn that they had come at any pieces of eight, which were the things they seemed most to aim at.' Before starting on the homeward journey to London, Defoe explains to the reader that he had once intended to make the whole circuit of Britain by sea, and had even provided himself with a yacht and an able com-mander, or skipper. But this commander, who was an old, experienced seaman, apparently dissuaded him from such an undertaking: the difficulty

> was the necessity of getting pilots to every part of the coast, as to every port, river and creek; and the danger of not getting them . . . it would be impractical any single man that knew so perfectly the whole coast . . . so I laid it aside, as I say, as hopeless and too dangerous an adventure and satisfied myself, to make the circuit very near as perfect by land, which I have done with much less hazard, though with much more pains and expense: the fruit of which you have, in part, communicated in these letters.

This is a splendid piece of codding at the expense of the reader, for of course Defoe had never possessed a private yacht with its own 'commander': nor had he suffered the 'pains and expenses' of making these circuits. Because he was ill and getting old, and once more going broke, Defoe was obliged to piece together the *Tour* from memory, books, reports in the Press, and the exercise of imagination – quite a different thing from invention or lying. Just as in the novels he imagines himself as a Londoner in the Plague Year, a Cavalier in the Civil War, or a castaway on a desert island, so in the *Tour* Defoe imagines himself as a traveller round England. This man is an Anglican, who has travelled widely in Europe and even Arabia, and he sees many things that Defoe did not. For example, Defoe probably witnessed the storm at Plymouth in 1705 but not the shoal of pilchards: that sounds too much like an incident in the Civil War, when Fairfax's army fed on what they regarded as a miraculous draught of fishes at Dartmouth. The narrator frequently refers to experiences that are Defoe's, but sometimes omits them for reasons of discretion. Sadly, this part of the

Tour says nothing of his experiences during the Monmouth Rebellion of 1685.

Making his way home through Devon and Somerset, Defoe is apparently on friendly ground. At Bideford he is delighted to find a very large, well-built meeting house for Dissenters, 'and by the multitude of people I saw coming out of it and the appearance of them, I thought all the town had gone there, and began to enquire for the church; but when I came to the church, I found that also large, spacious and well filled too, and that with people of the best fashion.' Perhaps he means that the gentry attended the Church of England. He then goes on to describe the Dissenting minister, as though from a prejudiced point of view: 'The person who officiates at the meeting house in the town, I happened to have some conversation with, and found him to be not only a learned man and master of good reading, but a most acceptable, gentlemanly person, and one, who, contrary to our received opinion of these people . . . had abundance of good manners, and good humour; nothing sour, cynical or morose in him . . .' The word 'cynical' in Defoe's time meant surly or captious – one of the bad qualities thought to be typical of Dissenters.

Entering Wellington, in Somerset, Defoe and his riding companions are mobbed by beggars: 'It was our misfortune at first, that we threw them some farthings, and halfpence, such as we had among them; for thinking by this to be rid of them, on the contrary, it brought such a crowd of them, as if the whole town was come out into the street, and they ran in this manner after us . . .' He finds no beggars at Taunton, a large, wealthy and populous town, but his comments on the employment of children have shocked modern readers of the *Tour*:

> One of the chief manufacturers of the town told us, that there was at that time so good a trade . . . that they had then eleven hundred looms going for the weaving of . . . stuffs . . . He farther added that there was not a child in the town, or in the villages round it, of above five years old, but if it was not neglected by its parents, and untaught, could earn its own bread. This was what I never met with in any place in England, except at Colchester in Essex.

It may be recalled that the child Moll Flanders was proud of being able to earn her own bread; but she did not start as young as five.

Defoe continues to Bridgwater, where he had ventured his life in the Battle of Sedgemoor, then slowly back to London, with less apprehension than he had travelled forty years earlier.

The *Tour*: London, the Midlands and Wales

HAVING TOURED East Anglia and the whole of southern England, Defoe decides he has reached 'the centre of this work', and pauses from travel to write of London, his home and the heart and engine of Britain's empire. Defoe often judges the worth of any county by how much produce it sends up to London, as though he regards the inhabitants of the provinces as worker ants, or bees, whose only duty is to the nest or hive. So great is his veneration for London that just for once we accept his expressions of regret at not having the space to treat it more fully.

Defoe was born and had lived most of his life in London, and regarded it as the capital of the Protestant world. Moreover, he had seen the transformation of London from a medieval city of wooden houses and Gothic churches into a modern city of stone and brick, expanding rapidly into the country and glorified by the classical buildings of Wren and his colleagues. The catalyst for the rise of the new London had been the Great Fire of 1666, which cleared the way for the building boom. Following the rebuilding of the City of London a second property boom developed in Covent Garden, Holborn, Soho, Westminster, Mayfair and south of the river, in Surrey and Kent. According to Defoe, London was stretching northwards, to Islington, Cavendish Square, Hyde Park Corner, Brentford Road and almost to Marylebone on the Acton Road. He predicts that Greenwich, Knightsbridge and Chelsea will all in a few years form part of London: 'How much further it may spread, who knows? New squares and new streets rising up every day in such a prodigy of buildings, that nothing in the world does, or ever did, equal it, except old Rome in Trajan's time, when the walls were fifty miles in compass, and the number of inhabitants six million, eight hundred thousand souls.'

After describing the spread of London, Defoe praises some of its new public buildings, such as the Monument to the recent Fire, the Royal Exchange, 'the greatest and finest of its kind in the whole world', and the much enlarged Customs House, which will 'when it is finished, outshine all the customs-houses in Europe'. He considers some of the new London churches 'rather convenient than fine, not adorned with pomp and pageantry as in Popish countries', and commends St Bride's, off Fleet Street, St Clement Danes and St Mary-le-Strand. This is merely a prelude to one of Defoe's rare but wonderful bursts of panegyric, expressing his deep-felt patriotism and Protestant ardour:

> But the beauty of all the churches in the city, and of all the Protestant churches in the world, is the cathedral of St Paul's; a building exceeding beautiful and magnificent; tho some authors are pleased to expose their ignorance, by pretending to find fault with it; tis easy to find fault with the works even of God Himself, when we view them in the gross, without regard to the particular beauties of every part separately considered, and without searching into the reason and nature of the particulars ... The vast extent of the Dome, that mighty arch, on which so great a weight is supported [meaning the upper towers or lanthorn of stone work seventy feet high] may well account for the strength of the pillars and butments below; yet those common observers of the superficial parts of the building, complain, that the columns are too gross, that the work looks heavy, and the lower figures near the eye are too large, as if the Doric and the Attic were not each of them as beautiful as the Corinthian.
>
> The wise architect, like a complete master of his business, had the satisfaction, in his lifetime, of hearing those ignorant reprovers of his work confuted by the approbation of the best masters in Europe; and the church of St Peter's in Rome, which is owned to be the most finished piece in the world, only exceeds St Paul's in the magnificence of its inside work; the painting, the altars, the oratories, and the variety of its imagery; things, which, in a Protestant church, however ornamental, are not allowed of.
>
> If all the square columns, the great pilasters, and the flat pannel work, as well within as without, which they now allege

are too heavy and look too gross, were filled with pictures, adorned with carved work and gilding, and crowded with adorable images of the saints and angels, the kneeling crowd would not complain of the grossness of the work; but tis the Protestant plainness that divesting those columns, etc of their ornaments, makes the work, which in itself is not so large and gross as that of St Peter's, be called gross and heavy; whereas neither by the rules of order, or by the necessity of the building, to be proportioned and sufficient to the height and weight of the work, could they have been less, or any otherwise than they are.

Nay, as it was, those gentlemen who in Parliament opposed Sir Christopher Wren's request at having the dome covered with copper, and who moved to have had the lanthorn on the top made shorter and built of wood; I say, those gentlemen pretending skill in the art, and offering to reproach the judgment of the architect, alleged that the copper and the stone lanthorn would be too heavy, and that the pillars below would not support it. To which Sir Christopher answered, that he had maintained the building with such sufficient columns, and the buttment was everywhere so good, that he would answer for it with his head, that it should bear the copper covering and the stone lanthorn, and seven thousand ton weight laid upon it more than was proposed, and that nothing below should give way, no not one half quarter of an inch; but that on the contrary, it should all be firmer and stronger for the weight that should be laid on it; adding that it was with this view that the work was brought up from its foundation, in such manner, as made common observers rather think the first range of the buildings too gross for its upper part; and that if they pleased, he would undertake to raise a spire of stone upon the whole, a hundred foot higher than the cross now stands . . .

In view of the outrage during the 1950s over the ugly new buildings that blighted the view of St Paul's, it is odd to hear from Defoe that Sir Christopher Wren was unhappy about its location. He would have moved it a little to the north to stand in the street called Paternoster Row, so that the north side stood open to Newgate Street and the south side on to the place where the church now stands. Newgate Street led to the infamous prison, which stood on the site of the present

Old Bailey, the Central Criminal Court. Paternoster Row received its name from the makers of holy beads during the Middle Ages, and later became a centre for booksellers and publishers. It was here, in 1719, at the sign of the Ship, that William Taylor published *Robinson Crusoe*. Defoe maintains that if Sir Christopher Wren had got his way on the siting of St Paul's, 'the common thoroughfare of the city would have been removed at a little further distance from the work, and we should not then have been obliged to walk just under the very wall as we do now, which makes the work appear quite out of all perspective, and is the chief reason of the objections I speak of; whereas had it been viewed at a little distance, the building would have been infinitely to more advantage.'

Defoe examines the changed relations between the City, the centre of London's commerce and wealth, and the Court, the centre of 'its gallantry and splendour'. He begins with the great city financial houses, 'whose stocks support the prodigious paper commerce called stock-jobbing, a trade which once bewitched the nation almost to its ruin, and which, though reduced very much, and recovered from that terrible infatuation which once overspread the whole body of the people, yet is still a negotiation which is so vast in its extent, that almost all the men of substance in England are more or less concerned in it . . .'

He goes on to discuss the former 'emulation' or rivalry between the Court and the City, 'for the Court envied the City's greatness, and the citizens were ever jealous of the Court's designs'. Now, he says, the two parties work to their common advantage, with the bank and the trading companies finding the money for all the projects pro-posed by Parliament and the Treasury. According to Trevelyan, the English victory in the recent war with France had been due as much to Godolphin's Treasury system as to Marlborough's military genius: 'The possibility that Parliamentary government might be superior to despotism, as a system of finance and national efficiency, had been demonstrated in the twenty year contest . . . The complicated system of relationship between Treasury experience, Cabinet policy and Par-liamentary control was the most original and least advertised invention of the English genius under the last Stuart reigns.' Defoe, writing in the *Review* two centuries earlier (18 July 1710), had also recognized the importance of Godolphin's efforts, and his *Essay on Credit* helped to ensure that his system worked as well under Harley's management.

Defoe examines in detail various City institutions, such as insurance companies, 'in all which offices a premio is so small and the recovery, in case of loss, so easy and certain, where no fraud is suspected, that nothing can be shown like it in the whole world, especially that of insuring houses from fire, which has now obtained such a universal approbation, that I am told there are above seventy thousand houses thus insured in London, and the parts adjacent'. The Post Office, an efficient service, now runs packets as far as Portugal and also delivers throughout London, 'so you may send a letter from Limehouse in the east to the farthest part of Westminster for a penny, and that several times in the same day'. He goes on to admire the Customs House and its quays and wharves on the river, from which it receives £40,000 a year. The porters or dockers are 'poor working men, who, though themselves not worth perhaps, twenty pounds in the world, are trusted with great quantities of valuable goods, sometimes to the value of several thousand pounds, and yet tis very rarely to be heard that any loss or embezzlement is made'.

Next follows a description of the London markets for fish, meat, vegetables, fruit, corn, hay, hides, leather, coal, baize, broad cloth and live cattle, the last four being 'without question' the largest in the world. While the live cattle are sold at Smithfield, the beef goes to fourteen 'flesh markets': in only one of these, Leadenhall, as much meat is sold in a month 'as would suffice all Spain for a year'. Defoe calls the whole river from London Bridge to Blackwall one great naval arsenal. Although there are more ships built at Amsterdam than at London, that is because the English build for themselves alone, and the Dutch for all the world. Moreover, while all the Dutch ships are built in Amsterdam, London produces only a fifth of England's total. Defoe also explains the arcane language of Billingsgate coal market: 'The brokers or buyers of these coals are called crimps, for what reason . . . is likewise a mystery peculiar to this trade; for these people are noted for giving such dark names to the several parts of their trade; so the vessels they load their ships with at Newcastle are called keels, and the ships that bring them are called cats, and hags, or hag boats, and fly boats and the like.'

Defoe remarks grimly that there are more prisons in London, the capital of a land at liberty, than any city in Europe – perhaps in all the cities of Europe put together. After giving a list of the 'open gaols', sponging houses and lunatic asylums, he describes three hospitals, all of which have survived into the late twentieth century. St Bartholomew's, or Bart's, was flourishing in the last year, 1718, for which Defoe has statistics:

Cured and discharged of sick, maimed and wounded, from all parts	3088
Buried at the expense of the house	198
Remaining under care	513

St Thomas's Hospital in Southwark had comparable figures of 3608, 216 and 566. A new, third hospital was 'built at the sole charge and expense of one Mr Thomas Guy, a bookseller in Lombard Street, who lived to see the said hospital not only designed, the ground purchased and cleared, but the building begun, and a considerable progress made in it, and died while these sheets were in the press'. Guy is a 'thriving frugal man, who God was pleased exceedingly to bless, in whatever he set his mind to, knowing to what good purpose he laid up his gains'. He never married and lived to be over eighty. Defoe cites Guy's Hospital as a proof that 'this age has produced some of the most eminent acts of public charity . . . that can be found within the reach of our English history . . . so that the Papists have no reason to boast that there were greater benefactions and acts of charity to the poor given in their time, than in our Protestant time'.

In this letter on London Defoe is contemptuous of the two most famous buildings left from Papist times. Westminster Hall, where Dr Sacheverell went on trial in March 1710 is

> a very noble Gothic building, ancient, vastly large, and the finest roof of its kind in England, being one hundred feet wide; but what a wretched figure does it make without doors [i.e., from outside], tis like a great pile of something, but a stranger would be much at a loss to know what; and whether it was a house or a church, or, indeed a heap of churches; being huddled all together with differing and distant roofs, some higher, some lower, some standing east and west, some north and south, some one way, and some another.

This pile or heap of a Great Hall was nevertheless the only part of the old Palace of Westminster that survived the fire of 1843, as it did the incendiary bombs in 1941. Time has spared another medieval relic which Defoe disliked: 'The Abbey, or Collegiate Church of Westminster, stands next to this: a venerable old pile of building it is indeed, but so old and weak, that had it not been taken in hand some years ago, and great care bestowed in upholding and repairing it, we might, by this time, have called it a heap, not a pile, not a church, but the ruins of a church.' Even the Roman Catholic James II submitted to coronation here by a Protestant bishop, but 'our kings and queens make always two solemn visits to this church, and very rarely, if ever come here any more, viz. to be crowned and to be buried'. Defoe claims that Westminster Abbey 'begins to be crowded with the bodies of citizens, poets, seamen and parsons, nay, even with very mean persons, if they have but any way made themselves known in the world; so that in time the royal ashes will be thus mingled with common dust, that it will leave no more room either for king or common people, or at least not for their monuments, some of which are more pompously foolish than solid and to the purpose'.

Defoe's next letter, 'Containing the description of part of the counties of Middlesex, Hertford, Bucks, Oxford, Wilts, Somerset, Gloucester, Warwick, Worcester, Hereford, Monmouth and the several counties of South and North Wales', begins with a ride north-east from the City, through Hackney and then the Newington suburb where he had studied at Dr Morton's Academy, and was now living and writing the *Tour*. These northern suburbs, he says, are now so increased in population as to appear a continual street of houses, most of them occupied by 'the middle sort of mankind, grown wealthy by trade, and who still taste of London; some of them live both in the city and in the country at the same time; yet many of them are immensely rich'.

Turning east to Hampstead and Highgate, Defoe observes: 'The Jews have particularly fixed upon this town for their country retreats, and some of them are very wealthy; they live there in good figure, and have several trades particularly depending upon them, and especially butchers of their own to supply them with provisions killed their own way; also I am told, they have a private synagogue here'. Like Epsom, Hampstead had prospered from its mineral springs and the fashionable people who gathered there:

> This consequently raised the rate of lodgings, and that in-
> creased buildings, till the place grew from a little village, to a
> magnitude equal to some cities; nor could the uneven surface,
> inconvenient for building, uncompact and unpleasant, check
> the humour of the town, for even on the very steep of the
> hill, where there's no walking twenty yards together, without
> tugging up a hill, or straddling down a hill, yet tis all one, the

buildings increased to that degree, that the town almost spreads the whole side of the hill.

From Hampstead Defoe makes an excursion to Edgworth, the modern Edgware, on the road that already in those days ran from 'Hide-Park Corner, just where Tyburn stands' to St Albans in Hertfordshire. On the way there he praises the palace or mansion house of the Duke of Chandos, Handel's patron, who had also set a fashion for Italian stucco embellishments. Two miles from the Duke's palace Defoe crosses Bushy Heath in the company of two foreign gentlemen:

> I cannot but remember, with some satisfaction . . . how they looked at one another, and then again turning their eyes every way in a kind of wonder, one of them said to the other, that England was not like other countries, but it was all a planted garden. They had there on the right hand, the town of St Alban's in their view; and all the space between, and further beyond it looked indeed like a garden. The enclosed corn-fields made one grand parterre [arrangement of flower-beds], the thick planted hedge-rows, like a wilderness or labyrinth, divided in espaliers [a lattice-work of wood to train trees on]; the villages interspersed, looked like so many noble seats of gentlemen at a distance. In a word, it was all nature, and yet looked all like art . . .

After doubling back to admire 'the great houses and palaces' of Chelsea and Hammersmith, Defoe sets a course through Aylesbury and Tring to Oxford, 'a name known throughout the learned world'. While apparently viewing the city with approval, Defoe cannot resist some banter against the citadel of the High Church Tories, such as his old antagonist Dr Sacheverell. Moreover, he had been barred from studying there by the Act of Conformity. He begins by saying that Oxford is 'so eminent for the goodness of its air, and healthy situation, that our courts have no less than three times . . . resorted hither when London has been visited by the pestilence, and here they have been always safe'. After this jibe at Charles II for running away during the Plague Year, Defoe takes a swipe at Charles I, who made Oxford his capital in the Civil War: 'Oxford has also several times been the retreat of our princes, when the rest of the kingdom had been embroiled in war and rebellion; and here they have found both safety and support; at least, as long at the loyal inhabitants were able to protect them.'

He then reminds the present High Churchmen how, during the reign of the Roman Catholic Queen Mary (or 'Bloody Mary', as she was called by Puritans), the Oxford clergymen Latimer and Ridley 'made here their ... bold disputations against the Papists, in behalf of the Protestant religion; and their triumphant closing the debates, by laying down their lives for the truths which they asserted'.

The Bodleian Library comes in for praise, and Defoe gives potted histories of the seventeen colleges, but will not join in the argument about whether Oxford or Cambridge is the older university: 'As they have not decided it themselves, who am I?' However, he seems to believe that Oxford is three centuries older than it really is. Contesting the Papist claim that it was built from pious donations during the Middle Ages, he maintains that

> although these learned foundations have stood 800 years, and the Reformation, as they say, is not yet of 200 years standing, yet learning has more increased and the universities flourished more; more great scholars been produced, greater libraries been raised, and more fine buildings been erected in these 200 years than in the 800 years of Popery; and I might add, as many great benefactions have been given, notwithstanding this very momentous difference, that the Protestant's gifts are merely acts of charity in the world, and acts of bounty, in reverence to learning and learned men, without the grand excitement of the health of the souls of their fathers, to be prayed out of purgatory, and got a ready admission into heaven and the like.

Defoe continues to Woodstock to see the recently finished Blenheim Palace, a gift to the Duke of Marlborough after the battle for which it was named. Here, for the last time, he salutes the man whose reputation had been so effectively tarnished by the malice of Swift:

> The magnificence of the buildings does not here ... as at other palaces of the nobility, express the genius and the opulence of the possessor, but it represents the bounty, the gratitude, or what else posterity please to call it of the English nation, to the man whom they delighted to honour. Posterity, when they view in this house the trophies of the Duke of Marlborough's fame, and the glories of his great achievements will not celebrate his name only; but will look on Blenheim House, as a

monument to the generosity of the English nation; who in so glorious a manner rewarded the services of those who acted for them as he did. Nor can any nation in Europe show the like munificence to any general, no not the greatest in the world.

After admiring the bridge, or rialto – a single arch costing £20,000 – the gardens of nearly 100 acres, 'the outhouses fit for a regiment of the guards', the salons, galleries and royal apartments, Defoe suggests that Blenheim may one day be, as Woodstock was in the Middle Ages, the summer residence of the monarch: 'I shall enter no further into the description, because tis yet a house unfurnished, and it can only be properly said what it is to be, not what it is; but as the Duke is dead, the Duchess old, and the heir abroad, when and how it shall be all performed, requires more of the gift of prophecy than I am master of.' Defoe could not foresee that, during a ball at Blenheim Palace on 30 November 1874, the American wife of Lord Randolph Churchill would give birth to a boy, Winston, whose fame and whose services to the country would exceed even those of the first Duke of Marlborough.

From Woodstock, Defoe makes a detour to Banbury to see the site of a Civil War battle: 'It was a vigorous action, and in which the king's forces may be said fairly to outgeneral their enemies, which really was not always their fate. I had the plan of that action before me, which I have had some years, and found out every step of the ground as it was disputed on both sides by inches, where the horse engaged and where the foot, and where Waller lost his cannon and where he retired.' Returning to Oxfordshire, he makes for the 'famous Cotswold Downs, so eminent for the best of sheep and fine wool', then rides along Ackerman's Street, called from the Saxon word 'aching-man', after the cripples who went to Bath in search of a cure. Defoe remarks that in ancient times people went there to bathe, as its name suggests, but during the last fifty years they had started to drink the water as well.

> In the morning you (supposing you to be a young lady) are fetched in a close chair, dressed in your bathing clothes, that is, stripped to the smock, to the Cross Bath. There the music plays you into the bath, and the women that tend you, present you with a little floating wooden dish, like a basin; in which the lady puts a handkerchief, and a nosegay, of late the snuff-box is added, and some patches; though the bath occasioning a little perspiration, the patches do not stick as kindly as they should.

Here the ladies and the gentlemen pretend to keep some distance, and each to their proper side, but frequently mingle
here too, as in the King and Queen Bath, though not so often;
and the place being but narrow, they converse freely, and talk,
rally, make vows, and sometimes love.

Defoe was one of a long line of authors who coupled the waters of
Bath with sexual immorality. Chaucer's Wife of Bath in *The Canterbury
Tales* has been five times married, and boasts of how she controlled
her rich, elderly husbands by shrewishness, and by forcing them to
their marital duties:

> As help me God, I laugh when that I think,
> How piteously at night I made them swink [toil].

Like Moll, with the married man she meets at the spa, Chaucer's Wife
of Bath is aroused by alcohol:

> For after wine, on Venus most I think;
> For also sicker [just as surely] as cold engendereth hail,
> A liquorous mouth must have a lecherous tail.

Defoe occasionally quotes from Chaucer, and once uses the term 'a
Canterbury Tale' to mean a long, rambling story. Moll's description
of Bath as a place 'where men may find a mistress but very rarely look
for a wife' is closer in spirit to Chaucer than to the subsequent writers
about the resort, such as Tobias Smollett, Jane Austen and Dickens.

Following the course of the river Avon, Defoe reaches Bristol, 'the
greatest, the richest and the best port of trade in Great Britain, London
only excepted'. The Bristol merchants have a virtual monopoly on
trade in the West of England and South Wales: 'and as to their trade
to Ireland, it is not only great in itself, but is prodigiously increased
in these last thirty years, since the Revolution, notwithstanding the
great increase and encroachment of the merchants of Liverpool, in
the Irish trade, and the great devastation of the war; the kingdom of
Ireland itself being wonderfully increased since that time.'

At Berkeley Castle Defoe looks at the room where Edward II was
held a prisoner; 'but they do not admit that he was killed there'. In
Gloucester Cathedral he pays his respects to John Hooper, the first
Protestant bishop there, 'set up by King Edward VI, and afterwards
martyred for his religion in the Marian tyranny: being burned to death
in the cemetery of his own cathedral'. At Tewkesbury he visits the site

of the last battle of the Wars of the Roses, then follows the Warwick-shire Avon up to Stratford:

> At this last town, going into the parish church, we saw the monument of old Shakespear, the famous poet, and whose dramatick performances so justly maintain his character among the British poets, and perhaps will do so to the end of time. The busto of his head is in the wall on the north side of the church, and a flat grave-stone covers the body, in the aisle just in front of him. On which grave-stone these lines are written,

> > Good friends, for Jesus's sake forbear
> > To move the dust that resteth here.
> > Blest be the man that spares these stone,
> > And curst be he that moves my bones,

which he also misquotes. Defoe recognizes that Shakespeare is an immortal poet, but fails to spot the irony of the doggerel verse on his tomb. But then Defoe, as a Puritan, had probably never allowed himself to see or read one of Shakespeare's plays.

Returning to Tewkesbury, Defoe then visits Worcester, 'all the way still on the bank of the Severn; and here we had the pleasing sight of the hedge-rows, being filled with apple trees and pear trees, and the fruit so common, that any passenger as they travel the road may gather and eat what they please; and here as well as in Gloucestershire, you meet with cider in the public-houses sold as beer and ale is in other parts of England, and as cheap'. He disapproves of the monuments in Worcester Cathedral to

> that famous Countess of Salisbury, who dancing before or with King Edward III in his great hall at Windsor, dropped her garter, which the king taking up, honoured it so much as to make it the denominating sign of his new order of knights . . . the most noble order of the Garter: What honour . . . redounds to that noble order, from its being derived from the garter of a — For tis generally agreed, she was the king's mistress, I will not enquire.

Continuing north through Herefordshire and Shropshire, Defoe follows the route he took on his mission for Harley in 1705, of which we have a detailed record. However, at this point in the *Tour* he crosses the border into Wales, which he never visited in Harley's service – nor, very likely, on any other occasion. Even if Defoe knew Wales, he certainly did not know all the countries with which he compares it:

> We began with Brecknock[shire], being willing to see the highest of the mountains, which are said to be hereabouts; and indeed, except I had still an idea of the height of the Alps, and of those mighty mountains of America, the Andes, which we see very often in the South-Seas, 20 leagues from the shore: I say except that I had still an idea of those countries on my mind, I should have been surprised at the sight of these hills . . .

Defoe has to concede that even wildest Brecknockshire, or 'Breakneckshire', as he calls it, is not totally barren; indeed one of the lakes, 'as is said of the River Thysse in Hungary is two thirds water, and one third fish . . . nor are these mountains useless even to the city of London . . . for from hence they send yearly, great herds of black cattle to England, and which are known to fill our fairs and markets, even that of Smithfield itself'.

In Radnorshire Defoe had planned to visit the Cataract of the Wye, 'but we did not go to see it, by reason of a great flood at that time, which made the way dangerous. There is a kind of desert too, on that side, which is scarce habitable or passable.' After Brecknockshire and Radnorshire he ventures into Glamorgan:

> Entering this shire . . . we were saluted with Monuchdenny-Hill on our left, and the Black Mountain on the right, and all a ridge of horrid rocks and precipices between, over which if we had not had trusty guides, we should never have found our way; and indeed we began to repent our curiosity, as not having met with anything worth the trouble; and a country looking so full of horror, that we thought to have given over the enterprise, and have left Wales out of our circuit: But after a day and night conversing with rocks and mountains, our guide brought us down into a most agreeable vale . . . and in the evening we came to the ancient city of Llandaff, and Cardiff, standing almost together.

Defoe is happier when he reaches Pembroke, 'the most flourishing town of all South Wales . . . Here are a great many English merchants, and they told us there were near 200 sail of ships belonged to the town; in a word all this part of Wales is a rich and flourishing country . . . and is so well cultivated, that tis called by distinction, Little

England, beyond Wales.' After this home from home he returns to darkest Wales at Aberystwyth, 'a very dirty, black, smoky place, and we found the people looked as if they lived continually in the coal or lead mines. However they are rich and the place is very populous.'

In North Wales Defoe traverses a ridge of mountains, 'so that for almost a whole week's travel, we seemed to be conversing with the upper regions; for we were often above the clouds, I'm sure, a very great way, and the names of some of these hills seemed as barbarous to us, who spoke no Welch, as the hills themselves.' He reports that 'Snowden Hill is a monstrous height, and according to its name had snow on the top in the beginning of June, and perhaps had so till the next June, that is to say, all the year.' The mountains of Caernarfonshire are

> indeed so like the Alps, that except for the language of the people, one could hardly avoid thinking he is passing from Grenobles to Susa, or rather passing the country of the Grisons. The lakes also which are so numerous here, make the similitude the greater, nor are the fables which the country people tell of these lakes, much unlike the stories which we meet with among the Switzers, of the famous lakes in their country . . .

Defoe ends his fabulous tour of Wales with a visit to Denbigh, and then to the nearby Holy Well, where he boasts of the toleration accorded to Roman Catholics:

> The stories of this Well of St Winifrid are, that the pious virgin, being ravished and murthered, this healing water sprung out of her body when buried; but this smells too much of the legend, to take up any of my time; the Romanists indeed believe it, as tis evident from their thronging hither to receive the healing sanative virtue of the water, which they do not hope for as it is a medicinal water, but as it is a miraculous water, and heals them by virtue of the intercession and influence of the famous virgin, St Winifrid; of which I believe as much as comes to my share . . .
>
> There is a little town near the well, which may, indeed, be said to have risen from the confluence of the people hither, for almost all the houses are either public houses, or let into lodgings; and the priests that attend there, and are very numer-

ous, appear in disguise: Sometimes they are physicians, sometimes surgeons, sometimes gentlemen, and sometimes patients, or anything as occasion presents . . .

No body takes any notice of them, as to their profession, though they know them well enough, no not the Roman Catholics themselves; but in private, they have their proper oratories in certain places, whither the votaries resort; and good manners has prevailed so far, that however the Protestants know who and who's together; no body takes notice of it, or enquires where one another goes, or has been gone.

Defoe now crosses the Dee to Chester to start Letter Seven, 'Containing a Description of Part of Cheshire, Shropshire, Wales, Staffordshire, Warwickshire, Northamptonshire, Leicestershire, Lincolnshire, Rutlandshire and Bedfordshire'. Now that he is safely back in England, he cannot resist giving his readers another reminder of what he went through in Wales:

I must confess, I that have seen the Alps, on so many occasions, have gone under so many of the most frightful passes in the country of the Grisons, and in the mountains of Tirol, never believed there was anything in this island of Britain that came near, much less that exceeded those hills, in the terror of their aspect, or in the difficulty of access to them; but certainly, if they are outdone anywhere in the world, it is here: Even Hannibal himself would have found it impossible to have marched his army over Snowden, or over the rocks of Merioneth and Montgomery shires . . .

This is a glorious leg-pull, since Defoe had almost certainly never set foot in Switzerland, and probably not in Wales – or at least only in the region bordering England. However, we know that he met and conversed with the Welsh in Hereford, Ludlow and Shrewsbury, and seemed to have gained a favourable impression:

The Welsh gentlemen are very civil, hospitable and kind; the people very obliging and conversible, and especially to strangers; but when we let them know, we travelled merely in curiosity to view the country, and be able to speak well of them to strangers, their civility was heightened to such a degree, that nothing could be more friendly, willing to tell us everything that belonged to their country, and to show us everything that we desired to see . . . They value themselves much upon their antiquity: The ancient race of their houses, and families, and the like; and above all upon their ancient heroes: their King Caractacus, Owen ap Tudor, Prince Lewellin, and the like noblemen and princes of British extraction; and as they believe their country to be the pleasantest and most agreeable in the world, so you cannot oblige them more, than to make them think you believe so too.

Defoe calls Chester 'a very ancient city, and to this day the buildings are very old' – as always, a mark of his disapproval. However, he added in Chester's favour 'that the streets are very broad and fair, and run through the whole city in strait lines, crossing in the middle of the city as at Chichester'. Both cities were built by the ancient Romans, whom Defoe admires as much as he despises the modern Popish Romans. He tells us that the prisoners taken at Preston during the 1715 rising were held in Chester Castle's 'a great while, till compassion to their misery moved the clemency of their conqueror, to deliver them'. It was here at Chester in 1689 that the 'first army of King William, designed for the war in Ireland and commanded by the great Duke Schomberg, encamped for a considerable time before they embarked'. Since Defoe remarks a few lines later that he himself was in Chester 'about the year 1690', some have surmised that he came here with William, but once again we do not know. Indeed, he mentions the earlier visit only in order to admire the recent installation of piped water: 'When I was formerly at the city . . . they had no water to supply their ordinary occasions, but what was carried from the River Dee upon horses, in great leather vessels, like a pair of bakers panniers; just the very same for shape and use, as they have to this day in the streets of Constantinople and Belgrade . . .'

From Chester, Defoe rides into Whitchurch and Bangor Bridge, which was famous for being the birthplace of Pelagius (c. 360–c. 420):

But as for the town or monastery, scarce any of the ruins were to be seen, and as all the people spoke Welch, we could find no body that could give us any intelligence. So effectually had time in so few years, rased the very foundations of the place. I will not say, as some do, that this is miraculous, and that it is the particular judgment of God upon the place, for being the birth-place of that arch heretick Pelagius . . .

Just over the Dee in Denbighshire, he mentions the birthplace of another, more recent enemy of his religion: 'From hence we turned south and passing by Wem, the title given by James II to the late Lord Chancellor Jefferies, we saw the house where his father, then but a private gentleman lived, and in but middling circumstances.'

Defoe continues to Shrewsbury, 'a large, pleasant town ... full of gentry, yet full of trade too ... This is really a town of mirth and gaiety; something like Bury in Suffolk, or Durham to the North, but much bigger than each of them, or indeed than both together.' Shrewsbury, he says, will ever be famous for the reception it gave Charles I, after his first discouragement when he raised the flag at Nottingham. Thanks to the zeal and loyalty of the people of Shropshire, the King 'completed a strong army in less time than could be imagined, insomuch that to the surprise of the Parliament ... he was in the field before them'. Among the Shropshire men who rallied to Charles was the fictional narrator of *The Memoirs of a Cavalier*.

At Penkridge, in Staffordshire, Defoe is surprised to find what he calls the greatest horse-fair in the world:

> And those not ordinary and common draught-horses ... such as we generally see at county fairs: But here were really incredible numbers of the finest and most beautiful horses that can anywhere be seen; being brought hither from Yorkshire, the Bishopric of Durham, and all the horse-breeding counties; we were told that there were not less than an hundred jockeys and horse-copers, as they call them there, from London, to buy horses for sale. Also an incredible number of gentlemen attended with their grooms to buy gallopers, or race-horses, for their Newmarket sport ... How dextrous the northern grooms and breeders are in their looking after them, and ordering them: These fellows take such indefatigable pains with them, that they bring them out, like pictures of horses, not a hair amiss in them; they lie constantly in the stables with them, and feed them by weight and measure; keep them so clean and so fine, I mean in their bodies as well as their outsides, that in short, nothing can be so nice. Here were several horses sold for 150 guineas a horse; but then they were such as were famous for the breed, and known by their race, almost as well as the Arabians know the genealogy of their horses.

Defoe calls Lichfield 'a place of good conversation and good company, above all the towns in this county, or the next, I mean Warwickshire or Derbyshire'. At the time Defoe was writing the *Tour* a young man in Lichfield, Samuel Johnson, was gaining the knowledge, wisdom and wit that would eventually make him a by-word for good company and conversation. The elderly Puritan and the young High Churchman would not have been kindred spirits, yet Boswell tells us that Johnson read Defoe and 'allowed a considerable share of merit to a man, who, bred a tradesman, had written so variously and so well'. At Coventry Defoe recalls the street battles fought during the 1705 General Elections, when Whigs and Tories fell on each other with clubs and staves: 'Nor were these the scum and rabble of the town, but in short the burgesses and chief inhabitants, nay even magistrates, aldermen, and the like.' At Althorp in Northamptonshire Defoe admires the house of the late Earl of Sunderland, who had done him some favours in 1708 and again ten years later. At Houghton, he inspects 'the noble seat of the Duke of Montague', singling out for particular praise the park which 'is walled round with brick, and so finely planted with trees, and in such an excellent order, as I saw nothing more beautiful, no not in Italy itself, except that the walls of trees were not orange and lemon, and citron, as it is in Naples and the Abruzzo, and other southern parts of Italy'. On the way to Leicester Defoe turns aside to 'see an old town called Lutterworth, famous for being the birth-place of honest John Wickliff, the first preacher of the Reformation in England, whose disciples were afterwards called Lollards; when we came there we saw nothing worth notice, nor did the people, as I could find, so much as know in general, that this great man was born amongst them'. In fact John Wyclif (*c.* 1329–84) was probably born near Richmond in Yorkshire, and went to live in his Lutterworth parish only in 1382, after his writing had been condemned and he was expelled from Oxford.

Fired by the memory of this early Protestant hero, Defoe savages Lincoln, which he appears to regard as typifying the Popish, unreformed Church:

Lincoln is an ancient, ragged, decayed or still decaying city; it is so full of the ruins of monasteries and religious houses; that in short, the very barns, stables, out-houses, and, as they showed me, some of the very hog-styes, were built church-fashion; that is to say, with stone walls and arched windows and doors. There are here 13 churches, but the meanest to look at that are anywhere to be seen; the cathedral indeed and the ruins of the old castle are very venerable pieces of antiquity.

Defoe then heads up to the north-east corner of the county, where he had once taken a ferry over the Humber to Hull:

an ill-favoured dangerous passage . . . where in an open boat, in which we had about fifteen horses, and ten or twelve cows, mingled with about seventeen or eighteen passengers, called Christians; we were about four hours tossed about on the Humber; whether I was sea-sick or not, is not worth notice, but that we were all sick of the passage, any one may suppose, and particularly I was so uneasy at it, that I chose to go round by York, rather than return to Barton, at least for that time.

Following the coast down from Grimsby, Defoe enters that part of the Fens

very properly called Holland, for tis a flat, level and often drowned country like Holland itself; here the very ditches are navigable, and the people pass from town to town in boats as in Holland; here we have the uncouth music of the bittern, a bird formerly counted ominous and presaging, and who, as fame tells us, (but as I believe no body knows) thrusts its bill into a reed, and then gives the dull, heavy groan or sound, like a sigh, which it does so loud, that with a deep base, like the sound of a gun at a great distance, tis heard two or three miles, (say the people) but perhaps not quite so far.

He admires the Boston Stump, the largest and highest church tower in England, and calls the nearby town of Spalding pretty well built and populous, 'But for the healthiness and pleasantness of it, I have no more to say than this, that I was very glad when I got out of it, and out of the rest of the fen country; for tis a horrid air for a stranger to breathe in.'

Before leaving the Fenlands, Defoe gives an account of decoy ducks, demonstrating the humour and pathos with which he writes on the animal kingdom. The art of catching the wild duck, mallard, widgeon and teal depends on breeding and training the decoys – or duckoys, as they are also called. The decoy ducks are hatched and brought up on the decoy ponds, becoming so tame that they feed from the hand of the decoy man:

> When they fly abroad, or as might be said, are sent abroad, they go none knows where; but tis believed by some they fly quite over the seas in Holland and Germany; There they meet with others of their acquaintance, that is to say of their own kind, where sorting with them, and observing how poorly they live, how all the rivers are frozen up, and the lands covered with snow, and that they are almost starved, they fail not to let them know, (in language that they make one another understand) that in England, from whence they came, the case is quite altered; that the English ducks live much better than they do in those cold climates; that they have open lakes, and sea shores full of food, the tides flowing freely into every creek; that they have also within the land, large lakes, refreshing springs of water, open ponds, covered and secured from human eyes, with large rows of grown trees and impenetrable groves; that the lands are full of food, the stubbles yielding constant supplies of corn, left by the negligent husbandmen . . . that tis not once in a wild duck's age, that they have any long frosts or deep snows . . .
>
> By these representations, made in their own duck language . . . they draw together a vast number of the fowls, and, in a word, kidnap them from their own country; for being once brought out of knowledge, they follow the decoys, as a dog follows the huntsman . . .
>
> When they have brought them over, the first thing they do is to settle with them in the decoy ponds, to which they [the decoy ducks] belong. Here they chatter and gabble to them in their own language, as if they were telling them, that these are the ponds they told them of . . .

The decoy men, from the hides they have made of reeds, throw corn into the water to lure the ducks to the place where nets are prepared in the trees:

> The decoy ducks greedily fall upon it, and calling their foreign guests, seem to tell them, that now they may find their words good, and how well the ducks live in England; so inviting or

rather wheedling them forward, till by degrees they are gotten under the arch or sweep of the net, which is on the trees, and which by degrees . . . declines lower and lower, and also narrower and narrower, till at the further end it comes to a point like a purse . . .

When the whole quantity are thus greedily following the leading ducks or decoys, and feeding plentifully as they go . . . on a sudden a dog, who is perfectly taught his business, rushes from behind the reeds, and jumps into the water, swimming directly after the ducks, and (terribly to them) barking as he swims . . . till by degrees the net growing lower and narrower, they are hurried to the very end, where another decoy man takes them out alive with his hands.

As for the traitors, that drew the poor ducks into this snare, they are taught to rise but a little way, and so not reaching to the net, they fly back to the ponds, and make their escape; or else being used to the decoy-man, they go to him fearless, and are taken out as the rest; but instead of being killed with them, are stroked, made much of, and put into a little pond just by him, and fed and made much of for their services.

Defoe finally leaves the Fens, 'longing to be delivered from fogs and stagnate air, and water the colour of brewed ale', returning hurriedly to London through Bedfordshire. He ends the second volume of the *Tour* with an appendix on turnpikes and roads in general, producing from this unlikely subject one of his most brilliant essays.

He begins by explaining why the roads are especially bad in the Midlands, through which he has just been travelling. The soil in this part of the country, 'even from sea to sea, is of a deep stiff clay, or marly kind, and it carries a depth of near fifty miles at least, in some places much more, nor is it possible to go from London to any part of Britain, north, without crossing this clayey, dirty part'. Since the Midland counties do a big trade with London, and also lie on the carriage route to the North, the roads are deeply rutted and always in need of repair. Parliament therefore enacted that turnpikes or toll-bars should be set up on all the great roads of England, beginning at London 'and proceeding through almost all those dirty, deep roads, in the midland counties especially, at which carriages, droves of cattle, and travellers on horseback, are obliged to pay an easy toll, that is to say, a horse a penny, a coach three pence, a cart four pence, at some six pence to eight pence, a waggon six pence, at some a shilling; cattle pay by the score, or by the head . . .'

Although the turnpikes have brought improvement, Defoe believes that the modern roads cannot compare with the network built by the Romans, when there was only a five-hundredth part of the trade:

> The causeways and roads or streetways of the Romans, were perfect solid buildings, the foundations were laid so deep, and the materials so good, however far they were obliged to fetch them, that if they had been vaulted and arched, they could not have been more solid: I have seen the bottom of them dug up in several places, where I have observed flint-stones, chalk-stones, hard gravel, solid hard clay, and several other sorts of earth, laid in layers, like the veins of ore in a mine; a laying of clay of a solid binding quality, then flint-stones, then chalk, then upon the chalk rough ballast of gravel, till the whole work has been raised six or eight foot from the bottom; then it has been covered with a crown or rising ridge in the middle, gently sloping to the sides, that the rain might run off everyway, and not soak into the work: This I have seen as fair and firm, after having stood, as we may conclude, at least 12 or 1600 years, as if it had been made just the year before.

To those who doubt the truth of his observations, Defoe recommends seeing the Fosse causeway from Cirencester, in Gloucestershire, to Bath, or the causeway from Castleford Bridge to York:

> In several parts of this causeway, the country being hard, and the way good on either side, travellers have not made much use of the causeway, it being very high, and perhaps exposing them too much to the wind and weather, but have rather chosen to go on either side, so that the causeway in some places, lies as flat and smooth on the top, as if it had never been made use of at all; and perhaps it has not, there being not so much as the mark of a wheel upon it, or of a horse foot for a good way together, for which I refer to a curious traveller that goes that way.

Defoe admits that the Romans were able to build these roads because they were 'lords of the world', and could force the native population, as well as their armies, to join in these undertakings: 'But now the case is altered, labour is dear, wages high, no man works for bread

and water now; our labourers do not work in the road and drink in
the brook; so that as rich as we are, it would exhaust the whole nation
to build the edifices, the causeways, the aqueducts, lines, castles, fortifications, and other public works, which the Romans built with very
little expense.' But the turnpike system had brought an improvement
to some of the worst stretches of road, like Baldock Lane between
Hatfield and Stevenage, famous for being so impassable that travellers
often paid to ride through the neighbouring fields

> rather than plunge in sloughs and holes, which no horse could
> wade through . . . But the repair of the roads . . . in Bedford-
> shire, is not so easy a work as in some parts of England. The
> drifts of cattle, which come this way out of Lincolnshire and
> the fens of the Isle of Ely . . . are so great, and so constantly
> coming up to London markets, that it is made more difficult
> to make the ways good, where they are constantly trodden by
> the feet of the large, heavy bullocks.

Better roads would also mean that cheese could be brought from
Cheshire to London far more quickly, and fish from the sea ports to
the inner parts of the kingdom.

> By this carriage of herrings and mackerel . . . to all the inland
> counties, with them sweet and good, which tis plain they might
> do, were the roads made good, even as far as Northampton
> and Coventry, and farther too. I might give example where
> the herrings, which are not the best fish to keep neither, are,
> even as it is, carried to those towns, and up to Warwick,
> Birmingham, Tamworth and Stafford, and though they fre-
> quently stink before they come thither, yet the people are so
> eager for them, that they buy them, and give dear for them
> too . . .

The *Tour*: Northern England and Scotland

IN A PREFACE to the third and final volume of the *Tour*, covering northern England and Scotland, Defoe mentions some of the building completed since the first two volumes were published: Houghton, Walpole's mansion in Norfolk, for instance, and Guy's Hospital in Southwark, 'the noblest foundation of the age for one private charity, finished and filled at the foot of above an hundred thousand pounds gift, if common fame may be believed'. The new East India House and the South Sea Company House meet with his approval, 'both lofty and magnificent'. He also applauds the South Sea Company's 'cookery', as they call it, for boiling the blubber of whales from their Greenland enterprise, 'being the largest magazine for all sorts of materials for the shipping, fishing &. that is belonging to any private branch of commerce'. Having promoted the South Sea Company in pamphlets and in *Robinson Crusoe*, Defoe now gives them a puff in the *Tour*, for which one can only hope he was well rewarded.

After the preface comes an introduction, explaining how he intends to describe the northern parts of Britain, whose people, 'their customs and genius differing so much from others, will add to our entertainment'. He promises that Scotland, 'a kingdom so famous in the world for great and gallant men, as well statesmen as soldiers, but especially the last, can never leave us bare of subject, or empty of something to say of her'. However, he makes plain his view that, since the Union, Scotland is no longer a separate nation but only a part of Great Britain:

> I might enlarge here upon the honour it is to Scotland to be
> a part of the British Empire, and to be incorporated with so
> powerful a people under the crown of so great a monarch;

their being united in name as one, Britain and their enjoying
all the privileges of, and in common with, a nation who have
the greatest privileges, and enjoy the most liberty of any people
in the world. But I should be told, and perhaps justly too, that
this was talking like an Englishman, rather than like a Briton;
that I was gone from my declared impartiality, and that the
Scots would perhaps talk a different style when I came among
them. Nor is it my business to enquire which nation have the
better end of the staff in the late coalition, or how the articles
on which it is established, are performed on one side or other.

Defoe had discussed the politics of the Union in literally hundreds of
articles, tens of pamphlets and several fat books. He left to the *Tour*
his amusing observations on Scottish customs and manners.

Defoe starts his eighth letter at Nottingham on the river Trent,
which he sees as a demarcation line between North and South, for he
nowhere mentions the old political borders of Northumbria and Mer-
cia. To Defoe, this was the region 'which the Scots and Northumber-
landers, and others on that side, call North by Trent'. The Trent, he
says, is one of the six great rivers that cross the island from west to
east, their names all starting with T; the Thames, Tees, Tyne, Tweed
and Tay. The country 'south by Trent' is richer and more populous,
because of the greatness of London and the commerce of the Thames;
however, the southern cities of Exeter, Bristol and Norwich will soon
be 'matched if not out-done by the growing towns of Liverpool, Hull,
Leeds, Newcastle, and Manchester, and the cities of Edinburgh and
Glasgow, as shall be shown in its place'. Long before the Industrial
Revolution Defoe was predicting the rise of the North.

Defoe starts his travels 'north by Trent' at Nottingham, set on the
slope of a sandy rock 'so soft, that they easily work into it for making
vaults and cellars, and yet so firm as to support the roofs of those cellars
two or three under one another'. Moreover, he adds, 'the bountiful
inhabitants generally keep these cellars well stocked with excellent ALE;
nor are they uncommunicative in bestowing it among their friends, as
some in our company experienced to a degree not fit to be made
matter of history'. This is the first of several flattering references to
the beer of 'north by Trent', which helps to account for the genial
mood of this final part of the *Tour*. Although they disapprove of drunkenness, the Puritans of the seventeenth and early eighteenth centuries
never regarded alcohol as a moral or social evil; that did not come

about until the late eighteenth, nineteenth and, once again, in the late twentieth century.

Defoe visits Sherwood Forest, noting that the woods which formerly made it so famous for thieves are wasted, 'and if there was such a man as Robin Hood, a famous outlaw and deer-stealer . . . he would hardly find shelter for one week'. In another part of the forest that once covered this county Defoe 'had the diversion of seeing the ancient meeting of the gentry at the horse-races near Nottingham'. As on other occasions, the horses made him think of the Greek Olympic Games or the Circus Maximus in Rome:

> It is true, in those races the young Roman and Grecian gentlemen rode, or rather drove themselves; whereas in our races the horses, not the riders, make the show; and they are generally ridden by grooms and boys, chiefly for lightness; sometimes indeed the gentlemen ride themselves, as I have often seen the Duke of Monmouth, natural son to King Charles II, ride his own horses at a match, and win it too, though he was a large man, and must weigh heavy.
>
> But the illustrious company at the Nottingham races was in my opinion the glory of the day . . . greater than ever I saw at Newmarket, except when the king has been there in ceremony; for I cannot but say that in Charles II's time when his majesty used to be frequently at Newmarket, I have frequently known the assembly there have been with far less company than this at Nottingham and if I might go back to one of these Nottingham meetings, when the Mareschal de Tallard [the French general captured by Marlborough at Blenheim] was there, I should say, that no occasion at Newmarket, in my memory, ever came up to it, except the first time that King William was there after the Peace of Ryswick.

Once again, we have no idea if Defoe had attended any or all of these meetings at Newmarket and Nottingham, or whether he saw the Duke of Monmouth before joining the doomed rebellion of 1685. This and many similar passages in the *Tour* make it quite clear that Defoe was a devotee of the racecourse.

On leaving Nottinghamshire, Defoe gives a long and spritely account of Derbyshire, where he had gone for his health in the autumn of 1712. He finds the waters at Matlock 'milk or rather blood warm, very pleasant to go into and very sanative, especially for rheumatick pains, bruises etc.' As for Buxton baths, 'which they call one of the wonders of the Peak . . . to us, who had been at Bath in Somersetshire, and at Aix-la-Chapelle in Germany, it is nothing at all'. He also savours the Derbyshire beer: 'The nearer we approached to Yorkshire . . . so the ale advanced nearer to its perfection.'

Defoe is reluctantly taken to see the mountains, rocks, caverns and precipices which poets had called the wonders of Derbyshire. 'The Peak people,' he grumbles, 'who are mightily fond of having strangers showed everything they can, and of calling everything a wonder, told us here of another high mountain, where a giant was buried, and which they called the Giant's Tomb.' In exasperation, he sneers that the greatest wonder of Derbyshire is why such a noble palace as Chatsworth was built where no one would ever see it.

The chief delight of Derbyshire for Defoe was visiting the lead mines and the 'wretches' who worked in them. He calls them a rude, boorish people but 'bold, daring and desperate' and therefore often engaged as sappers in the army. He describes the Barmoot Court, which adjudges disputes among the miners, 'and in a word keeps the peace among them; which by the way may be called the greatest of all the wonders of the Peak, for they are of a strange, turbulent, quarrelsome temper, and very hard to be reconciled to one another in their subterranean affairs'. On his way to see the supposed Giant's Tomb, Defoe noticed a garden, a dog and some children next to the face of a cliff, but not within sight of habitation. When he approached, he saw a small opening in the rock, and the noise he made brought out a woman, holding a baby in her arms. Defoe asked her where she lived: 'Here, Sir, says she and points to the hole in the rock. Here! says I; and do all these children live here too? Yes sir, says she, they were all born here. Pray how long have you dwelt here then? said I. My husband was born here, said she, and his father before him.' Defoe and his party are given permission to enter the large cave: 'The habitation was poor tis true, but things within did not look so like misery as I expected. Everything was clean and neat . . . There were shelves with earthen ware, and some pewter and brass. There was, which I observed in particular, a whole flitch or side of bacon, hanging up in the chimney.' The poor woman said her husband worked in the lead mines where, if he was lucky, he could earn five pence a day:

> Then I asked what she did? She said when she was able to
> work she washed the ore: But, looking down at her children,

and shaking her head, she intimated that they found her so much business, she could do but little, which I easily granted must be true. But what can you get at washing the ore, said I, when you can work? She said if she worked hard she could gain three-pence a day. So that, in short, here was but eight-pence a day, when they both worked hard, and that not always, and perhaps not often, and all this to maintain a man, his wife and five small children, and yet they seemed to live very pleasantly, the children looked plump and fat, ruddy and wholesome, and the woman was tall, well-shaped, clean and (for the place) a very well-looking, comely woman.

The sight of the cave-dwellers so affected the tourists that they collected almost a crown in coins to give the woman, Defoe having the honour to be the almoner for the company:

And as I told into the poor woman's hand, I could perceive such a surprise in her face, that had she not given vent to her joy by a sudden flux of tears, I found she would have fainted away . . . We asked her if she had a good husband; she smiled, and said, yes, she thanked God for it, and that she was very happy in that . . . In a word it was a lecture to us all, and that such, I assure you, as made the whole company very grave all the rest of the day.

Defoe and his party then visited a hill where the woman had said they would find the 'grooves' or mouths of the shafts by which men descended into the lead mines:

And as we were standing still to look at one of them, admiring how small they were, and scarce believing a poor man who shewed it us when he told us that they went down those narrow pits or holes to so great a depth in the earth; I say while we were wondering, and scarce believing the fact, we were agreeably surprised with seeing a hand, and then an arm, and quickly after a head, thrust up out of the very ground we were looking at. Immediately we rode closer up to the place, where we see the poor wretch working and heaving himself up gradually, as we thought with difficulty; but when he showed us that it was by setting his feet upon pieces of wood fixed across the angles of the groove like a ladder, we found that the difficulty was not much; and if the groove had been larger they could not either go up or down so easily, or with so much safety . . .

When he reached the surface, the miner presented an uncouth spectacle, 'for he was lean as a skeleton, pale as a dead corpse, his hair and beard a deep black, his flesh lank, and as we thought, something of the colour of the lead itself'. Besides his tool-bag, the miner carried about three-quarters of a hundredweight of ore, which explained his heaving and struggling at the mouth of the shaft. Defoe learned through an interpreter of the miner's dialect that he worked at a depth of sixty fathoms, but wished he was with his colleagues even deeper, where there were richer veins of ore.

> If we blessed ourselves before, [says Defoe] when we saw how poor the woman and her five children lived in the hole or cave in the mountain, how much [more] we had to acknowledge to our Maker, that we were not appointed to get our bread thus, one hundred and fifty yards under ground, or in a hole as deep in the earth as the cross upon St Paul's cupola is high out of it. Nor was it possible to see these miserable people without such reflections, unless you will suppose a man as stupid and senseless as the horse he rides on. But to leave moralizing to the reader, I proceed.

The tourists examined the ore and asked the miner's permission to carry away a sample, for which they gave him 'two pieces of better metal, called shillings', or more than he got in three days underground: 'And we found soon after that the money was so much, that it made him move off immediately towards the alehouse, to melt some of it into good Pale Derby; but to his further good luck, we were gotten to the same alehouse before him; where, when we saw him come, we gave him some liquor too, and made him keep his money, and promise us to carry it home to his family, which they told us lived hard by.'

Defoe was the first and surely the best of all those middle-class writers, such as Friedrich Engels, Charles Dickens, Henry Mayhew, Émile Zola, Winifred Holtby and George Orwell, who in their time attempted to give an account of working-class conditions. In describing the life of the woman with five children, and later the work of the man underground, Defoe brilliantly uses the story-telling art of surprise, first in the discovery of the cave's hidden entrance, and then in the spectacle of the miner rising from the ground. Although it is very likely that he had indeed visited the cave and the mine-shaft on a conducted tour, he makes them appear as astonishing as the single footprint in the sand on Robinson Crusoe's island. Again, instead of descending into the mine, as some of his party wanted to do, Defoe employs his imagination to tell us what it is like to work deep under the earth. Although he is moved by what he has seen, he refrains from giving a lecture to his readers. Best of all, he does not scold the miner for going into an alehouse, but gives him a drink on top of the two shillings.

Defoe mentions in the *Tour* that he has travelled through northern England five times, presumably referring to his four round trips to Scotland and the journey he made to Newcastle in 1712. Although he claims to have varied his route in order to see as many places as possible, one can guess that he normally followed the great northern post-road between London and Edinburgh. Thus in the *Tour* he first enters Yorkshire at Bawtry, just before Doncaster, which, 'as it stands upon the great northern post-road, it is very full of great inns'. So important were inns to the economy of Doncaster that Defoe's host was also the mayor of the town, was rich enough to keep a pack of hounds and mingled easily with the local gentry.

From Doncaster, Defoe turns west to Sheffield, a large and populous town, whose houses are black from the constant smoke of the forges. To prove the antiquity of the Sheffield knives, or whittles, he quotes 'those famous lines of Geoffrey Chaucer on the miller of Trumpington, which however they vary from the print in Chaucer, as now extant, I give you as I find it:

> At Trumpington, not far from Cambridge,
> There dwelt a miller upon a bridge;
> With a rizzled beard, and a hooked nose,
> And a Sheffield whittle in his hose.'

These lines do indeed 'vary from the print in Chaucer', being a garbled botch of the opening of the Reeve's Tale, which gives the miller a 'camuse' or flat nose, a skull as 'piled' or hairy as an ape's, but does not mention his beard. Defoe seldom bothered to check his references, so that the *Tour* often leaves blank such things as the distance between two towns, or even the names of the towns themselves.

Having ventured as far as Sheffield and 'Black Barnsley', Defoe describes another visit to Yorkshire, starting from Rochdale in Lancashire then crossing the Pennines to Halifax, Leeds, York and Hull.

When Defoe and his friends leave Rochdale, 'though it was but at the middle of August, and in some places the harvest was hardly got in, we saw the mountains covered with snow, and felt the cold very acute and piercing'. However, they find that the locals manage to keep warm, for 'the store of good ale which flows plentifully in the most mountainous part of this country, seems abundantly to make up for all the inclemency of the season . . . also plenty of coals for firing, which all these hills are full of.' They start to climb the hills in the early morning, well primed with beer, 'but as we ascended higher it began to snow again, that is to say we ascended into that part where it was snowy, and had no doubt been snowing all night, as we could see by the thickness of the snow'. From then on Defoe's crossing of the Pennines in August starts to sound like Robinson Crusoe's crossing of the Pyrennees in December:

> It is not easy to express the consternation we were in when we came up near the top of the mountain; the wind blew exceeding hard, and blew the snow so directly in our faces, and that so thick, that it was impossible to keep our eyes open to see our way. The ground also was so covered with snow, that we could see no track, or when we were in the way, or when out; except when we were shewed it by a frightful precipice on one hand, and uneven ground on the other; even our horses discovered [showed] their uneasiness at it; and a poor spaniel dog that was my fellow traveller, and usually diverted us by giving us a mark for our gun, turned tail to it and cried.

After braving a thunderstorm, while walking their horses along the edge of a precipice, Defoe and his friends have entered Yorkshire and 'thought we were come into a Christian country' again, but find they have yet another mountain to cross in the snow. Strangest of all, they find these mountains covered in houses: 'And though we saw no people stirring without doors, yet they were all full within; for in short this whole country, however mountainous . . . is yet infinitely full of people; those people are full of business; not a beggar, not an idle person to be seen, except here and there an alms house, where people ancient, decrepid and past labour, might perhaps be found . . .'

Defoe has led us over the mountains, during an August snowstorm, into a lost world or Shangri-La, where there are many houses but no sign as yet of the people who live there, although we are told they are all hard at work. At last Defoe explains who these people are and what it is they do:

> This business is the clothing trade, for the convenience of which the houses are thus scattered and spread upon the sides of the hills ... The reason is this; such has been the bounty of nature to this otherwise frightful country, that two things essential to the business, as well to the ease of the people are found here; I mean coals and running water upon the tops of the highest hills ... Having thus fire and water at every dwelling, there is no need to enquire why they dwell thus dispersed upon the highest hills, the convenience of the manufacturers require it. Among the manufacturers houses are likewise scattered an infinite number of cottages or small dwellings, in which dwell the workmen which are employed, the women and children of which are always busy carding, spinning &. so that no hands are unemployed, all can gain their bread, even from the youngest to the ancient; hardly anything above four years old, but its hands are sufficient to itself.

Those who condemn Defoe for this and similar observations at Taunton and Colchester should remember that he is talking of children working at home, not in factories or their masters' workshops, which in those days were the preserve of men, as he goes on to explain: 'This is the reason why we see so few people without doors; but if we knocked at the door of any of the master-manufacturers, we presently saw a house full of lusty fellows, some at the dye-vat, some dressing the cloths, some in the loom, some one thing, some another, all hard at work ...'

Defoe continues through Sowerby Bridge to Halifax, where he gives us a blood-curdling explanation of that famous prayer:

> From Hell, Hull and Halifax,
> Good Lord, deliver us.

Henry VII tried to protect English cloth by banning the export of wool and instead inviting foreigners to manufacture in this country in the appropriate places – for example, bays in Colchester, says in Sudbury, broadcloth in Wiltshire, and kersies and narrow cloth in Halifax:

> When this trade began to settle, nothing was more frequent than for young workmen to leave their cloths out all night

upon the tenters, and the idle fellows would come in upon them, and tearing them off without notice, steal the cloth. Now as it was absolutely necessary to preserve this trade in its infancy, this severe law was made, giving the power of life and death so far into the hands of the magistrates of Halifax, as to see the law executed upon them.

This law applied only to stealing cloth, and the magistrates could not pass sentences except in one of the following cases:

1. Hand napping, that is, to be taken in the very fact, or, as the Scots call it in the case of murther, red hand.
2. Back bearing, that is, when the cloth was found on the person carrying it off.
3. Tongue confessing, that part needs no further explanation.

The method of execution was by a mechanically operated axe, predating by more than 300 years the engine of Dr Guillotin. The story of the beheading machine of Halifax was just the kind Defoe enjoyed:

They tell us of a custom which prevailed here, in the case of a criminal being to be executed, (viz.) that if after his head was laid down, and the signal given to pull out the pin, he could be so nimble as to snatch out his head between the pulling out the pin and the falling down of the ax, and could get up upon his feet, jump off of the scaffold, run down a hill that lies just before it, and get through the river before the executioner could overtake him and seize upon him, he was to escape; and though the executioner did take him on the other side of the river, he was not to bring him back, at least he was not to be executed.

But as they showed me the form of the scaffold, and the weight of the ax, as it was, in my opinion, next to impossible, any man should be so quick-eyed as to see the pulling out of the pin, and so quick with his head, as to snatch it out; yet they tell a story of one fellow that did it, and was so bold after he had jumped off the scaffold, and was running down the hill, with the executioner at his heels, to turn about and call to the people to give him his hat; that having afterwards jumped into the river, which is but a little one, and not deep, he stopped, intending to drown the hangman, if he had come up to him; at which the poor fellow stopped too, and was afraid to go into the water to seize him. But this story is said to be too long ago to have any vouchers, though the people indeed all receive it for truth.

The force of this engine is so strong, the head of the axe being loaded with a weight of lead to make it fall heavy, and the execution is so sure, that it takes away all possibility of its failing to cut off the head; and to this purpose, the Halifax people tell you another story of a country woman, who was riding by upon her doffers or hampers to Halifax market, for the execution was always on a market day (the third after the fact) and passing just as the ax was let fall upon the neck of the criminal, it chopped it through with such force, that the head jumped off into one of her hampers, and that the woman not perceiving it, she carried it away to the market.

All the use I shall make of this unlikely story, is this, that it seems executions were so frequent, that it was not thought a sight worth the peoples running out to see; that the woman should ride along so close to the scaffold, and that she should go on, and not so much as stop to see the ax fall, or take any notice of it. But these difficulties seem to be much better solved, by saying, that tis as reasonable to think that the whole tale is a little Yorkshire, which, I suppose, you will understand well enough.

The Halifax beheading machine was removed in 1620, during the reign of James I, and the local custom of prosecution abolished, so that cloth stealers were left to the ordinary courts of justice. However, Defoe explains, the method of execution continued in Scotland, where it came to be known as the Maiden:

For in the reign of the same prince, the Earl of Morton, Regent or Prime Minister of Scotland under King James, passing through Halifax, and seeing one of the executions, was so pleased with the performance, that he caused a model to be taken and carried into Scotland, where it is preserved and constantly used for executions to this day. But one thing must not be forgotten in this part of the story, namely that his lordship's own head was the first that was cut off with it; and it being many years before that happened, the engine was called the Maiden, as not having so long been handselled [inaugurated], and still retains the name, though it has cut off many a head since that.

From Halifax, Defoe goes on to Leeds, through a countryside busy making cloth:

> A noble scene of industry and application is spread before you here, and which, joined to the market at Leeds, where it chiefly centers, is such a surprising thing, that they who had pretended to give an account of Yorkshire, and have left this out, must betray an ignorance not to be accounted for, or excused; tis what is well worth the curiosity of a stranger to go on purpose to see; and many travellers and gentlemen have come over from Hamburg, nay, even from Leipsig in Saxony, on purpose to see it.

Defoe is always excited by markets and matters of trade, as at Stourbridge in Cambridgeshire, the horse-fair in Staffordshire, or the wagons of corn at Farnham in Surrey; but at Leeds his excitement borders on ecstasy. He calls the cloth market a prodigy of its kind, not to be equalled anywhere in the world, and quite impossible to describe, though he spends many pages trying to do so. He explains how when the church bells ring at six in the morning, the rows of trestles in the street are within minutes covered by cloth, without noise, hurry or any disorder; how the merchants inspect the cloth and quietly do their bargaining; so that in less than an hour, ten or twenty thousands of pounds worth of merchandise has been bought and sold: 'And that which is most admirable is, tis all managed with the most profound silence, and you cannot hear a word spoken in the whole market, I mean by the persons buying and selling; tis all done in whisper.'

The West Riding cloth is carried by pack horse for sale to the rest of England, or shipped down to London for export to the American colonies, 'which take off great quantities of those coarse goods, especially New England, New York, Virginia &. as also to the Russia merchants, who send an exceeding quantity to Petersburgh, Riga, Dantzig and to Sweden and Pomerania'. At Leeds market there are also merchants from Holland and Hamburg, dealing with buyers as far away as Nuremberg and Vienna. Defoe explains how the Aire and Calder rivers are now navigable from Leeds and Wakefield to Hull, and from there to Holland, Bremen, Hamburg and the Baltic. This was the start of the great canal system in central Britain, which played so big a part in the Industrial Revolution.

Defoe is impressed by the fine stone bridges of Yorkshire, contrasting them with the wooden structures over the Thames at Kingston, Chertsey, Staines, Windsor, Maidenhead, Reading, Henley and Marlow. Indeed, the size of the stonework spanning a stream at Harwood put him in mind of the bridge at Madrid, 'of which a Frenchman of quality looking upon it, said to the Spaniards that were about him, That the King of Spain ought either to buy them some water, or they should sell their bridge'. However, on returning to the Harwood bridge soon after a heavy fall of rain, he saw that the water came up to the crown of the arches, and that some of the arches were quite submerged. He then calls at Knaresborough Spa, or Spaw, as it was spelled and pronounced at that time, in order to sample its mineral springs, including the Stinking Spaw, whose water is crystal-clear, 'but foetid and nauseous to the smell, so that those who drink it are obliged to hold their noses when they drink.'

Moving into his ninth letter, 'Containing a description of part of the counties of Yorkshire, Durham and Northumberland', Defoe comes to York, but as usual makes light of its claims to antiquity: 'It boasts of being the seat of some of the Roman emperors, and the station of their forces for the north of Britain, and itself a Roman colony, and the like, all of which I leave as I find it.' However, he has to concede that 'Here Constantine the Great took upon him the purple, and began the first Christian empire in the world; and this is truly and really an honour to the city of York; and this is all I shall say of her antiquity.'

In view of his often contemptuous comments on medieval churches – at Ely and Lincoln, for instance – the reader may be surprised to find that Defoe admires York Minster.

> It is a Gothic building, [he is forced to admit] but with all the most modern addenda that order of building can admit ...
> The royal chapel at Windsor, and King's College Chapel at Cambridge, are indeed very gay things, but neither of them can come to the minster of York on many accounts; also the great tower of the cathedral church at Canterbury is named to match with this at York; but this is but a piece of a large work, the rest of the same building being mean and gross, compared with this at York.

While staying at York, Defoe takes a day off to visit Marston Moor, the site of the Civil War battle which he described in *The Memoirs of a Cavalier*. As in the novel, he says that Prince Rupert 'a third time, by his excess of valour, and defect of conduct, lost the royal army, and had a victory wrung out of his hands, after he had all the advantage . . .' Defoe went to the battlefield in the company of an old soldier whose father had fought at Marston Moor: 'And he accordingly described it in so lively a manner to me, that I thought it was as if I had just now seen the two armies engaging. His relation of Prince Rupert's ill-conduct, put me in mind of the quite different conduct of old General Tilly, who commanded the imperial army at the great battle of Leipsig in Germany, against that glorious Prince Gustavus Adolphus.'

As in *The Memoirs of a Cavalier*, Defoe honours Gustavus Adolphus but barely mentions Oliver Cromwell, the victor at Marston Moor, who was still too unpopular as a regicide to be given his proper due as a military genius. Judging by references to Cromwell in the *Review* and some of the pamphlets, Defoe was not a whole-hearted admirer. For one thing, Cromwell had been a religious Independent, critical of the Presbyterian Church to which Defoe adhered. Defoe approved of Cromwell's aim of uniting Scotland with England, but not the brutal methods he used to further it. In the *Tour* Defoe is careful not to reveal which side he takes in the Civil War, as we see from this bland and even banal reflection: 'I came back extremely well pleased with the view of Marston Moor, and the account my friend had given of the battle; twas none of our business to concern our passion in the cause, or regret the misfortune of that day; the thing was over beyond our ken; time had levelled the victors with the vanquished . . . so we returned to York the same night.'

At Beverley Defoe tells the story of one John, Archbishop of York, 'a learned and devout man [who] out of mere pious zeal for religion and contempt for the world, quitted or renounced his honours and superiority in the Church, and laying aside the pall and the mitre, retired to Beverley, and lived all the rest of his time a recluse'. Defoe commends the good example of John of Beverley, who had died in 721, or just over 1,000 years ago, 'But as to sainting him, and praying to him, and offering at his shrine and such things, that we Protestants must ask their leave to have nothing to say to.'

Defoe moves on to Hull, from where Robinson Crusoe sailed on his first adventure, and explains the convoy system used in the recent war to protect Britain's merchant fleets from French privateers. He then follows the coast northwards, stopping at Scarborough to taste its purgative waters, and enters County Durham at Stockton-on-Tees. Having praised York Minster, Defoe makes no comment upon the architecture of Durham Cathedral, but mentions instead the opulence of the bishop's palace and 'the fine houses of the clergy, where they live in all the magnificency and splendour imaginable'. According to him, the bishopric is the richest and most sought after in England.

Inside Durham Cathedral Defoe inspects with delighted horror 'the old Popish vestments of the clergy, before the Reformation, and which on high days, some of the residents put on still.' Like many Puritans, he was fascinated as well as appalled by the costumes of the Scarlet Woman: 'They are so rich with embroidery and embossed with work of silver, that indeed it was a kind of load to stand under them.' This suggests that he tried the vestments on. In spite of abhorring the Popish practices of the Church of England, Defoe believes in freedom of conscience, for he says that the town of Durham is 'full of Roman Catholics, who live peaceably and disturb no body, and no body them; for we being there on a holiday, saw them going as publicly to mass as the Dissenters did on other days to their meeting-house'.

Heading north to Chester-le-Street, Defoe gives a further account of the mining disaster he had covered in the *Review* of 4 September 1708:

> Here we had an account of a melancholy accident, and in itself strange also, which happened in or near Lumley Park, not long before we passed through the town. A new coal pit being dug or digging, the workmen worked on the vein of coals till they came to a cavity, which, as was supposed, had formerly been dug from some other pit; but be it what it will, as soon as upon the breaking into the hollow part, the pent up air got vent, it blew up like a mine of a thousand barrels of powder, and, getting vent at the shaft of the pit, burst out with such a terrible noise, as made the very earth tremble for some miles round, and terrified the whole country. There were near three score poor people lost their lives in the pit, and one or two, as we were told, who were at the bottom of the shaft, were blown quite out, though sixty fathoms deep, and were found dead upon the ground.

In spite of such disasters, County Durham produced a never-failing supply of coal to London: the southerners were amazed at where it all came from. But when in the North, Defoe explains, 'We see the prodigious heaps, I might say mountains of coals, which are dug up at every pit, and how many of these pits there are; we are filled with equal wonder to consider where the people should live that can consume them.' While most of the Tyneside coal is shipped to London, some is burned by the salt pans at Shields and the Newcastle glass works. These factories make so much smoke, 'that we saw it ascend in clouds over the hills, four miles before we came to Durham, which is at least sixteen miles from the place.' The smoke makes Newcastle itself 'not the pleasantest place in the world to live in'.

Crossing the Tyne into Northumberland, Defoe looks at some of the battlefields in the wars between England and Scotland, notably Cheviot Chase (1388), Flodden Field (1513) and Hexham (1644), where Charles I's army ran away. Before leaving the county, he remarks on the speech defect of the locals, the 'shibboleth upon their tongues, namely a difficulty in pronouncing the letter *r*, which they cannot deliver from their tongues, without a hollow jarring in the throat, by which they are plainly known, as a foreigner is in pronouncing the *th*: This they call the Northumbrian *r*, and the natives value themselves upon their imperfection, because, forsooth, it shows the antiquity of their blood.'

In the seventh letter of volume two of the *Tour* Defoe made an excursion from Cheshire over the Mersey to visit the town he there called Leverpool. Now, at the start of Letter Ten, 'Containing a Description of Part of the Counties of Lancashire, Westmoreland and Cumberland', he returns to the town he now calls Liverpoole, 'one of the wonders of Britain, and that more in my opinion, than any of the wonders of the Peak'. Crossing again by ferry from Cheshire, he has a bumpy arrival:

> We land on the flat shore on the other side, and are contented to ride through the water for some length, not on horseback but on the shoulders of some honest Lancashire clown, who comes knee deep to the boat side, to truss you up, and then runs away with you, as nimbly as you desire to ride, unless his trot were easier; for I was shaken by him that I had the luck to be carried by, more than I cared for, and much worse than a hard trotting horse would have shaken me.

When Defoe first visited Liverpool – apparently in about 1680 – it was already a handsome, well-built city. On his second visit in 1690 the locals said that the population had doubled over the previous twenty years; 'But I think I may safely say that at this my third seeing it, it was more than double what it was at the second.' Liverpool not only rivals but will shortly overtake Bristol in trade with Virginia and the West Indies, as well as with Hamburg, the Baltic and Holland, 'so that, in a word, they are almost become like the Londoners, universal merchants.' While Bristol serves the south of Ireland, Liverpool has all the trade of the east and north from Dublin round to Londonderry.

Defoe approves of the new St Peter's Church, with its beautiful tower of eight good bells, 'and in a word there is no town in England, London excepted, that can equal Liverpool for the fineness of the streets, and beauty of the buildings.' He exaggerates both its size and importance; the city did not overtake Bristol for about 100 years. Nor does he point out that its wealth derived from the infamous three-way traffic – cloth to Africa, slaves across the Atlantic in the 'middle passage', and then a voyage home with tobacco and sugar.

Since Liverpool had no fortifications, it suffered some anxious days in 1715, when Scottish Jacobite rebels came as far south as Preston. According to Defoe, if the Scotsmen had moved on to Warrington,

> seized the pass there, and taken Manchester, as they would certainly have done in three days more, it would have fared but ill for Liverpool . . . Besides the invaders would here have found not the sweets of plunder only, but arms, ammunition, powder and lead, all which they extremely wanted; they would have had ships also to have facilitated a communication with their fellows in Ireland, who would have thronged over upon the least view of their success, if it had been only in hopes of plunder.

Defoe is raising the spectre of Catholic Irish invasion, which had terrified Protestant England during the Civil War and again in 1688, when Lord Tyrconnel's men occupied Reading and 'Lillibullero' was whistled throughout the country. In 1715, as in 1745, 1798 and 1916, the Irish were seen as instruments of Britain's continental enemy.

In writing of Manchester, Defoe once again seems to be prophesying its future greatness rather than giving a true account of the present. He calls Manchester the largest village in England, but goes on to estimate its population at 50,000 or even more:

If then, this calculation is just, as I believe it really is, you have then an open village, which is greater and more populous than many, nay, than most cities in England, not York, Lincoln, Chester, Salisbury, Winchester, Worcester, Gloucester, no not Norwich itself, can come up to it; and for lesser cities, two or three put together would not equal it, such as Peterborough, Ely and Carlisle, or such as Bath, Wells and Lichfield.

In Manchester, as in Sheffield, Leeds, Newcastle and Liverpool, Defoe stresses the early importance of what we have come to regard as cities of the Industrial Revolution – of factories, steam power, machines and railways. We often imagine that Lancashire's fame as 'King Cotton' began with Arkwright's spinning jenny and Crompton's mule; yet Defoe tells us that Manchester cotton was famous in Queen Elizabeth's time, 'when woollen manufacture was in its infancy, or at least not at full age; [so] we may reasonably believe that cotton was the elder manufacture of the two.'

Defoe heads north to Preston, where, in his novel, Colonel Jack fought on the side of the Highlanders in the 1715 rebellion. Defoe clearly finds Preston not as interesting as Liverpool or Manchester, because it is outside the trading area: 'Here's no manufacture; the town is full of attorneys, proctors and notaries . . . The people are gay here, though not perhaps the richer for that, but it has by this obtained the name Proud Preston. Here is a great deal of company, but not so much, they say, as before the late bloody action with the northern rebels . . .' At least Preston resisted the Scottish invaders, unlike Penrith in Cumberland: there, the local militia confronted the Scots on a moor to the north of the town, but in spite of 'making a brave appearance, and infinitely outnumbering the Highlanders . . . they ran away as soon as the Scots began to advance to charge them.'

On the Cumberland coast Defoe reaches the cape or headland named St Bees, after a lady who was the subject of various legends, 'viz. about her procuring, by her prayers, a deep snow on Midsummer Day, her taming a wild bull that did great damage in the country; these and the like tales, I leave where I find them, (viz.) among the rubbish of the old women and the Romish priests'. He is more interested in the nearby port of Whitehaven, the main supplier of coal to the ports of Ireland. It was apparently not uncommon in time of war, or when a cross-wind was blowing, to have 200 ships at a time sailing from there to Dublin. Before leaving England for Scotland, Defoe stops at Burgh upon the Sands, near Carlisle, to see the tomb and monument of Edward I, 'the greatest and truest hero of all our kings of the English or Saxon race'. Rather tactlessly, in view of where he is heading, Defoe hails Edward I as 'the terror of Scotland, and the first complete conqueror of their country, who brought away the sacred stone at Scone Abbey, on which their kings were crowned, also the regalia, and, in a word, made their whole country submit to his victorious arms.'

In an 'Introduction to the Account and Description of Scotland' Defoe explains why his is a pioneering venture: 'Hitherto all the descriptions of Scotland which have been published in our day, have been written by natives of that country, and that with such an air of the most scandalous partiality, that it has been far from pleasing the gentry or nobility of Scotland themselves, and much further has it been from doing any honour to the nation or to the country.' He mentions an author who boasted of Scotland's commerce with China, India, Turkey and the Levant, 'where I believe never Scottish ship yet sailed, unless it was in the service of English merchants, or some other foreign nation'. Another wrote of the country seats of the Scotch nobility and gentry, but in so fulsome a manner that few who read his description would have recognized their homes. Defoe vows to be truthful: 'I have so much honour for the noblemen and gentlemen of Scotland, that I am persuaded they will be as well pleased to see justice done them and their country, as to see themselves flattered, and the world imposed upon about them.'

At the start of the eleventh letter Defoe crosses the border just north of Berwick, and comes to the brow of a very high hill, which afforded a wide view of Scotland:

> But we were welcomed into it with such a Scots gale of wind, that, besides the steepness of the hill, it obliged us to quit our horses, for real apprehensions of being blown off, the wind blowing full north, and the road turning towards the north, it blew directly in our faces. And I can truly say, I never was sensible to so fierce a wind, so exceedingly keen and cold, for it pierced our very eyes that we could scarcely bear to hold them open.

Coming down into Mordintown, Defoe finds himself in an utterly foreign country, 'nor is there the least appearance of anything English, either in customs, habits, usages of the people, or in the way of living, eating, dress or behaviour; any more than if they had never heard of an English nation; nor was there an Englishman to be seen, or an English family to be found among them.' Indeed, there was a Scottish influence even south of the border, found in customs, words and, above all, in building. At Alnwick in Northumberland, Defoe had noticed the Scottish type of house, divided into flats with the stairs to the second floor on the outside, so that different families have separate entrances. In Northumberland he had also observed the Scottish custom of stacking the corn outdoors, rather than keeping it in a barn.

Defoe comes to the port of Eyemouth, best known at the time as one of the titles of the Duke of Marlborough, the Marquis of Blandford and Baron Eyemouth of Scotland. However, the Duke had scarcely been to the town and had certainly not made any changes there. Defoe then crosses Coldingham Moor, 'upon which, for about eight miles, you see hardly a hedge, or a tree, except in one part, and that at a good distance, nor do you meet with but one house in all the way, and that no house of entertainment, which we thought was but poor reception for Scotland to give her neighbours, who were strangers, at their very first entrance to her bounds'.

Having passed this desert, 'which indeed makes a stranger think Scotland a terrible place', Defoe enters the fruitful and pleasant Lothian valley. Here he visits the house of Sir James Hall, 'a gentleman so hospitable, so courteous to strangers, so addicted to improve and cultivate his estate ... that we began to see here that Scotland was not so naturally barren, as some people represent it, but, with application and judgment, in the proper methods of improving land, might be made to equal, not England only, but even the richest, most fruitful, most pleasant and best improved part of England'. Among Defoe's recommendations for Scottish agriculture are more enclosed pasture, keeping the sheep in folds, and letting the ploughed land lie fallow every fourth year.

Defoe stops at Dunbar and Musselburgh; there he is taken to see the site of the English victory over the Scots at the Battle of Pinkie, but tactfully says that he will not 'mingle any of our trophies and triumphs with my account of Scotland'. Before entering Edinburgh, Defoe explains that it is best to approach it from the north, for 'if you take a view of it from the east, you have really but a confused idea of the city'. The great street, stretching a mile and a half or more from the palace gate to the castle, 'is perhaps the largest, longest and finest street for buildings and number of inhabitants, not in Britain only, but in the world'.

To Defoe, who had suffered from altitude sickness on Hampstead Heath, the higher slopes of this great street must have been daunting:

> Together with this continual ascent, which, I think, tis easy to form an idea of in the mind, you are to suppose the edge or top of the ascent so narrow, that the street, and the row of houses on each side of it, take up the whole breadth; so that which way soever you turn, either to the right, or to the left, you go down hill immediately, and that so steep, as is very troublesome to those who walk in those side lanes which they call Wynds, especially if their lungs are not very good. So that, in a word, the city stands upon the narrow ridge of a long ascending mountain.

He explains how the city began as a fortress or 'a retreat from the outrages and attempts of the Picts and Irish, or whatever other enemies they had to fear'. As it stood on top of the ridge of a hill, with an impregnable castle behind and a loch on either side, there was nothing to fortify but the eastern gate. But because of Edinburgh's rocky and mountainous situation, its people were forced to crowd into houses of between seven and ten or twelve storeys high, with dire results for its sanitation. Almost every English visitor to the city, from medieval times to the nineteenth century, mentioned the infamous Edinburgh custom of emptying slops from the upstairs windows after a warning shout of 'gardyloe', supposedly from the French *gare de l'eau* or *gare l'eau* ('watch out for the water').

Defoe was more understanding. He explains why, because of its situation, Edinburgh is 'by its enemies made a subject of scorn and reproach; as if the people were not as willing to live sweet and clean as other nations, but delighted in stench and nastiness'. He argues convincingly that if English people had to live in such tall buildings, with such a scarcity of water, 'we should find a London or a Bristol as dirty as Edinburgh, and, perhaps, less able to make their dwellings tolerable, at least in so narrow a compass; for though many cities have more people in them, yet, I believe, this may be said with truth, that in no city in the world so many people live in so little room as at Edinburgh.' He also perceived that the buildings were handsome and strong, as well as tall:

all, or the greatest part of free-stone, and so firm is everything made, that though in so high a situation, and in a country where storms and violent winds are so frequent, tis very rare that any damage is done here. No blowing of tiles about the street, to knock people on the head as they pass: no stacks of chimneys and gable-ends of houses falling in to bury the inhabitants in their ruins, as we often find it in London, and other of our paper-built cities in England; but all is fixed, and strong to the top, though you have, in that part of the city called the Parliament-close, houses, which, on the south side, appear to be eleven or twelve storeys high, and inhabited to the very top.

Between 1706 and 1714 Defoe had written incessantly on the religious quarrel in Scotland. Here, in the *Tour*, he scarcely gives it a mention, except to say that in Scotland the Episcopalians are the Dissenters, 'as the Presbyterians are dissenters in England'. He notes that the ten Presbyterian churches in Edinburgh are full on Sunday, 'for the people of Scotland do not wander about on the sabbath-days, as in England, and even those who may have no more religion than enough, yet custom has made it almost natural to them, they all go to the kirk'.

They have also one very good custom as to their behaviour in the church, which I wish were practised here, namely, that after the sermon is over, and the blessing given, they all look round upon their friends, and especially to persons of distinction, and make their civilities and bows as we do here, for by the way the Scots do not want manners. But if any person come in when the worship is begun, he takes notice of no body, nor any body of him; whereas here we make our bows and our cringes in the middle of our very prayers.

After this foray into the Lothians and the capital city, Edinburgh, Defoe makes a different approach in Letter Twelve, 'Containing a Description of the South-Western part of Scotland, including the City of Glasgow'. Crossing the border near Carlisle, he passes through Annan to Dumfries, one of the west country ports which had prospered from Union. Dumfries had always been full of merchants – by which Defoe means 'not mercers and drapers, shopkeepers &., but merchant-adventurers' – and these were now trading with England and the American plantations. From Dumfries, Defoe makes a twelve-mile excursion to see Drumlanrig Castle, the home of James Douglas, the late Duke of Queensberry, who had been Lord Commissioner at the time of the Act of Union, and also a confidant of Defoe.

Defoe compares Drumlanrig Castle with Chatsworth in Derbyshire, as 'like a fine picture in a dirty grotto, or like an equestrian statue set up in a barn; tis environed with mountains, and those of the wildest and most hideous aspect in all the south of Scotland; as particularly that of Entekin, the frightfullest pass and the most dangerous that I met with . . .' He was the more surprised to find in this desolate place 'a palace so glorious, gardens so fine and everything so truly magnificent'. The interior was as beautiful as the outside, its gallery filled from end to end with portraits of the family of the Duke, most of them full length and wearing their robes of office. Charles I had made Lord Drumlanrig the Earl of Queensberry, and the title had passed to the late Duke, who died in 1711:

> The last mentioned Duke would require a history rather than a bare mention in a work of this kind . . . I shall sum it up all in this, that as I had the honour to be known to his Grace, so I had the opportunity to see and read by his permission, several letters written to him by the late King William, with his own hand, and several more by Queen Anne, written also by her majesty's own hand, with such expressions of their satisfaction in his fidelity and affection to their majesties' service, his ability and extraordinary judgment in the office entrusted to him; his knowledge of, and zeal for the true interest of his country, and their dependence upon his councils and conduct, that no minister of state in Europe could desire greater testimonials of his services, or a better character from his sovereign, and this from differing princes and at the distance of several years from one another, and to be sure without any manner of corresponding one with another.
>
> That this noble person was Lord Commissioner at the time of the Union, sat in the throne at the last Parliament of Scotland, and touched with the sceptre the Act of Parliament, which put an end to parliaments for ever in that part of Great Britain, will always be a matter of history to the end of time; whether the Scots will remember it to the advantage of the Duke's character, in their opinion, that must be as their several opinions guide them.

This fragment of memoir in the anonymous *Tour* is all Defoe will tell us about the time when he too played a part in the great affairs of nations. The Duke of Queensberry would not have shown him the letters from William and Anne if he had not known that Defoe was an emissary of Harley, and therefore the Queen. It is characteristic of Defoe that he should write this tribute to a man who was long since dead, rather than to a living statesman who might repay him with money or patronage.

'But I dwell too long here', Defoe says of Drumlanrig, as though to shake himself out of his reveries. He tells instead of how on a nearby moor he witnessed one of the Covenanter 'field meetings', or services in the open air, at which John Hepburn, a Cameronian, preached to a congregation of 7,000, sitting in rows on a hillside:

> he held his auditory, with not above an intermission of half an hour, almost seven hours, and many of the poor people had come fifteen or sixteen miles to hear him, and all the way to go home again on foot ... if there was an equal zeal to this in our part of the world, and for that worship which we acknowledge to be true, and of a sacred institution, our churches would be more thronged, and our ale-houses and fields less thronged on the sabbath-day, than they are now.

This account of a Cameronian meeting was given to Defoe by one of his agents, and passed on to Harley on 26 December 1706. In the angry mood of Scotland just before the Act of Union, it would not have been safe for an Englishman to visit Dumfriesshire, a hot-bed of Covenanter fanatics.

Defoe gives a hair-raising account of 'the famous pass at Enterkin, or Introkin Hill', the most dangerous he has experienced:

> ... being come about half way, you have a steep, unpassable height on the left, and a monstrous calm or ditch on your right; deep almost as the monument is high [meaning presumably the London Monument to the Great Fire]; and the path or way, just broad enough for you to lead your horse on it, and if his foot slips, you have nothing to do but let go the bridle, lest he pulls you with him, and then you will have the satisfaction of seeing him dashed to pieces, and lie at the bottom with four shoes uppermost.

On the first two occasions that he made this trip, the weather was good and the road dry and safe, but even then 'one of our company was so frightened with it, that in a kind of ecstasy, when he got to the bottom, he looked back and swore heartily that he would never come that way again'. On a third occasion Defoe traversed the pass soon after a spell of ice and snow: 'I looked down the frightful precipice, and saw no less than five horses in several places, lying at the bottom with their skins off, which had, by the slipperiness of the snow, lost their feet, and fallen irrecoverably to the bottom; where the mountaineers who make light of the place, had found means to come at them, and get their hides off.'

Defoe moves west to Kirkcudbright, or 'Kirkcubry', as it was pronounced then, as now, a place that surprises the stranger, 'especially one whose business is observation, as mine was'. He does indeed react surprisingly to a town which was famous even in Scotland for Puritan zeal and strict sabbath observance, but not, apparently, for its industry and enterprise:

Here is a pleasant situation, and yet nothing pleasant to be seen. Here is a harbour without ships, a port without trade, a fishery without nets, a people without business; and, that which is worse than all, they do not seem to desire business, much less do they understand it. I believe they are all very good Christians at Kirkubry, for they are in the very letter of it, they obey the text, and are contented with such things as they have. They have all the materials for trade, but no genius to it; all the opportunities for trade, but no inclination to it. In a word they have no notion of being rich and populous, and thriving by commerce. They have a fine river, navigable for the greatest ships to the town quay; a haven, deep as a well, safe as a mill-pond ... But alas! there is not a vessel that deserves the name of a ship, belongs to it; and, though here is an extraordinary salmon fishing, the salmon come and offer themselves, and go again, and cannot obtain the privilege of being made useful to mankind for they take very few of them. They have also white fish, but cure none; and herrings, but pickle none. In a word, it is to me the wonder of all the towns of North-Britain; especially, being so near England, that it has all the invitations to trade that Nature can give them, but they take no notice of it. A man might say of them, that they have the Indies at their door, and will not dip into the wealth of them; a gold mine at their door, and will not dig it.

Defoe then tackles the question of whether the people of Kirkcudbright are poor because they are slothful, or slothful because they are poor, and therefore lacking the money to build ships, hire seamen and buy nets. If only they had the investment, he believes, they would soon get a taste for the sweets of labour; 'when they found the money coming, they would soon work'. He blames the local gentry for turning their backs on commerce: 'They had rather see their sons made foot soldiers (than which, as officers treat them now, there is not a more abject thing on earth), than see them apply to trade, nay, to merchandise, or to the sea, because these things are not (forsooth) fit for gentlemen.' As a result, the common people of Kirkcudbright are not only poor but look poor: 'they appear dejected and discouraged, as if they had given over all hope of ever being otherwise than what they are'.

This description of Kirkcudbright is startling, for two quite different reasons: modern Kirkcudbright is renowned for its enterprise and industry, notably in the catching of scallops for sale all over Europe. Moreover, the tone of Defoe's remarks on Kirkcudbright in 1726 is uncannily like that of the English talking about the Roman Catholic Irish over the next two centuries. It was constantly held against the west coast Irish that, even during the Famine, they would not learn how to fish. The English loved to contrast these Catholic Irishmen with the Presbyterian Scots of Antrim and Down, who made the most of their land and the seas around it. Later the sociologists told us that this was the Protestant Work Ethic. Why was the work ethic absent from what was famed as the most Protestant town in Scotland, where during the reign of Charles II two young women were staked to the seashore and drowned at high tide rather than disavow their solemn Covenant? Even Defoe was impressed by the godliness of the inhabitants:

> They are, indeed, a sober, grave, religious people, and that more, ordinarily speaking, than in any other part of Scotland; far from what it is in England; I assure you, they have no assemblies here, or balls; and far from what it is in England, you hear no oaths, or profane words in the streets; and if a mean boy, such as we call shoe-blackers, or black-guard boys, should be heard to swear, the next gentleman in the street, if

any happened to be near him, would cane him, and correct him; whereas, in England, nothing is more frequent, or less regarded now, than the most horrid oaths and blasphemies in the open streets, and that by the little children that hardly know what an oath means.

From Kirkcudbright, Defoe goes west to Wigtown and Port Patrick, from where the ferry crosses to Belfast and other Irish ports. The boats are uncomfortable, he tells us, but none has been lost in living memory, 'except one full of cattle, which heeling to one side more than ordinary, also the cattle run to that side, and as it were, slid out into the sea; but the loading being out, the boat came to rights again, and was brought safe into the port, and none but the four-footed passengers were drowned'. By this time Defoe says he is sick of Galloway, where travel is very rough, and glad to move on to Ayr, 'a decaying town but one that, like an old beauty, shows the ruins of a good face'. He reaches the Clyde, and proposes making a ship canal to join it with the Tweed, and thus connect the North and Irish seas, like France's recently built Canal du Midi in the Languedoc, connecting the Mediterranean with the Atlantic.

Defoe then crosses the Clyde to Glasgow, which he calls 'the cleanest and most beautiful and best built city in Britain, London excepted', forgetting that he had said much the same about Liverpool. The old cathedral has a handsome spire, 'the highest that I saw in Scotland, and indeed the only one that is to be called high'. He omits to explain that Glasgow Cathedral was one of the few old churches to have escaped the destruction wrought by Knox's Calvinist brutes in the sixteenth century. However, he does acknowledge the darker side of the Calvinists, for he says, 'there are very few of the episcopal dissenters here; and the mob fell upon one of their meetings so often, that they were obliged to lay it down, or, if they do meet, tis very privately'.

The same Glasgow rabble had tried to prevent the Act of Union, 'yet now they know better, for they have the greatest addition to their trade by it imaginable; and I am assured that they send near fifty sail of ships every year to Virginia, New England, and other English colonies in America, and are every year increasing'. Its trade with America and the Mediterranean has given a boost to Glasgow's industry, such as cloth, linen, distilling of spirits and cured herrings which last now rival the Dutch. Defoe mentions the great number of Scots who go as indentured labour or 'servants' to the American plantations, and on much better terms than the English,

> without the scandalous art of kidnapping, making drunk, wheedling, betraying, and the like; the poor people offering themselves fast enough, and thinking it their advantage to go, as indeed it is to those who go with sober resolutions, namely to serve out their time, and then become diligent planters for themselves; and this would be a much wiser course in England than to turn thieves, and worse, and then be sent over by force, and on a pretext of mercy to save them from the gallows.

Here Defoe is referring to the kidnapping of 'servants', which happened to Colonel Jack, or the transportation from Newgate of the likes of Moll Flanders, her mother and highwayman husband. Defoe argues that these volunteer Scots will prove better Americans than the criminal English: 'This may be given as a reason, and, I believe, is the only reason, why so many of the Scots servants, which go over to Virginia, settle and thrive there, than of the English, which is so certainly true, that if it goes on for many years more, Virginia may be rather called a Scots than an English plantation.'

At Linlithgow Defoe honours the memory of James Stewart, the Earl of Moray and Regent of Scotland, who was murdered by Papists in 1570: 'But they got little by his death, for the reformers were in with the same zeal and never left, till they had entirely driven Mary [Queen of Scots], and all her Papist adherents out of the kingdom ...' With the same Calvinist relish, Defoe rejoices over the ruin of Melrose Abbey:

> There are several fragments of the house itself, and of the particular offices belonging to it; the court, the cloister and other buildings are so visible that tis easy to know it was a most magnificent place in those days. But the Reformation has triumphed over all these things, and the pomp and glory of Popery is sunk, now into the primitive simplicity of the true Christian profession, nor can any Protestant mourn the loss of these seminaries of superstition upon any principles that agree either with his own profession, or with the Christian pattern prescribed in the scriptures. So I leave Mailross with a singular satisfaction, at seeing what it now is, much more than that of remembering what it once was.

Defoe travels to Kelso and from there makes an excursion back into England to climb the Cheviot Hills with a party of tourists. When he tells us that the highest of these, the Master Hill, 'at a distance looks like the Pico-Tenerife at the Canaries', we now we are in for one of his adventure yarns, and sure enough, his party are soon beset by terror of reaching the summit, 'and with these apprehensions we all sat down upon the ground, and said we would go no further'. The guide re-assures this timid band that they need not fear being blown off the edge of a precipice, and after another half hour they come to the peak where Defoe makes fun of his own trepidation:

> Nor were we so afraid now as when we first mounted the sides of the hill, and especially we were made ashamed of those fears, when to our amazement, we saw a clergyman, and another gentleman, and two ladies, all on horseback, come up to the top of the hill, with a guide also as we had, and without alighting at all, and only to satisfy their curiosity, which they did it seems. This indeed made us look upon one another with a smile, to think how we were frighted, at our first coming up the hill. And thus it is in most things in nature; fear magnifies the object, and represents things frightful at first sight, which are presently made easy when they grow familiar.

In the thirteenth and final letter of the *Tour*, 'Containing a description of the North of Scotland', Defoe starts on the Fife or northern coast of the Firth of Forth. It is here that he sees men practise 'an odd kind of trade, or sport rather (viz.) of shooting of porpoises, of which very great numbers are seen almost continually in the firth'. The men boil off the fat for train, or whale-oil; and sometimes they capture grampuses, or the whales themselves. Defoe claims to have seen eight or nine of these 'fish' at the eastern Weems (East Wemyss), some of them twenty feet or more in length.

Porpoise-hunting cannot prevent the decay which Defoe observes on the northern side of the Firth of Forth and in Fife generally. The linen trade is stagnant, while 'the people who work in the coal mines ... what with their poverty and hard labour, and what with the colour or discolouring which comes from the coal, both to their clothes and complexions, are indeed frightful fellows at first sight.' Defoe blames the decay of Fife on the removal of the Court and nobility of Scotland to England. Before the Union, he says, the lords lived at home, spending the income from their estates among their neighbours. The export of coal, salt, corn, fish, cattle and linen brought goods and money from abroad, while the local manufacturers, though not so good and cheap as those from England, helped to employ the poor. Now, he complains, the Scottish noblemen gain and spend their money in England, so that their own country decays. This does not mean that Defoe now regrets the Union; rather he is chiding the Scots for not using it to their advantage, instead of making the country even poorer than it was:

> I know this is abundantly answered by saying that Scotland is now established in a lasting tranquillity; the wars between the nations are at an end, the wastings and plunderings, the ravages and blood are all over; the lands in Scotland will now be improved, their estates doubled, the charges of defending her abroad and at home lies upon England; the taxes are easy and ascertained, and the West Indies trade abundantly pours in wealth upon her; and this is all true; and, in the end, I am still of opinion Scotland will be the gainer. But, I must add, that her own nobility, would they be true patriots, should then put their helping hand to the rising advantages of their own country, and spend some of the large sums they get in England, in applying to the improvement of their country, erecting manufacture, employing the poor, and propagating the trade at home, which they may see plainly has made their united neighbours of England so rich.

Defoe then comes to St Andrews, the ancient pre-Reformation ecclesiastical centre whose two most famous archbishops led the resistance to Calvinism during the sixteenth and seventeenth centuries. The first was the Roman Catholic Cardinal Archbishop David Beaton (1494–1546), who in the fashion of the time was father to three and possibly seven children by Marion Ogilvy, his mistress. Beaton was one of the regents during the early reign of Mary Queen of Scots, and in 1546 ordered the Protestant George Wishart to be burnt at the stake. 'Here it was, that old limb of St Lucifer, Cardinal Beaton, massacred and murthered that famous sufferer and martyr of the Scots Church, Mr William [*sic*] Wishart, whom he caused to be burnt in the parade of his castle, he himself sitting in his balcony to feed and glut his eyes with the sight of it.' Three months later Cardinal Beaton was murdered near St Andrews. The same fate was in store for the Protestant Archbishop James Sharp (1613–79), who at the start of the reign of Charles II first turned on the Covenanters and then conducted their persecution by the 'boot', the thumbscrew and the gallows. On 3 May 1679 twelve Covenanters came upon Sharp by chance, dragged him out of his coach and then murdered him.

The old cathedral at St Andrews was an immense structure, longer by twenty-five feet than St Paul's in London, but now largely demolished and sunk to a parish church: 'The story of St Andrew and of his bones being buried here; of the first stone of the cathedral church being laid upon one of St Andrew's legs or thigh bone, and of those bones being brought from Patras in the Morea, near the Gulf of Lepanto; these things are too ancient and sound too much of the legend for me to meddle with.'

The story of Archbishop Sharp, whose body lies in the new church at St Andrews, is also becoming something of a legend: 'There is a fine monument in marble over his grave, with his statue kneeling on the upper part, and the manner of his murther is cut in brass relief below. This murther is matter of history, but is so foolishly, or so partially, or so imperfectly related by all that have yet written of it, that posterity will lose both the fact and the cause of it in a few years more.' Defoe calls Sharp a furious and merciless persecutor, even a murderer of many innocent people, who merely attended field meetings such as the one he claims to have witnessed near Drumlanrig. The Covenanter assassins of the Archbishop were already outlaws, whom any man might kill, and who, if captured, would have been put to death:

> They always went armed, and were, at that time, looking for another man, when unexpectedly they saw the bishop coming towards them in his coach, when one of them says to the other, we have not found the person we looked for; but lo, God has delivered our enemy, and the murtherer of our brethren into our hands, against whom we cannot obtain justice by the law, which is perverted. But remember the words of the text, If ye let him go, thy life shall be required for his life.

> In a word, they immediately resolved to fall upon him, and cut him to pieces; I say they resolved, all but one (viz.) Hackston of Rathellett, who was not willing to have his hand in the blood, though he acknowledged he deserved to die. So that when they attacked the bishop, Hackston went off and stood at a distance. Nor did he hold their horses, as one has ignorantly

published; for they attacked him all mounted; nor could they well have stopped a coach and six horses, if they had been on foot. I mention this part, because, however providence ordered it, so it was, that none of the murtherers ever fell into the hands of justice, but this Hackston of Rathelett, who was most cruelly tortured, and afterwards had his hands cut off, and was then executed at Edinburgh.

The story of Sharp and the justification used by his murderers is told by Sir Walter Scott in *Old Mortality*, his rousing novel about the Covenanters.

Defoe reaches Perth, which had for a time been the stronghold of the Pretender during the 1715 rebellion, 'but I cannot say it was unhappy for the town, for the townsmen get so much money by both parties, that they are evidently enriched by it'. Defoe realizes that this bald statement needs amplification, for he adds:

It seems a little enigmatic to us in the south, that a rebellion could enrich any place; but a few words will explain it. First I must premise that the Pretender and his troops lay near, or in this place a considerable time; now the bare consumption of victuals and drink, is a very considerable advantage in Scotland, and therefore tis frequent in Scotland for towns to petition the government to have regiments of soldiers quartered upon them, which in England would look monstrous, nothing being more terrible and uneasy to our towns in England.

The *Tour* then visits the sites of two of the battles that followed the rebellion, first at Dunblane and then at Sheriffmuir, where King George's small army under the Duke of Argyll held off the Jacobites under the Earl of Mar. Defoe wonders how it was possible that 'a rabble of 5,000 Highlanders, armed in haste, appearing in rebellion, and headed by a person never in arms before, nor of the least experience, should come so near to the overthrow of an army of regular, disciplined troops, and led by experienced officers and so great a general.'

Early on in his tour of Scotland Defoe had promised not to boast of English military triumphs, yet cannot now resist a visit to Scone, which was 'famous for the old chair in which the kings of Scotland were crowned, and which Edward I, king of England, having pierced through the whole kingdom, and nothing being able to withstand him, brought away with him'. And from Scone to Dunkeld it was so little distance that Defoe went to see the place 'where the first skirmish was fought between the forces of King William, after the Revolution, and the Laird of Claverhouse, after called Viscount of Dundee, but Dundee's men though 5,000, were gallantly repulsed by a handful, even of new raised men'.

Defoe accepts the view of the antiquarian William Camden that the Firth of Tay was the utmost bounds of the Roman Empire in Britain. The general Julius Agricola went on further into the Highlands, 'yet seeing no end of the barbarous country, and no advantage by the conquest of a few Barbarian mountaineers, withdrew and fixed the Roman eagles here'. Edward I, as already mentioned, had crossed the Tay to rifle the abbey at Scone, but Defoe says that he never ventured into the mountains of Ross, Murray, Caithness and Sutherland. Oliver Cromwell had pushed to the farthest points of the island,

> and that he might rule them with a rod of iron ... he built citadels and forts in all the angles and extremities, where he found it needful to place his stationary legions, just as the Romans did ... and just now, we find King George's forces marching to the remotest corners, nay, ferrying over into the western and north-western islands; but this is not as a foreigner and a conqueror but as a sovereign, a lawful governor and father of the country, to deliver from, not entangle her in the chains of tyranny and usurpation.

Twenty years after the *Tour* was published the Highlanders rose again in the Forty-Five on behalf of the Young Pretender, or Bonny Prince Charlie, but that was the end of the wars in Scotland.

Defoe pushed on to Dundee, 'a pleasant, large populous city, and well deserves the title of Bonny Dundee, so often given it in discourse as well as in song'. On the way to Montrose he finds that he does not receive such a friendly reception among the common people of Angus and neighbouring counties as in the other parts of Scotland. The hostility to the English 'did not lie so much against us on account of the late successes at, and after the rebellion, and the forfeiture of the many noblemen's and gentlemen's estates ... though that might add to the disgust. But it was on account of the Union, which they almost universally exclaimed against, though sometimes against all manner of just reasoning.'

Defoe's observations on public opinion in Angus were at least fifteen years out of date, even supposing he had ever been there. We know from his letters to Harley that he had studied the trade of Aberdeen, and had even talked of becoming a wool merchant there, but the *Tour* shows no evidence of a first-hand acquaintance. For instance, he says that Aberdonians favour episcopacy, but this was common knowledge. Between 1706 and 1711 he constantly wrote in the *Review* of the 'rabbling' of Presbyterians in north-east Scotland by episcopal zealots like Isbel Macka of Dingwall, who called herself an ambassadress and boasted of having 'about 300 under her command, most part of them women and the rest of them in women's clothes'.

In parts of north-east Scotland, as at Bury St Edmunds and Hampton Court in England, Defoe betrays his rancour against the pre-Reformation Church:

> In this rich country is the city, or town rather, of Elgin; I say city, because in ancient times the monks claimed it for a city; and the cathedral shows, by its ruins, that it was a place of great magnificence. Nor must it be wondered at, if in so pleasant, so rich, and so agreeable a part of the country, all the rest being so different from it, the clergy should seat themselves in a proportioned number, seeing we must do them the justice to say, that if there is any place richer and more fruitful, and pleasant than another, they seldom fail to find it out.

Defoe's puritanical hatred of the medieval Church, especially its art and architecture, appears at its most unattractive in Scotland.

Oliver Cromwell, he says, made Inverness a citadel, garrisoned by a large body of veteran English troops. After the Civil War and the inter-regnum, or 'at the end of those troublesome days', many disbanded English soldiers elected to stay in this cheap and fertile region of Scotland. Defoe claims to notice two results of this English settlement:

> 1. That the English falling to husbandry, and cultivation of the earth after their own manner, were instrumental, with the help of a rich and fruitful soil, to bring all that part of the country into so good a method and management, as is observed to outdo all the rest of Scotland to this day; for as they reap early, so they sow early, and manure and help the soil by all the regular arts of husbandry, as is practised in England.
>
> 2. As Cromwell's soldiers initiated them into the arts and industry of the husbandmen, so they left them the English

accent upon their tongues, and they preserve it also to this day; for they speak perfect English, even much better than in the most southerly provinces of Scotland; nay, some will say that they speak it as well as in London; though I do not grant that neither.

According to Defoe, geographers are almost as much at a loss to describe the north of Scotland as the Romans were to conquer it, filling it with hills and mountains 'as they do in the inner parts of Africa, for want of knowing what else to place there'. His own account of the Highlands is almost as vague as Captain Singleton's of his journey through Africa. He claims to have reached John o' Groats, before turning south and west in the general direction of Skye. He recommends that would-be travellers should form a party and take tents and provisions, so as not to make themselves burdensome to the Highland chiefs, 'though there I can assure them they would always meet with good treatment and great hospitality'. At the town of Tain, almost the only one to be mentioned in this part of the *Tour*, Defoe complains: 'We could understand nothing of what the people said, any more than if we had been in Morocco, and all the remedy we had was, that we found most of the gentlemen spoke French, and some few spoke broad Scots: we found it also much for convenience to make the common people believe we were French' – just as, in *The Memoirs of a Cavalier*, the hero makes the people of Lyons believe he is Scottish.

The Highlands are not as barbarous as some writers have suggested. Defoe points out that those Mackenzies, McLeans, Dundonalds, Gordons and McKays who have appeared at Court and in the British army are as polite and finished gentlemen as those of any country, including England. These mountaineers are well provisioned with bread, venison 'which they kill with their guns where they find it', with salmon in such quantity as is scarcely credible, and with cattle and sheep, though 'the latter are so wild, that sometimes, were they not by their own disposition, used to flock together, they would be much harder to kill than the deer'.

Defoe appears to regard the Highlands and Islands as virtually pagan; he commends the Church of Scotland's Society for the Propagation of Christian Knowledge, of which he had been an active member. He says of the Highlanders that 'if at any time any glimpse of light has been infused into them, and they had been taught any knowledge of superior things, it has been by the diligence of the Popish clergy, who to do them justice, have shown more charity, and taken more pains that way, than some whose work it has been, and who it might much more have been expected from'. Like many Puritans, Defoe was ignorant about the early Church in Britain. Just as in Northumberland he did not mention Lindisfarne, so in Scotland he does not mention the equally holy island of Iona. For a worthy description of that and the other islands of the Hebrides we must wait fifty years for the two splendid companion books on their travels by James Boswell and Samuel Johnson.

In writing of Scotland, twenty years after the Act of Union, Defoe does not try to pretend that this was wholly successful. Nevertheless, in the *Tour*, he is able to stand by most of the arguments he used in his pamphlets and the *Review* of 1706–8. One can say with confidence that Defoe would not sympathise with modern Scottish demands for independence, a separate parliament, or even more devolution.

Old Age and Death in Hiding:
1725–31

WHILE WRITING THE *Tour*, Defoe suffered such pain from his bladder stones that in 1725 he decided to have an operation. In the days before anaesthetics such an ordeal would have daunted even the bravest, and helps us to understand the strength of Defoe's 'passive courage'. Squeamish readers should skip even this brief account of an operation in which the patient was strapped down on a board, tied hand and foot, held down by three attendants, as a surgeon passed a tube through the penis to the urethra, then cut him open between the anus and the scrotum to insert a catheter so that the stones could be found and removed, or crushed. Defoe later described the operation as follows: 'Here's a man . . . torn and mangled by the merciless surgeons, cut open alive, and bound hand and foot to force him to bear it; the very apparatus is enough to chill the blood and sink a man's soul within him. What does he suffer less than he that is broken alive on the Wheel?' This rhetorical question helps to explain why eighteenth-century people condoned these ghastly executions – in France the wheel, and in England hanging, drawing and quartering.

Although he survived the torture of the operation and did not contract any subsequent infection, Defoe was now a partial invalid, and still less able to deal with the troubles that afflicted him. These mostly involved the land he had bought at Colchester, and the trading and farming ventures he had set up there. In addition to his dealings in timber, corn, cattle, cloth, honey, oysters and even anchovies, Defoe had decided in 1723 to start a tile factory, similar to the one he had owned at Tilbury until he was sent to prison in 1703. He offered a partnership to John Ward, a Warwickshire mercer and linen draper, persuading him to invest in the project and move to Colchester. But Ward had neither the expertise nor the capital to stock a farm and establish a tile works, so he went back to Warwickshire in 1725. Defoe, living more than forty miles away and a semi-invalid, was so out of touch that he could not even cope with collecting the rents, let alone supervising the trading projects. When Ward and others later took him to court for the recovery of their money, Defoe could not produce any proper accounts.

Defoe's behaviour was much like that of some of the feckless characters in his novels. Like Robinson Crusoe, who was not content with the 'middle station wherein God and Nature had placed him' and left his Brazilian plantation to go on a slaving venture to Africa, Defoe was not content to live off his farm, but expanded into trading and the manufacture of tiles. Roxana says of her first husband, when he was left the brewery by his father: 'But this addition to his stock was his ruin, for he had no genius to business, he had no knowledge of accounts . . . It was below him to inspect the books, he committed all this to his clerks and book-keepers; and while he found money in cash to pay the malt-man, and the excise, and put some in his pocket, he was perfectly easy and indolent.' And Mary Defoe must often have agreed with Roxana's advice to young women: 'If you have any regard to your future happiness, any view to living comfortably with a husband; any hope of protecting your fortunes, or recovering them after any disaster; never, ladies marry a fool.'

Mary Defoe, who had seen her dowry of £3,700 disappear in the brankruptcy of 1692, was lucky enough to escape the débâcle at Colchester. In 1725 her brother Samuel Tuffley died, leaving her several properties worth at least £6,000. Defoe characteristically wrote to his partner John Ward to tell him that the death of a relative gave him 'a considerable estate', but Tuffley had been wise enough to leave his money to Mary alone. She was now financially independent and does not appear to have used her fortune to rescue Defoe from the consequence of his folly. Not all the family escaped unharmed. Defoe's daughter Hannah had bought a share of the Colchester land, and after her marriage mortgaged this property. Defoe's second son Daniel later stepped in to try to help his father out of his legal and financial mess; though he received small thanks for this.

The principal sufferer from his folly was Defoe's youngest daughter and favourite child, Sophia, who had been born in 1701. She was one of the three 'lovely daughters' whom Henry Baker had met when he visited Defoe in 1724. He soon decided to marry her, as he later wrote in his self-satisfied memoirs:

> Mr Baker very soon discovered the superior excellence of Miss Sophia, the younger daughter, of whose person and manner he speaks in strains of the highest eulogium ... her elegance of form, where all was just proportion, her graceful mien, her fine turned neck and bosom, her beauteous fair blue eyes, beaming all goodness, her auburn glossy tresses, her face where every feature spoke perfection, and over all the bloom of health that tinctured every charm.

But Mr Baker, as he calls himself, was a hard-headed as well as a warm-hearted young man, and did not intend to marry Sophia without a substantial dowry:

> He knew nothing of Mr Defoe's circumstances, only imagined from his very genteel way of living, that he must be able to give his daughter a good portion; he did not suppose a large one. On speaking to Mr Defoe he [Defoe] sanctioned the proposals, and said, he hoped he should be able to give her a certain sum; but when urged to the point some time afterwards, his answer was ... that when they talked before, he did not know the true state of his affairs, that he found he could not part with any money at present, but at his death, his daughter's portion would be more than he had promised, and he offered his bond as a guarantee for the payment.

It appears from this that, shortly after the start of Baker's courtship of Sophia in 1724, Defoe had learned the extent of his troubles at Colchester, and the likelihood of his losing the court case brought against him by his former partner, Ward. The hapless Sophia was clearly in love with Baker, but nevertheless supported her father in this wrangle. It was not until she had suffered a nervous breakdown in 1729 that the two men agreed to consider her happiness, rather than their own self-importance.

In spite of his failing health and financial worries, Defoe continued to write as well and as fast as ever. In the seven years remaining to him after the publication of *Roxana* he did not attempt another novel, unless one includes his bogus *Memoirs of an English Officer*. His abandonment of fiction after the period 1719–24 should not be seen as a sign of failing power or imagination. On the contrary, he was writing better than ever; moreover, some of the books that we call non-fiction, such as the *Tour*, are just as truly works of imagination as are some of those we call novels. The two-volume *General History of the Pirates*, for example, published in 1726, is far more exciting and readable than his pirate story *Captain Singleton*, which would not still be in print were it not a 'novel' by Defoe.

For some of his later writing Defoe adopted the pseudonym and persona of 'Andrew Moreton', a crusty old gentleman who very much disapproved of most things happening in the modern world. Although 'Andrew Moreton's' opinions are largely his own, Defoe exaggerates them to the point of absurdity, to produce a pompous old fogey of the kind that today would be caricatured as 'Disgusted of Tunbridge Wells'. Most of his writing as 'Andrew Moreton' appeared in the form of pamphlets, addressing such social problems as prostitution, shoe-shine boys and the theatre, especially the huge success in 1723 of John Gay's *The Beggar's Opera*. While 'Andrew Moreton' complains that *The Beggar's Opera* glamorizes Newgate villains such as Macheath, the highwayman, and Polly Peachum, his sweetheart, Defoe is of course aware that he had done exactly the same in *Moll Flanders*.

Some of the 'Andrew Moreton' essays are quite as amusing as Steele and Addison at their best, and show an advance in Defoe's artistry as a writer. One of the most entertaining is *Everybody's Business in Nobody's Business, or the Pride, Insolence and Exorbitant Wages of our Women Servants*:

> Let us trace this from the beginning, and suppose a person has a servant maid sent him out of the country at 50 shillings or 3 pounds a year. The girl has scarce been a week, nay a day in service, but a committee of servant wenches are appointed to examine her, who advise her to raise her wages or give warning [notice] ... Her neat's leathern shoes are now transformed into laced shoes with high heels; her yarn stockings are turned into fine worsted ones with silk clocks [ornaments], and her high wooden pattens are kicked away for leathern clogs ... If she has any share of cunning, the apprentice or her master's son is enticed away and ruined by her ... The apparel of our women servants should be next regulated, that we may know the mistress from the maid. I remember that I was once put very much out by the blush, being at a friend's home, and by him required to salute the ladies, I kissed a chamber-jade into the bargain, for she was as well dressed as the best.

In another huffing and puffing pamphlet 'Andrew Moreton' rails at his local government enemies in *Parochial Tyranny, Or the House-keeper's Complaint against the insupportable executions and partial Assessments of Select Vestries*. Through 'Andrew Moreton' Defoe is attacking those Church of England vestries, or parish councils, that enriched themselves by appointing Dissenters to office, then making them pay a fine in lieu of service, as he had himself paid £10 in Newington. He begins by saying that parish government, like most well-intentioned organizations, had been so much abused as to become a nuisance, and should therefore be reformed. He blames 'designing men who enhanced parish taxes to above treble their old standard, and yet the poor are not nearly so well provided for'. While the King cannot raise money without the Lords or Commons, or they without the royal assent, 'our parish tyrants are more arbitrary, they assess, re-assess and distress at pleasure', taking a Parson's Rate, a Church Rate and a Poor Rate, besides taxes for highways, sewers, rubbish collection and the Watch, or local police force.

> But woe to those house-keepers who disoblige the Vestry-Gentry, who are of a different party or principle [religion] who have or may refuse to vote in all elections, national or parochial, according to their direction, these shall be saddled with offices, fines and double taxes, as has been the case of but many since the last election. In most villages adjacent to London, where the gentry and tradesmen retire for health and air, they are sure to be rid to death by these parish jockeys, who know no mercy and I doubt not make a good living out of them. It is shameful to think what taxes are paid where there are but a few poor, except for church-wardens &, who grow rich at the parochial charge.

Defoe accuses the Church of England vestrymen of spending on wine the money that should be given to the few deserving poor, and notes that the Quakers are quite excluded from this parochial charity. There is evidence that Defoe himself was good to the Quakers in Newington, for one of them, Thomas Webb, gave this written testimony, discovered by the historian A. J. Shirren: '. . . And poor distressed I, left alone, and no one to go and speak to, save only Mr Deffoe, who hath acted a noble and generous part towards me and my poor children.'

The reading public bought and therefore clearly enjoyed these essays by 'Andrew Moreton', so that Defoe put the name to one of his full-length books, published in 1729 – *The Universal History of Apparitions. Whether Angelical, Diabolical or Human-Soul Departed*. Even when he was writing about the supernatural, under the pseudonym of his alter ego, Defoe could not resist airing his old obsessions:

> We have heard tales imposed upon the world about apparitions showing themselves to an abundance of people before, at, and after the late massacre in Ireland, Anno 1641 . . . Nor could they be so much blamed as in other cases, for here were people escaped from the murderers, even out of their very hands, some that had seen their wives, children, fathers, husbands, neighbours butchered before their face . . . No wonder if they saw clouds of Irish armies in the air, heard shouts of dying, murthered women and children . . . In Ireland the priests and zealots, nay, the very women, boasted of the number they had killed; showed the daggers with which they cut the throats of the Protestants.

The Catholic Irish again appear in a bad light in Defoe's *Political History of the Devil*, one of the most light-hearted and entertaining of all his books. It also contains a penetrating critical study of *Paradise Lost*, one of the first to suggest that Milton was exalting the Devil and turning him into the hero of the poem. Defoe begins by pointing out that Milton had failed to resolve the main difficulty: '(viz.) How the Devil came to fall, and how sin came into Heaven.' He quotes the lines:

> His Pride
> Had cast him out of heaven and all his host
> Of rebel angels, by whose aid aspiring
> He trusted to have equalled the most High.

'His Pride!' Defoe exclaims, 'but how came Satan while an Arch-angel to be proud? How did it consist that Pride and perfect Holiness should meet in the same person? Here we must bid Mr Milton good night; for in plain terms he is in the dark about it, and so we are all.'

In spite of his bantering tone, Defoe is raising a serious question, and even suggests that Milton is close to the Arian heresy.* Others may think that Milton was more of a Manichaean, the heresy that

---

* That Jesus was of similar, but not of the same, substance as the Father, nor co-eternal with him.

attributes equal power to good and evil, to God and Satan. There are some who hold that Protestantism, especially the Calvinist brand of Milton and Defoe, is inspired by these ancient heresies and must eventually lead to the abandonment of religion. If Defoe was troubled by religious doubts, he disguises them in the jokey style he adopts throughout *The Political History of the Devil* – for example, in the heading to Chapter Six: 'What became of the Devil and his host of fallen Spirits after their being expelled from Heaven, and his wandering condition till the Creation; with some more of Mr Milton's absurdities on that subject.' According to Defoe, Milton's account of the Fall is based neither on scripture nor on philosophy: 'But let that lie as Mr Milton's extraordinary genius pleases to place it; his passage it seems is just nine days between Heaven and Hell', a distance not as great 'as according to Sir Isaac Newton and the rest of our men of science, we take it to be'. He ends the chapter by saying that 'Mr Milton is a good poet but a bad historian.'

After dealing with Satan in *Paradise Lost*, Defoe explains that the Devil 'has very much changed hands in his modern management of the world . . . and now walks about in beaus, wits and fools, yet I must not omit to tell you that he has not dismissed his former regiments, but like officers in time of peace, he keeps them all on half-pay'. He then goes on to describe how the Devil tempted a man who, we can almost certainly say, was Defoe himself:

> I know a person who the Devil so haunted with naked women, fine beautiful ladies in bed with him, and ladies of his acquaintance too, offering their favours to him, and all in his sleep; so that he seldom slept without some such entertainment; the particulars are too gross for my story, but he gave me several long accounts of his Night's amours, and being a man of virtuous life and good morals it was the greatest surprise imaginable; for you cannot doubt but that the cunning Devil made everything he acted to the life with him, and in a manner most wicked; he owned with grief to me, that the very first attempt the Devil made upon him, was with a very beautiful lady of his acquaintance, who he had been really something freer than ordinary with in their common conversation. This lady he brought to him in a Posture for Wickedness, and wrought up his inclination so high in his sleep that he, as he thought, actually was about to debauch her, she not at all resisting; but

that he waked in the very moment, to his particular satisfaction.

From this, as from *Conjugal Lewdness* and passages of *Moll Flanders* and *Roxana*, one gets the impression that during the 1720s naked ladies figured large in Defoe's waking and sleeping thoughts, which throws into doubt the happiness of his married life, or at least the physical side of it. One might even suppose that sex as well as money contributed to the troubles of his final years. However, the passage just quoted also suggests that Defoe sincerely wanted to fight the temptation, whether or not he believed it was sent by the Devil. Moreover, these pangs of lust were probably mild compared to the torments he suffered over his bankruptcy. These are described in another late book, *The Complete English Tradesman*.

It has been remarked that Defoe's most imaginative and brilliant writing is often reserved for what might appear the most mundane subjects, such as road-making, lead mines and 'Publick Credit'. And just as he used *The Political History of the Devil* to tell us about his erotic dreams, so he used *The Complete English Tradesman* to tell us about his financial troubles. It was published in 1726, when his Colchester projects were already in disarray. There can be few examples in literature of an author less able to practise what he preached than Defoe in *The Complete English Tradesman*. On every brilliant and lucid page he enjoins the would-be trader to stick to the rules that he himself was unable to keep and to avoid the pitfalls into which he stumbled. He warns against shopkeepers getting involved in shipping and merchant venture, against bubbles and projects, and failing to keep the books. Almost the only advice that he himself took was on writing a simple business letter: 'He that affects a rumbling and bombastic style, and fills his letters with compliments and flourishes, should turn poet instead of tradesman, and set up for a wit, not a shopkeeper.'

The chapter on 'Tradesmen in Distress' begins with a description that must have been taken from his own experience, though we do not know if he ever took refuge in one of the debtor's havens, such as the Mint or the Fryars:

> In former times it was a dismal and calamitous thing for a tradesman to break: when it befell a family, it put all into confusion and disturbance; the man in the utmost terror, fright and distress, ran away with what goods he could get off, as if the house was on fire, to get into the Fryars or the Mint; the family fled one way, and one another, like people in desper-

ation; the wife to her father and mother if she had any, and the children some to one relation, some to another; a statute (so they vulgarly called a commission of bankruptcy) came out and swept away all and oftentimes consumed it too, and left little or nothing, either to pay the creditors or relieve the bankrupt. This made the bankrupt desperate, and made him fly to those places of shelter with his goods, where, hardened by the cruelty of his creditors, he chose to spend all the effects which should have been paid the creditors and at last perished in misery.

In recent times, Defoe continues, the treatment of bankrupts has changed for the better, and often the family stays in the house. The law obliges a man to give a full account of himself, on oath, to the Commissioners of the bankruptcy court, who, if they accept his integrity, 'may effectively deliver him from all further molestation, give him a part even of the creditor's estate, and so he may into the world again, and try whether he may not retrieve his fortunes . . .' He goes on:

> Some have said this law is too favourable to the bankrupt, that it makes tradesmen careless, that they value not breaking at all . . . yet the terror of ruining a man's family, sinking his fortunes, blasting his credit, and throwing him out of business, and into the worst of disgrace that a tradesman can fall into, this is not taken away or abated at all; and this, to an honest trading man, is as bad as all the rest ever was or could be . . . Breaking is the death of a tradesman; he is mortally stabbed, or, as we may say, shot through the head in his trading capacity; his shop is shut up as it is when a man is buried; his credit, the life and blood of his trade, is stagnated, and his attendance, which was the pulse of his business, is stopped, and beats no more . . .
>
> But the difficulty which I am proposing to speak of, is when the poor tradesman distressed . . . in point of credit, finds the melancholy truth there too plain to be concealed, finds that his stock is diminished, or perhaps entirely sunk . . . What course shall be taken?

Defoe then advises his readers to do exactly what he himself should have done with regard to his Colchester projects:

When he perceives his case as above, and knows that if his new adventures or projects should fail, he cannot by any means stand or support himself, I not only give it as my advice to all tradesmen, as their interest, but insist upon it, as they are honest men, they shall break, that is, stop in time: Fear not to do that which necessity obliges you to do; but above all, fear not to do that early, which if omitted, necessity will oblige you to do later . . .

By breaking *in time*, you will first obtain the character of an honest, tho unfortunate man; tis owing to the contrary course, which indeed is the ordinary practice of tradesmen, namely, not to break till they run the bottom quite out and have little or nothing to pay; I say tis owing to this, that some people think all men that break are knaves . . . I say *break in time*, you will certainly be received by your creditors with compassion, and with a generous treatment, and whatever happens, you will be able to begin the world again with the title of an honest man; even the same creditors will embark with you again, and be more forward to give you credit than before . . .

Although Defoe was perhaps a little sanguine about the forgiving nature of creditors, he knew from experience how little mercy one could expect from trying to stay on in business:

What shall we say to the peace and satisfaction of mind in breaking, which the tradesman will always have when he acts the honest part, breaks betimes, compared to that guilt and chagrin of the mind, occasioned by a running on, as I said, to the last gasp, when they have little to pay: Indeed, as the Tradesman can expect no quarter from his creditors, so he will have no quiet in himself.

I might instance here the miserable, anxious, perplexed life which the poor tradesman lives under before he breaks; the distress and extremities of his declining state; how harassed and tormented for money; what shifts he is driven to for supporting himself; how many little mean, and even wicked things will even the most religious tradesman stoop to in his distress, to deliver himself; even such things as his very soul would abhor at any other time, and for which he goes, perhaps, with a wounded conscience all his life after?

Even as he was writing these words, Defoe's financial affairs were heading for disaster – not as total as that of 1692 but just as disturbing, for he was now in poor health and fearful of ending his life in prison. He was already engaged in a number of legal actions with Ward and his other creditors over his Essex property, now heavily mortgaged and no longer profitable. Then, in 1728, he was once more pursued by creditors from the bankruptcy thirty-six years earlier. Two elderly ladies, the widows of former business associates, went to court to demand the money they said Defoe had never paid. They were able to show a promissory note for £800, which Defoe had signed in September 1691. One of these women, Mary Brooke, pursued Defoe for this money until the end of his life and for two years afterwards, hoping to claim his library or any other possessions.

At the beginning of 1729 Defoe's would-be son-in-law Henry Baker seems to have realized that he could not expect a handsome dowry, and agreed to the sum of £500 from Defoe's will, guaranteed by the lease on the Stoke Newington house. Baker and Sophia were married on 30 April 1729, and from their own account lived happily for the next thirty-odd years. Defoe disappeared from Stoke Newington, finding a refuge first near Greenwich and finally in lodgings in the City. He was now on the run, not only from his implacable creditor but from his legal actions, and even the vestrymen of Newington, for he had defaulted on the rates. He was able to pay his expenses from the pamphlets he continued to write up until his death.

It is from this very late stage of Defoe's life that we have his only surviving family letters, the first to his daughter Sophia, the second and last to her husband Baker, now living at Enfield. This betrays symptoms of persecution mania over the behaviour of Daniel, his younger son, who certainly did not leave his mother and sister to starve, since Mary Defoe was now a rich woman. Nor is it clear why Defoe believed that his family could not visit him. But he was probably right to think that Mary Brooke, his principal creditor, wanted to have him arrested and put in jail or a sponging-house. We do not know whether the gloomy tone of these letters reflected Defoe's constant mood during these last years in hiding, or whether, like Mr Micawber, he sometimes recovered his cheerfulness and drank a few glasses of punch. The first of these letters was written on 7 June 1729, to 'Mrs Sophia Defoe Baker', apparently after she had said or written something to hurt him:

If I have been more sensibly grieved at what I thought unkind in my Sophia (say it was only that I thought so), if I took fire more than another would have done, it was because I loved you more than ever any loved or will or can love you (he that has you excepted). Had Deb [perhaps a nickname for one of the other daughters] the hasty, the rash, and so far weak, said ten times as much to me, it had made no impression at all: but from Sophia, thee Sophia! whose image sits close to my affections, and who I love beyond the power of expressing: I acknowledge it wounded my very soul; and my weakness is so much the more, as that affection is strong ... Perhaps I do not write like a father. But perhaps I do too, if it be considered that love is the same, let the relation be what it will; besides, a father, I hope, may be allowed not to love in a less exalted and sublime manner, but a greater; and from thence I still infer, as my affection made my grief the greater, so the same affection doubled the satisfaction I have at my dear Sophia's return; I received your letter my Dear, with a joy not to be described, but in the deepest silence, or expressed but by tears.

Defoe's last extant letter, to Henry Baker, is written from an address 'about two miles from Greenwich, Kent', and is dated Tuesday 12 August 1730:

Dear Mr Baker, I have your kind and affectionate letter of the 1st. But not come to my hand till the 10th; when it had been delayed I know not. As your kind manner and kinder thought, from which it flows ... was a particular satisfaction to me; so the stop of a letter, however it happened, deprived me of that cordial too many days, considering how much I stood in need of it, to support a mind sinking under the weight of affliction too heavy for my strength, and looking on myself as abandoned of every comfort, every friend and every relative, except such only as are able to give me no assistance ...

I was sorry you should say at the beginning of your letter you were debarred seeing me. Depend upon my sincerity for this, I am far from debarring you. On the contrary it would be a greater comfort to me than I can now enjoy, that I could have your enjoyable visits with safety, and could see both you and my dear Sophia, could it be without the grief of seeing her father *in tenebris* [shadows] and under the load of insupportable sorrows. I am sorry I must open my grief so far as to tell her, it is not the blow I received from a wicked, perjured and contemptible enemy, that has broken in upon my spirit; which as she well knows, has carried me on through greater disasters than these. But it has been the injustice, unkindness and I may say, inhuman dealing of my own son, which has both ruined my family, and in a word has broken my heart; and as I am at this time under a weight of very heavy illness, which I think will be a fever, I take this occasion to vent my grief in the breasts who I know will make a prudent use of it, and tell you that nothing but this has conquered or could conquer me. Et tu! Brute. I depended upon him, I trusted him, I gave up my two dear unprotected children into his hands; but he has no compassion, but suffers them and their poor dying mother to beg their bread at his door, and to crave as it were an alms, what he is bound under hand and seal, besides the most sacred promises, to supply them with; himself at the same time, living in a profusion of plenty. It is too much for me. Excuse my infirmity, I can say no more; my heart is too full. I only ask one thing of you as a dying request. Stand by them when I am gone, and let them not be wronged, while he is able to do them right: Stand by them as a brother; and if you have any-thing in you owing to my memory, who have bestowed on you the best gift I have to give, let them not be injured and trampled on by false pretence and unnatural reflections . . .

It adds to my grief that it is so difficult to me to see you. I am at a distance from London in Kent; nor have I a lodging in London . . .

I have not seen my son or daughter, wife or child many weeks, and know not which way to see them. They dare not come by water, and by land there is no coach, and I know not what to do. It is not possible to come to Enfield, unless you could find a retired lodging for me where I might not be known, and might have the comfort of seeing you both now and then . . .

I would say (I hope) with comfort, that tis yet well. I am so near my journey's end, and am hastening to the place where the weary are at rest, and where the wicked cease to trouble; be it that the passage is rough, and the day stormy, by what way soever He pleases to bring me to the end of it, I desire to finish life with this temper of soul in all cases: Te Deum Laudamus . . .

It adds to my grief that I must never see the pledge of your mutual love, my little grandson. Give him my blessing, and may he be to you both your joy in youth and your comfort in age, and never add a sigh to your sorrow. But, alas! that is not to be expected. Kiss my dear Sophy once more for me; and if I must not see her no more, tell her this is from a Father that has loved her above all his comforts, to his last breath.

Your unhappy,
D.F.

In spite of his sorrows, Defoe continued to write and, as late as December 1730, published *An Effective Scheme for the Immediate Preventing of Street Robbers*. He was writing *Of Royal Education* when he died on 24 April 1731 at lodgings in Rope Maker's Alley, near where he had lived as a child. His death was registered in the same church, St Giles in Cripplegate, where the Foes had worshipped before the expulsion of Annesley in 1662. The cause of death was given as a lethargy, a variety of apoplexy, or what we would now call a stroke. One newspaper obituary wrote of 'the famous Mr Daniel Defoe', and another called him a 'Person well known for his numerous and various publications'; and perhaps this was how he had come to think of himself, though he was never self-conscious about his writing. What afforded him most satisfaction was his lifelong battle for his beliefs, so that the words he wrote on his murdered rival John Tutchin in 1707 were probably meant for himself:

That he was a man of misfortune, that he had run through infinite difficulties; this may call him unhappy, but not dishonest . . . a man may be an honest man, and not be able to do every honest thing he would do . . . he may be an honest man that cannot pay his debts but he cannot be honest that can and will not . . . If you will say he was an enemy to persecution, to Jacobites and Highflyers . . . he was indeed an enemy to all these, and GOD made him a wall of brass against them; he was neither to be silenced by the noise; nor terrified by their figure; he stood out the battle to the last gasp . . . Had he been unpersecuted by insulting enemies and unmerciful creditors, that his temper had not been ruffled and irritated beyond his own government, he had appeared in a more agreeable shape, and abstracted from them, was really a very valuable person.

Defoe was buried in Bunhill Fields, in Finsbury, the cemetery for Dissenters, which also houses the remains of John Bunyan, Isaac Watts and William Blake. In the following year, 1732, Defoe was joined in his grave by his long-suffering wife Mary. It was not until 1870 that the present obelisk was erected from contributions by the boy and girl readers of the weekly *Christian World*. The original tombstone was taken to Southampton, where it remained until after the Second World War. It now stands with a bust of Defoe in Stoke Newington Church Street Public Library, which had been founded by philanthropists at the end of the nineteenth century. Defoe, who was an early advocate of public libraries, would have liked the institution across the road from his home, especially the reference section, which contained several books on Defoe himself. In 1960 Stoke Newington Public Libraries Committee published *Defoe in Stoke Newington* by A. J. Shirren, one of its members.

In subsequent local government reorganizations, Stoke Newington Borough Council was absorbed by the London Borough of Hackney, which closed down the Church Street Reference Library, and sold or 'dispersed' most of the books from the lending department.* But the tombstone and bust remain there.

The story of the tombstone roughly suggests how Defoe's reputation has fared since his death. For the first fifty years, until about 1780, he was remembered as a political pamphleteer, for the *Tour* and certain moral tracts – but, above all, for *Robinson Crusoe*. The first two decades after his death saw the emergence of three pioneers of the novel: Samuel Richardson (1689–1761), Henry Fielding (1704–54) and Tobias Smollett (1721–71). Richardson was, like Defoe, the father of three daughters, and wrote his most famous novels, *Pamela* and *Clarissa*, 'to cultivate the principles of virtue and religion', as Defoe had set out to do with his *Family Instructor* and *Religious Courtship*. Henry Fielding was at one time Justice of the Peace for Westminster, and he shared Defoe's interest in the criminal world. Twenty years after Defoe, Fielding also wrote a life of the thief-taker turned criminal, Jonathan Wild, who went to the scaffold in 1725.

---

* For a fuller account of what happened at Stoke Newington and dozens of other libraries, see W. J. West's *The Strange Rise of Semi-Literate England. The Dissolution of the Libraries*. Duckworth 1991.

The Scottish novelist Smollett followed Defoe's example in writing tales of the low life; and *Humphry Clinker* takes the form of a tour of England and Scotland not dissimilar to Defoe's. Like Defoe's *The Memoirs of a Cavalier*, Smollett begins *Roderick Random* with an account of his mother's dreams in pregnancy. If Smollett was indebted to Defoe, he certainly does not admit the fact. Indeed, in his hugely successful history of England, published in 1757–8, he calls Defoe 'a scurrilous party-writer in very little estimation'. Later in the history he makes partial amends by admitting Defoe to the ranks of 'the most remarkable political writers of his age', along with Swift, Steele, Addison and Bolingbroke. By contrast, Oliver Goldsmith, whose *History of England* fails to mention Defoe among the century's leading authors, brings into his novel *The Vicar of Wakefield* reference both to *Religious Courtship* and *Robinson Crusoe*.

Defoe's most famous book continued to go from strength to strength. The prophet of the French Revolution, Jean-Jacques Rousseau, prescribed *Robinson Crusoe* for natural education, just as later Karl Marx, the prophet of the Russian Revolution, used the book to explain his theories of labour value. It was Samuel Johnson, the first critic fully to comprehend the genius of Shakespeare, who paid Defoe the most graceful of compliments: 'Was there ever yet anything written by mere man that was wished longer by its readers, excepting *Don Quixote*, *Robinson Crusoe* and *The Pilgrim's Progress*?' As Johnson's remark makes clear, *Robinson Crusoe* was not regarded during the eighteenth century as a children's book, but stood as a work of moral value comparable with the Bible. Its later reputation developed as generations of children found that the book they were given to improve their minds was also thrilling.

The reputation of *Robinson Crusoe* encouraged some late eighteenth-century scholars to re-examine some of the other books believed to be by Defoe. A writer in the *Monthly Review* of March 1775 explained:

> Few novels are better known than the story of the Lewd Roxana, which now is ascribed to the famous De Foe. It is not improbable that this is one of Daniel's productions; for he wrote books of all kinds, romantic as well as religious; moral as well as immoral. History, politics, poetry; in short all subjects were alike to Daniel – The versatility of the man's genius procured him the admiration of the age in which he lived . . .

The *Gentleman's Magazine* of May 1783 ran a review of the eighth
edition of the *Tour*, 'originally written by, I think Daniel Defoe',
but now so emended as to appear 'the strangest jumble and hodge-
podge that ever was put together'. A correspondence ensued, in
which one reader enquired: 'Who was the author of that singular
book *The Memoirs of a Cavalier*, I almost despair of learning. I think
Robinson Crusoe is allowed to be the work of Defoe, but I know no
particulars of Defoe's life or what other books he wrote.' Another
reader correctly credited Defoe with *A Journal of the Plague Year* and
Colonel Jack.

An antiquarian, George Chalmers, did some research into Defoe's
bibliography, and his findings appeared in a *Life* appended to new
editions of *The History of the Union* (1786) and *Robinson Crusoe* (1790).
According to Pat Rogers, Chalmers's 'checklist of about eighty
"canonical" works and twenty supposititious items was an essential base
for nineteenth century reappraisals of Defoe'. Chalmers calls Defoe a
novelist of 'the foremost rank', an historian with few equals, and also
praises his writing on politics: 'Defoe, it must be allowed was a party
writer. But were not Swift and Prior, Steel and Addison . . . and Bolingbroke, party writers? De Foe being a party writer upon settled principles did not change with the change of parties: Addison and Steel,
Prior and Swift, connected as they were with persons, changed their
note as persons were elevated or deposed.' A reviewer of Chalmers's
Life expanded upon the theme of Defoe's integrity:

> De Foe with great abilities, extensive knowledge and a ready
> pen, living in troubled times, became a busy controversial
> writer: he steadily supported the Whig interest, but could
> not (and what considerate honest man can?) go all lengths
> with his party: therefore while he provoked the hatred of the
> Tories, he could not gain the entire love of the Whigs; and
> between both, his character has been transmitted to us under
> various misrepresentations [John Noorthouck, *Monthly
> Review*, December 1790].

Defoe's work was widely praised by writers of the Romantic Revival,
notably Coleridge, Wordsworth, Hazlitt and Lamb, but most percep-
tively by Sir Walter Scott, who especially enjoyed the historical books.
According to Scott, even if Defoe had never written *Robinson Crusoe*,
he 'deserved immortality for *A Journal of the Plague Year*', and *The
Memoirs of a Cavalier* 'reflect additional lustre even on the author of

Robinson Crusoe. As an Episcopalian Tory, Scott dismisses as 'incorrect' Defoe's *History of the Church of Scotland*, and he calls *The History of the Union* 'little more than a dry journal of what passed in the Scottish Parliament upon that remarkable occasion'. However, he acknowledges: 'Defoe must have had an interesting tale to tell, if he had chosen it. But writing under Harley's patronage, he cramped his genius, probably to avoid giving offence to the irritable Scottish nation.' Scott may have felt sympathetic to Defoe, since he too was writing to pay off the debts from a bankruptcy.

During the Nonconformist Revival in the mid nineteenth century Defoe, like Bunyan, came to be seen as one of the martyrs of the faith. His first full-length biographer, George Lee, a superintendent inspector in the Board of Health, presented him as a social reformer as well as the champion of the Dissenters. One of the illustrations in Lee's book depicts Defoe in the pillory, receiving the cheers and bouquets of a sympathetic crowd. Like many Victorians, Lee was perturbed by the bawdy scenes in some of the novels, but managed to convince himself that these had been written for worthy reasons. For instance, he writes of *Roxana*:

> There are many incidents in the story, very distasteful to a pure and virtuous mind . . . yet no reader can possibly mistake the lessons designed to be taught, namely that prosperous wickedness has a worm at the root . . . and the moral and religious reflections that run through the work, could not fail to benefit readers who having fallen themselves, were incapable of being injured by the relation of Roxana's crimes. This, it should be remembered, was the class for whom Defoe wrote the book . . . He did not tell the story for the sake of amusement; but that he might infuse with it moral instruction and good principles, as an essential part of the narrative . . . and I cannot but hope that many poor degraded women would be brought, by the perusal, to think seriously; and through repentance, seek to lead new and better lives.

Defoe's patriotism and pride in Britain's overseas empire were both highly acceptable in the late Victorian age. Although the Nonconformists and Evangelical Christians, who formed the bulk of Defoe's admirers, were enemies of the slave trade and supporters of emancipation, none of them seems to have noticed that Robinson Crusoe was shipwrecked while on his way to Africa to purchase a cargo of 'servants'.

The Life of Daniel Defoe

His reputation was at its highest in 1870, when readers of *Christian World* subscribed to the tombstone in Bunhill Fields. From about that time the Nonconformists, like their old tormentors the High Church Anglicans, were beginning a slow descent towards apathy and agnosticism. The Nonconformists enjoyed a revival in 1905, when a Liberal government came to power on a vote to disestablish the Church of England, but then came the First World War, the rise of the Labour party, the rapid decline of the Liberals, and with them the Nonconformists. The last and best loved of the Nonconformist bodies, the Salvation Army, was edged out of its work of helping the needy by the professional social workers.

The relics of the Dissenting tradition can still be seen at Abney Park Cemetery, across the road from the site of Defoe's house in Stoke Newington Church Street. The cemetery was opened in 1840 in the grounds of the house of Sir Thomas Abney, the former Lord Mayor. For thirty years Isaac Watts, the hymn-writer, lived in Abney's house, and a statue of Watts now stands near the site. During the nineteenth century Abney Park Cemetery was given a Gothic chapel and an Egyptian lodge and was carefully planted with trees and shrubs. William Booth, the founder of the Salvation Army, is among the famous Dissenters buried there.

By the 1970s Abney Park Cemetery had become overgrown, untended and vandalized, so it was sold for £1 to the London Borough of Hackney, which promised to carry out restoration. A Hackney Borough noticeboard by the Church Street entrance calls the cemetery: 'Abney Park Local Nature Reserve Architectural Conservation Area. This project has received grant-aid from English Nature under the Community Action for Wildlife ... After a long period of neglect, wildlife has flourished, with plants and creepers framing the monuments and chapel.'

Whether Abney Park is a cemetery, a nature reserve or an architectural conservation area, it inspires gloomy reflections on the decline of the Nonconformist tradition which gave to English Christians some of their most inspiring hymns, from Milton, through Bunyan to the Wesleys, Blake and Booth, whose Salvation Army popularized 'Onward, Christian Soldiers'. Isaac Watts himself was once honoured and sometimes mocked as the archetypal Dissenter; indeed some of his verses are better known by the Lewis Carroll parodies ('Tis the voice of the turtle, I hear him declare') than by the almost forgotten originals:

Tis the voice of the sluggard, I hear him complain,
You have waked me too soon, I would slumber again.

It was Watts who insisted that 'Birds in their little nests agree', and
offered up thanks to heaven:

> Lord I ascribe it to thy grace
>   And not to chance as others do,
> That I was born of Christian race
>   And not a Heathen or a Jew.

Yet the same Isaac Watts wrote 'There is a Land of Pure Delight',
'When I Survey the Wondrous Cross', and 'O God, Our Help in Ages
Past'.

The decline of the Puritan faith, from which Defoe drew courage
and inspiration, meant that much of his writing was incomprehensible
to followers of the successor creeds such as Marxism, Freudianism,
feminism and sociology. Defoe's independence of mind and readiness
to declare that 'all the world is mistaken but himself' were unacceptable
to an age which believed that all thoughts and attitudes are determined
by society.

Defoe's political principles, for which he had stood in the pillory
and suffered in Newgate Prison, were no longer fashionable in the
twentieth century. A new generation of scholars debunked what they
called the 'Whig interpretation of history', once put forward by Burke,
Macaulay and G. M. Trevelyan. With the debunking there came a
reaction against the Whig hero, William of Orange. Scottish and Irish
nationalists, for their different reasons, turned against William and his
admirer, Defoe. The Irish writer Seán O'Faoláin once lamented: 'It
is the greatest pity in the world that the novel began in the eighteenth
century. The press-reporter Defoe laid his stodgy hand on [it] and his
finger prints are still all over it' (quoted in Moore, *Defoe in the Pillory*,
p. 189).

The author of a recent book on black inhabitants of Britain during
the eighteenth century complains of Defoe's 'equivocal' attitude to
slavery. Unfortunately he supported it, and the infamous transatlantic
trade. On this, as in his attitude to the Irish Roman Catholics, the
High Church Tory Dr Johnson was more in tune with modern
opinion. School history books and educational television frequently
cite the *Tour* to prove that Defoe and the rulers of eighteenth-century
England condoned child labour. They seldom point out that the child

spinners and weavers of Taunton, Colchester and the West Riding worked in very much better conditions than their nineteenth-century counterparts.

In her widely acclaimed book, *Britons, Forging the Nation 1707–1837*, Linda Colley presents Defoe as a paid apologist for the British ruling class:

> Even Defoe, committed publicist for Great Britain as the Protestant Israel though he was, conceded that 'notwithstanding we are a nation of liberty', there were more prisons in London than in 'any city in Europe, perhaps as many as in all the capital cities of Europe put together'. And most Britons were very poor. In Wales, between a third and a half of the population at this time lived out their unknown lives at subsistence level. Knowing all this, it is tempting to believe – and some historians have actually argued – that the sublime confidence running through Handel's oratorios or Defoe's political and economic writings was little more than the propaganda of an affluent and atypical minority. After all, why should men and women living lives of no promise whatsoever believe that Britain was in any sense a promised land?

At the time of writing this final chapter Defoe's reputation appears to be making a come-back, this time in the cinema and on television. Feature films of *Robinson Crusoe* and *Moll Flanders* have been made while *Moll* has also been seen in a four-hour costume drama from Granada TV. Whether Moll's story on the screen 'is all applied, with the utmost care to virtuous and religious uses', as Defoe in his preface claims to have done in the book, the viewers will have to decide for themselves.

NOTES FOR FURTHER READING

Although Daniel Defoe was one of the most prolific writers in the language, most of his energy went into journalism, pamphlets and other ephemeral works. Apart from *Robinson Crusoe*, few of his books have ever been widely known to the general public, and are insufficient to earn him a place on the English literature syllabus of our modern universities. As a result, Defoe has been largely ignored by biographers of both the popular and academic kinds. In the concluding chapter of this book, I mentioned the biographical works of George Chalmers and William Lee in the eighteenth and nineteenth centuries. These were followed by the lives by Brian Fitzgerald, James R. Sutherland and John R. Moore, who also published the biographical *Checklist of the Writings of Daniel Defoe* and an interesting volume of essays, *Defoe in the Pillory, and other Studies*. Even Moore, the best of these biographers, was inclined to accept as fact some of the legends told about Defoe, not least by Defoe himself. For example, Moore accepts the *Tour* as evidence that Defoe had lived on the Continent, when he probably never left Britain.

Paula R. Backscheider broke new ground with her exhaustive research into every aspect of Defoe's career, including such dismal topics as his bankruptcy and his operation for bladder stones. In general I have followed Mrs Backscheider on details of Defoe's career; however, she does not mention the theory that he went to school at Dorking in Surrey. Professor Pat Rogers, the editor of the Penguin *Tour*, goes along with earlier biographers on this point, which gains support from Defoe's remarks on Dorking in the *Tour*. Pat Rogers also edited the useful *Defoe. The Critical Heritage*. For Defoe's correspondence, I used *The Letters of Daniel Defoe*, edited by George Harris Healey (1955). Some of the British Museum's copies of Defoe's *Review* were destroyed by enemy action during the Second World War. Luckily, an American scholar, Arthur Wellesley Secord, had edited a complete run of the paper in twenty-two books. I have referred to extracts by the date rather than volume and page number. Yale University Press has recently brought out a lavishly illustrated edition of the *Tour*.

Two of Britain's greatest historians have written about the period when Defoe was active. When Lord Macaulay's *History of England* first appeared in the 1850s, the factory workers of Manchester clubbed together to have each volume read out loud at evening gatherings. Although some of Macaulay's likes and dislikes are too strongly expressed, most of his judgements have stood the test of time, and his prose is a joy to read. His chapter on the siege of Londonderry, and its legacy of bitterness to the people of Ulster, should be compulsory reading for all modern British and Irish politicians.

Macaulay was dying when he completed the final volume, describing the death of William II, but his great-nephew, G. M. Trevelyan, carried on the work with a three-volume history, *England Under Queen Anne*. Trevelyan writes at length on Defoe's political role, as does William Thomas Morgan in *English Political Parties and Leaders in the Reign of Queen Anne*. Both capture the personality of Robert Harley, Defoe's patron, better than any more recent historian or biographer.

Some enterprising historian should make a study of Defoe in Scotland, especially now that some nationalists want to dissolve the Union and even revive the Parliament which he helped to abolish. In the chapters on Scotland I found space for only a fraction of the entertaining material in Defoe's books, pamphlets and journalism. The Scottish historian John Stuart Milne has pointed out to me some of Defoe's errors of fact, especially his over-estimate of the strength of the Presbyterians, but I have not attempted to tone down Defoe's anti-Jacobite bias, which will be apparent to readers.

Almost all Defoe's surviving correspondence is found in *The Letters of Daniel Defoe*, edited by George Harris Healey (Oxford, 1955). The British Museum Library has virtually all his known books and pamphlets, as well as the twenty-two books of the facsimile *Review*, edited with an introduction by Arthur Wellesley Secord, published in 1922.

For further reading on Defoe's contemporaries, Addison, Swift and Prior, Samuel Johnson's *Lives of the Poets* is as delightful as it is informative. There is also a brilliant portrait of Steele in the *Life of Savage*. There is a good Penguin anthology of the *Tatler* and *Spectator*. Until Victoria Glendinning's forthcoming biography of Swift, the best popular work is John Middleton Murry's. Much as I dislike Swift, I greatly enjoyed the *Journal to Stella*. Samuel Pepys was active during Defoe's early life. His politics were dramatically opposite but he had also endured an operation for bladder stones, an occasion he marked each year with a thanksgiving celebration.

INDEX

Alex Kershaw

Jack London

A Life

Born illegitimate in San Francisco, Jack London (1876–1916) was a legend before he was out of his teens: oyster pirate, seal-hunter, hobo, Klondike goldminer in Alaska – and spectacular drinker. London sailed the seven seas in his yacht the *Snark*, introduced surfing to the West Coast and was a war correspondent in Korea and Mexico. His books (including *Call of the Wild*, *Martin Eden*, *White Fang*, *The Iron Heel*, *The People of the Abyss* and *The Sea Wolf*) continue in print as world classics in many languages.

'For sheer excitement, it cannot be beat.'
MICHAEL SHELDEN, *Daily Telegraph*

'Money, love, passion is the troika that powers [Kershaw's] book . . . his brilliant portrait ripples . . . this compelling book fits its subject marvellously.' JAMES WOOD, *Guardian*

'Kershaw tells with gusto the story of his wayward, tousled handsome socialist hero . . . This biography is, I think, the best . . . in these pages is a love story to break your heart.'
MICHAEL FOOT, *New Statesmen*

'Kershaw infects us with his own delight in London's terrific struggle from apparently hopeless poverty in the Oakland of the 1880s . . . the book's strength lies in its dedication.'
OWEN DUDLEY EDWARDS, *Independent*

'A compelling and smartly written celebration of London's extra-ordinary life and work.' SCOTT BRADFIELD, *Mail on Sunday*

0 00 654848 2

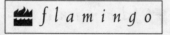 *flamingo*

Tiziano Terzani

A Fortune-Teller Told Me

Earthbound Travels in the Far East

Warned by a Hong Kong fortune-teller not to risk flying, Tiziano Terzani – a seasoned traveller and Far Eastern correspondent for *Der Spiegel* – took the advice. For a whole year he travelled by rail, road and sea as well as on foot through Burma, Thailand, Laos, Cambodia, Vietnam, China, Mongolia, Japan, Indonesia, Singapore and Malaysia. Consulting fortune-tellers and shamans wherever he went, he learnt to understand and respect older ways of life and beliefs now threatened by the crasser forms of Western modernity.

The consequences of Terzani's decision was a year full of unexpected events and encounters, in which he reflects entertainingly on his own fate and on that of the people he meets. 'It turned out to be one of the most extraordinary years I have ever spent: I was marked for death and instead I was reborn,' he recalled afterwards.

'[A] beautifully written adventure story . . . a voyage of self-discovery . . . He sees fortune-tellers, soothsayers, astrologers, chiromancers, seers, shamans, magicians, palmists, frauds, men and women of god (many gods) all over Asia and in Europe too . . . Almost every page and every story celebrates the mystical and the unknowable. It is a fabulous story of renewal and change . . . Terzani is already something of a legend. He has written magnificently all his life. Never better than now.'

WILLIAM SHAWCROSS, *Literary Review*

0 00 655071 1

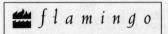